CW01045472

NON-LEAGUE FOOTBALL TABLES 1889-2014

EDITOR
Michael Robinson

FOREWORD

In selecting the Leagues to be included in this twelfth edition of Non-League Football Tables we have again chosen those forming the pinnacle of the Non-League Football Pyramid, i.e. The Football Conference and it's three direct feeders, the Southern League, Isthmian League and Northern Premier League.

In addition we have once more included the briefly-lived Football Alliance which became, effectively, the 2nd Division of the Football League in 1892 and this edition also includes tables for the London League, the Aetolian League and the Spartan League.

Furthermore, as league sponsors change frequently, we have not used sponsored names (eg. Rymans League) other than in an indicative way on the cover and in the contents page.

We are indebted to Mick Blakeman for providing tables for the new Leagues included in this edition of the book.

British Library Cataloguing in Publication Data
A catalogue record for this book is available from the British Library

ISBN: 978-1-86223-299-0

Copyright © 2014   Soccer Books Limited, 72 St. Peters Avenue, Cleethorpes, DN35 8HU, United Kingdom   (01472 696226)

Printed in the UK by 4edge Ltd.

CONTENTS

Football Alliance 1889-1892 ....Page 4

Southern League 1894-2014 (current sponsors Evo-Stik) .... Pages 4-44

Football Conference 1979-2014 (current sponsors Skrill) .... Pages 45-56

Isthmian League 1905-2014 (current sponsors Ryman) .... Pages 57-89

Northern Premier League 1968-2014 (current sponsors Evo-Stik) ... Pages 90-107

London League 1896-1964 .... Page 108-125

Aetolian League 1959-1964 .... Pages 126-127

Spartan League 1907-1975 .... Pages 128-147

FOOTBALL ALLIANCE

1889-90

Sheffield Wednesday	22	15	2	5	70	39	32
Bootle	22	13	2	7	66	39	28
Sunderland Albion	21	12	2	7	64	39	28
Grimsby Town	22	12	2	8	58	47	26
Crewe Alexandra	22	11	2	9	68	59	24
Darwen	22	10	2	10	70	75	22
Birmingham St George	21	9	3	9	62	49	21
Newton Heath	22	9	2	11	40	44	20
Walsall Town Swifts	22	8	3	11	44	59	19
Small Heath	22	6	5	11	44	67	17
Nottingham Forest	22	6	5	11	31	62	17
Long Eaton Rangers	22	4	2	16	35	73	10

Sunderland Albion record includes 2 points awarded when Birmingham St George refused to fulfil a fixture which the Alliance committee had ordered to be replayed.

1890-91

Stoke	22	13	7	2	57	39	33
Sunderland Albion	22	12	6	4	69	28	30
Grimsby Town	22	11	5	6	43	27	27
Birmingham St George	22	12	2	8	64	62	26
Nottingham Forest	22	9	7	6	66	39	23
Darwen	22	10	3	9	64	59	23
Walsall Town Swifts	22	9	3	10	34	61	21
Crewe Alexandra	22	8	4	10	59	67	20
Newton Heath	22	7	3	12	37	55	17
Small Heath	22	7	2	13	58	66	16
Bootle	22	3	7	12	40	61	13
Sheffield Wednesday	22	4	5	13	39	66	13

Nottingham Forest had 2 points deducted.

1891-92

Nottingham Forest	22	14	5	3	59	22	33
Newton Heath	22	12	7	3	69	33	31
Small Heath	22	12	5	5	53	36	29
Sheffield Wednesday	22	12	4	6	65	35	28
Burton Swifts	22	12	2	8	54	52	26
Crewe Alexandra	22	7	4	11	44	49	18
Ardwick	22	6	6	10	39	51	18
Bootle	22	8	2	12	42	64	18
Lincoln City	22	6	5	11	37	65	17
Grimsby Town	22	6	6	10	40	39	16
Walsall Town Swifts	22	6	3	13	33	59	15
Birmingham St George	22	5	3	14	34	64	11

Grimsby Town and Birmingham St. George both had 2 points deducted.

SOUTHERN LEAGUE

1894-95

First Division

Millwall Athletic	16	12	4	0	68	19	28
Luton Town	16	9	4	3	36	22	22
Southampton St Mary's	16	9	2	5	34	25	20
Ilford	16	6	3	7	26	40	15
Reading	16	6	2	8	33	38	14
Chatham	16	4	5	7	22	25	13
Royal Ordnance Factories	16	3	6	7	20	30	12
Clapton	16	5	1	10	22	38	11
Swindon Town	16	4	1	11	24	48	9

Second Division

New Brompton	12	11	0	1	57	10	22
Sheppey United	12	6	1	5	25	23	13
Old St Stephen's	12	6	0	6	26	26	12
Uxbridge	12	4	3	5	14	20	11
Bromley	12	4	1	7	23	30	9
Chesham	12	3	3	6	20	42	9
Maidenhead	12	2	4	6	19	33	8

1895-96

First Division

Millwall Athletic	18	16	1	1	75	16	33
Luton Town	18	13	1	4	68	14	27
Southampton St Mary's	18	12	0	6	44	23	24
Reading	18	11	1	6	45	38	23
Chatham	18	9	2	7	43	45	20
New Brompton	18	7	4	7	30	37	18
Swindon Town	18	6	4	8	38	41	16
Clapton	18	4	2	12	30	67	10
Royal Ordnance Factories	18	3	3	12	23	44	9
Ilford	18	0	0	18	10	81	0

Second Division

Wolverton L & NW Railway	16	13	1	2	43	10	27
Sheppey United	16	11	3	2	60	19	25
1st Scots Guards	16	8	5	3	37	22	21
Uxbridge	16	9	1	6	28	23	19
Old St Stephen's	16	6	3	7	34	21	15
Guildford	16	7	1	8	29	41	15
Maidenhead	16	4	1	11	20	49	9
Chesham	16	2	3	11	15	48	7
Bromley	16	2	2	12	16	49	6

1896-97

First Division

Southampton St Mary's	20	15	5	0	63	18	35
Millwall Athletic	20	13	5	2	63	24	31
Chatham	20	13	1	6	54	29	27
Tottenham Hotspur	20	9	4	7	43	29	22
Gravesend United	20	9	4	7	35	34	22
Swindon Town	20	8	3	9	33	37	19
Reading	20	8	3	9	31	49	19
New Brompton	20	7	2	11	32	42	16
Northfleet	20	5	4	11	24	46	14
Sheppey United	20	5	1	14	34	47	11
Wolverton L & NW Railway	20	2	0	18	17	74	4

Second Division

Dartford	24	16	4	4	83	19	36
Royal Engineers Training Battalion	24	11	9	4	49	37	31
Freemantle	24	12	4	8	58	40	28
Uxbridge	24	11	5	8	62	37	27
Wycombe Wanderers	24	10	6	8	37	54	26
Chesham	24	11	3	10	41	55	25
Southall	24	9	6	9	55	52	24
1st Scot Guards	24	9	6	9	49	50	24
West Herts	24	11	1	12	41	49	23
Warmley (Bristol)	24	10	2	12	44	43	22
Old St Stephen's	24	5	7	12	36	52	17
Maidenhead	24	4	8	12	33	64	16
1st Coldstream Guards	24	3	6	15	30	66	12

1897-98

First Division

	P	W	D	L	F	A	Pts
Southampton	22	18	1	3	53	18	37
Bristol City	22	13	7	2	67	33	33
Tottenham Hotspur	22	12	4	6	52	31	28
Chatham	22	12	4	6	50	34	28
Reading	22	8	7	7	39	31	23
New Brompton	22	9	4	9	37	37	22
Sheppey United	22	10	1	11	40	49	21
Gravesend United	22	7	6	9	28	39	20
Millwall Athletic	22	8	2	12	48	45	18
Swindon Town	22	7	2	13	36	48	16
Northfleet	22	4	3	15	29	60	11
Wolverton L & NW Railway	22	3	1	18	28	82	7

Second Division

	P	W	D	L	F	A	Pts
Royal Artillery (Portsmouth)	22	19	1	2	75	22	39
Warmley (Bristol)	22	19	0	3	108	15	38
West Herts	22	11	6	5	50	48	28
Uxbridge	22	11	2	9	39	57	24
St Albans	22	9	5	8	47	41	23
Dartford	22	11	0	11	68	55	22
Southall	22	8	2	12	49	61	18
Chesham	22	8	2	12	38	48	18
Olsd St Stephen's	22	7	2	13	47	66	16
Wycombe Wanderers	22	7	2	13	37	55	16
Maidenhead	22	4	4	14	27	81	12
Royal Engineers Training Battalion	22	4	2	16	26	62	10

1898-99

First Division

	P	W	D	L	F	A	Pts
Southampton	24	15	5	4	54	24	35
Bristol City	24	15	3	6	55	33	33
Millwall Athletic	24	12	6	6	59	35	30
Chatham	24	10	8	6	32	23	28
Reading	24	9	8	7	31	24	26
New Brompton	24	10	5	9	38	30	25
Tottenham Hotspur	24	10	4	10	40	36	24
Bedminster	24	10	4	10	35	39	24
Swindon Town	24	9	5	10	43	49	23
Brighton United	24	9	2	13	37	48	20
Gravesend United	24	7	5	12	42	52	19
Sheppey United	24	5	3	16	23	53	13
Royal Artillery (Portsmouth)	24	4	4	16	17	60	12

Second Division (London Section)

	P	W	D	L	F	A	Pts
Thames Ironworks	22	19	1	2	64	16	39
Wolverton L & NW Railway	22	13	4	5	88	43	30
Watford	22	14	2	6	62	35	30
Brentford	22	11	3	8	59	39	25
Wycombe Wanderers	22	10	2	10	55	57	22
Southall	22	11	0	11	44	55	22
Chesham	22	9	2	11	45	62	20
St Albans	22	8	3	11	45	59	19
Shepherds Bush	22	7	3	12	37	53	17
Fulham	22	6	4	12	36	44	16
Uxbridge	22	7	2	13	29	48	16
Maidenhead	22	3	2	17	33	86	8

Second Division (South West Section)

	P	W	D	L	F	A	Pts
Cowes	10	10	0	0	58	8	20
Ryde	10	7	0	3	30	11	14
Freemantle	10	4	1	5	18	31	9
Sandown	10	4	0	6	20	29	8
Eastleigh	10	2	1	7	17	37	5
Andover	10	2	0	8	14	41	4

1899-1900

First Division

	P	W	D	L	F	A	Pts
Tottenham Hotspur	28	20	4	4	67	26	44
Portsmouth	28	20	1	7	58	27	41
Southampton	28	17	1	10	70	33	35
Reading	28	15	2	11	41	28	32
Swindon Town	28	15	2	11	50	42	32
Bedminster	28	13	2	13	44	45	28
Millwall Athletic	28	12	3	13	36	37	27
Queens Park Rangers	28	12	2	14	49	57	26
Bristol City	28	9	7	12	43	47	25
Bristol Rovers	28	11	3	14	46	55	25
New Brompton	28	9	6	13	39	49	24
Gravesend United	28	10	4	14	38	58	24
Chatham	28	10	3	15	38	58	23
Thames Ironworks	28	8	5	15	30	45	21
Sheppey United	28	3	7	18	24	66	13

Cowes resigned and disbanded in December 1899 and their record was deleted when it stood as: 13 3 1 9 17 43 7
Brighton United resigned and disbanded in February 1900 and their record at the time was deleted: 22 3 3 16 22 56 9

Second Division

	P	W	D	L	F	A	Pts
Watford	20	14	2	4	57	25	30
Fulham	20	10	4	6	44	23	24
Chesham Town	20	11	2	7	43	37	24
Wolverton L & NW Railway	20	9	6	5	46	36	24
Grays United	20	8	6	6	63	29	22
Shepherds Bush	20	9	4	7	45	37	22
Dartford	20	8	3	9	36	44	19
Wycombe Wanderers	20	8	3	9	35	50	19
Brentford	20	5	7	8	31	48	17
Southall	20	6	3	11	21	44	15
Maidenhead	20	1	2	17	16	64	4

1900-01

First Division

	P	W	D	L	F	A	Pts
Southampton	28	18	5	5	58	26	41
Bristol City	28	17	5	6	54	27	39
Portsmouth	28	17	4	7	56	32	38
Millwall Athletic	28	17	2	9	55	32	36
Tottenham Hotspur	28	16	4	8	55	33	36
West Ham United	28	14	5	9	40	28	33
Bristol Rovers	28	14	4	10	46	35	32
Queens Park Rangers	28	11	4	13	43	48	26
Reading	28	8	8	12	24	25	24
Luton Town	28	11	2	15	43	49	24
Kettering	28	7	9	12	33	46	23
New Brompton	28	7	5	16	34	51	19
Gravesend United	28	6	7	15	32	85	19
Watford	28	6	4	18	24	52	16
Swindon Town	28	3	8	17	19	47	14

Chatham resigned and disbanded in December 1900 and their record was deleted when it stood as: 10 1 2 7 6 32 4

Second Division

	P	W	D	L	F	A	Pts
Brentford	16	14	2	0	63	11	30
Grays United	16	12	2	2	62	12	26
Sheppey United	16	8	1	7	44	26	17
Shepherds Bush	16	8	1	7	30	30	17
Fulham	16	8	0	8	38	26	16
Chesham Town	16	5	1	10	26	39	11
Maidenhead	16	4	1	11	21	49	9
Wycombe Wanderers	16	4	1	11	23	68	9
Southall	16	4	1	11	22	68	9

1901-02

First Division

Portsmouth	30	20	7	3	67	24	47
Tottenham Hotspur	30	18	6	6	61	22	42
Southampton	30	18	6	6	71	28	42
West Ham United	30	17	6	7	45	28	40
Reading	30	16	7	7	57	24	39
Millwall Athletic	30	13	6	11	48	31	32
Luton Town	30	11	10	9	31	35	32
Kettering	30	12	5	13	44	39	29
Bristol Rovers	30	12	5	13	43	39	29
New Brompton	30	10	7	13	39	38	27
Northampton	30	11	5	14	53	64	27
Queens Park Rangers	30	8	7	15	34	56	23
Watford	30	9	4	17	36	60	22
Wellingborough	30	9	4	17	34	75	22
Brentford	30	7	6	17	34	61	20
Swindon Town	30	2	3	25	17	93	7

Second Division

Fulham	16	13	0	3	51	19	26
Grays United	16	12	1	3	49	14	25
Brighton & Hove Albion	16	11	0	5	34	17	22
Wycombe Wanderers	16	7	3	6	36	30	17
West Hampstead	16	6	4	6	39	29	16
Shepherds Bush	16	6	1	9	31	31	13
Southall	16	5	2	9	28	52	12
Maidenhead	16	3	1	12	23	59	7
Chesham Town	16	2	2	12	24	64	6

1902-03

First Division

Southampton	30	20	8	2	83	20	48
Reading	30	19	7	4	72	30	45
Portsmouth	30	17	7	6	69	32	41
Tottenham Hotspur	30	14	7	9	47	31	35
Bristol Rovers	30	13	8	9	46	34	34
New Brompton	30	11	11	8	37	35	33
Millwall Athletic	30	14	3	13	52	37	31
Northampton Town	30	12	6	12	39	48	30
Queens Park Rangers	30	11	6	13	34	42	28
West Ham United	30	9	10	11	35	49	28
Luton Town	30	10	7	13	43	44	27
Swindon Town	30	10	7	13	38	46	27
Kettering	30	8	11	11	33	40	27
Wellingborough	30	11	3	16	36	56	25
Watford	30	6	4	20	35	87	16
Brentford	30	2	1	27	16	84	5

Second Division

Fulham	10	7	1	2	27	7	15
Brighton & Hove Albion	10	7	1	2	34	11	15
Grays United	10	7	0	3	28	12	14
Wycombe Wanderers	10	3	3	4	13	19	9
Chesham Town	10	2	1	7	9	37	5
Southall	10	1	0	9	10	35	2

1903-04

First Division

Southampton	34	22	6	6	75	30	50
Tottenham Hotspur	34	16	11	7	54	37	43
Bristol Rovers	34	17	8	9	66	42	42
Portsmouth	34	17	8	9	41	38	42
Queens Park Rangers	34	15	11	8	53	37	41
Reading	34	14	13	7	48	35	41
Millwall	34	16	8	10	64	42	40
Luton Town	34	14	12	8	38	33	40
Plymouth Argyle	34	13	10	11	44	34	36
Swindon Town	34	10	11	13	30	42	31
Fulham	34	9	12	13	33	34	30
West Ham United	34	10	7	17	38	43	27
Brentford	34	9	9	16	34	48	27
Wellingborough	34	11	5	18	44	63	27
Northampton Town	34	10	7	17	36	69	27
New Brompton	34	6	13	15	26	43	25
Brighton & Hove Albion	34	6	12	16	45	79	24
Kettering	34	6	7	21	30	78	19

Second Division

Watford	20	18	2	0	70	15	38
Portsmouth Reserves	20	15	2	3	85	25	32
Millwall Reserves	20	9	4	7	35	39	22
Southampton Reserves	20	9	3	8	59	35	21
Grays United	20	9	3	8	25	55	21
Fulham Reserves	20	8	4	8	40	34	20
Swindon Town Reserves	20	8	3	9	50	44	19
Reading Reserves	20	8	2	10	43	42	18
Wycombe Wanderers	20	5	5	10	29	64	15
Southall	20	4	2	14	25	62	10
Chesham Town	20	1	2	17	19	65	4

1904-05

First Division

Bristol Rovers	34	20	8	6	74	36	48
Reading	34	18	7	9	57	38	43
Southampton	34	18	7	9	54	40	43
Plymouth Argyle	34	18	5	11	57	39	41
Tottenham Hotspur	34	15	8	11	53	34	38
Fulham	34	14	10	10	46	34	38
Queens Park Rangers	34	14	8	12	51	46	36
Portsmouth	34	16	4	14	61	56	36
New Brompton	34	11	11	12	40	41	33
West Ham United	34	12	8	14	48	42	32
Brighton & Hove Albion	34	13	6	15	44	45	32
Northampton Town	34	12	8	14	43	54	32
Watford	34	14	3	17	41	44	31
Brentford	34	10	9	15	33	38	29
Millwall	34	11	7	16	38	47	29
Swindon Town	34	12	5	17	41	59	29
Luton Town	34	12	3	19	45	54	27
Wellingborough	34	5	3	26	25	104	13

Second Division

Fulham Reserves	22	16	4	2	78	25	36
Portsmouth Reserves	22	14	2	6	75	28	30
Swindon Town Reserves	22	12	3	7	54	47	27
Grays United	22	11	3	8	61	40	25
Southampton Reserves	22	10	5	7	52	35	25
Brighton & Hove Albion	22	9	3	10	48	49	21
West Ham United Reserves	22	8	5	9	45	47	21
Clapton Orient	22	7	7	8	47	56	21
Watford Reserves	22	5	6	11	30	62	16
Southall	22	7	2	13	31	66	16
Wycombe Wanderers	22	6	2	14	37	70	14
Reading Reserves	22	4	4	14	24	57	12

1905-06

First Division

Fulham	34	19	12	3	44	15	50
Southampton	34	19	7	8	58	39	45
Portsmouth	34	17	9	8	61	35	43
Luton Town	34	17	7	10	64	40	41
Tottenham Hotspur	34	16	7	11	46	29	39
Plymouth Argyle	34	16	7	11	52	33	39
Norwich City	34	13	10	11	46	38	36
Bristol Rovers	34	15	5	14	56	56	35
Brentford	34	14	7	13	43	52	35
Reading	34	12	9	13	53	46	33
West Ham United	34	14	5	15	42	39	33
Millwall	34	11	11	12	38	41	33
Queens Park Rangers	34	12	7	15	58	44	31
Watford	34	8	10	16	38	57	26
Swindon Town	34	8	9	17	31	52	25
Brighton & Hove Albion	34	9	7	18	30	55	25
New Brompton	34	7	8	19	20	62	22
Northampton Town	34	8	5	21	32	79	21

Second Division

Crystal Palace	24	19	4	1	66	14	42
Leyton	24	16	6	2	61	18	38
Portsmouth Reserves	24	12	8	4	52	24	32
Fulham Reserves	24	11	6	7	52	39	28
Southampton Reserves	24	7	9	8	39	41	23
Southern United	24	8	7	9	45	49	23
St Leonard's United	24	9	4	11	54	50	22
Watford Reserves	24	8	5	11	43	47	21
West Ham United Reserves	24	7	5	12	46	48	19
Grays United	24	8	3	13	24	77	19
Reading Reserves	24	6	5	13	36	49	15
Swindon Town Reserves	24	5	5	14	36	51	15
Wycombe Wanderers	24	5	3	16	36	83	13

1906-07

First Division

Fulham	38	20	13	5	58	32	53
Portsmouth	38	22	7	9	64	36	51
Brighton & Hove Albion	38	18	9	11	53	43	45
Luton Town	38	18	9	11	52	52	45
West Ham United	38	15	14	9	60	41	44
Tottenham Hotspur	38	17	9	12	63	45	43
Millwall	38	18	6	14	71	50	42
Norwich City	38	15	12	11	57	48	42
Watford	38	13	16	9	46	43	42
Brentford	38	17	8	13	57	56	42
Southampton	38	13	9	16	49	56	35
Reading	38	14	6	18	57	47	34
Leyton	38	11	12	15	38	60	34
Bristol Rovers	38	12	9	17	55	54	33
Plymouth Argyle	38	10	13	15	43	50	33
New Brompton	38	12	9	17	47	59	33
Swindon Town	38	11	11	16	43	54	33
Queens Park Rangers	38	11	10	17	47	55	32
Crystal Palace	38	8	9	21	46	66	25
Northampton Town	38	5	9	24	29	88	19

Second Division

Southend United	22	14	5	3	58	23	33
West Ham United Reserves	22	14	3	5	64	30	31
Portsmouth Reserves	22	11	6	5	53	24	28
Fulham Reserves	22	11	4	7	47	32	26
Hastings & St Leonards	21	10	4	7	46	31	24
Tunbridge Wells Rangers	22	10	1	11	46	36	21
Salisbury City	22	9	2	11	40	42	20
Southampton Reserves	22	8	2	12	37	56	18
Swindon Town Reserves	22	7	3	12	35	43	17
Reading Reserves	22	6	4	12	32	47	16
Royal Engineers (Aldershot)	21	5	4	12	27	58	14
Wycombe Wanderers	22	4	6	12	28	68	14

The match between Tunbridge Wells Rangers and Royal Engineers (Aldershot) was not completed.

1907-08

First Division

Queens Park Rangers	38	21	9	8	82	57	51
Plymouth Argyle	38	19	11	8	50	31	49
Millwall	38	19	8	11	49	32	46
Crystal Palace	38	17	10	11	54	51	44
Swindon Town	38	16	10	12	55	40	42
Bristol Rovers	38	16	10	12	59	56	42
Tottenham Hotspur	38	17	7	14	59	48	41
Northampton Town	38	15	11	12	50	41	41
Portsmouth	38	17	6	15	63	52	40
West Ham United	38	15	10	13	47	48	40
Southampton	38	16	6	16	51	60	38
Reading	38	15	6	17	55	50	36
Bradford Park Avenue	38	12	12	14	53	54	36
Watford	38	12	10	16	47	49	34
Brentford	38	14	5	19	49	52	33
Norwich City	38	12	9	17	46	49	33
Brighton & Hove Albion	38	12	8	18	46	59	32
Luton Town	38	12	6	20	33	56	30
Leyton	38	8	11	19	51	73	27
New Brompton	38	9	7	22	44	75	25

Second Division

Southend	18	13	3	2	47	16	29
Portsmouth Reserves	18	10	5	3	39	22	25
Croydon Common	18	10	3	5	35	25	23
Hastings & St Leonard's	18	10	2	6	43	29	22
Southampton Reserves	18	7	4	7	54	46	18
Tunbridge Wells Rangers	18	7	3	8	42	38	17
Salisbury City	18	6	4	8	35	46	16
Swindon Town Reserves	18	5	5	8	36	40	15
Brighton & Hove Albion Reserves	18	4	4	10	34	47	12
Wycombe Wanderers	18	1	1	16	16	72	3

1908-09

First Division

Northampton Town	40	25	5	10	90	45	55
Swindon Town	40	22	5	13	96	55	49
Southampton	40	19	10	11	67	58	48
Portsmouth	40	18	10	12	68	60	46
Bristol Rovers	40	17	9	14	60	63	43
Exeter City	40	18	6	16	56	65	42
New Brompton	40	17	7	16	48	59	41
Reading	40	11	18	11	60	57	40
Luton Town	40	17	6	17	59	60	40
Plymouth Argyle	40	15	10	15	46	47	40
Millwall	40	16	6	18	59	61	38
Southend United	40	14	10	16	52	54	38
Leyton	40	15	8	17	52	55	38
Watford	40	14	9	17	51	64	37
Queens Park Rangers	40	12	12	16	52	50	36
Crystal Palace	40	12	12	16	62	62	36
West Ham United	40	16	4	20	56	60	36
Brighton & Hove Albion	40	14	7	19	60	61	35
Norwich City	40	12	11	17	59	75	35
Coventry City	40	15	4	21	64	91	34
Brentford	40	13	7	20	59	74	33

Second Division

Croydon Common	12	10	0	2	67	14	20
Hastings & St Leonard's	12	8	1	3	42	18	17
Depot Battalion Royal Engineers	12	8	1	3	23	22	17
2nd Grenadier Guards	12	5	0	7	21	33	10
South Farnborough Athletic	12	2	4	6	20	39	8
Salisbury City	12	3	1	8	24	36	7
Chesham Town	12	2	1	9	17	52	5

1909-10

First Division

Brighton & Hove Albion	42	23	13	6	69	28	59
Swindon Town	42	22	10	10	92	46	54
Queens Park Rangers	42	19	13	10	56	47	51
Northampton Town	42	22	4	16	90	44	48
Southampton	42	16	16	10	64	55	48
Portsmouth	42	20	7	15	70	63	47
Crystal Palace	42	20	6	16	69	50	46
Coventry City	42	19	8	15	71	60	46
West Ham United	42	15	15	12	69	56	45
Leyton	42	16	11	15	60	46	43
Plymouth Argyle	42	16	11	15	61	54	43
New Brompton	42	19	5	18	76	74	43
Bristol Rovers	42	16	10	16	37	48	42
Brentford	42	16	9	17	50	58	41
Luton Town	42	15	11	16	72	92	41
Millwall	42	15	7	20	45	59	37
Norwich City	42	13	9	20	59	78	35
Exeter City	42	14	6	22	60	69	34
Watford	42	10	13	19	51	76	33
Southend United	42	12	9	21	51	90	33
Croydon Common	42	13	5	24	52	96	31
Reading	42	7	10	25	38	73	24

Second Division - Section A

Stoke	10	10	0	0	48	9	20
Ton Pentre	10	4	2	4	17	21	10
Merthyr Town	9	4	1	4	16	21	9
Salisbury City	8	2	1	5	7	18	5
Burton United	6	2	0	4	8	21	4
Aberdare	7	1	0	6	6	11	2

Second Division - Section B

Hastings & St Leonard's	9	6	3	0	26	11	15
Kettering	10	6	0	4	34	19	12
Chesham Town	10	5	2	3	25	25	12
Peterborough City	10	4	2	4	16	23	10
South Farnborough Athletic	10	4	1	5	23	19	9
Romford	9	0	0	9	7	33	0

1910-11

First Divison

Swindon Town	38	24	5	9	80	31	53
Northampton Town	38	18	12	8	54	27	48
Brighton & Hove Albion	38	20	8	10	58	35	48
Crystal Palace	38	17	13	8	55	48	47
West Ham United	38	17	11	10	63	46	45
Queens Park Rangers	38	13	14	11	52	41	40
Leyton	38	16	8	14	57	52	40
Plymouth Argyle	38	15	9	14	54	55	39
Luton Town	38	15	8	15	67	63	38
Norwich City	38	15	8	15	46	48	38
Coventry City	38	16	6	16	65	68	38
Brentford	38	14	9	15	41	42	37
Exeter City	38	14	9	15	51	53	37
Watford	38	13	9	16	49	65	35
Millwall	38	11	9	18	42	54	31
Bristol Rovers	38	10	10	18	42	55	30
Southampton	38	11	8	19	42	67	30
New Brompton	38	11	8	19	34	65	30
Southend United	38	10	9	19	47	64	29
Portsmouth	38	8	11	19	34	53	27

Second Division

Reading	22	16	3	3	55	11	35
Stoke	22	17	1	4	72	21	35
Merthyr Town	22	15	3	4	52	22	33
Cardiff City	22	12	4	6	48	29	28
Croydon Common	22	11	3	8	61	26	25
Treharris	22	10	3	9	38	31	23
Aberdare	22	9	5	8	38	33	23
Ton Pentre	22	10	3	9	44	40	23
Walsall	22	7	4	11	37	41	18
Kettering	22	6	1	15	34	68	13
Chesham Town	22	1	3	18	16	93	5
Salisbury City	22	0	3	19	16	92	3

1911-12

First Division

Queens Park Rangers	38	21	11	6	59	35	53
Plymouth Argyle	38	23	6	9	63	31	52
Northampton Town	38	22	7	9	82	41	51
Swindon Town	38	21	6	11	82	50	48
Brighton & Hove Albion	38	19	9	10	73	35	47
Coventry City	38	17	8	13	66	54	42
Crystal Palace	38	15	10	13	70	46	40
Millwall	38	15	10	13	60	57	40
Watford	38	13	10	15	56	68	36
Stoke	38	13	10	15	51	63	36
Reading	38	11	14	13	43	69	36
Norwich City	38	10	14	14	40	60	34
West Ham United	38	13	7	18	64	69	33
Brentford	38	12	9	17	60	65	33
Exeter City	38	11	11	16	48	62	33
Southampton	38	10	11	17	46	63	31
Bristol Rovers	38	9	13	16	41	62	31
New Brompton	38	11	9	18	35	72	31
Luton Town	38	9	10	19	49	61	28
Leyton	38	7	11	20	27	62	25

Second Division

Merthyr Town	26	19	3	4	60	14	41
Portsmouth	26	19	3	4	73	20	41
Cardiff City	26	15	4	7	55	26	34
Southend United	26	16	1	9	73	24	33
Pontypridd	26	13	6	7	39	24	32
Ton Pentre	26	12	3	11	56	45	27
Walsall	26	13	1	11	44	41	27
Treharris	26	11	5	10	44	47	27
Aberdare	26	10	3	13	39	44	23
Kettering	26	11	0	15	37	62	22
Croydon Common	26	8	2	15	43	45	18
Mardy	26	6	6	12	37	51	18
Cwm Albion	26	5	1	16	27	70	11
Chesham Town	26	1	0	25	18	131	2

1912-13

First Division

Plymouth Argyle	38	22	6	10	78	36	50
Swindon Town	38	20	8	10	66	41	48
West Ham United	38	18	12	8	66	46	48
Queens Park Rangers	38	18	10	10	46	36	46
Crystal Palace	38	17	11	10	55	36	45
Millwall	38	19	7	12	62	43	45
Exeter City	38	18	8	12	48	44	44
Reading	38	17	8	13	59	55	42
Brighton & Hove Albion	38	13	12	13	49	47	38
Northampton Town	38	12	12	14	61	48	36
Portsmouth	38	14	8	16	41	49	36
Merthyr Town	38	12	12	14	43	61	36
Coventry City	38	13	8	17	53	59	34
Watford	38	12	10	16	43	50	34
Gillingham	38	12	10	16	36	53	34
Bristol Rovers	38	12	9	17	55	65	33
Southampton	38	10	11	17	40	72	31
Norwich City	38	10	9	19	39	50	29
Brentford	38	11	5	22	42	55	27
Stoke	38	10	4	24	39	75	24

Second Division

Cardiff City	24	18	5	1	54	15	41
Southend United	24	14	6	4	43	23	34
Swansea Town	24	12	7	5	29	23	31
Croydon Common	24	13	4	7	51	29	30
Luton Town	24	13	4	7	52	39	30
Llanelly	24	9	6	9	33	39	24
Pontypridd	24	6	11	7	30	28	23
Mid Rhondda	24	9	4	11	33	31	22
Aberdare	24	8	6	10	38	40	22
Newport County	24	7	5	12	29	36	19
Mardy	24	6	3	15	38	38	15
Treharris	24	5	2	17	18	60	12
Ton Pentre	24	3	3	18	22	69	9

1913-14

First Division

Swindon Town	38	21	8	9	81	41	50
Crystal Palace	38	17	16	5	60	32	50
Northampton Town	38	14	19	5	50	37	47
Reading	38	17	10	11	43	36	44
Plymouth Argyle	38	15	13	10	46	42	43
West Ham United	38	15	12	11	61	60	42
Brighton & Hove Albion	38	15	12	11	43	45	42
Queens Park Rangers	38	16	9	13	45	43	41
Portsmouth	38	14	12	12	57	48	40
Cardiff City	38	13	12	13	46	42	38
Southampton	38	15	7	16	55	54	37
Exeter City	38	10	16	12	39	38	36
Gillingham	38	13	9	16	48	49	35
Norwich City	38	9	17	12	49	51	35
Millwall	38	11	12	15	51	56	34
Southend Unied	38	10	12	16	41	66	32
Bristol Rovers	38	10	11	17	46	67	31
Watford	38	10	9	19	50	56	29
Merthyr Town	38	9	10	19	38	61	28
Coventry City	38	6	14	18	43	68	26

Second Division

Croydon Common	30	23	5	2	76	14	51
Luton Town	30	24	3	3	92	22	51
Brentford	30	20	4	6	80	18	44
Swansea Town	30	20	4	6	66	23	44
Stoke	30	19	2	9	71	34	40
Newport County	30	14	8	8	49	38	36
Mid Rhondda	30	13	7	10	55	37	33
Pontypridd	30	14	5	11	43	38	33
Llanelly	30	12	4	14	45	39	28
Barry	30	9	8	13	44	70	26
Abertillery	30	8	4	18	44	57	20
Ton Pentre	30	8	4	18	33	61	20
Mardy	30	6	6	18	30	60	18
Caerphilly	30	4	7	19	21	103	15
Aberdare	30	4	5	21	33	87	13
Treharris	30	2	4	24	19	106	8

1914-15

First Division

Watford	38	22	8	8	67	47	52
Reading	38	21	7	10	68	43	49
Cardiff City	38	22	4	12	72	38	48
West Ham United	38	18	9	11	58	47	45
Northampton Town	38	16	11	11	56	52	43
Southampton	38	19	5	14	78	74	43
Portsmouth	38	16	10	12	54	42	42
Millwall	38	16	10	12	51	51	42
Swindon Town	38	15	11	12	77	59	41
Brighton & Hove Albion	38	16	7	15	46	47	39
Exeter City	38	15	8	15	50	41	38
Queens Park Rangers	38	13	12	13	55	56	38
Norwich City	38	11	14	13	53	56	36
Luton Town	38	13	8	17	61	73	34
Crystal Palace	38	13	8	17	47	61	34
Bristol Rovers	38	14	3	21	53	75	31
Plymouth Argyle	38	8	14	16	51	61	30
Southend United	38	10	8	20	44	64	28
Croydon Common	38	9	9	20	47	63	27
Gillingham	38	6	8	24	44	82	20

Second Division

Stoke	24	17	4	3	62	15	38
Stalybridge Celtic	24	17	3	4	47	22	37
Merthyr Town	24	15	5	4	46	20	35
Swansea Town	24	16	1	7	48	21	33
Coventry City	24	13	2	9	56	33	28
Ton Pentre	24	11	6	7	42	43	28
Brentford	24	8	7	9	35	45	23
Llanelly	24	10	1	13	39	32	21
Barry	24	6	5	13	30	35	17
Newport County	24	7	3	14	27	42	17
Pontypridd	24	5	6	13	31	58	16
Mid Rhondda	24	3	6	15	17	40	12
Ebbw Vale	24	3	1	20	23	88	7

1919-20

First Division

Portsmouth	42	23	12	7	73	27	58
Watford	42	26	6	10	69	42	58
Crystal Palace	42	22	12	8	69	43	56
Cardiff City	42	18	17	7	70	43	53
Plymouth Argyle	42	20	10	12	57	29	50
Queens Park Rangers	42	18	10	14	62	50	46
Reading	42	16	13	13	51	43	45
Southampton	42	18	8	16	72	63	44
Swansea Town	42	16	11	15	53	45	43
Exeter City	42	17	9	16	57	51	43
Southend United	42	13	17	12	46	48	43
Norwich City	42	15	11	16	64	57	41
Swindon Town	42	17	7	18	65	68	41
Millwall	42	14	12	16	52	55	40
Brentford	42	15	10	17	52	59	40
Brighton & Hove Albion	42	14	8	20	60	72	36
Bristol Rovers	42	11	13	18	61	78	35
Newport County	42	13	7	22	45	70	33
Northampton Town	42	12	9	21	64	103	33
Luton Town	42	10	10	22	51	76	30
Merthyr Town	42	9	11	22	47	78	29
Gillingham	42	10	7	25	34	74	27

Second Division

Mid Rhondda	20	17	3	0	79	10	37
Ton Pentre	20	12	7	1	50	14	31
Llanelly	20	10	5	5	47	30	25
Pontypridd	20	10	3	7	33	29	23
Ebbw Vale	20	7	7	6	38	40	21
Barry	20	7	5	8	32	27	19
Mardy	20	7	5	8	29	30	19
Abertillery	20	6	5	9	29	40	17
Porth Athletic	20	4	4	12	30	74	12
Aberaman Athletic	20	4	3	13	28	48	11
Caerphilly	20	1	3	16	20	74	5

1920-21

English Section

Brighton & Hove Albion Reserves	24	16	3	5	65	29	35
Portsmouth Reserves	24	13	7	4	44	20	33
Millwall Reserves	24	12	4	8	46	24	28
Southampton Reserves	24	10	7	7	53	35	27
Boscombe	24	10	6	8	25	40	26
Reading Reserves	24	11	3	10	41	34	25
Luton Town Reserves	24	8	8	8	38	35	24
Charlton Athletic	24	8	8	8	41	41	24
Watford Reserves	24	9	4	11	43	45	22
Norwich City Reserves	24	7	7	10	31	39	21
Gillingham Reserves	24	6	5	13	32	47	17
Chatham	24	5	6	13	24	47	16
Thornycrofts	24	4	6	14	29	74	14

Welsh Section

Barry	20	13	4	3	35	12	30
Aberdare Athletic	20	12	3	5	29	23	27
Ebbw Vale	20	10	5	5	34	23	25
Pontypridd	20	10	3	7	34	23	23
Mid Rhondda	20	10	3	7	26	18	23
Abertillery Town	20	8	5	7	35	24	21
Ton Pentre	20	7	5	8	32	34	19
Aberaman Athletic	20	5	7	8	30	33	17
Llanelly	20	7	2	11	28	46	16
Mardy	20	2	6	12	18	39	10
Porth Athletic	20	3	3	14	28	54	9

1921-22

English Section

Plymouth Argyle Reserves	36	22	5	9	91	38	49
Bristol City Reserves	36	18	8	10	73	50	44
Portsmouth Reserves	36	17	10	9	63	41	44
Southampton Reserves	36	19	5	12	70	47	43
Gillingham Reserves	36	17	9	10	65	47	43
Charlton Athletic Reserves	36	18	6	12	69	54	42
Boscombe	36	17	5	14	38	55	39
Luton Town Reserves	36	17	4	15	50	54	38
Watford Reserves	36	15	7	14	65	53	37
Brighton & Hove Albion Reserves	36	12	13	11	60	52	37
Bath City	36	16	5	15	55	53	37
Swindon Town Reserves	36	14	7	15	59	46	35
Bristol Rovers Reserves	36	13	7	16	50	82	33
Millwall Reserves	36	13	4	19	49	53	30
Reading Reserves	36	11	7	18	46	59	29
Exeter City Reserves	36	10	9	17	42	63	29
Guildford United	36	11	6	19	44	56	28
Norwich City Reserves	36	10	6	20	47	86	26
Southend United Reserves	36	9	3	24	47	92	21

Welsh Section

Ebbw Vale	16	11	3	2	33	11	25
Ton Pentre	16	9	4	3	35	14	22
Aberaman Athletic	16	7	5	4	25	19	19
Porth Athletic	16	6	6	4	31	20	18
Pontypridd	16	7	4	5	28	19	18
Swansea Town Reserves	16	7	4	5	24	17	18
Barry	16	3	3	10	14	35	9
Abertillery Town	16	3	2	11	21	45	8
Mardy	16	2	3	11	14	43	7

1922-23

English Section

Bristol City Reserves	38	24	5	9	84	39	53
Boscombe	38	22	7	9	67	34	51
Portsmouth Reserves	38	23	3	12	93	51	49
Bristol Rovers Reserves	38	20	8	10	59	41	48
Plymouth Argyle Reserves	38	20	7	11	74	41	47
Torquay United	38	18	8	12	63	38	44
Brighton & Hove Albion Reserves	38	20	3	15	95	60	43
Luton Town Reserves	38	16	11	11	67	56	43
Southend United Reserves	38	18	6	14	69	68	42
Southampton Reserves	38	18	5	15	65	54	41
Millwall Reserves	38	15	10	13	61	55	40
Coventry City Reserves	38	15	8	15	56	61	38
Guildford United	38	15	7	16	65	59	37
Swindon Town Reserves	38	13	6	19	54	73	32
Bath City	38	10	8	20	44	71	28
Watford Reserves	38	11	6	21	34	79	28
Yeovil & Petters United	38	10	6	22	56	104	26
Norwich City Reserves	38	9	7	22	42	68	25
Exeter City Reserves	38	10	5	23	43	81	25
Reading Reserves	38	7	6	25	43	95	20

Welsh Section

Team	P	W	D	L	F	A	Pts
Ebbw Vale	12	6	5	1	22	15	17
Aberaman Athletic	12	7	2	3	30	19	16
Swansea Town Reserves	12	6	2	4	25	14	14
Pontypridd	12	6	2	4	18	18	14
Barry	12	4	3	5	15	11	11
Bridgend Town	12	4	2	6	15	21	10
Porth Athletic	12	0	2	10	18	24	2

1923-24

Eastern Section

Team	P	W	D	L	F	A	Pts
Peterborough & Fletton United	30	20	2	8	54	31	42
Leicester City Reserves	30	19	3	8	72	30	41
Southampton Reserves	30	18	5	7	60	36	41
Millwall Reserves	30	18	3	9	56	38	39
Portsmouth Reserves	30	16	2	12	66	37	34
Brighton & Hove Albion Reserves	30	13	7	10	55	42	33
Norwich City Reserves	30	13	6	11	46	34	32
Folkestone	30	12	5	13	61	51	29
Coventry City Reserves	30	10	8	12	39	40	28
Watford Reserves	30	11	6	13	36	48	28
Reading Reserves	30	11	6	13	32	43	28
Northampton Town Reserves	30	9	10	11	32	47	28
Luton Town Reserves	30	10	7	13	40	49	27
Guildford United	30	7	5	18	38	72	19
Kettering	30	5	8	17	30	67	18
Bournemouth Reserves	30	4	5	21	40	85	13

Western Section

Team	P	W	D	L	F	A	Pts
Yeovil & Petters United	34	25	3	6	71	30	53
Plymouth Argyle Reserves	34	21	5	8	74	37	47
Pontypridd	34	19	8	7	81	44	46
Torquay United	34	19	7	8	59	25	45
Bristol City Reserves	34	17	9	8	63	39	43
Swansea Town Reserves	34	19	5	10	62	38	43
Bristol Rovers Reserves	34	17	6	11	69	43	40
Cardiff City Reserves	34	15	4	15	55	31	34
Exeter City Reserves	34	11	11	12	48	47	33
Weymouth	34	15	3	16	48	60	33
Llanelly	34	14	5	15	47	62	33
Swindon Town Reserves	34	11	6	17	36	60	28
Bridgend Town	34	11	5	18	57	72	27
Newport County Reserves	34	10	7	17	57	79	27
Ebbw Vale	34	8	8	18	38	62	24
Bath City	34	6	9	19	32	71	21
Barry	34	6	7	21	36	74	19
Aberaman Athletic	34	6	4	24	41	87	16

1924-25

Eastern Section

Team	P	W	D	L	F	A	Pts
Southampton Reserves	32	17	10	5	65	30	44
Kettering Town	32	17	6	9	67	39	40
Brighton & Hove Albion Reserves	32	15	10	7	68	42	40
Millwall Reserves	32	15	10	7	65	48	40
Peterborough & Fletton United	32	15	9	8	56	29	39
Bournemouth Reserves	32	15	9	8	66	48	39
Leicester City Reserves	32	15	7	10	61	45	37
Portsmouth Reserves	32	15	7	10	51	40	37
Folkestone	32	13	11	8	55	46	37
Norwich City Reserves	32	13	8	11	65	58	34
Coventry City Reserves	32	12	9	11	51	41	33
Luton Town Reserves	32	12	5	15	48	63	32
Northampton Town Reserves	32	10	5	17	38	59	25
Watford Reserves	32	7	7	18	44	71	21
Nuneaton Town	32	8	2	22	37	62	18
Reading Reserves	32	8	1	23	38	87	17
Guildford United	32	4	3	25	40	107	11

Western Section

Team	P	W	D	L	F	A	Pts
Swansea Town Reserves	38	25	4	9	73	26	54
Plymouth Argyle Reserves	38	22	10	6	97	35	54
Pontypridd	38	24	4	10	81	39	52
Bridgend Town	38	20	11	7	74	52	51
Mid Rhondda United	38	21	6	11	79	48	48
Weymouth	38	21	4	13	77	50	46
Cardiff City Reserves	38	18	6	14	56	44	42
Newport County Reserves	38	17	8	13	71	60	42
Swindon Town Reserves	38	17	8	13	48	46	42
Bristol City Reserves	38	18	5	15	51	43	41
Yeovil & Petters United	38	15	10	13	49	50	40
Exeter City Reserves	38	16	6	16	78	55	38
Taunton Unied	38	15	6	17	55	51	36
Bristol Rovers Reserves	38	13	6	19	45	50	32
Torquay United	39	9	11	18	41	73	29
Llanelly	38	6	12	20	49	94	24
Ebbw Vale	38	9	6	23	40	91	24
Bath City	38	8	8	22	28	85	24
Barry	38	8	6	24	38	82	22
Aberaman Athletic	38	6	7	25	39	95	19

1925-26

Eastern Section

Team	P	W	D	L	F	A	Pts
Millwall Reserves	34	24	6	4	106	37	54
Leicester City Reserves	34	23	2	9	105	60	48
Brighton & Hove Albion Reserves	34	21	4	9	105	69	46
Kettering Town	34	19	5	10	98	66	43
Peterborough & Fletton United	34	19	3	12	76	62	41
Portsmouth Reserves	34	17	5	12	76	67	39
Norwich City Reserves	34	17	4	13	85	90	38
Bournemouth Reserves	34	15	7	12	76	67	37
Southampton Reserves	34	14	7	13	65	72	35
Fulham Reserves	34	13	6	15	86	77	32
Grays Thurrock United	34	13	5	16	63	77	31
Guildford United	34	11	8	15	71	87	30
Watford Reserves	34	12	2	20	62	94	26
Luton Town Reserves	34	11	3	20	70	78	25
Folkestone	34	9	6	19	67	93	24
Reading Reserves	34	10	3	21	58	84	23
Coventry City Reserves	34	9	5	20	54	93	23
Nuneaton Town	34	7	3	24	61	113	17

Western Section

Team	P	W	D	L	F	A	Pts
Plymouth Argyle Reserves	26	20	1	5	67	31	41
Bristol City Reserves	26	16	4	6	48	28	36
Bristol Rovers Reserves	26	13	4	9	51	35	30
Swindon Town Reserves	26	13	4	9	57	40	30
Ebbw Vale	26	13	3	10	60	46	29
Torquay United	26	12	5	9	59	46	29
Yeovil & Petters United	26	9	8	9	43	48	26
Mid-Rhondda United	26	12	1	13	47	49	25
Weymouth	26	10	3	13	64	60	23
Exeter City Reserves	26	8	5	13	40	49	21
Barry	26	8	4	14	47	55	20
Taunton United	26	9	2	15	44	60	20
Pontypridd	26	7	5	14	44	77	19
Bath City	26	7	1	18	38	86	15

1926-27

Eastern Section

Brighton & Hove Albion Reserves	32	21	6	5	86	47	48
Peterborough & Fletton United	32	18	9	5	80	39	45
Portsmouth Reserves	32	19	6	7	95	65	44
Kettering Town	32	15	10	7	66	41	40
Millwall Reserves	32	16	5	11	67	56	37
Bournemouth Reserves	32	14	6	12	69	64	34
Norwich City Reserves	32	14	5	13	79	74	33
Dartford	32	13	7	12	60	71	33
Reading Reserves	32	12	8	12	75	79	32
Luton Town Reserves	32	10	11	11	75	70	1
Leicester City Reserves	32	12	5	15	94	72	29
Watford Reserves	32	10	8	14	74	84	28
Southampton Reserves	32	10	6	16	57	77	26
Poole	32	9	6	17	55	86	24
Grays Thurrock United	32	10	3	19	49	66	23
Guildford United	32	6	7	19	57	106	19
Folkestone	32	7	4	21	57	98	18

Western Section

Torquay United	26	17	4	5	63	30	38
Bristol City Reserves	26	14	10	2	77	37	38
Plymouth Argyle Reserves	26	15	4	7	56	38	34
Ebbw Vale	26	14	2	10	67	45	30
Bristol Rovers Reserves	26	12	4	10	51	43	28
Swindon Town Reserves	26	11	5	10	60	57	27
Barry	26	11	4	11	65	50	26
Exeter City Reserves	26	10	6	10	62	49	26
Weymouth	26	12	2	12	48	65	26
Newport County Reserves	26	9	6	11	57	53	24
Bath City	26	7	9	10	44	52	23
Yeovil & Petters United	26	9	5	12	49	66	23
Taunton United	26	4	4	18	36	83	12
Mid Rhondda United	26	2	5	19	22	89	9

1927-28

Eastern Section

Kettering Town	34	23	6	5	90	39	52
Peterborough & Fletton United	34	21	3	10	73	43	45
Northfleet United	34	17	7	10	83	54	41
Brighton & Hove Albion Reserves	34	20	0	14	90	63	40
Norwich City Reserves	34	17	6	11	69	69	40
Southampton Reserves	34	16	7	11	92	70	39
Aldershot Town	34	17	5	12	85	66	39
Sittingbourne	34	16	5	13	64	70	37
Millwall Reserves	34	15	6	13	66	59	36
Poole	34	15	5	14	69	84	35
Folkestone	34	12	6	16	71	91	30
Guildford City	34	12	5	17	65	89	29
Dartford	34	12	4	18	46	49	28
Gillingham Reserves	34	10	7	17	72	84	27
Sheppey United	34	11	3	20	57	87	25
Chatham	34	10	4	20	49	70	24
Grays Thurrock United	34	10	3	21	48	88	23
Bournemouth Reserves	34	9	4	21	48	62	22

Western Section

Bristol City Reserves	30	20	3	7	95	51	43
Exeter City Reserves	30	18	4	8	104	56	40
Bristol Rovers Reserves	30	16	3	11	80	64	35
Plymouth Argyle Reserves	30	16	2	12	88	53	34
Newport County Reserves	30	13	8	9	99	70	34
Ebbw Vale	30	15	3	12	67	74	33
Swindon Town Reserves	30	13	4	13	80	74	30
Aberdare & Aberaman	30	12	6	12	62	68	30
Yeovil & Petters United	30	11	7	12	64	57	29
Torquay United Reserves	30	11	6	13	51	67	28
Bath City	30	12	3	15	64	68	27
Taunton Town	30	11	5	14	60	65	27
Weymouth	30	10	6	14	50	83	26
Merthyr Town Reserves	30	9	4	17	50	77	22
Barry	30	8	6	16	45	87	22
Mid Rhondda United	30	7	6	17	36	81	20

1928-29

Eastern Section

Kettering Town	36	24	4	8	96	46	52
Peterborough & Fletton United	36	21	5	10	86	44	47
Brighton & Hove Albion Reserves	36	19	9	8	91	56	47
Millwall Reserves	36	21	4	11	90	67	46
Bournemouth Reserves	36	20	5	11	82	58	45
Aldershot Town	36	18	5	13	68	52	41
Sheppey United	36	17	7	12	58	58	41
Folkestone	36	17	6	13	83	80	40
Northfleet United	36	17	4	15	87	65	38
Gillingham Reserves	36	15	8	13	68	70	38
Guildford City	36	13	11	12	85	78	37
Southampton Reserves	36	14	6	16	86	79	34
Poole	36	13	8	15	62	66	34
Thames Association	36	13	5	18	67	74	31
Dartford	36	10	6	20	55	106	26
Chatham	36	8	8	20	47	81	24
Sittingbourne	36	11	1	24	59	98	23
Norwich City Reserves	36	8	6	22	48	96	22
Grays Thurrock United	36	6	6	24	47	91	18

Western Section

Plymouth Argyle Reserves	26	15	6	5	69	27	36
Newport County Reserves	26	15	2	9	64	58	32
Bristol Rovers Reserves	26	14	3	9	54	45	31
Bristol City Reserves	26	14	2	10	70	46	30
Torquay United Reserves	26	13	4	9	52	42	30
Bath City	26	13	4	9	43	59	30
Exeter City Reserves	26	11	6	9	69	53	28
Lovells Athletic	26	11	6	9	54	48	28
Swindon Town Reserves	26	11	5	10	68	74	27
Yeovil & Petters United	26	11	2	13	49	57	24
Taunton Town	26	9	5	12	58	66	23
Ebbw Vale	26	9	5	12	56	66	23
Barry	26	6	3	17	38	66	15
Merthyr Town Reserves	26	3	1	22	37	92	7

1929-30

Eastern Section

Aldershot Town	32	21	6	5	84	39	48
Millwall Reserves	32	21	3	8	75	56	45
Thames Association	32	17	6	9	80	60	40
Peterborough & Fletton United	32	18	3	11	66	39	39
Northampton Town Reserves	32	17	4	11	86	60	38
Southampton Reserves	32	14	7	11	73	62	35
Sheppey United	32	15	5	12	76	69	35
Kettering Town	32	13	7	12	70	69	33
Dartford	32	14	5	13	57	59	33
Norwich City Reserves	32	14	3	15	69	69	31
Guildford City	32	13	2	17	65	97	28
Bournemouth Reserves	32	10	7	15	59	63	27
Brighton & Hove Albion Reserves	32	12	2	18	56	79	26
Folkestone	32	13	0	19	56	82	26
Sittingbourne	32	10	5	17	55	59	25
Northfleet United	32	6	7	19	53	77	19
Grays Thurrock United	32	7	2	23	54	101	16

Western Section

Bath City	28	16	6	6	85	52	38
Bristol Rovers Reserves	28	16	4	8	66	50	36
Taunton Town	28	14	7	7	50	40	35
Barry	28	15	3	10	65	55	33
Yeovil & Petters United	28	12	7	9	63	47	31
Plymouth Argyle Reserves	28	14	3	11	68	52	31
Newport County Reserves	28	13	4	11	68	76	30
Lovells Athletic	28	13	2	13	59	57	28
Exeter City Reserves	28	11	6	11	49	54	28
Bristol City Reserves	28	11	5	12	59	63	27
Swindon Town Reserves	28	10	6	12	69	67	26
Torquay United Reserves	28	10	6	12	76	77	26
Llanelly	28	10	4	14	55	52	24
Ebbw Vale	28	5	6	17	52	97	16
Merthyr Town Reserves	28	5	1	22	48	93	11

1930-31

Eastern Section

Dartford	16	9	5	2	39	18	23
Aldershot Town	16	10	3	3	50	28	23
Norwich City Reserves	16	9	1	6	47	38	19
Peterborough & Fletton United	16	6	5	5	35	29	17
Thames Association Reserves	16	7	2	7	38	31	16
Millwall Reserves	16	7	0	9	47	40	14
Folkestone	16	4	3	9	31	46	11
Guildford City	16	5	1	10	28	53	11
Sheppey United	16	4	2	10	31	63	10

Western Section

Exeter City Reserves	22	15	2	5	59	28	32
Llanelly	22	10	8	4	72	39	28
Merthyr Town	22	12	3	7	62	49	27
Plymouth Argyle Reserves	22	12	2	8	55	34	26
Bath City	22	10	6	6	47	39	26
Torquay United Reserves	22	9	5	8	66	49	23
Swindon Town Reserves	22	7	7	8	48	52	21
Bristol Rovers Reserves	22	7	6	9	58	64	20
Barry	22	7	5	10	29	39	19
Taunton Town	22	5	7	10	36	62	17
Newport County Reserves	22	6	2	14	36	66	14
Ebbw Vale	22	5	1	16	32	79	11

1931-32

Eastern Section

Dartford	18	12	3	3	53	18	27
Folkestone	18	12	2	4	58	27	26
Guildford City	18	11	1	6	33	24	23
Norwich City Reserves	18	9	2	7	46	33	20
Millwall Reserves	18	9	2	7	41	39	20
Tunbridge Wells Rangers	18	7	5	6	23	25	19
Bournemouth Reserves	18	6	4	8	43	61	16
Peterborough & Fletton United	18	4	5	9	28	29	13
Aldershot Town	18	3	5	10	17	30	11
Sheppey United	18	2	1	15	16	72	5

Western Section

Yeovil & Petters United	24	16	4	4	65	31	36
Plymouth Argyle Reserves	24	15	5	4	81	31	35
Bath City	24	12	7	5	50	33	31
Llanelly	24	12	4	8	65	46	28
Taunton Town	24	13	2	9	53	58	28
Newport County Reserves	24	10	6	8	70	51	26
Exeter City Reserves	24	9	7	8	59	43	25
Merthyr Town	24	9	4	11	66	73	22
Bristol Rovers Reserves	24	8	4	12	54	47	20
Swindon Town Reserves	24	8	4	12	54	95	20
Barry	24	7	3	14	58	76	17
Torquay United Reserves	24	5	6	13	43	66	16
Ebbw Vale	24	3	2	19	34	102	8

1932-33

Eastern Section

Norwich City Reserves	14	9	2	3	34	22	20
Dartford	14	8	2	4	26	23	18
Folkestone	14	7	1	6	35	32	15
Bournemouth Reserves	14	5	4	5	36	33	14
Tunbridge Wells Rangers	14	5	2	7	23	24	12
Guildford City	14	5	2	7	22	28	12
Millwall Reserves	14	5	1	8	27	31	11
Aldershot Reserves	14	3	4	7	24	34	10

Western Section

Bath City	20	13	4	3	62	34	30
Exeter City Reserves	20	12	3	5	62	46	27
Torquay United Reserves	20	12	1	7	56	37	25
Plymouth Argyle Reserves	20	11	2	7	68	38	24
Yeovil & Petters United	20	11	2	7	59	44	24
Llanelly	20	10	2	8	53	33	22
Bristol Rovers Reserves	20	7	3	10	53	65	17
Newport County Reserves	20	6	4	10	42	55	16
Merthyr Tydfil	20	7	1	12	39	58	15
Barry	20	3	4	13	30	72	10
Taunton Town	20	4	2	14	21	63	10

1933-34

Eastern Section

Norwich City Reserves	16	9	4	3	41	15	22
Margate	16	8	3	5	23	20	19
Millwall Reserves	16	7	4	5	28	28	18
Clapton Orient Reserves	16	8	1	7	33	34	17
Bournemouth Reserves	16	6	3	7	28	30	15
Tunbridge Wells Rangers	16	6	2	8	25	36	14
Folkestone	16	5	3	8	26	26	13
Guildford City	16	5	3	8	27	33	13
Dartford	16	4	5	7	15	24	13

Western Section

Plymouth Argyle Reserves	20	13	6	1	62	22	32
Bristol Rovers Reserves	20	14	3	3	56	27	31
Bath City	20	11	3	6	43	25	25
Torquay United Reserves	20	9	4	7	54	36	22
Yeovil & Petters United	20	10	1	9	35	39	21
Exeter City Reserves	20	8	3	9	54	47	19
Merthyr Town	20	8	2	10	39	50	18
Llanelly	20	8	1	11	25	39	17
Barry	20	4	5	11	37	64	13
Newport County Reserves	20	4	3	13	36	54	11
Taunton Town	20	5	1	14	27	65	11

Central Section

Plymouth Argyle Reserves	18	16	1	1	47	14	33
Clapton Orient Reserves	18	9	3	6	35	25	21
Norwich City Reserves	18	8	4	6	41	27	20
Yeovil & Petters United	18	7	4	7	34	38	18
Bath City	18	7	3	8	31	36	17
Dartford	18	6	4	8	28	26	16
Tunbridge Wells Rangers	18	7	1	10	26	37	15
Llanelly	18	6	2	10	28	39	14
Folkestone	18	6	1	11	30	41	13
Guildford City	18	6	1	11	28	45	13

1934-35

Eastern Section

Norwich City Reserves	18	12	1	5	52	21	25
Dartford	18	8	6	4	36	22	22
Margate	18	7	6	7	38	30	20
Bournemouth Reserves	18	8	3	8	34	26	19
Guildford City	18	7	5	6	41	34	19
Aldershot Reserves	18	7	3	8	29	43	17
Folkestone	18	5	6	7	30	39	16
Tunbridge Wells Rangers	18	6	4	8	32	56	16
Clapton Orient Reserves	18	5	4	9	33	35	14
Millwall Reserves	18	3	6	9	26	45	12

Western Section

Yeovil & Petters United	16	11	2	3	49	18	24
Newport County Reserves	16	8	5	3	45	29	21
Plymouth Argyle Reserves	16	7	5	4	40	24	19
Exeter City Reserves	16	7	2	7	38	32	16
Bath City	16	6	4	6	35	32	16
Bristol Rovers Reserves	16	5	5	6	33	37	15
Barry	16	6	3	7	30	40	15
Torquay United Reserves	16	5	3	8	24	29	13
Taunton Town	16	1	3	12	13	66	5

Central Section

Folkestone	20	11	4	5	43	31	26
Guildford City	20	11	4	5	43	39	26
Plymouth Argyle Reserves	20	6	9	5	40	28	21
Torquay United Reserves	20	7	6	7	34	35	20
Bristol Rovers Reserves	20	8	4	8	38	46	20
Margate	20	8	3	9	40	34	19
Dartford	20	8	3	9	43	38	19
Aldershot Reserves	20	8	3	9	33	44	19
Tunbridge Wells Rangers	20	8	2	10	33	37	18
Yeovil & Petters United	20	8	1	11	45	51	17
Bath City	20	6	3	11	34	43	15

1935-36

Eastern Section

Margate	18	13	2	3	49	16	28
Folkestone	18	11	3	4	46	23	25
Dartford	18	9	3	6	47	25	21
Tunbridge Wells Rangers	18	9	1	8	26	41	19
Clapton Orient Reserves	18	7	4	7	39	31	18
Millwall Reserves	18	7	3	8	42	39	17
Norwich City Reserves	18	8	0	10	39	38	16
Guildford City	18	6	3	9	32	52	15
Aldershot Reserves	18	6	1	11	24	45	13
Bournemouth Reserves	18	3	2	13	25	59	8

Western Section

Plymouth Argyle Reserves	16	12	3	1	51	18	27
Bristol Rovers Reserves	16	8	3	5	35	30	19
Newport County Reserves	16	8	3	5	29	30	19
Torquay United Reserves	16	7	1	8	25	28	15
Bath City	16	5	5	6	18	26	15
Cheltenham Town	16	6	2	8	32	28	14
Yeovil & Petters United	16	5	3	8	31	35	13
Barry	16	5	2	9	29	41	12
Exeter City Reserves	16	4	2	10	24	38	10

Central Section

Margate	20	14	3	3	57	18	31
Bristol Rovers Reserves	20	13	1	6	51	37	27
Plymouth Argyle Reserves	20	12	2	6	53	32	26
Aldershot Reserves	20	9	4	7	37	37	22
Folkestone	20	9	3	8	51	36	21
Tunbridge Wells Rangers	20	7	4	9	40	41	18
Dartford	20	7	3	10	34	42	17
Guildford City	20	7	3	10	33	47	17
Cheltenham Town	20	5	5	10	32	45	15
Bath City	20	5	5	10	34	52	15
Yeovil & Petters United	20	3	5	12	40	75	11

1936-37

Ipswich Town	30	19	8	3	68	35	46
Norwich City Reserves	30	18	5	7	70	35	41
Folkestone	30	17	4	9	71	62	38
Margate	30	15	4	11	64	49	34
Guildford City	30	15	4	11	54	60	34
Bath City	30	14	5	11	65	55	33
Yeovil & Petters United	30	15	3	12	77	69	33
Plymouth Argyle Reserves	30	11	8	11	64	58	30
Newport County Reserves	30	11	8	11	72	68	30
Barry	30	12	4	14	58	72	28
Cheltenham Town	30	10	4	16	61	70	24
Dartford	30	9	5	16	41	55	23
Exeter City Reserves	30	8	7	15	57	78	23
Tunbridge Wells Rangers	30	8	6	16	62	64	22
Torquay United Reserves	30	8	5	17	46	76	21
Aldershot Reserves	30	7	6	17	47	74	20

Midweek Section

Margate	18	12	1	5	48	24	25
Bath City	18	10	5	3	38	28	25
Norwich City Reserves	18	9	5	4	44	27	23
Folkestone	18	7	6	5	32	36	20
Millwall Reserves	18	8	3	7	44	47	19
Portsmouth Reserves	18	6	5	7	40	27	17
Tunbridge Wells Rangers	18	5	4	9	30	41	14
Aldershot Reserves	18	6	2	10	20	30	14
Guildford City	18	3	6	9	24	36	12
Dartford	18	4	3	11	19	43	11

1937-38

Guildford City	34	22	5	7	94	60	49
Plymouth Argyle Reserves	34	18	9	7	98	58	45
Ipswich Town	34	19	6	9	89	54	44
Yeovil & Petters United	34	14	14	6	72	45	42
Norwich City Reserves	34	15	11	8	77	55	41
Colchester United	34	15	8	11	90	58	38
Bristol Rovers Reserves	34	14	8	12	63	62	36
Swindon Town Reserves	34	14	7	13	70	76	35
Tunbridge Wells Rangers	34	14	6	14	68	74	34
Aldershot Reserves	34	10	12	12	42	55	32
Cheltenham Town	34	13	5	16	72	68	31
Exeter City Reserves	34	13	5	16	71	75	31
Dartford	34	9	11	14	51	70	29
Bath City	34	9	9	16	45	65	27
Folkestone	34	10	6	18	58	82	26
Newport County Reserves	34	10	6	18	56	86	26
Barry	34	8	7	19	50	88	23
Torquay United Reserves	34	8	7	19	46	81	23

Midweek Section

Millwall Reserves	18	13	3	2	59	21	29
Colchester United	18	13	1	4	42	23	27
Aldershot Reserves	18	11	3	4	38	29	25
Norwich City Reserves	18	9	1	8	45	39	19
Portsmouth Reserves	18	5	5	8	31	30	15
Dartford	18	6	3	9	32	35	15
Folkestone	18	6	3	9	34	38	15
Tunbridge Wells Rangers	18	5	4	9	28	36	14
Bath City	18	5	3	10	27	45	13
Guildford City	18	4	0	14	21	61	8

1938-39

Colchester United	44	31	5	8	110	37	67
Guildford City	44	30	6	8	126	52	66
Gillingham	44	29	6	9	104	57	64
Plymouth Argyle Reserves	44	26	5	13	128	63	57
Yeovil & Petters United	44	22	10	12	85	70	54
Arsenal Reserves	44	21	9	14	92	57	51
Cardiff City Reserves	44	24	3	17	105	72	51
Tunbridge Wells Rangers	44	22	6	16	93	76	50
Norwich City Reserves	44	23	4	17	86	76	50
Chelmsford City	44	18	8	18	74	73	44
Bath City	44	16	12	16	58	74	44
Barry	44	18	7	19	76	90	43
Cheltenham Town	44	16	9	19	76	105	41
Ipswich Town Reserves	44	14	12	18	64	76	40
Worcester City	44	13	14	17	72	90	40
Folkestone	44	16	6	22	74	85	38
Newport County Reserves	44	13	10	21	74	108	36
Exeter City Reserves	44	12	9	23	51	107	33
Torquay United Reserves	44	12	8	24	53	89	32
Swindon Town Reserves	44	11	9	24	66	101	31
Aldershot Reserves	44	12	6	26	69	92	30
Bristol Rovers Reserves	44	9	11	24	66	85	29
Dartford	44	8	5	31	53	119	21

Midweek Section

Tunbridge Wells Rangers	16	8	7	1	37	18	23
Colchester United	16	9	2	5	36	21	20
Norwich City Reserves	16	7	4	5	40	26	18
Millwall Reserves	16	7	4	5	33	23	18
Portsmouth Reserves	16	5	4	7	21	29	14
Guildford City	16	4	6	6	24	39	14
Aldershot Reserves	16	4	5	7	22	25	13
Folkestone	16	4	5	7	24	35	13
Dartford	16	4	3	9	24	45	11

1939-40

Eastern Section

Chelmsford City	7	5	0	2	29	9	10
Guildford City	8	4	1	3	26	13	9
Tunbridge Wells Rangers	7	2	3	2	21	16	7
Dartford	7	2	1	4	17	30	5
Norwich City Reserves	7	2	1	4	9	34	5

Western Section

Lovells Athletic	14	11	1	2	53	22	23
Worcester City	14	9	2	3	55	30	20
Hereford United	14	8	0	6	45	31	16
Yeovil & Petters United	14	7	2	5	30	24	16
Gloucester City	14	5	0	9	35	49	10
Barry	14	4	1	9	31	56	9
Cheltenham Town	13	3	2	8	21	38	8
Bath City	13	3	2	8	21	41	8

1945-46

Chelmsford City	18	15	1	2	66	23	34
Hereford United	20	13	3	4	59	31	29
Bath City	20	12	2	6	62	32	26
Cheltenham Town	18	9	1	8	35	54	22
Barry Town	20	8	4	8	42	42	20
Yeovil & Petters United	18	7	1	10	57	52	18
Worcester City	20	8	2	10	60	58	18
Colchester United	20	7	3	10	29	47	17
Bedford Town	16	4	1	11	30	49	15
Swindon Town Reserves	18	4	3	11	36	65	14
Cardiff City Reserves	20	4	5	11	39	60	13

1946-47

Gillingham	31	20	6	5	103	45	47
Guildford City	32	21	4	7	86	39	46
Merthyr Tydfil	31	21	2	8	104	37	45
Yeovil Town	32	19	6	7	100	49	44
Chelmsford City	31	17	3	11	90	60	38
Gravesend & Northfleet	32	17	4	11	82	58	38
Barry Town	30	14	6	10	89	61	36
Colchester United	31	15	4	12	65	60	35
Cheltenham Town	31	14	3	14	68	75	32
Millwall	24	8	5	11	59	57	29
Dartford	32	10	5	17	71	100	25
Bedford Town	32	8	8	16	63	98	24
Hereford United	32	8	7	17	37	85	23
Worcester City	31	8	5	18	55	90	22
Exeter City Reserves	32	10	2	20	69	126	22
Bath City	32	7	7	18	52	93	21
Gloucester City	32	8	1	23	57	120	17

1947-48

Merthyr Tydfil	34	23	7	4	84	38	53
Gillingham	34	21	5	8	81	43	47
Worcester City	34	21	3	10	74	45	45
Colchester United	34	17	10	7	88	41	44
Hereford United	34	16	10	8	77	53	42
Lovells Athletic	34	17	6	11	74	50	40
Exeter City Reserves	34	15	7	12	65	57	37
Yeovil Town	34	12	11	11	56	50	35
Chelmsford City	34	14	7	13	62	58	35
Cheltenham Town	34	13	9	12	71	71	35
Bath City	34	12	8	14	55	62	32
Barry Town	34	10	9	15	60	70	29
Gravesend & Northfleet	34	11	6	17	52	81	28
Guildford City	34	11	4	19	69	74	26
Dartford	34	10	6	18	35	62	26
Gloucester City	34	8	6	20	45	78	22
Torquay United Reserves	34	6	9	19	43	95	21
Bedford Town	34	6	3	25	41	104	15

1948-49

Gillingham	42	26	10	6	104	48	62
Chelmsford City	42	27	7	8	115	64	61
Merthyr Tydfil	42	26	8	8	133	54	60
Colchester United	42	21	10	11	94	61	52
Worcester City	42	22	7	13	87	56	51
Dartford	42	21	9	12	73	53	51
Gravesend & Northfleet	42	20	9	13	60	46	49
Yeovil Town	42	19	9	14	90	53	47
Cheltenham Town	42	19	9	14	71	64	47
Kidderminster Harriers	42	19	6	17	77	96	44
Exeter City Reserves	42	18	7	17	83	73	43
Hereford United	42	17	6	19	83	84	40
Bath City	42	15	8	19	72	87	38
Hastings United	42	14	10	18	69	93	38
Torquay United Reserves	42	15	7	20	73	93	37
Lovells Athletic	42	14	8	20	73	74	36
Guildford City	42	12	12	18	58	85	36
Gloucester City	42	12	10	20	78	100	34
Barry Town	42	12	10	20	55	95	34
Tonbridge	42	9	7	26	54	105	25
Chingford Town	42	6	9	27	43	94	21
Bedford Town	42	5	8	29	32	101	18

1949-50

Merthyr Tydfil	46	34	3	9	143	62	71
Colchester United	46	31	9	6	109	51	71
Yeovil Town	46	29	7	10	104	45	65
Chelmsford City	46	26	9	11	121	64	61
Gillingham	46	23	9	14	93	61	55
Dartford	46	20	9	17	70	65	49
Worcester City	46	21	7	18	85	80	49
Guildford City	46	18	11	17	79	73	47
Weymouth	46	19	9	18	80	82	47
Barry Town	46	18	10	18	78	72	46
Exeter City Reserves	46	16	14	16	73	83	46
Lovells Athletic	46	17	10	19	86	78	44
Tonbridge	46	16	12	18	65	76	44
Hastings United	46	17	8	21	92	140	42
Gravesend & Northfleet	46	16	9	21	88	82	41
Torquay United Reserves	46	14	12	20	80	89	40
Bath City	46	16	7	23	61	78	39
Gloucester City	46	14	11	21	72	101	39
Hereford United	46	15	8	23	74	76	38
Cheltenham Town	46	13	11	22	75	96	37
Headington United	46	15	7	24	72	97	37
Bedford Town	46	12	11	23	63	79	35
Kidderminster Harriers	46	12	11	23	65	108	35
Chingford Town	46	10	6	30	61	151	26

1950-51

Merthyr Tydfil	44	29	8	7	156	66	66
Hereford United	44	27	7	10	110	69	61
Guildford City	44	23	8	13	88	60	54
Chelmsford City	44	21	12	11	84	58	54
Llanelly	44	19	13	12	89	73	51
Cheltenham Town	44	21	8	15	91	61	50
Headington United	44	18	11	15	84	83	47
Torquay United Reserves	44	20	6	18	93	79	46
Exeter City Reserves	44	16	12	16	90	94	44
Weymouth	44	16	12	16	82	88	44
Tonbridge	44	16	12	16	79	87	44
Gloucester City	44	16	11	17	81	76	43
Yeovil Town	44	13	15	16	72	72	41
Worcester City	44	15	11	18	69	78	41
Bath City	44	15	10	19	66	73	40
Dartford	44	14	11	19	61	70	39
Bedford Town	44	15	9	20	64	94	39
Gravesend & Northfleet	44	12	14	18	65	83	38
Kettering Town	44	13	11	20	87	87	37
Lovells Athletic	44	12	13	19	81	93	37
Kidderminster Harriers	44	13	9	22	58	103	35
Barry Town	44	13	7	24	54	104	33
Hastings United	44	11	6	27	91	143	28

1951-52

Merthyr Tydfil	42	27	6	9	128	60	60
Weymouth	42	22	13	7	81	42	57
Kidderminster Harriers	42	22	10	10	70	40	54
Guildford City	42	18	16	8	66	47	52
Hereford United	42	21	9	12	80	59	51
Worcester City	42	23	4	15	86	73	50
Kettering Town	42	18	10	14	83	56	46
Lovells Athletic	42	18	10	14	87	68	46
Gloucester City	42	19	8	15	68	55	46
Bath City	42	19	6	17	75	67	44
Headington United	42	16	11	15	55	53	43
Bedford Town	42	16	10	16	75	64	42
Barry Town	42	18	6	18	84	89	42
Chelmsford City	42	15	10	17	67	80	40
Dartford	42	15	9	18	63	65	39
Tonbridge	42	15	6	21	63	84	36
Yeovil Town	42	12	11	19	56	76	35
Cheltenham Town	42	15	4	23	59	85	34
Exeter City Reserves	42	13	7	22	76	106	33
Llanelly	42	13	6	23	70	111	32
Gravesend & Northfleet	42	12	7	23	68	88	31
Hastings United	42	3	5	34	41	131	11

1952-53

Headington United	42	23	12	7	93	50	58
Merthyr Tydfil	42	25	8	9	117	66	58
Bedford Town	42	24	8	10	91	61	56
Kettering Town	42	23	8	11	88	50	54
Bath City	42	22	10	10	71	46	54
Worcester City	42	20	11	11	100	66	51
Llanelly	42	21	9	12	95	72	51
Barry Town	42	22	3	17	89	69	47
Gravesend & Northfleet	42	19	7	16	83	76	45
Gloucester City	42	17	9	16	50	78	43
Guildford City	42	17	8	17	64	60	42
Hastings United	42	18	5	19	75	66	41
Cheltenham Town	42	15	11	16	70	89	41
Weymouth	42	15	10	17	70	75	40
Hereford United	42	17	5	20	76	73	39
Tonbridge	42	12	9	21	62	88	33
Lovells Athletic	42	12	8	22	68	81	32
Yeovil Town	42	11	10	21	75	99	32
Chelmsford City	42	12	7	23	58	92	31
Exeter City Reserves	42	13	4	25	71	94	30
Kidderminster Harriers	42	12	5	25	54	85	29
Dartford	42	6	5	31	40	121	17

1953-54

Team	P	W	D	L	F	A	Pts
Merthyr Tydfil	42	27	8	7	97	55	62
Headington United	42	22	9	11	68	43	53
Yeovil Town	42	20	8	14	87	76	48
Bath City	42	17	12	13	73	67	46
Kidderminster Harriers	42	18	9	15	62	59	45
Weymouth	42	18	8	16	83	72	44
Barry Town	42	17	9	16	108	91	43
Bedford Town	42	19	5	18	80	84	43
Gloucester City	42	16	11	15	69	77	43
Hastings United	42	16	10	16	73	67	42
Kettering Town	42	15	12	15	65	63	42
Hereford United	42	16	9	17	66	62	41
Llanelly	42	16	9	17	80	85	41
Guildford City	42	15	11	16	56	60	41
Gravesend & Northfleet	42	16	8	18	76	77	40
Worcester City	42	17	6	19	66	71	40
Lovells Athletic	42	14	11	17	62	60	39
Tonbridge	42	15	9	18	85	91	39
Chelmsford City	42	14	10	18	67	71	38
Exeter City Reserves	42	11	13	18	61	72	35
Cheltenham Town	42	11	12	19	56	83	34
Dartford	42	6	13	23	42	89	25

1954-55

Team	P	W	D	L	F	A	Pts
Yeovil Town	42	23	9	10	105	66	55
Weymouth	42	24	7	11	105	84	55
Hastings United	42	21	9	12	94	60	51
Cheltenham Town	42	21	8	13	85	72	50
Guildford City	42	20	8	14	72	59	48
Worcester City	42	19	10	13	80	73	48
Barry Town	42	16	15	11	82	87	47
Gloucester City	42	16	13	13	66	54	45
Bath City	42	18	9	15	73	80	45
Headington Town	42	18	7	17	82	62	43
Kidderminster Harriers	42	18	7	17	84	86	43
Merthyr Tydfil	42	19	4	19	67	78	42
Exeter City Reserves	42	17	8	17	97	94	42
Lovells Athletic	42	15	11	16	71	68	41
Kettering Town	42	15	11	16	70	69	41
Hereford United	42	17	5	20	91	72	39
Llanelly	42	16	7	19	78	81	39
Bedford Town	42	16	3	23	75	103	35
Tonbridge	42	11	8	23	68	91	30
Dartford	42	9	12	21	55	76	30
Chelmsford City	42	11	6	25	73	111	28
Gravesend & Northfleet	42	9	9	24	62	97	27

1955-56

Team	P	W	D	L	F	A	Pts
Guildford City	42	26	8	8	74	34	60
Cheltenham Town	42	25	6	11	82	53	56
Yeovil Town	42	23	9	10	98	55	55
Bedford Town	42	21	9	12	99	69	51
Dartford	42	20	9	13	78	62	49
Weymouth	42	19	10	13	83	63	48
Gloucester City	42	19	9	14	72	60	47
Lovells Athletic	42	19	9	14	91	78	47
Chelmsford City	42	18	10	14	67	55	46
Kettering Town	42	16	11	15	105	86	43
Exeter City Reserves	42	17	9	16	75	76	43
Gravesend & Northfleet	42	17	8	17	79	75	42
Hereford United	42	17	7	18	90	90	41
Hastings United	42	15	10	17	90	76	40
Headington United	42	17	6	19	82	86	40
Kidderminster Harriers	42	14	7	21	86	108	35
Llanelly	42	14	6	22	64	98	34
Barry Town	42	11	11	20	91	108	33
Worcester City	42	12	9	21	66	83	33
Tonbridge	42	11	11	20	53	74	33
Merthyr Tydfil	42	7	10	25	52	127	24
Bath City	42	7	10	25	43	107	24

1956-57

Team	P	W	D	L	F	A	Pts
Kettering Town	42	28	10	4	106	47	66
Bedford Town	42	25	8	9	89	52	58
Weymouth	42	22	10	10	92	71	54
Cheltenham Town	42	19	15	8	73	46	53
Gravesend & Northfleet	42	21	11	10	74	58	53
Lovells Athletic	42	21	7	14	99	84	49
Guildford City	42	18	11	13	68	49	47
Hereford United	42	19	8	15	96	60	46
Headington United	42	19	7	16	64	61	45
Gloucester City	42	18	8	16	74	72	44
Hastings United	42	17	9	16	70	58	43
Worcester City	42	16	10	16	81	80	42
Dartford	42	16	10	16	79	88	42
Chelmsford City	42	16	9	17	73	85	41
Tonbridge	42	14	12	16	74	65	40
Yeovil Town	42	14	11	17	83	85	39
Bath City	42	15	8	19	56	78	38
Exeter City Reserves	42	10	10	22	52	89	30
Merthyr Tydfil	42	9	11	22	72	95	29
Barry Town	42	6	11	25	39	84	23
Kidderminster Harriers	42	7	10	25	60	83	20
Llanelly	42	5	8	29	39	123	18

1957-58

Team	P	W	D	L	F	A	Pts
Gravesend & Northfleet	42	27	5	10	109	71	59
Bedford Town	42	25	7	10	112	64	57
Chelmsford City	42	24	9	9	93	57	57
Weymouth	42	25	5	12	90	61	55
Worcester City	42	23	7	12	95	59	53
Cheltenham Town	42	21	10	11	115	66	52
Hereford United	42	21	6	15	79	56	48
Kettering Town	42	18	9	15	99	76	45
Headington Town	42	18	7	17	90	83	43
Poole Town	42	17	9	16	82	81	43
Hasting United	42	13	15	14	78	77	41
Gloucester City	42	17	7	18	70	70	41
Yeovil Town	42	16	9	17	70	84	41
Dartford	42	14	9	19	66	92	37
Lovells Athletic	42	15	6	21	60	83	36
Bath City	42	13	9	20	65	64	35
Guildford City	42	12	10	20	58	92	34
Tonbridge	42	13	7	22	77	100	33
Exeter City Reserves	42	12	8	22	60	94	32
Barry Town	42	11	9	22	72	101	31
Kidderminster Harriers	42	10	10	22	60	101	30
Merthyr Tydfil	42	9	3	30	69	137	21

1958-59

North-Western Zone

Team	P	W	D	L	F	A	Pts
Hereford United	34	22	5	7	80	37	49
Kettering Town	34	20	7	7	83	63	47
Boston United	34	18	8	8	73	47	44
Cheltenham Town	34	20	4	10	65	47	44
Worcester City	34	19	4	11	74	47	42
Bath City	34	17	5	12	89	62	39
Wellington Town	34	15	9	10	74	58	39
Nuneaton Borough	34	17	5	12	76	66	39
Wisbech Town	34	16	5	13	77	54	37
Headington United	34	16	3	15	76	61	35
Barry Town	34	15	5	14	64	67	35
Merthyr Tydfil	34	16	3	15	54	59	35
Gloucester City	34	12	6	16	50	65	30
Corby Town	34	10	8	16	59	79	28
Lovells Athletic	34	10	3	21	51	70	23
Rugby Town	34	7	6	21	45	93	20
Kidderminster Harriers	34	7	3	24	42	94	17
Burton Albion	34	3	3	28	41	104	9

South-Eastern Zone

Bedford Town	32	21	6	5	90	41	48
Gravesend & Northfleet	32	21	2	9	79	54	44
Dartford	32	20	3	9	77	41	43
Yeovil Town	32	17	8	7	60	41	42
Weymouth	32	13	11	8	61	43	37
Chelmsford City	32	12	12	8	74	53	36
King's Lynn	32	14	5	13	70	63	33
Poole Town	32	12	8	12	60	65	32
Cambridge City	32	12	7	13	61	54	31
Hastings United	32	13	5	14	60	59	31
Tonbridge	32	14	3	15	51	59	31
Cambridge United	32	11	8	13	55	77	30
Trowbridge Town	32	12	4	16	53	75	28
Exeter City Reserves	32	7	12	13	47	71	26
Guildford City	11	7	6	19	45	67	20
Clacton Town	32	6	7	19	44	81	19
Yiewsley	32	3	7	22	36	78	13

1959-60

Premier Division

Bath City	42	32	3	7	116	50	67
Headington United	42	23	8	11	78	61	54
Weymouth	42	22	9	11	93	69	53
Cheltenham Town	42	21	6	15	82	68	48
Cambridge City	42	18	11	13	81	72	47
Chelmsford Town	42	19	7	16	90	70	45
Bedford Town	42	21	3	18	97	85	45
King's Lynn	42	17	11	14	89	78	45
Boston United	42	17	10	15	83	80	44
Wisbech Town	42	17	10	15	81	84	44
Yeovil Town	42	17	8	17	81	73	42
Hereford United	42	15	12	15	70	74	42
Tonbridge	42	16	8	18	79	73	40
Hastings United	42	16	8	18	63	77	40
Wellington Town	42	13	11	18	63	78	37
Dartford	42	15	7	20	64	82	37
Gravesend & Northfleet	42	14	8	20	69	84	36
Worcester City	42	13	10	19	72	89	36
Nuneaton Borough	42	11	11	20	64	78	33
Barry Town	42	14	5	23	78	103	33
Poole Town	42	10	8	24	69	96	28
Kettering Town	42	9	10	23	60	90	28

First Division

Clacton Town	42	27	5	10	106	69	59
Romford	42	21	11	10	65	40	53
Folkestone Town	42	23	5	14	93	71	51
Exeter City Reserves	42	23	3	16	85	62	49
Guildford City	42	19	9	14	79	56	47
Sittingbourne	42	20	7	15	66	55	47
Margate	42	20	6	16	88	77	46
Trowbridge Town	42	18	9	15	90	78	45
Cambridge United	42	18	9	15	71	72	45
Yiewsley	42	17	10	15	83	69	44
Bexleyheath & Welling	42	16	11	15	85	77	43
Merthyr Tydfil	42	16	10	16	63	65	42
Ramsgate Athletic	42	16	8	18	83	84	40
Ashford Town	42	14	12	16	61	70	40
Tunbridge Wells United	42	17	5	20	77	73	39
Hinckley Athletic	42	14	8	20	62	75	36
Gloucester City	42	13	9	20	56	84	35
Dover	42	14	6	22	59	85	34
Kidderminster Harriers	42	14	6	22	59	97	34
Corby Town	42	15	3	24	75	91	33
Burton Albion	42	11	10	21	52	79	32
Rugby Town	42	10	11	21	67	91	31

1960-61   Premier Division

Oxford United	42	27	10	5	104	43	64
Chelmsford City	42	23	11	8	91	55	57
Yeovil Town	42	23	9	10	109	54	55
Hereford United	42	21	10	11	83	67	52
Weymouth	42	21	9	12	78	63	51
Bath City	42	18	14	10	74	52	50
Cambridge City	42	16	12	14	101	71	44
Wellington Town	42	17	9	16	66	68	43
Bedford Town	42	18	7	17	94	97	43
Folkestone Town	42	18	7	17	75	86	43
King's Lynn	42	13	16	13	68	66	42
Worcester City	42	15	11	16	69	69	41
Clacton Town	42	15	11	16	82	83	41
Romford	42	13	15	14	66	69	41
Guildford City	42	14	11	17	65	62	39
Tonbridge	42	16	6	20	79	85	38
Cheltenham Town	42	15	7	20	81	81	37
Gravesend & Northfleet	42	15	7	20	75	101	37
Dartford	42	13	11	18	57	90	37
Hastings United	42	8	9	25	60	100	25
Wisbech Town	42	9	6	27	58	112	24
Boston United	42	6	8	28	62	123	20

Oxford United were previously known as Headington United.

First Division

Kettering Town	40	26	7	7	100	55	59
Cambridge United	40	25	5	10	100	53	55
Bexleyheath & Welling	40	22	8	10	93	46	52
Merthyr Tydfil	40	23	6	11	88	65	52
Sittingbourne	40	21	10	9	77	63	52
Hinckley Athletic	40	17	13	10	74	59	47
Ramsgate Athletic	40	19	7	14	77	56	45
Rugby Town	40	18	9	13	89	71	45
Corby Town	40	16	10	14	82	73	42
Poole Town	40	18	5	17	71	65	41
Barry Town	40	16	9	15	65	74	41
Yiewsley	40	17	7	16	65	76	41
Trowbridge Town	40	14	10	16	71	73	38
Ashford Town	40	14	8	18	61	67	36
Margate	40	11	12	17	62	75	34
Dover	40	12	7	21	67	74	31
Canterbury City	40	10	10	20	52	75	30
Nuneaton Borough	40	11	7	22	60	91	29
Burton Albion	40	12	4	24	63	85	28
Tunbridge Wells United	40	8	5	27	56	115	21
Gloucester City	40	7	7	26	40	102	21

1961-62   Premier Division

Oxford United	42	28	5	9	118	46	61
Bath City	42	25	7	10	102	70	57
Guildford City	42	24	8	10	79	49	56
Yeovil Town	42	23	8	11	97	59	54
Chelmsford City	42	19	12	11	74	60	50
Weymouth	42	20	7	15	80	64	47
Kettering Town	42	21	5	16	90	84	47
Hereford United	42	21	2	19	81	68	44
Cambridge City	42	18	8	16	70	71	44
Bexleyheath & Welling	42	19	5	18	69	75	43
Romford	42	15	9	18	63	70	39
Cambridge United	42	13	12	17	76	78	38
Wellington United	42	14	10	18	75	78	38
Gravesend & Northfleet	42	17	4	21	59	92	38
Bedford Town	42	16	5	21	73	79	37
Worcester City	42	15	7	20	51	64	37
Merthyr Tydfil	42	13	11	18	62	80	37
Clacton Town	42	13	10	19	74	91	36
Tonbridge	42	10	14	18	71	92	34
King's Lynn	42	12	8	22	59	74	32
Folkestone Town	42	12	6	24	64	103	30
Cheltenham	42	9	7	26	48	86	25

First Division

Wisbech Town	38	21	11	6	76	42	53
Poole Town	38	23	6	9	81	47	52
Dartford	38	21	8	9	89	50	50
Rugby Town	38	20	9	9	82	49	49
Margate	38	20	6	12	73	55	46
Corby Town	38	19	6	13	82	60	44
Sittingbourne	38	16	12	10	69	51	44
Dover	38	19	6	13	66	55	44
Yiewsley	38	18	6	14	64	51	42
Barry Town	38	14	11	13	55	51	39
Ashford Town	38	14	11	13	66	70	39
Hinckley Athletic	38	15	8	15	75	65	38
Burton Albion	38	16	5	17	70	79	37
Nuneaton Borough	38	12	12	14	63	69	36
Tunbridge Wells United	38	12	7	19	60	85	31
Canterbury City	38	11	8	19	60	82	30
Ramsgate Athletic	38	10	9	19	48	70	29
Trowbridge Town	38	9	9	20	45	69	27
Gloucester City	38	6	4	28	46	104	16
Hastings United	38	5	4	29	45	115	14

1962-63

Premier Division

Cambridge City	40	25	6	9	99	64	56
Cambridge United	40	23	7	10	74	50	53
Weymouth	40	20	11	9	82	43	51
Guildford City	40	20	11	9	70	50	51
Kettering Town	40	22	7	11	66	49	51
Wellington Town	40	19	9	12	71	49	47
Dartford	40	19	9	12	61	54	47
Chelmsford City	40	18	10	12	63	50	46
Bedford Town	40	18	8	14	61	45	44
Bath City	40	18	6	16	58	56	42
Yeovil Town	40	15	10	15	64	54	40
Romford	40	14	11	15	73	68	39
Bexleyheath & Welling	40	13	11	16	55	63	37
Hereford United	40	14	7	19	56	66	35
Merthyr Tydfil	40	15	4	21	54	71	34
Rugby Town	40	14	5	21	65	76	33
Wisbech Town	40	15	3	22	64	84	33
Worcester City	40	12	9	19	47	65	33
Poole Town	40	10	12	18	54	66	32
Gravesend & Northfleet	40	10	3	27	62	91	23
Clacton Town	40	3	7	30	50	135	13

First Division

Margate	38	21	13	4	86	47	55
Hinckley Athletic	38	22	9	7	66	38	53
Hastings United	38	22	8	8	86	36	52
Nuneaton Borough	38	21	10	7	82	41	52
Tonbridge	38	22	8	8	81	51	52
Dover	38	22	7	9	78	56	51
Corby Town	38	19	8	11	79	50	46
King's Lynn	38	19	7	15	76	66	45
Cheltenham Town	38	18	7	13	83	52	43
Folkestone Town	38	15	10	13	79	57	40
Canterbury City	38	14	8	16	42	56	36
Yiewsley	38	11	10	17	63	71	32
Ramsgate Athletic	38	12	7	19	58	82	31
Trowbridge Town	38	11	9	18	50	81	31
Burton Albion	38	10	10	18	48	76	30
Gloucester City	38	9	11	18	42	78	29
Sittingbourne	38	12	3	23	56	75	27
Ashford Town	38	9	6	23	58	76	24
Barry Town	38	6	5	27	35	75	17
Tunbridge Wells United	38	6	2	30	43	118	14

1963-64

Premier Division

Yeovil Town	42	29	5	8	93	36	63
Chelmsford City	42	26	7	9	99	55	59
Bath City	42	24	9	9	88	51	57
Guildford City	42	21	9	12	90	55	51
Romford	42	20	9	13	71	58	49
Hastings United	42	20	8	14	75	61	48
Weymouth	42	20	7	15	65	53	47
Bedford Town	42	19	9	14	71	68	47
Cambridge United	42	17	9	16	92	77	43
Cambridge City	42	17	9	16	76	70	43
Wisbech Town	42	17	8	17	64	68	42
Bexley United	42	16	10	16	70	77	42
Dartford	42	16	8	18	56	71	40
Worcester City	42	12	15	15	70	74	39
Nuneaton Borough	42	15	8	19	58	61	38
Rugby Town	42	15	8	19	68	86	38
Margate	42	12	13	17	68	81	37
Wellington Town	42	12	9	21	73	85	33
Merthyr Tydfil	42	12	8	22	69	108	32
Hereford United	42	12	7	23	58	86	31
Kettering Town	42	10	5	27	49	89	25
Hinckley Athletic	42	7	6	29	51	104	20

First Division

Folkstone Town	42	28	7	7	82	38	63
King's Lynn	42	28	5	9	94	44	61
Cheltenham Town	42	25	10	7	92	49	60
Tonbridge	42	24	11	7	98	54	59
Corby town	42	24	7	11	114	56	55
Stevenage Town	42	21	6	15	70	59	48
Ashford Town	42	19	9	14	73	57	47
Burton Albion	42	19	8	15	76	70	46
Poole Town	42	17	11	14	75	61	45
Dover	42	18	9	15	86	75	45
Canterbury City	42	16	12	14	66	66	44
Crawley Town	42	20	2	20	81	71	42
Trowbridge Town	42	16	9	17	71	78	41
Clacton Town	42	19	1	22	76	88	39
Gloucester City	42	17	4	21	88	89	38
Yiewsley	42	15	8	19	63	77	38
Sittingbourne	42	15	8	19	52	70	38
Ramsgate Athletic	42	13	9	20	57	55	35
Tunbridge Wells Rangers	42	10	8	24	47	89	28
Gravesend & Northfleet	42	7	9	26	43	96	23
Deal Town	42	5	7	30	48	106	17
Barry Town	42	3	6	33	33	137	12

1964-65 Premier Division

Weymouth	42	24	8	10	99	50	56
Guildford City	42	21	12	9	73	49	54
Worcester City	42	22	6	14	100	62	50
Yeovil Town	42	18	14	10	76	55	50
Chelmsford City	42	21	8	13	86	77	50
Margate	42	20	9	13	88	79	49
Dartford	42	17	11	14	74	64	45
Nuneaton Borough	42	19	7	16	57	55	45
Cambridge United	42	16	11	15	78	66	43
Bedford Town	42	17	9	16	66	70	43
Cambridge City	42	16	9	17	72	69	41
Cheltenham Town	42	15	11	16	72	78	41
Folkestone Town	42	17	7	18	72	79	41
Romford	42	17	7	18	61	70	41
King's Lynn	42	13	13	16	56	79	39
Tonbridge	42	10	16	16	66	75	36
Wellington Town	42	13	10	19	63	78	36
Rugby Town	42	15	6	21	71	98	36
Wisbech Town	42	14	6	22	75	91	34
Bexley United	42	14	5	23	67	74	33
Hastings United	42	9	14	19	58	86	32
Bath City	42	13	3	26	60	86	29

First Division

Hereford United	42	34	4	4	124	39	72
Wimbledon	42	24	13	5	108	52	61
Poole Town	42	26	6	10	92	56	58
Corby Town	42	24	7	11	88	55	55
Stevenage Town	42	19	13	10	83	43	51
Hillingdon Borough	42	21	7	14	105	63	49
Crawley Town	42	22	5	15	83	52	49
Merthyr Tydfil	42	20	9	13	75	59	49
Gloucester City	42	19	10	13	68	65	48
Burton Albion	42	20	7	15	83	75	47
Canterbury City	42	13	16	13	73	53	42
Kettering Town	42	14	13	15	74	64	41
Ramsgate Athletic	42	16	8	18	51	59	40
Dover	42	14	10	18	54	59	38
Hinckley Athletic	42	13	9	20	56	81	35
Trowbridge Town	42	13	5	24	68	106	31
Ashford Town	42	11	8	23	60	98	30
Barry Town	42	11	7	24	47	103	29
Deal Town	42	7	13	22	61	127	27
Tunbridge Wells Rangers	42	10	6	26	51	107	26
Gravesend & Northfleet	42	9	7	26	57	101	25
Sittingbourne	42	8	5	29	58	103	21

1965-66 Premier Division

Weymouth	42	22	13	7	70	35	57
Chelmsford City	42	21	12	9	74	50	54
Hereford United	42	21	10	11	81	49	52
Bedford Town	42	23	6	13	80	57	52
Wimbledon	42	20	10	12	80	47	50
Cambridge City	42	19	11	12	67	52	49
Romford	42	21	7	14	87	72	49
Worcester City	42	20	8	14	69	54	48
Yeovil Town	42	17	11	14	91	70	45
Cambridge United	42	18	9	15	72	64	45
King's Lynn	42	18	7	17	75	72	43
Corby Town	42	16	9	17	66	73	41
Wellington Town	42	13	13	16	65	70	39
Nuneaton Borough	42	15	8	19	60	74	38
Folkestone Town	42	14	9	19	53	75	37
Guildford City	42	14	8	20	70	84	36
Poole Town	42	14	7	21	61	75	35
Cheltenham Town	42	13	9	20	69	99	35
Dartford	42	13	7	22	62	69	33
Rugby Town	42	11	10	21	67	95	32
Tonbridge	42	11	6	25	63	101	28
Margate	42	8	10	24	66	111	26

First Division

Barnet	46	30	9	7	114	49	69
Hillingdon Borough	46	27	10	9	101	46	64
Burton Albion	46	28	8	10	121	60	64
Bath City	46	25	13	8	88	50	63
Hastings United	46	25	10	11	104	59	60
Wisbech Town	46	25	9	12	98	54	59
Canterbury City	46	25	8	13	89	66	58
Stevenage Town	46	23	9	14	86	49	55
Kettering Town	46	22	9	15	77	74	53
Merthyr Tydfil	46	22	6	18	95	68	50
Dunstable Town	46	15	14	17	76	72	44
Crawley Town	46	17	10	19	72	71	44
Bexley United	46	20	4	22	65	71	44
Trowbridge Town	46	16	11	19	79	81	43
Dover	46	17	8	21	59	62	42
Barry Town	46	16	10	20	72	94	42
Gravesend & Northfleet	46	16	9	21	84	86	41
Gloucester City	46	14	12	20	75	98	40
Sittingbourne	46	11	12	23	77	121	34
Ramsgate Athletic	46	9	15	22	35	76	33
Hinckley Athletic	46	10	12	24	59	93	32
Tunbridge Wells Rangers	46	12	8	26	47	88	32
Ashford Town	46	9	10	27	44	92	28
Deal Town	46	3	4	39	29	165	10

1966-67

Premier Division

Romford	42	22	8	12	80	60	52
Nuneaton Borough	42	21	9	12	82	54	51
Weymouth	42	18	14	10	64	40	50
Wimbledon	42	19	11	12	88	60	49
Barnet	42	18	13	11	86	66	49
Guildford City	42	19	10	13	65	51	48
Wellington Town	42	20	7	15	70	67	47
Cambridge United	42	16	13	13	75	67	45
Chelmsford City	42	15	15	12	66	59	45
Hereford United	42	16	12	14	79	61	44
King's Lynn	42	15	14	13	78	72	44
Cambridge City	42	15	13	14	66	70	43
Cheltenham Town	42	16	11	15	60	71	43
Yeovil Town	42	14	14	14	66	72	42
Burton Albion	42	17	5	20	63	71	39
Corby Town	42	15	9	18	60	75	39
Poole Town	42	14	11	17	52	65	39
Hillingdon Borough	42	11	13	18	49	70	35
Bath City	42	11	12	19	51	74	34
Worcester City	42	11	8	23	59	79	30
Bedford Town	42	8	13	21	54	72	29
Folkestone Town	42	6	15	21	44	81	27

First Division

	P	W	D	L	F	A	Pts
Dover	46	29	12	5	92	35	70
Margate	46	31	7	8	127	54	69
Stevenage Town	46	29	8	9	90	32	66
Hastings United	46	25	16	5	89	45	66
Kettering United	46	27	9	10	105	62	63
Crawley Town	46	26	8	12	81	48	60
Ramsgate Athletic	46	23	8	15	79	62	54
Dartford	46	19	15	12	92	67	53
Tonbridge	46	21	10	15	91	69	52
Trowbridge Town	46	20	12	14	73	60	52
Ashford Town	46	18	8	20	74	68	44
Merthyr Tydfil	46	17	9	20	81	71	43
Gloucester City	46	18	6	22	69	83	42
Canterbury City	46	17	8	21	57	75	42
Wisbech Town	46	16	9	21	87	93	41
Bexley United	46	13	15	18	53	69	41
Banbury United	46	13	14	19	88	100	40
Rugby Town	46	15	7	24	57	77	37
Dunstable Town	46	14	6	26	55	87	34
Barry Town	46	11	11	24	62	89	33
Gravesend & Northfleet	46	11	9	26	63	106	31
Hinckley Athletic	46	10	8	28	44	100	28
Tunbridge Wells Rangers	46	4	15	27	31	96	23
Sittingbourne	46	5	10	31	44	136	20

1967-68

Premier Division

	P	W	D	L	F	A	Pts
Chelmsford City	42	25	7	10	85	50	57
Wimbledon	42	24	7	11	85	47	55
Cambridge United	42	20	13	9	73	42	53
Cheltenham Town	42	23	7	12	97	67	53
Guildford City	42	18	13	11	56	43	49
Romford	42	20	8	14	72	60	48
Barnet	42	20	8	14	81	71	48
Margate	42	19	8	15	80	71	46
Wellington Town	42	16	13	13	70	66	45
Hillingdon Borough	42	18	9	15	53	54	45
King's Lynn	42	18	8	16	66	57	44
Yeovil Town	42	16	12	14	45	43	44
Weymouth	42	17	8	17	65	62	42
Hereford United	42	17	7	18	58	62	41
Nuneaton Borough	42	13	14	15	62	64	40
Dover	42	17	6	19	54	56	40
Poole Town	42	13	10	19	55	74	36
Stevenage Town	42	13	9	20	57	75	35
Burton Albion	42	14	6	22	51	73	34
Corby Town	42	7	13	22	40	77	27
Cambridge City	42	10	6	26	51	81	26
Hastings United	42	4	8	30	33	94	16

First Division

	P	W	D	L	F	A	Pts
Worcester City	42	23	14	5	92	35	60
Kettering Town	42	24	10	8	88	40	58
Bedford Town	42	24	7	11	101	40	55
Rugby Town	42	20	15	7	72	44	55
Dartford	42	23	9	10	70	48	55
Bath City	42	21	12	9	78	51	54
Banbury United	42	22	9	11	79	59	53
Ramsgate Athletic	42	17	7	8	70	37	51
Merthyr Tydfil	42	18	13	11	80	66	49
Tonbridge	42	18	9	15	76	71	45
Canterbury City	42	16	11	15	66	63	43
Ashford Town	42	18	6	18	73	78	42
Brentwood Town	42	16	9	17	63	73	41
Bexley United	42	12	13	17	56	64	37
Trowbridge Town	42	12	11	19	64	70	35
Gloucester City	42	12	9	21	54	68	33
Wisbech Town	42	11	10	21	43	78	32
Crawley Town	42	10	8	24	54	85	28
Folkestone Town	42	10	7	25	49	80	27
Dunstable Town	42	8	10	24	44	94	26
Barry Town	42	7	12	23	36	81	26
Gravesend & Northfleet	42	6	7	29	28	112	19

1968-69　Premier Division

	P	W	D	L	F	A	Pts
Cambridge United	42	27	5	10	72	39	59
Hillingdon Borough	42	24	10	8	68	47	58
Wimbledon	42	21	12	9	66	48	54
King's Lynn	42	20	9	13	68	60	49
Worcester City	42	19	11	12	53	47	49
Romford	42	18	12	12	58	52	48
Weymouth	42	16	15	11	52	41	47
Yeovil Town	42	16	13	13	52	50	45
Kettering Town	42	18	8	16	51	55	44
Dover	42	17	9	16	66	61	43
Nuneaton Borough	42	17	7	18	74	58	41
Barnet	42	15	10	17	72	66	40
Chelmsford City	42	17	6	19	56	58	40
Hereford United	42	15	9	18	66	62	39
Telford United	42	14	10	18	62	61	38
Poole Town	42	16	6	20	75	76	38
Burton Albion	42	16	5	21	55	71	37
Margate	42	14	7	21	79	90	35
Cheltenham Town	42	15	5	22	55	64	35
Bedford Town	42	11	12	19	46	63	34
Rugby Town	42	10	6	26	38	83	26
Guildford City	42	7	11	24	41	73	25

First Division

	P	W	D	L	F	A	Pts
Brentwood Town	42	26	12	4	44	37	64
Bath City	42	26	10	6	96	40	62
Gloucester City	42	25	9	8	100	53	59
Crawley Town	42	21	13	8	65	32	55
Corby Town	42	22	6	14	81	65	50
Dartford	42	20	8	14	79	51	48
Ramsgate Athletic	42	19	9	14	72	57	47
Salisbury	42	20	6	16	69	52	46
Cambridge City	42	18	10	14	73	63	46
Banbury United	42	16	12	14	67	72	44
Trowbridge Town	42	15	8	19	70	60	44
Folkestone Town	42	19	5	18	53	59	43
Canterbury City	42	17	7	18	67	63	41
Ashford Town	42	16	8	18	72	73	40
Bexley United	42	15	9	18	62	75	39
Hastings United	42	15	9	18	58	69	39
Wisbech Town	42	11	13	18	57	70	35
Dunstable Town	42	14	6	22	73	99	34
Merthyr Tydfil	42	10	7	25	49	101	27
Barry Town	42	8	10	24	39	78	26
Gravesend & Northfleet	42	8	9	25	51	79	25
Tonbridge	42	2	6	34	36	137	10

1969-70 Premier Division

Cambridge United	42	26	6	10	86	49	58
Yeovil Town	42	25	7	10	78	48	57
Chelmsford City	42	20	11	11	76	58	51
Weymouth	42	18	14	10	59	37	50
Wimbledon	42	19	12	11	64	52	50
Hillingdon Borough	42	19	12	11	56	50	50
Barnet	42	16	15	11	71	54	47
Telford United	42	18	10	14	61	62	46
Brentwood Town	42	16	13	13	61	38	45
Hereford United	42	18	9	15	74	65	45
Bath City	42	18	8	16	63	55	44
King's Lynn	42	16	11	15	72	68	43
Margate	42	17	8	17	70	64	42
Dover	42	15	10	17	51	50	40
Kettering Town	42	18	3	21	64	75	39
Worcester City	42	14	10	18	35	44	38
Romford	42	13	11	18	50	62	37
Poole Town	42	8	19	15	48	57	35
Gloucester City	42	12	9	21	53	73	33
Nuneaton Borough	42	11	10	21	52	74	32
Crawley Town	42	6	15	21	53	101	27
Burton Albion	42	3	9	30	24	82	15

First Division

Bedford Town	42	26	9	7	93	37	61
Cambridge City	42	26	8	8	104	43	60
Dartford	42	24	11	7	33	46	58
Ashford Town	42	19	15	8	71	43	53
Rugby Town	42	20	10	12	82	66	50
Trowbridge Town	42	20	8	14	72	65	48
Hastings United	42	18	11	13	67	51	47
Guildford City	42	19	9	14	68	58	47
Banbury United	42	19	8	15	86	72	46
Cheltenham Town	42	20	5	17	78	81	45
Canterbury City	42	15	13	14	61	57	43
Corby Town	42	14	15	13	58	53	43
Folkestone Town	42	19	5	18	57	55	43
Ramsgate Athletic	42	14	13	15	53	57	41
Salisbury	42	13	13	16	48	53	39
Gravesend & Northfleet	42	13	11	18	62	71	37
Bexley United	42	10	11	21	58	76	31
Dunstable Town	42	11	9	22	52	82	31
Merthyr Tydfil	42	9	11	22	40	80	29
Barry Town	42	11	6	25	39	76	28
Wisbech Town	42	8	9	25	58	116	25
Tonbridge	42	4	10	28	46	101	18

1970-71 Premier Division

Yeovil Town	42	25	7	10	66	31	57
Cambridge City	42	22	11	9	67	38	55
Romford	42	23	9	10	63	42	55
Hereford United	42	23	8	11	71	53	54
Chelmsford City	42	20	11	11	61	32	51
Barnet	42	18	14	10	69	49	50
Bedford Town	42	20	10	12	62	46	50
Wimbledon	42	20	8	14	72	54	48
Worcester City	42	20	8	14	61	46	48
Weymouth	42	14	16	12	64	48	44
Dartford	42	15	12	15	53	51	42
Dover	42	16	9	17	64	63	41
Margate	42	15	10	17	64	70	40
Hillingdon Borough	42	17	6	19	61	68	40
Bath City	42	13	12	17	48	68	38
Nuneaton Borough	42	12	12	18	43	66	36
Telford United	42	13	8	21	64	70	34
Poole Town	42	14	6	22	57	75	34
King's Lynn	42	11	7	24	44	67	29
Ashford Town	42	8	13	21	52	86	29
Kettering Town	42	8	11	23	48	84	27
Gloucester City	42	6	10	26	34	81	21

First Division

Guildford City	38	22	10	6	76	36	54
Merthyr Tydfil	38	19	12	7	52	33	50
Gravesend & Northfleet	38	19	10	9	74	42	48
Folkestone	38	20	8	10	83	53	48
Burton Albion	38	19	10	9	56	37	48
Rugby Town	38	17	14	7	58	40	48
Ramsgate Athletic	38	20	5	13	83	54	45
Trowbridge Town	38	19	7	12	78	55	45
Bexley United	38	17	11	10	57	45	45
Crawley Town	38	15	11	12	84	68	41
Hastings United	38	13	12	13	51	50	38
Banbury United	38	13	11	14	58	53	37
Corby Town	38	14	8	16	57	60	36
Salisbury	38	13	7	18	56	60	33
Cheltenham Town	38	8	15	15	44	58	31
Stevenage Athletic	38	12	7	19	55	79	21
Tonbridge	38	8	8	22	48	83	24
Barry Town	38	9	6	23	35	82	24
Dunstable Town	38	8	4	26	32	81	20
Canterbury City	38	5	4	29	37	105	14

1971-72

Premier Division

Chelmsford City	42	28	6	8	109	46	62
Hereford United	42	24	12	6	68	30	60
Dover	42	20	11	11	67	45	51
Barnet	42	21	7	14	80	57	49
Dartford	42	20	8	14	75	68	48
Weymouth	42	21	5	16	69	43	47
Yeovil Town	42	18	11	13	67	51	47
Hillingdon Borough	42	20	6	16	64	58	46
Margate	42	19	8	15	74	68	46
Wimbledon	42	19	7	16	75	64	45
Romford	42	16	13	13	54	49	45
Guildford City	42	20	5	17	71	65	45
Telford United	42	18	7	17	83	68	43
Nuneaton Borough	42	16	10	16	46	47	42
Bedford Town	42	16	9	17	59	66	41
Worcester City	42	17	7	18	46	57	41
Cambridge City	42	12	14	16	68	71	38
Folkestone	42	14	7	21	58	64	35
Poole Town	42	9	11	22	43	72	29
Bath City	42	11	4	27	45	86	26
Merthyr Tydfil	42	7	8	27	29	93	22
Gravesend & Northfleet	42	5	6	31	30	110	16

First Division (North)

Kettering Town	34	23	6	5	70	27	52
Burton Albion	34	18	13	3	58	27	49
Cheltenham Town	34	20	4	10	72	51	44
Rugby Town	34	18	7	9	52	36	43
Wellingborough Town	34	15	10	9	73	44	40
Stourbridge	34	13	14	7	59	42	40
King's Lynn	34	14	11	9	62	45	39
Corby Town	34	15	9	10	47	35	39
Ilkeston Town	34	14	11	9	44	38	39
Banbury United	34	14	5	15	54	46	33
Bury Town	34	14	5	15	47	44	33
Wealdstone	34	14	5	15	51	58	33
Lockheed Leamington	34	15	3	16	41	52	33
Gloucester City	34	8	8	18	46	61	24
Stevenage Athletic	34	8	8	18	41	69	24
Bletchley	34	7	7	20	36	70	21
Dunstable Town	34	5	7	22	29	75	17
Barry Town	34	1	7	26	22	84	9

First Division (South)

Team	P	W	D	L	F	A	Pts
Waterlooville	30	15	9	6	40	22	39
Ramsgate Athletic	30	14	11	5	42	27	39
Maidstone United	30	14	10	6	48	28	38
Crawley Town	30	15	5	10	67	55	35
Metropolitan Police	30	15	3	12	48	41	33
Tonbridge	30	12	9	9	37	34	33
Bexley United	30	14	4	12	52	46	32
Basingstoke Town	30	14	4	12	37	36	32
Andover	30	11	9	10	32	34	31
Ashford Town	30	12	4	14	43	48	28
Salisbury	30	10	7	13	45	44	27
Winchester City	30	10	7	13	40	47	27
Hastings United	30	10	7	13	28	42	27
Trowbridge Town	30	8	7	15	41	49	23
Canterbury City	30	7	8	15	39	56	22
Woodford Town	30	4	6	20	22	52	14

First Division (South)

Team	P	W	D	L	F	A	Pts
Maidstone United	42	25	12	5	90	38	62
Tonbridge	42	26	7	9	70	44	59
Ashford Town	42	24	7	11	90	40	55
Bideford	42	19	14	9	70	43	52
Minehead	42	20	12	10	65	47	52
Gravesend & Northfleet	42	22	7	13	81	55	51
Bath City	42	18	11	13	56	54	47
Wealdstone	42	16	12	14	81	61	44
Bletchley Town	42	14	13	15	54	51	41
Hastings United	42	14	13	15	53	53	41
Andover	42	15	11	16	62	70	41
Canterbury City	42	14	12	16	51	59	40
Basingstoke Town	42	14	12	16	48	57	40
Crawley Town	42	14	11	17	59	76	39
Metropolitan Police	42	15	8	19	82	75	38
Trowbridge Town	42	15	8	19	65	77	38
Bexley United	42	12	14	16	54	64	38
Salisbury	42	14	10	18	49	60	38
Bognor Regis Town	42	12	9	21	41	66	33
Dorchester Town	42	10	12	20	47	73	32
Winchester City	42	7	11	24	41	79	25
Dunstable Town	42	4	10	28	38	105	18

1972-73

Premier Division

Team	P	W	D	L	F	A	Pts
Kettering Town	42	20	17	5	74	44	57
Yeovil Town	42	21	14	7	67	61	56
Dover	42	23	9	10	61	68	55
Chelmsford City	42	23	7	12	75	43	53
Worcester City	42	20	13	9	68	47	53
Weymouth	42	20	12	10	72	51	52
Margate	42	17	15	10	80	60	49
Bedford Town	42	16	15	11	43	36	47
Nuneaton Borough	42	16	14	12	51	41	46
Telford United	42	12	20	10	57	47	44
Cambridge City	42	14	15	13	64	53	43
Wimbledon	42	14	14	14	50	50	42
Barnet	42	15	11	16	60	59	41
Romford	42	17	5	20	51	65	39
Hillingdon Borough	42	16	6	20	52	58	38
Dartford	42	12	11	19	49	63	35
Folkestone	42	11	11	20	41	72	33
Guildford City	42	10	11	21	59	84	31
Ramsgate	42	9	13	20	35	61	31
Poole Town	42	10	10	22	50	88	30
Burton Albion	42	9	7	26	43	81	25
Waterlooville	42	4	16	22	33	63	24

1973-74　Premier Division

Team	P	W	D	L	F	A	Pts
Dartford	42	22	13	7	67	37	57
Grantham	42	18	13	11	70	49	49
Chelmsford City	42	19	10	13	62	49	48
Kettering Town	42	16	16	10	62	51	48
Maidstone United	42	16	14	12	54	43	46
Yeovil Town	42	13	20	9	45	39	46
Weymouth	42	19	7	16	60	41	45
Barnet	42	18	9	15	55	46	45
Nuneaton Borough	42	13	19	10	54	47	45
Cambridge City	42	15	12	15	45	54	42
Atherstone Town	42	16	9	17	61	59	41
Wimbledon	42	15	11	16	50	56	41
Telford United	42	12	16	14	51	57	40
Dover	42	11	17	14	41	46	39
Tonbridge	42	12	15	15	38	45	39
Romford	42	11	17	14	39	52	39
Margate	42	15	8	19	56	63	38
Guildford City	42	13	11	18	48	67	37
Worcester City	42	11	14	17	53	67	36
Bedford Town	42	11	14	17	38	51	36
Folkestone	42	11	12	19	56	65	34
Hillingdon Borough	42	9	15	18	44	65	33

First Division (North)

Team	P	W	D	L	F	A	Pts
Grantham	42	29	8	5	113	41	66
Atherstone Town	42	23	11	8	82	48	57
Cheltenham Town	42	24	8	10	87	47	56
Rugby Town	42	20	10	12	60	47	50
Kidderminster Harriers	42	19	12	11	67	56	50
Merthyr Tydfil	42	17	12	13	51	40	46
Corby Town	42	14	16	12	62	56	44
Stourbridge	42	16	11	15	70	64	43
Gloucester City	42	18	7	17	55	64	43
Bromsgrove Rovers	42	17	8	17	63	54	42
Redditch United	42	18	6	18	58	59	42
Banbury United	42	18	5	19	60	53	41
Wellingborough Town	42	17	7	18	58	71	41
King's Lynn	42	14	12	16	45	49	40
Lockheed Leamington	42	13	12	17	51	58	38
Enderby Town	42	12	14	16	50	61	38
Stevenage Athletic	42	12	13	17	50	63	37
Tamworth	42	14	8	20	45	65	36
Bury Town	42	13	9	20	52	69	35
Barry Town	42	11	10	21	45	71	32
Ilkeston Town	42	9	6	27	35	68	24
Bedworth United	42	10	3	29	42	94	23

First Division (North)

Team	P	W	D	L	F	A	Pts
Stourbridge	42	29	11	2	103	36	69
Burton Albion	42	27	9	6	88	32	63
Cheltenham Town	42	24	8	10	75	51	56
AP Leamington	42	21	12	9	82	45	54
Enderby Town	42	19	14	9	60	36	52
Witney Town	42	20	10	12	69	55	50
Stevenage Athletic	42	19	11	12	65	46	49
Banbury United	42	19	11	12	69	57	49
King's Lynn	42	19	10	13	65	50	48
Kidderminster Harriers	42	15	14	13	67	53	44
Merthyr Tydfil	42	16	12	14	70	61	44
Redditch United	42	14	11	17	56	73	39
Bromsgrove Rovers	42	14	10	18	54	61	38
Bedworth United	42	14	10	18	50	77	38
Tamworth	42	13	11	18	42	51	37
Corby Town	42	12	11	19	40	57	35
Bletchley Town	42	10	15	17	47	71	35
Barry Town	42	10	8	24	53	85	29
Bury Town	42	10	6	26	57	84	26
Gloucester City	42	10	6	26	52	81	26
Wellingborough Town	42	7	9	26	42	87	23
Dunstable Town	42	5	11	26	26	83	21

First Division (South)

Wealdstone	38	26	7	5	75	35	59
Bath City	38	20	8	10	55	34	48
Waterlooville	38	16	15	7	55	38	47
Minehead	38	16	15	7	69	52	47
Bideford	38	17	12	9	61	51	46
Poole Town	38	18	9	11	67	47	45
Bexley United	38	18	7	13	50	42	43
Hastings United	38	16	9	13	45	36	41
Basingstoke Town	38	14	11	13	55	44	39
Gravesend & Northfleet	38	13	13	12	58	52	39
Bognor Regis Town	38	13	12	13	48	54	38
Ashford Town	38	14	8	16	41	42	36
Ramsgate	38	13	9	16	46	44	35
Dorchester Town	38	10	13	15	40	48	33
Canterbury City	38	9	12	17	37	46	30
Trowbridge Town	38	8	14	16	44	61	30
Salisbury	38	10	9	19	40	60	29
Metropolitan Police	38	9	11	18	37	61	29
Andover	38	11	3	24	38	70	25
Crawley Town	38	6	9	23	35	79	21

First Division (South)

Gravesend & Northfleet	38	24	12	2	70	30	60
Hillingdon Borough	38	22	8	8	87	45	52
Minehead	38	21	9	8	74	33	51
Ramsgate	38	19	11	8	70	37	49
Bexley United	38	19	7	12	61	44	45
Waterlooville	38	17	11	10	67	49	45
Ashford Town	38	16	12	10	64	55	44
Basingstoke Town	38	16	11	11	64	50	43
Canterbury City	38	16	9	13	54	43	41
Hastings United	38	13	14	11	54	45	40
Poole Town	38	11	13	14	50	60	35
Metropolitan Police	38	11	13	14	54	66	35
Folkestone & Shepway	38	10	14	14	53	57	34
Andover	38	12	8	18	52	71	32
Bognor Regis Town	38	10	11	17	49	64	31
Salisbury	38	9	11	18	45	66	29
Trowbridge Town	38	10	9	19	48	76	29
Bideford	38	10	8	20	40	71	28
Dorchester Town	38	8	10	20	40	63	26
Crawley Town	38	3	5	30	31	102	11

1974-75

Premier Division

Wimbledon	42	25	7	10	63	33	57
Nuneaton Borough	42	23	8	11	56	37	54
Yeovil Town	42	21	9	12	64	34	51
Kettering Town	42	20	10	12	73	41	50
Burton Albion	42	18	13	11	54	48	49
Bath City	42	20	8	14	63	50	48
Margate	42	17	12	13	64	64	46
Wealdstone	42	17	11	14	62	61	45
Telford United	42	16	13	13	55	56	45
Chelmsford City	42	16	12	14	62	51	44
Grantham	42	16	11	15	70	62	43
Dover	42	15	13	14	43	53	43
Maidstone United	42	15	12	15	52	50	42
Atherstone Town	42	14	14	14	48	53	42
Weymouth	42	13	13	16	66	58	39
Stourbridge	42	13	12	17	56	70	38
Cambridge	42	11	14	17	51	56	36
Tonbridge	42	11	12	19	44	66	34
Romford	42	10	13	19	46	62	33
Dartford	42	9	13	20	52	70	31
Barnet	42	10	9	23	44	76	29
Guildford & Dorking United	42	10	5	27	45	82	25

1975-76

Premier Division

Wimbledon	42	26	10	6	74	29	62
Yeovil Town	42	21	12	9	68	35	54
Atherstone Town	42	18	15	9	56	55	51
Maidstone United	42	17	16	9	52	39	50
Nuneaton Borough	42	16	18	8	41	33	50
Gravesend & Northfleet	42	16	18	8	49	47	50
Grantham	42	15	14	13	56	47	44
Dunstable Town	42	17	9	16	52	43	43
Bedford Town	42	13	17	12	55	51	43
Burton Albion	42	17	9	16	52	53	43
Margate	42	15	12	15	62	60	42
Hillingdon Borough	42	13	14	15	61	54	40
Telford United	42	14	12	16	54	51	40
Chelmsford City	42	13	14	15	52	52	40
Kettering Town	42	11	17	14	48	52	39
Bath City	42	11	16	15	62	57	38
Weymouth	42	13	9	20	51	67	35
Dover	42	8	18	16	51	60	34
Wealdstone	42	12	9	21	61	82	33
Tonbridge AFC	42	11	11	20	45	70	33
Cambridge City	42	8	15	19	41	67	31
Stourbridge	42	10	9	23	38	72	29

First Division (North)

Bedford Town	42	28	9	5	85	33	65
Dunstable Town	42	25	8	9	105	61	58
AP Leamington	42	25	7	10	68	48	57
Redditch United	42	22	12	8	76	40	56
Worcester City	42	24	8	10	84	50	56
Cheltenham Town	42	21	9	12	72	53	51
Tamworth	42	21	8	13	74	53	50
King's Lynn	42	19	10	13	71	64	48
Enderby Town	42	17	12	13	61	48	46
Banbury United	42	18	10	14	52	51	46
Stevenage Athletic	42	16	13	13	62	48	45
Bromsgrove Rovers	42	18	9	15	63	52	45
Merthyr Tydfil	42	11	15	16	53	64	37
Witney Town	42	16	4	22	57	76	36
Corby Town	42	11	13	18	60	57	35
Kidderminster Harriers	42	12	11	19	50	66	35
Gloucester City	42	13	8	21	55	75	34
Wellingborough Town	42	9	13	20	42	61	31
Barry Town	42	10	10	22	49	73	30
Bedworth United	42	9	9	24	60	91	27
Milton Keynes City	42	7	5	30	48	100	19
Bury Town	42	5	7	30	36	119	17

First Division (North)

Redditch United	42	29	11	2	101	39	69
AP Leamington	42	27	10	5	85	31	64
Witney Town	42	24	9	9	66	40	57
Worcester City	42	24	8	10	90	49	56
Cheltenham Town	42	20	10	12	87	55	50
Barry Town	42	19	10	13	52	47	48
King's Lynn	42	17	14	11	52	48	48
Tamworth	42	18	11	13	65	43	47
Barnet	42	15	12	15	56	56	42
Oswestry Town	42	16	8	18	63	71	40
Enderby Town	42	16	6	20	48	51	38
Banbury United	42	15	8	19	58	67	38
Merthyr Tydfil	42	11	15	16	59	67	37
Bromsgrove Rovers	42	13	11	18	49	65	37
Milton Keynes City	42	15	6	21	51	63	36
Bury Town	42	12	11	19	52	72	35
Gloucester City	42	13	9	20	49	78	35
Kidderminster Harriers	42	13	8	21	54	70	34
Bedworth United	42	8	18	16	41	66	34
Corby Town	42	11	10	21	50	65	32
Wellingborough Town	42	9	11	22	42	68	29
Stevenage Athletic	42	6	6	30	46	105	18

First Division (South)

Minehead	38	27	8	3	102	35	62
Dartford	38	26	4	8	84	46	56
Romford	38	21	9	8	66	37	51
Salisbury	38	17	11	10	73	53	45
Hastings United	38	15	15	8	67	51	45
Poole United	38	20	2	16	57	57	42
Bexley United	38	14	13	11	62	53	41
Waterlooville	38	13	13	12	62	54	39
Basingstoke Town	38	13	12	13	69	71	38
Ashford Town	38	14	8	16	67	73	36
Canterbury City	38	11	13	14	53	60	35
Folkestone & Shepway	38	10	14	14	36	51	34
Metropolitan Police	38	9	14	15	46	58	32
Trowbridge Town	38	11	10	17	48	75	32
Guildford & Dorking United	38	9	13	16	43	50	31
Bognor Regis Town	38	6	17	15	44	72	29
Ramsgate	38	9	10	19	57	76	28
Crawley Town	38	9	10	19	46	66	28
Andover	38	9	10	19	42	62	28
Dorchester Town	38	11	6	21	45	69	28

First Division (South)

Barnet	34	23	8	3	65	25	54
Hastings United	34	18	11	5	47	18	47
Waterlooville	34	19	6	9	50	25	44
Dorchester Town	34	16	11	7	48	30	43
Salisbury	34	15	11	8	57	39	41
Romford	34	18	5	11	47	32	41
Poole Town	34	17	7	10	40	35	41
Trowbridge Town	34	15	8	11	47	39	38
Crawley Town	34	14	9	11	53	42	37
Folkestone & Shepway	34	12	11	11	39	42	35
Basingstoke Town	34	12	10	12	51	43	34
Canterbury City	34	6	16	12	36	46	28
Bognor Regis Town	34	9	9	16	33	50	27
Tonbridge AFC	34	9	9	16	33	50	27
Metropolitan Police	34	5	12	17	37	61	22
Andover	34	4	11	19	17	49	19
Ashford Town	34	5	8	21	32	65	18
Aylesbury United	34	5	6	23	27	68	16

1976-77

Premier Division

Wimbledon	42	28	7	7	64	22	63
Minehead	42	23	12	7	73	39	58
Kettering Town	42	20	16	6	66	46	56
Bath City	42	20	15	7	51	30	55
Nuneaton Borough	42	20	11	11	52	35	51
Bedford Town	42	17	14	11	54	47	48
Yeovil Town	42	15	16	11	54	42	46
Dover	42	13	16	13	46	43	42
Grantham	42	14	12	16	55	50	40
Maidstone United	42	13	14	15	46	50	40
Gravesend & Northfleet	42	13	13	16	38	43	39
AP Leamington	42	12	15	15	44	53	39
Redditch United	42	12	14	16	45	54	38
Wealdstone	42	13	12	17	54	66	38
Hillingdon Borough	42	14	10	18	45	59	38
Atherstone Town	42	14	9	19	41	49	37
Weymouth	42	16	5	21	53	73	37
Dartford	42	13	10	19	52	57	36
Telford United	42	11	12	19	36	50	34
Chelmsford City	42	9	13	20	56	68	31
Burton Albion	42	10	10	22	41	52	30
Margate	42	9	10	23	47	85	28

First Division (North)

Worcester City	38	32	5	1	97	22	69
Cheltenham Town	38	23	8	7	85	35	54
Witney Town	38	21	8	9	48	31	50
Bromsgrove Rovers	38	20	8	10	61	37	48
Barry Town	38	19	8	11	62	45	46
Cambridge City	38	17	10	11	68	43	44
Stourbridge	38	17	9	12	48	35	43
Kidderminster Harriers	38	17	6	15	74	65	40
Banbury United	38	15	10	13	51	47	40
Gloucester City	38	18	4	16	70	81	40
Enderby Town	38	15	9	14	50	44	39
King's Lynn	38	13	11	14	47	53	37
Corby Town	38	11	13	14	56	64	35
Tamworth	38	11	13	14	49	58	35
Merthyr Tydfil	38	12	6	20	60	69	30
Oswestry Town	38	8	10	20	30	60	26
Wellingborough Town	38	8	7	23	37	73	23
Dunstable	38	7	7	24	38	84	21
Bedworth United	38	5	10	23	28	68	20
Milton Keynes City	38	7	6	25	31	76	20

1977-78

Premier Division

Bath City	42	22	18	2	83	32	62
Weymouth	42	21	16	5	64	36	58
Maidstone United	42	20	11	11	59	41	51
Worcester City	42	20	11	11	67	50	51
Gravesend & Northfleet	42	19	11	12	57	42	49
Kettering Town	42	18	11	13	58	48	47
Barnet	42	18	11	13	63	58	47
Wealdstone	42	16	14	12	54	48	46
Telford United	42	17	11	14	52	45	45
Nuneaton Borough	42	15	14	13	38	36	44
Dartford	42	14	15	13	57	65	43
Yeovil Town	42	14	14	14	57	49	42
Hastings United	42	15	9	18	49	60	39
Cheltenham Town	42	12	14	16	43	52	38
Hillingdon Borough	42	13	9	20	45	54	35
Atherstone Town	42	10	15	17	41	56	35
Redditch United	42	15	5	22	40	55	35
AP Leamington	42	11	13	18	34	57	35
Minehead	42	11	12	19	43	48	34
Dover	42	9	13	20	41	63	31
Bedford Town	42	8	13	21	51	75	29
Grantham	42	11	6	25	40	66	28

First Division (North)

Witney Town	38	20	15	3	54	27	55
Bridgend Town	38	20	9	9	59	45	49
Burton Albion	38	17	11	10	48	32	45
Enderby Town	38	17	10	11	59	44	44
Bromsgrove Rovers	38	16	12	10	56	41	44
Banbury United	38	17	10	11	52	47	44
Kidderminster Harriers	38	16	11	11	58	41	43
Merthyr Tydfil	38	18	6	14	85	62	42
Cambridge City	38	14	12	12	56	45	40
Barry Town	38	14	11	13	58	48	39
Wellingborough Town	38	11	15	12	47	43	37
King's Lynn	38	12	13	13	55	55	37
Gloucester City	38	14	8	16	68	75	36
Corby Town	38	9	17	12	46	48	35
Dunstable Town	38	11	13	14	49	59	35
Stourbridge	38	9	15	14	52	53	33
Tamworth	38	10	11	17	37	48	31
Bedworth United	38	8	14	16	36	58	30
Milton Keynes City	38	5	11	22	26	74	21
Oswestry Town	38	6	8	24	29	85	20

First Division (South)

	P	W	D	L	F	A	Pts
Margate	38	24	10	4	92	32	58
Dorchester Town	38	23	10	5	67	31	56
Salisbury	38	21	10	7	60	27	52
Waterlooville	38	19	13	6	66	36	51
Romford	38	17	15	6	58	37	49
Aylesbury United	38	20	7	11	56	42	47
Trowbridge Town	38	16	11	11	65	59	43
Chelmsford City	38	15	11	12	58	46	41
Folkestone & Shepway	38	16	9	13	64	56	41
Taunton Town	38	15	10	13	57	54	40
Addlestone	38	14	10	14	57	60	38
Crawley Town	38	14	9	15	61	60	37
Basingstoke Town	38	11	11	16	44	50	33
Tonbridge AFC	38	13	5	20	64	77	31
Ashford Town	38	9	13	16	39	60	31
Hounslow	38	10	10	18	43	62	30
Bognor Regis Town	38	9	8	21	52	69	26
Poole Town	38	10	6	20	43	68	26
Andover	38	4	12	22	30	68	20
Canterbury City	38	2	6	30	31	113	10

1978-79

Premier Division

	P	W	D	L	F	A	Pts
Worcester City	42	27	11	4	92	33	65
Kettering Town	42	27	7	8	109	43	61
Telford United	42	22	10	10	60	39	54
Maidstone United	42	18	18	6	55	35	54
Bath City	42	17	19	6	59	41	53
Weymouth	42	18	15	9	71	51	51
AP Leamington	42	19	11	12	65	53	49
Redditch United	42	19	10	13	70	57	48
Yeovil Town	42	15	16	11	59	49	46
Witney Town	42	17	10	15	53	52	44
Nuneaton Borough	42	13	17	12	59	50	43
Gravesend & Northfleet	42	15	12	15	56	55	42
Barnet	42	16	10	16	52	64	42
Hillingdon Borough	42	12	16	14	50	41	40
Wealdstone	42	12	12	18	51	59	36
Atherstone Town	42	9	17	16	46	65	35
Dartford	42	10	14	18	40	56	34
Cheltenham Town	42	11	10	21	38	72	32
Margate	42	10	9	23	44	75	29
Dorchester Town	42	7	11	24	46	86	25
Hastings United	42	5	13	24	37	85	23
Bridgend Town	42	6	6	30	39	90	18

First Division (North)

	P	W	D	L	F	A	Pts
Grantham	38	21	10	7	70	45	52
Merthyr Tydfil	38	22	7	9	90	53	51
Alvechurch	38	20	10	8	70	42	50
Bedford Town	38	19	9	10	74	49	47
King's Lynn	38	17	11	10	57	46	45
Oswestry Town	38	18	8	12	63	43	44
Gloucester City	38	18	8	12	76	59	44
Burton Albion	38	16	10	12	51	40	42
Kidderminster Harriers	38	13	14	11	70	60	40
Bedworth United	38	13	14	11	41	34	40
Tamworth	38	15	8	15	47	45	38
Stourbridge	38	15	7	16	64	61	37
Barry Town	38	14	9	15	51	53	37
Enderby Town	38	14	8	16	46	55	36
Banbury United	38	10	13	15	42	58	33
Wellingborough Town	38	13	6	19	50	71	32
Cambridge City	38	9	9	20	37	62	27
Bromsgrove Rovers	38	6	14	18	33	61	26
Milton Keynes City	38	7	9	22	37	87	23
Corby Town	38	5	6	27	40	85	16

First Division (South)

	P	W	D	L	F	A	Pts
Dover	40	28	9	3	88	20	65
Folkestone & Shepway	40	22	6	12	84	50	50
Gosport Borough	40	19	11	10	62	47	49
Chelmsford City	40	20	7	13	65	61	47
Minehead	40	16	13	11	58	39	45
Poole Town	40	15	15	10	48	44	45
Hounslow	40	16	12	12	56	45	44
Waterlooville	40	17	10	13	52	43	44
Trowbridge Town	40	15	12	13	65	61	42
Aylesbury United	40	16	9	15	54	52	41
Taunton Town	40	16	9	15	53	51	41
Bognor Regis Town	40	17	7	16	58	58	41
Dunstable	40	18	4	18	57	55	40
Tonbridge AFC	40	15	10	15	43	47	40
Salisbury	40	13	10	17	47	51	36
Basingstoke Town	40	12	11	17	49	62	35
Addlestone	40	12	9	19	56	64	33
Andover	40	12	6	22	47	69	30
Ashford Town	40	10	10	20	28	53	30
Crawley Town	40	9	9	22	44	75	27
Canterbury City	40	6	3	31	31	98	15

1979-80   Midland Division

	P	W	D	L	F	A	Pts
Bridgend Town	42	28	6	8	85	39	62
Minehead	42	22	15	5	70	42	59
Bedford Town	42	20	12	10	71	42	52
Kidderminster Harriers	42	23	6	13	81	59	52
Merthyr Tydfil	42	20	11	11	70	47	51
Enderby Town	42	21	8	13	62	50	50
Stourbridge	42	19	11	12	67	49	49
Alvechurch	42	17	14	11	78	60	48
Trowbridge Town	42	19	9	14	62	61	47
Bromsgrove Rovers	42	18	10	14	67	56	46
Barry Town	42	15	12	15	64	58	42
King's Lynn	42	15	11	16	48	55	41
Banbury United	42	13	14	15	56	56	40
Taunton Town	42	16	8	18	55	62	40
Witney Town	42	10	19	13	43	45	39
Bedworth United	42	12	15	15	40	42	39
Milton Keynes City	42	15	7	20	46	59	37
Gloucester City	42	10	14	18	55	68	32
Cheltenham Town	42	13	5	24	49	70	31
Wellingborough Town	42	9	7	26	54	106	25
Cambridge City	42	6	9	27	30	73	21
Corby Town	42	5	9	28	40	94	19

Gloucester City had 2 points deducted

Southern Division

	P	W	D	L	F	A	Pts
Dorchester Town	46	25	12	9	81	53	62
Aylesbury United	46	25	11	10	73	40	61
Dover	46	22	13	11	78	47	57
Gosport Borough	46	21	15	10	70	50	57
Dartford	46	21	14	11	66	45	56
Bognor Regis Town	46	20	15	11	66	38	55
Hillingdon Borough	46	19	16	11	64	41	54
Dunstable	46	17	19	10	93	64	53
Addlestone	46	20	13	13	72	57	53
Hastings United	46	19	15	12	74	65	53
Fareham Town	46	16	16	14	61	53	48
Waterlooville	46	17	12	17	67	64	46
Andover	46	16	13	17	65	65	45
Poole Town	46	16	13	17	49	64	45
Canterbury City	46	15	14	17	56	60	44
Hounslow	46	14	15	17	44	57	43
Margate	46	17	8	21	51	62	42
Folkestone & Shepway	46	14	11	21	54	63	39
Ashford Town	46	12	14	20	54	71	38
Crawley Town	46	13	11	22	55	72	37
Chelmsford City	46	9	18	19	47	66	36
Basingstoke Town	46	9	15	22	48	79	33
Salisbury	46	10	12	24	47	58	32
Tonbridge AFC	46	3	9	34	30	128	15

1980-81

Midland Division

	P	W	D	L	F	A	Pts
Alvechurch	42	26	9	7	76	40	61
Bedford Town	42	25	11	6	63	32	61
Trowbridge Town	42	24	9	9	69	39	57
Kidderminster Harriers	42	23	9	10	67	41	55
Barry Town	42	21	9	12	60	40	51
Stourbridge	42	17	16	9	75	49	50
Enderby Town	42	21	8	13	71	47	50
Cheltenham Town	42	18	12	12	70	59	48
Bromsgrove Rovers	42	19	9	14	65	50	47
Corby Town	42	19	7	16	69	58	45
Bridgend Town	42	19	7	16	74	64	45
Minehead	42	19	7	16	54	60	45
Gloucester City	42	19	6	17	82	72	44
Merthyr Tydfil	42	15	12	15	60	50	42
Bedworth United	42	14	12	16	49	46	40
Banbury United	42	11	11	20	51	65	33
Taunton Town	42	10	9	23	48	68	29
Cambridge City	42	8	12	22	46	87	28
Witney Town	42	9	9	24	44	65	27
Wellingborough Town	42	10	7	25	43	91	27
Redditch United	42	11	4	27	54	92	26
Milton Keynes City	42	3	7	32	28	103	13

Southern Division

	P	W	D	L	F	A	Pts
Dartford	46	26	14	6	76	39	66
Bognor Regis Town	46	25	13	8	95	43	63
Hastings United	46	24	14	8	87	43	62
Gosport Borough	46	24	12	10	84	52	60
Waterlooville	46	19	21	6	67	50	59
Dorchester Town	46	21	13	12	84	56	55
Dover	46	22	10	14	70	50	54
Poole Town	46	19	14	13	70	56	52
Addlestone & Weybridge	46	21	9	16	66	57	51
Dunstable	46	19	13	14	73	68	51
Aylesbury United	46	20	10	16	66	60	50
Hounslow	46	17	13	16	65	55	47
Hillingdon Borough	46	16	15	15	50	49	47
Basingstoke Town	46	16	14	16	69	58	46
Crawley Town	46	18	4	24	64	78	40
Ashford Town	46	12	15	19	55	76	39
Tonbridge AFC	46	12	15	19	44	68	39
Chelmsford City	46	13	12	21	54	78	38
Canterbury City	46	12	13	21	40	59	37
Salisbury	46	14	8	24	57	76	36
Folkestone	46	11	11	24	47	65	33
Margate	46	11	7	28	65	117	29
Fareham Town	46	5	18	23	31	73	28
Andover	46	6	10	30	41	94	22

1981-82

Midland Division

	P	W	D	L	F	A	Pts
Nuneaton Borough	42	27	11	4	88	32	65
Alvechurch	42	26	10	6	79	34	62
Kidderminster Harriers	42	22	12	8	71	40	56
Stourbridge	42	21	10	11	69	47	52
Gloucester City	42	21	9	12	64	48	51
Bedworth United	42	20	10	12	59	40	50
Enderby Town	42	20	10	12	79	66	50
Witney Town	42	19	8	15	71	49	46
Barry Town	42	16	14	12	59	46	46
Corby Town	42	19	8	15	70	59	46
Merthyr Tydfil	42	16	12	14	63	54	44
Wellingborough Town	42	15	12	15	50	45	42
Bridgend Town	42	13	13	16	50	62	39
Bromsgrove Rovers	42	15	8	19	57	63	38
Bedford Town	42	12	13	17	45	54	37
Cheltenham Town	42	11	14	17	65	68	36
Taunton Town	42	12	8	22	46	76	32
Banbury United	42	11	8	23	63	91	30
Minehead	42	12	6	24	38	69	30
Cambridge City	42	10	8	24	38	80	28
Milton Keynes City	42	6	11	25	34	70	23
Redditch United	42	8	5	29	37	103	21

Southern Division

	P	W	D	L	F	A	Pts
Wealdstone	46	32	8	6	100	32	72
Hastings United	46	31	9	6	79	34	71
Dorchester Town	46	21	18	7	76	41	60
Gosport Borough	46	26	8	12	76	45	60
Fareham Town	46	20	14	12	58	48	54
Poole Town	46	19	15	12	92	63	53
Waterlooville	46	22	9	15	75	53	53
Welling United	46	19	13	14	70	48	51
Addlestone & Weybridge	46	17	17	12	71	53	51
Chelmsford City	46	20	11	15	64	53	51
Aylesbury United	46	19	12	15	79	61	50
Basingstoke Town	46	18	12	16	74	61	48
Dover	46	19	8	19	61	63	46
Ashford Town	46	16	14	16	52	56	46
Tonbridge AFC	46	19	7	20	62	70	45
Dunstable	46	18	8	20	63	68	44
Salisbury	46	16	10	20	64	81	42
Hounslow	46	15	11	20	59	83	41
Hillingdon Borough	46	14	10	22	46	58	38
Canterbury City	46	10	16	20	49	78	36
Crawley Town	46	9	12	25	46	81	30
Folkestone	46	10	6	30	49	101	26
Andover	46	4	11	31	39	100	19
Thanet United	46	5	7	34	37	110	17

1982-83

Premier Division

AP Leamington	38	25	4	9	78	50	79
Kidderminster Harriers	38	23	7	8	69	40	76
Welling United	38	21	6	11	63	40	69
Chelmsford City	38	16	11	11	57	40	59
Bedworth United	38	16	11	11	47	39	59
Dartford	38	16	8	14	48	38	56
Gosport Borough	38	14	13	11	47	43	55
Fareham Town	38	16	7	15	73	82	55
Dorchester Town	38	14	12	12	52	50	54
Gravesend & Northfleet	38	14	12	12	49	50	54
Gloucester City	38	13	12	13	61	57	51
Witney Town	38	12	13	13	60	48	47
Alvechurch	38	13	8	17	60	66	47
Stourbridge	38	12	11	15	48	54	47
Corby Town	38	12	11	15	58	67	47
Hastings United	38	11	11	16	48	61	44
Enderby Town	38	11	9	18	44	62	42
Waterlooville	38	10	9	19	62	83	39
Poole Town	38	9	9	20	57	73	36
Addlestone & Weybridge	38	5	10	23	24	62	25

Witney Town had 2 points deducted for fielding an ineligible player

Midland Division

Cheltenham Town	32	22	5	5	65	29	71
Sutton Coldfield Town	32	21	7	4	62	24	70
Forest Green Rovers	32	21	3	8	68	32	66
Merthyr Tydfil	32	17	7	8	64	45	58
Willenhall Town	32	17	6	9	74	49	57
Oldbury United	32	16	6	10	52	49	54
Banbury United	32	15	3	14	59	55	48
Bridgend Town	32	12	11	9	46	37	47
Wellingborough Town	32	13	7	12	49	37	46
Bromsgrove Rovers	32	13	5	14	47	47	44
Dudley Town	32	12	7	13	40	45	43
Bridgwater Town	32	12	6	14	42	43	42
Aylesbury United	32	12	5	15	37	51	41
Redditch United	32	8	6	18	51	73	30
Taunton Town	32	5	7	20	30	64	22
Minehead	32	5	7	20	24	62	22
Milton Keynes City	32	0	4	28	22	90	4

Southern Division

Fisher Athletic	34	23	5	6	79	34	74
Folkestone	34	22	6	6	79	41	72
RS Southampton	34	21	7	6	66	30	70
Dunstable	34	19	5	10	57	39	62
Hillingdon Borough	34	14	11	9	41	30	53
Salisbury	34	14	10	10	58	49	52
Crawley Town	34	14	9	11	51	43	51
Ashford Town	34	13	10	11	51	41	49
Tonbridge AFC	34	14	5	15	57	57	47
Hounslow	34	11	12	11	46	47	45
Canterbury City	34	12	9	13	52	63	45
Cambridge City	34	12	5	17	56	63	41
Dover	34	11	7	16	35	52	40
Thanet United	34	10	5	19	30	61	35
Basingstoke Town	34	8	10	16	37	56	34
Woodford Town	34	6	9	19	29	57	27
Andover	34	6	8	20	28	53	26
Erith & Belvedere	34	5	9	20	26	62	24

1983-84

Premier Division

Dartford	38	23	9	6	67	32	78
Fisher Athletic	38	22	9	7	80	42	75
Chelmsford City	38	19	9	10	67	45	66
Gravesend & Northfleet	38	18	9	11	50	38	63
Witney Town	38	18	6	14	75	50	60
King's Lynn	38	18	6	14	42	45	60
Folkestone	38	16	9	13	60	56	57
Cheltenham Town	38	16	7	15	63	56	55
Gloucester City	38	13	15	10	55	50	54
Hastings United	38	15	9	14	55	57	54
Bedworth United	38	15	9	14	51	55	54
Welling United	38	15	7	16	61	61	52
AP Leamington	38	14	9	15	73	83	51
Corby Town	38	12	14	12	55	54	50
Fareham Town	38	13	11	14	65	70	50
Alvechurch	38	12	12	14	56	62	48
Sutton Coldfield Town	38	10	14	14	49	53	44
Gosport Borough	38	6	15	17	31	64	33
Dorchester Town	38	4	8	26	40	69	20
Stourbridge	38	4	7	27	30	82	19

Midland Division

Willenhall Town	38	27	4	7	100	44	85
Shepshed Charterhouse	38	25	5	8	88	37	80
Bromsgrove Rovers	38	20	8	10	73	43	68
Dudley Town	38	18	13	7	71	43	67
Aylesbury United	38	17	15	6	62	35	66
Moor Green	38	18	12	8	63	44	66
Rushden Town	38	17	12	9	68	42	63
Merthyr Tydfil	38	18	8	12	63	44	62
Redditch United	38	17	9	12	67	67	60
VS Rugby	38	15	12	11	68	51	57
Forest Green Rovers	38	15	12	11	67	51	57
Bridgnorth Town	38	16	9	13	64	52	57
Leicester United	38	12	9	17	58	58	45
Oldbury United	38	10	13	15	53	51	43
Coventry Sporting	38	11	7	20	40	67	40
Bridgwater Town	38	10	8	20	39	65	38
Wellingborough Town	38	7	9	22	43	80	30
Banbury United	38	6	11	21	37	78	29
Milton Keynes City	38	3	9	26	31	110	18
Tamworth	38	2	7	29	25	118	13

Southern Division

RS Southampton	38	26	6	6	83	35	84
Crawley Town	38	22	9	7	68	28	75
Basingstoke Town	38	20	9	9	54	36	69
Tonbridge AFC	38	20	9	9	61	44	69
Addlestone & Weybridge	38	19	11	8	58	34	68
Poole Town	38	20	7	11	68	42	67
Hillingdon Borough	38	18	11	9	43	20	65
Ashford Town	38	19	5	14	65	47	62
Salisbury	38	17	8	13	61	48	59
Cambridge City	38	13	9	16	43	53	48
Canterbury City	38	12	9	17	44	52	45
Waterlooville	38	12	9	17	56	69	45
Dover Athletic	38	12	9	17	51	74	45
Chatham Town	38	11	10	17	46	56	43
Andover	38	12	6	20	35	54	42
Erith & Belvedere	38	11	9	18	43	68	42
Dunstable	38	10	8	20	38	65	38
Thanet United	38	9	8	21	40	65	35
Woodford Town	38	7	8	23	30	69	29
Hounslow	38	4	12	22	30	58	24

1984-85

Premier Division

	P	W	D	L	F	A	Pts
Cheltenham Town	38	24	5	9	83	41	77
King's Lynn	38	23	6	9	73	48	75
Crawley Town	38	22	8	8	76	52	74
Willenhall Town	38	20	8	10	57	38	68
RS Southampton	38	21	4	13	76	52	67
Welling United	38	18	11	9	55	38	65
Folkestone	38	19	6	13	70	54	63
Fisher Athletic	38	19	5	14	67	57	62
Chelmsford City	38	17	10	11	52	50	61
Shepshed Charterhouse	38	18	5	15	67	50	59
Corby Town	38	15	6	17	56	54	51
Bedworth United	38	14	8	16	48	52	50
Gravesend & Northfleet	38	12	12	14	46	46	48
Fareham Town	38	13	8	17	52	55	47
Alvechurch	38	11	7	20	53	59	40
Hastings United	38	11	7	20	46	71	40
Witney Town	38	9	12	17	51	58	39
Gloucester City	38	10	6	22	49	74	36
Trowbridge Town	38	10	5	23	45	83	35
AP Leamington	38	2	5	31	22	112	11

Midland Division

	P	W	D	L	F	A	Pts
Dudley Town	34	21	8	5	70	36	71
Aylesbury United	34	20	7	7	62	30	67
Hednesford Town	34	18	7	9	58	42	61
Moor Green	34	17	9	8	63	43	60
VS Rugby	34	17	9	8	59	41	60
Bromsgrove Rovers	34	16	10	8	53	42	58
Stourbridge	34	15	11	8	52	45	56
Redditch United	34	12	11	11	68	57	47
Sutton Coldfield Town	34	13	6	15	50	56	45
Bridgnorth Town	34	13	5	16	67	65	44
Coventry Sporting	34	11	9	14	45	52	42
Merthyr Tydfil	34	10	11	13	43	46	41
Rushden Town	34	10	7	17	42	52	37
Forest Green Rovers	34	9	10	15	49	65	37
Wellingborough Town	34	10	7	17	39	63	37
Oldbury United	34	10	6	18	52	66	36
Banbury United	34	9	5	20	33	59	32
Leicester United	34	3	6	25	17	62	15

Southern Division

	P	W	D	L	F	A	Pts
Basingstoke Town	38	24	9	5	61	22	81
Gosport Borough	38	22	6	10	78	41	72
Poole Town	38	20	12	6	69	38	72
Hillingdon	38	19	10	9	51	23	67
Thanet United	38	19	9	10	63	47	66
Salisbury	38	19	5	14	55	54	62
Sheppey United	38	18	6	14	49	45	60
Addlestone & Weybridge	38	16	9	13	68	54	57
Waterlooville	38	15	10	13	71	63	55
Canterbury City	38	15	7	16	61	64	52
Woodford Town	38	13	13	12	46	53	52
Tonbridge AFC	38	16	3	19	59	62	51
Andover	38	15	5	18	42	54	50
Dorchester Town	38	13	7	18	45	60	46
Cambridge City	38	11	11	16	59	71	44
Chatham Town	38	12	8	18	44	66	44
Ashford Town	38	10	9	19	54	69	39
Dunstable	38	8	10	20	35	56	34
Dover Athletic	38	7	7	24	39	78	28
Erith & Belvedere	38	6	8	24	36	65	26

1985-86

Premier Division

	P	W	D	L	F	A	Pts
Welling United	38	29	6	3	95	31	93
Chelmsford City	38	20	10	8	68	41	70
Fisher Athletic	38	20	7	11	67	45	67
Alvechurch	38	19	9	10	71	56	66
Worcester City	38	19	9	10	64	50	66
Crawley Town	38	18	5	15	76	59	59
Shepshed Charterhouse	38	19	1	18	51	52	58
Aylesbury United	38	14	10	14	52	49	52
Folkestone	38	14	10	14	56	56	52
Bedworth United	38	14	8	16	44	49	50
Willenhall Town	38	12	13	13	51	44	49
Dudley Town	38	15	4	19	58	62	49
Corby Town	38	14	7	17	61	67	49
King's Lynn	38	12	10	16	39	42	46
Basingstoke Town	38	13	4	21	36	67	43
RS Southampton	38	11	9	18	44	61	42
Witney Town	38	11	6	21	44	74	39
Gosport Borough	38	10	8	20	42	66	38
Fareham Town	38	8	13	17	40	62	37
Gravesend & Northfleet	38	9	9	20	29	55	36

Midland Division

	P	W	D	L	F	A	Pts
Bromsgrove Rovers	40	29	5	6	95	45	92
Redditch United	40	23	6	11	70	42	75
Merthyr Tydfil	40	21	10	9	60	40	73
VS Rugby	40	17	14	9	41	31	65
Stourbridge	40	15	14	11	62	39	59
Rusden Town	40	17	7	16	69	74	58
Bilston Town	40	15	12	13	60	48	57
Bridgnorth Town	40	13	18	9	56	45	57
Gloucester City	40	15	12	13	61	57	57
Grantham	40	16	7	17	46	59	55
Wellingborough Town	40	15	9	16	56	56	54
Sutton Coldfield Town	40	13	14	13	60	45	53
Hednesford Town	40	14	9	17	67	70	51
Forest Green Rovers	40	14	9	17	52	56	51
Mile Oak Rovers	40	14	8	18	57	73	50
Leicester United	40	13	10	17	41	48	49
Banbury United	40	13	8	19	38	55	47
Coventry Sporting	40	10	15	15	42	48	45
Moor Green	40	12	6	22	63	91	42
Leamington	40	10	6	24	40	77	36
Oldbury United	40	8	7	25	50	87	31

Southern Division

	P	W	D	L	F	A	Pts
Cambridge City	40	23	11	6	87	41	80
Salisbury	40	24	8	8	84	51	80
Hastings Town	40	23	9	8	83	51	78
Dover Athletic	40	23	6	11	89	53	75
Corinthian	40	20	9	11	78	45	69
Tonbridge AFC	40	17	13	10	65	51	64
Dunstable	40	17	11	12	70	61	62
Ruislip	40	17	6	17	67	66	57
Erith & Belvedere	40	14	12	14	35	40	54
Waterlooville	40	16	6	18	52	58	54
Burnham & Hillingdon	40	16	6	18	44	59	54
Canterbury City	40	13	13	14	58	58	52
Trowbridge Town	40	13	13	14	57	63	52
Sheppey United	40	14	10	16	43	53	52
Thanet United	40	13	7	20	58	63	46
Woodford Town	40	12	10	18	49	62	46
Poole Town	40	12	7	21	55	63	43
Ashford Town	40	10	12	18	45	65	42
Chatham Town	40	8	15	17	53	70	39
Andover	40	10	8	22	52	92	38
Dorchester Town	40	5	8	27	35	94	23

1986-87

Premier Division

Fisher Athletic	42	25	11	6	72	29	86
Bromsgrove Rovers	42	24	11	7	82	41	83
Aylesbury United	42	24	11	7	72	40	83
Dartford	42	19	12	11	76	43	69
Chelmsford City	42	17	13	12	48	45	64
Cambridge City	42	14	20	8	68	52	62
Redditch United	42	16	14	12	59	54	62
Alvechurch	42	18	8	16	66	62	62
Corby Town	42	14	17	11	65	51	59
Worcester City	42	16	11	15	62	55	59
Shepshed Charterhouse	42	16	10	16	59	59	58
Bedworth United	42	15	12	15	55	51	57
Crawley Town	42	14	11	17	59	60	53
Fareham Town	42	11	17	14	58	49	50
Willenhall Town	42	13	11	18	48	57	50
Basingstoke Town	42	12	12	18	53	78	48
Witney Town	42	12	12	18	29	56	48
Gosport Borough	42	11	13	18	42	57	46
Salisbury	42	12	7	23	52	82	43
King's Lynn	42	9	13	20	48	72	40
Dudley Town	42	9	9	24	39	76	36
Folkestone	42	8	11	23	36	79	35

Midland Division

VS Rugby	38	25	5	8	81	43	80
Leicester United	38	26	1	11	89	49	79
Merthyr Tydfil	38	23	6	9	95	54	75
Moor Green	38	22	6	10	73	55	72
Halesowen Town	38	19	12	7	72	50	69
Hednesford Town	38	21	5	12	84	56	68
Gloucester City	38	19	5	14	77	59	62
Coventry Sporting	38	17	8	13	55	54	59
Forest Green Rovers	38	16	9	13	65	53	57
Stourbridge	38	16	7	15	56	56	55
Grantham	38	15	9	14	74	54	54
Banbury United	38	14	7	17	55	65	49
Buckingham Town	38	13	9	16	55	59	48
Bridgnorth Town	38	12	9	17	59	63	45
Wellingborough Town	38	13	6	19	55	76	45
Mile Oak Rovers	38	11	10	17	50	63	43
Sutton Coldfield Town	38	8	10	20	56	78	34
Bilston Town	38	8	7	23	37	76	31
Leamington	38	4	13	21	37	80	25
Rushden Town	38	1	10	27	42	124	13

Southern Division

Dorchester Town	38	23	8	7	83	42	77
Ashford Town	38	23	7	8	63	32	76
Woodford Town	38	22	6	10	72	44	72
Hastings Town	38	20	10	8	74	54	70
Dover Athletic	38	20	6	12	66	43	66
Gravesend & Northfleet	38	18	7	13	67	46	61
Tonbridge AFC	38	16	10	12	73	67	58
Erith & Belvedere	38	15	12	11	57	50	57
Chatham Town	38	16	9	13	53	46	57
Thanet United	38	14	14	10	56	50	56
Waterlooville	38	16	8	14	66	65	56
Trowbridge Town	38	15	9	14	77	65	54
Dunstable	38	13	9	16	60	57	48
Corinthian	38	11	12	15	56	65	45
Sheppey United	38	9	12	17	43	65	39
Andover	38	9	9	20	51	80	36
Burnham & Hillingdon	38	7	11	20	32	62	32
Poole Town	38	8	6	24	50	90	30
Ruislip	38	6	12	20	35	75	30
Canterbury City	38	8	5	25	46	82	29

1987-88

Premier Division

Aylesbury United	42	27	8	7	79	35	89
Dartford	42	27	8	7	79	39	89
Cambridge City	42	24	8	10	84	43	80
Bromsgrove Rovers	42	22	11	9	65	39	77
Worcester City	42	22	6	14	58	48	72
Crawley Town	42	17	14	11	73	63	65
Alvechurch	42	17	13	12	54	52	64
Leicester United	42	15	14	13	68	59	59
Fareham Town	42	16	11	15	51	59	59
Corby Town	42	16	8	18	61	64	56
Dorchester Town	42	14	14	14	51	57	56
Ashford Town	42	12	16	14	45	54	52
Shepshed Charterhouse	42	13	11	18	53	62	50
Bedworth United	42	12	14	16	49	64	50
Gosport Borough	42	10	17	15	39	49	47
Burton Albion	42	11	14	17	62	74	47
VS Rugby	42	10	16	16	52	57	46
Redditch United	42	10	13	19	55	63	43
Chelmsford City	42	11	10	21	60	75	43
Willenhall Town	42	9	12	21	39	76	39
Nuneaton Borough	42	8	13	21	58	77	37
Witney Town	42	8	11	23	45	71	35

Midland Division

Merthyr Tydfil	42	30	4	8	102	40	94
Moor Green	42	26	8	8	91	49	86
Grantham Town	42	27	4	11	97	53	85
Atherstone United	42	22	10	10	93	56	76
Sutton Coldfield Town	42	22	6	14	71	47	72
Halesowen Town	42	18	15	9	75	59	69
Gloucester City	42	18	14	10	86	62	68
Dudley Town	42	20	5	17	64	55	65
Forest Green Rovers	42	14	16	12	67	54	58
Banbury United	42	17	7	18	48	46	58
Bridgnorth Town	42	16	7	19	59	75	55
Buckingham Town	42	15	9	18	74	75	54
King's Lynn	42	16	6	20	53	63	54
Wellingborough Town	42	14	10	18	67	70	52
Rushden Town	42	14	9	19	69	85	51
Trowbridge Town	42	14	3	25	53	82	45
Bilston Town	42	12	8	22	52	87	44
Hednesford Town	42	11	10	21	50	81	43
Mile Oak Rovers	42	9	14	19	43	65	41
Coventry Sporting	42	11	8	23	46	83	41
Stourbridge	42	10	10	22	46	79	40
Paget Rangers	42	10	9	23	49	89	39

Southern Division

Dover Athletic	40	28	10	2	81	28	94
Waterlooville	40	27	10	3	88	33	91
Salisbury	40	24	11	5	71	33	83
Gravesend & Northfleet	40	20	12	8	60	32	72
Thanet United	40	17	13	10	60	38	64
Andover	40	17	13	10	64	58	64
Dunstable	40	17	12	11	78	56	63
Burnham	40	17	10	13	61	45	61
Bury Town	40	17	7	16	80	67	58
Erith & Belvedere	40	16	9	15	52	56	57
Sheppey United	40	14	10	16	58	52	52
Hastings Town	40	14	10	16	62	70	52
Tonbridge AFC	40	14	8	18	51	56	50
Poole Town	40	13	10	17	69	70	49
Baldock Town	40	12	12	16	44	53	48
Hounslow	40	11	8	21	41	76	41
Folkestone	40	9	11	20	47	76	38
Corinthian	40	9	10	21	49	67	37
Ruislip	40	5	13	22	33	80	28
Canterbury City	40	7	6	27	33	87	27
Chatham Town	40	7	5	28	39	88	26

1988-89   Premier Division

	P	W	D	L	F	A	Pts
Merthyr Tydfil	42	26	7	9	104	58	85
Dartford	42	25	7	10	79	33	82
VS Rugby	42	24	7	11	64	43	79
Worcester City	42	20	13	9	72	49	73
Cambridge City	42	20	10	12	72	51	70
Dover Athletic	42	19	12	11	65	47	69
Gosport Borough	42	18	12	12	73	57	66
Burton Albion	42	18	10	14	79	68	64
Bath City	42	15	13	14	66	51	58
Bromsgrove Rovers	42	14	16	12	68	56	58
Wealdstone	42	16	10	16	60	53	58
Crawley Town	42	14	16	12	61	56	58
Dorchester Town	42	14	16	12	56	61	58
Alvechurch	42	16	8	18	56	59	56
Moor Green	42	14	13	15	58	70	55
Corby Town	42	14	11	17	55	59	53
Waterlooville	42	13	13	16	61	63	52
Ashford Town	42	13	13	16	59	76	52
Fareham Town	42	15	6	21	43	68	51
Leicester United	42	6	11	25	46	84	29
Redditch United	42	5	7	30	36	105	22
Bedworth United	42	4	7	31	36	102	19

Midland Division

	P	W	D	L	F	A	Pts
Gloucester City	42	28	8	6	95	37	92
Atherstone United	42	26	9	7	85	38	87
Tamworth	42	26	9	7	85	45	87
Halesowen Town	42	25	10	7	85	42	85
Grantham Town	42	23	11	8	66	37	80
Nuneaton Borough	42	19	9	14	71	58	66
Rushden Town	42	19	8	15	71	50	65
Spalding United	42	17	13	12	72	64	64
Dudley Town	42	16	13	13	73	62	61
Sutton Coldfield Town	42	18	7	17	56	56	61
Willenhall Town	42	16	12	14	65	71	60
Forest Green Rovers	42	12	16	14	64	67	52
Bilston Town	42	15	7	20	63	71	52
Ashtree Highfield	42	12	15	15	57	62	51
Hednesford Town	42	12	15	15	49	57	51
Banbury United	42	10	14	18	53	74	44
Bridgnorth Town	42	12	7	23	59	77	43
Stourbridge	42	11	10	21	37	65	43
King's Lynn	42	7	13	22	31	67	34
Coventry Sporting	42	6	13	23	39	91	31
Wellingborough Town	42	5	15	22	39	72	30
Mile Oak Rovers	42	5	10	27	46	98	25

Southern Division

	P	W	D	L	F	A	Pts
Chelmsford City	42	30	5	7	106	38	95
Gravesend & Northfleet	42	27	6	9	70	40	87
Poole Town	42	24	11	7	98	48	83
Bury Town	42	25	7	10	75	34	82
Burnham	42	22	13	7	78	47	79
Baldock Town	42	23	5	14	69	40	74
Hastings Town	42	21	11	10	75	48	74
Hounslow	42	21	6	15	75	60	69
Salisbury	42	20	5	17	79	58	65
Trowbridge Town	42	19	7	16	59	52	64
Folkestone	42	17	8	17	62	65	59
Corinthian	42	13	13	16	59	69	52
Canterbury City	42	14	8	20	52	60	50
Witney Town	42	13	11	18	61	71	50
Dunstable	42	11	14	17	42	57	47
Buckingham Town	42	12	10	20	56	79	46
Erith & Belvedere	42	11	10	21	48	63	43
Andover	42	11	9	22	56	90	42
Sheppey United	42	10	8	24	50	90	38
Thanet United	42	7	15	20	47	95	36
Tonbridge AFC	42	7	6	29	50	98	27
Ruislip	42	6	8	28	47	112	26

1989-90   Premier Division

	P	W	D	L	F	A	Pts
Dover Athletic	42	32	6	4	87	27	102
Bath City	42	30	8	4	81	28	98
Dartford	42	26	9	7	80	35	87
Burton Albion	42	20	12	10	64	40	72
VS Rugby	42	19	12	11	51	35	69
Atherstone United	42	19	10	13	60	52	67
Gravesend & Northfleet	42	18	12	12	44	50	66
Cambridge City	42	17	11	14	76	56	62
Gloucester City	42	17	11	14	80	68	62
Bromsgrove Rovers	42	17	10	15	56	48	61
Moor Green	42	18	7	17	62	59	61
Wealdstone	42	16	9	17	55	54	57
Dorchester Town	42	16	7	19	52	67	55
Worcester City	42	15	10	17	62	63	54
Crawley Town	42	13	12	17	53	57	51
Waterlooville	42	13	10	19	63	81	49
Weymouth	42	11	13	18	50	70	46
Chelmsford City	42	11	10	21	52	72	43
Ashford Town	42	10	7	25	43	75	37
Corby Town	42	10	6	26	57	77	36
Alvechurch	42	7	5	30	46	95	26
Gosport Borough	42	6	5	31	28	93	23

Worcester City had 1 point deducted.

Midland Division

	P	W	D	L	F	A	Pts
Halesowen Town	42	28	8	6	100	49	92
Rushden Town	42	28	5	9	82	39	89
Nuneaton Borough	42	26	7	9	81	47	85
Tamworth	42	22	8	12	82	70	74
Barry Town	42	21	8	13	67	53	71
Spalding United	42	20	7	15	73	63	67
Sutton Coldfield Town	42	18	10	14	72	69	64
Stourbridge	42	17	12	13	73	61	63
Dudley Town	42	18	9	15	69	64	63
Stroud	42	16	13	13	75	62	61
Leicester United	42	17	5	20	66	77	56
Bridgnorth Town	42	13	14	15	68	73	53
King's Lynn	42	16	5	21	57	69	53
Grantham Town	42	14	10	18	57	63	52
Bedworth United	42	14	9	19	50	60	51
Hednesford Town	42	11	14	17	50	62	47
Bilston Town	42	11	14	17	40	54	47
Redditch United	42	11	13	18	57	64	46
Racing Club Warwick	42	11	11	20	45	66	44
Willenhall Town	42	9	9	24	37	66	36
Banbury United	42	9	9	24	46	83	34
Sandwell Borough	42	6	12	24	46	79	30

Banbury United had 2 points deducted.

Southern Division

	P	W	D	L	F	A	Pts
Bashley	42	25	7	10	80	47	82
Poole Town	42	23	8	11	85	60	77
Buckingham Town	42	22	10	10	67	46	76
Dunstable	42	20	14	8	56	38	74
Salisbury	42	21	9	12	72	50	72
Hythe Town	42	20	12	10	69	48	72
Trowbridge Town	42	20	9	13	79	64	69
Hastings Town	42	20	9	13	64	54	69
Bury Town	42	18	12	12	76	62	66
Baldock Town	42	18	11	13	69	52	65
Burnham	42	17	11	14	77	52	62
Fareham Town	42	14	14	14	49	53	56
Yate Town	42	16	6	20	53	52	54
Witney Town	42	16	6	20	54	56	54
Canterbury City	42	14	10	18	52	52	52
Margate	42	12	15	15	46	45	51
Folkestone	42	14	9	19	61	83	51
Andover	42	13	11	18	54	70	50
Hounslow	42	11	5	26	39	82	38
Erith & Belvedere	42	8	11	23	34	73	35
Corinthian	42	6	10	26	44	93	28
Sheppey United	42	6	7	29	35	83	25

1990-91 Premier Division

Farnborough Town	42	26	7	9	79	43	85
Gloucester City	42	23	14	5	86	49	83
Cambridge City	42	21	14	7	63	43	77
Dover Athletic	42	21	11	10	56	37	74
Bromsgrove Rovers	42	20	11	11	68	49	71
Worcester City	42	18	12	12	55	42	66
Burton Albion	42	15	15	12	59	48	60
Halesowen Town	42	17	9	16	73	67	60
VS Rugby	42	16	11	15	56	46	59
Bashley	42	15	12	15	56	52	57
Dorchester Town	42	15	12	15	47	54	57
Wealdstone	42	16	8	18	57	58	56
Dartford	42	15	9	18	61	64	54
Rushden Town	42	14	11	17	64	66	53
Atherstone United	42	14	10	18	55	58	52
Moor Green	42	15	6	21	64	75	51
Poole Town	42	12	13	17	56	69	49
Chelmsford City	42	11	15	16	57	68	48
Crawley Town	42	12	12	18	45	67	48
Waterlooville	42	11	13	18	51	70	46
Gravesend & Northfleet	42	9	7	26	46	91	34
Weymouth	42	4	12	26	50	88	24

Midland Division

Stourbridge	42	28	6	8	80	48	90
Corby Town	42	27	4	11	99	48	85
Hednesford Town	42	25	7	10	79	47	82
Tamworth	42	25	5	12	84	45	80
Nuneaton Borough	42	21	11	10	74	51	70
Barry Town	42	20	7	15	61	48	67
Newport AFC	42	19	6	17	54	46	63
King's Lynn	42	17	9	16	53	62	60
Grantham Town	42	17	7	18	62	56	58
Redditch United	42	16	10	16	66	75	58
Hinckley Town	42	16	9	17	72	68	57
Sutton Coldfield Town	42	15	11	16	56	65	56
Bedworth United	42	15	9	18	57	73	54
Bilston Town	42	14	9	19	69	79	51
Leicester United	42	14	10	18	65	77	51
Racing Club Warwick	42	12	13	17	56	65	49
Bridgnorth Town	42	13	9	20	62	74	48
Stroud	42	11	14	17	51	64	47
Dudley Town	42	11	13	18	48	73	46
Alvechurch	42	10	8	24	54	92	38
Willenhall Town	42	10	10	22	58	69	37
Spalding United	42	8	9	25	35	70	33

Nuneaton Borough had 4 points deducted. Willenhall Town had 3 points deducted. Leicester United had 1 point deducted.

Southern Division

Buckingham Town	40	25	8	7	73	38	83
Trowbridge Town	40	22	12	6	67	31	78
Salisbury	40	22	11	7	63	39	77
Baldock Town	40	21	9	10	66	52	72
Ashford Town	40	22	5	13	82	52	71
Yate Town	40	21	8	11	76	48	71
Hastings Town	40	18	11	11	66	46	65
Hythe Town	40	17	9	14	55	44	59
Andover	40	16	6	18	69	76	54
Margate	40	14	11	15	52	55	53
Burnham	40	12	16	12	57	49	52
Bury Town	40	15	5	20	58	74	50
Sudbury Town	40	13	10	17	60	68	49
Newport IOW	40	13	9	18	56	62	48
Gosport Borough	40	12	11	17	47	58	47
Witney Town	40	12	11	17	57	75	47
Dunstable	40	9	15	16	48	63	42
Canterbury City	40	12	6	22	60	83	42
Erith & Belvedere	40	10	6	24	46	73	36
Fareham Town	40	9	9	22	46	74	36
Corinthian	40	5	12	23	34	78	27

Hythe Town had 1 point deducted.

1991-92 Premier Division

Bromsgrove Rovers	42	27	9	6	78	34	90
Dover Athletic	42	23	15	4	66	30	84
VS Rugby	42	23	11	8	70	44	80
Bashley	42	22	8	12	70	44	74
Cambridge City	42	18	14	10	71	53	68
Dartford	42	17	15	10	62	45	66
Trowbridge Town	42	17	10	15	69	51	61
Halesowen Town	42	15	15	12	61	49	60
Moor Green	42	15	11	16	61	59	56
Burton Albion	42	15	10	17	59	61	55
Dorchester Town	42	14	13	15	66	73	55
Gloucester City	42	15	9	18	67	70	54
Atherstone United	42	15	8	19	54	66	53
Corby Town	42	13	12	17	66	81	51
Waterlooville	42	13	11	18	43	56	50
Worcester City	42	12	13	17	56	59	49
Crawley Town	42	12	12	18	62	67	48
Chelmsford City	42	12	12	18	49	56	48
Wealdstone	42	13	7	22	52	69	46
Poole Town	42	10	13	19	46	77	43
Fisher Athletic	42	9	11	22	53	89	38
Gravesend & Northfleet	42	8	9	25	39	87	33

Midland Division

Solihull Borough	42	29	10	3	92	40	97
Hednesford Town	42	26	13	3	81	37	91
Sutton Coldfield Town	42	21	11	10	71	51	74
Barry Town	42	21	6	15	88	56	69
Bedworth United	42	16	15	11	67	63	63
Nuneaton Borough	42	17	11	14	68	53	62
Tamworth	42	16	12	14	66	52	60
Rushden Town	42	16	12	14	69	63	60
Stourbridge	42	17	8	17	85	62	59
Newport AFC	42	15	13	14	72	60	58
Yate Town	42	14	15	13	65	64	57
Bilston Town	42	15	10	17	56	67	55
Grantham Town	42	11	17	14	59	55	50
King's Lynn	42	13	11	18	61	68	50
Hinckley Town	42	14	8	20	61	87	50
Leicester United	42	12	13	17	56	63	49
Bridgnorth Town	42	12	12	18	61	74	48
Racing Club Warwick	42	11	14	17	45	61	47
Stroud	42	14	4	24	66	88	46
Redditch United	42	12	8	22	52	92	44
Alvechurch	42	11	10	21	54	88	43
Dudley Town	42	8	9	25	41	92	33

Southern Division

Hastings Town	42	28	7	7	80	37	91
Weymouth	42	22	12	8	64	35	78
Havant Town	42	21	12	9	67	46	75
Braintree Town	42	21	8	13	77	58	71
Buckingham Town	42	19	15	8	57	26	69
Andover	42	18	10	14	73	68	64
Ashford Town	42	17	12	13	66	57	63
Sudbury Town	42	18	9	15	70	66	63
Sittingbourne	42	19	10	13	63	41	61
Burnham	42	15	14	13	57	55	59
Baldock Town	42	16	10	16	62	67	58
Salisbury	42	13	16	13	67	51	55
Hythe Town	42	15	10	17	61	62	55
Margate	42	13	16	13	49	56	55
Newport IOW	42	13	10	19	58	63	49
Dunstable	42	12	12	18	55	67	48
Bury Town	42	14	4	24	52	94	46
Witney Town	42	11	12	19	55	76	45
Fareham Town	42	12	8	22	45	71	44
Erith & Belvedere	42	11	10	21	44	67	43
Canterbury City	42	8	14	20	43	69	38
Gosport Borough	42	6	9	27	32	65	27

Buckingham Town had 3 points deducted.
Sittingbourne had 6 points deducted.

1992-93　Premier Division

Team	P	W	D	L	F	A	Pts
Dover Athletic	40	25	11	4	65	23	86
Cheltenham Town	40	21	10	9	76	40	73
Corby Town	40	20	12	8	68	43	72
Hednesford Town	40	21	7	12	72	52	70
Trowbridge Town	40	18	8	14	70	66	62
Crawley Town	40	16	12	12	68	59	60
Solihull Borough	40	17	9	14	68	59	60
Burton Albion	40	16	11	13	53	50	59
Bashley	40	18	8	14	60	60	59
Halesowen Town	40	15	11	14	67	54	56
Waterlooville	40	15	9	16	59	62	54
Chelmsford City	40	15	9	16	59	69	54
Gloucester City	40	14	11	15	66	68	53
Cambridge City	40	14	10	16	62	73	52
Atherstone United	40	13	14	13	56	60	50
Hastings Town	40	13	11	16	50	55	50
Worcester City	40	12	9	19	45	62	45
Dorchester Town	40	12	6	22	52	74	42
Moor Green	40	10	6	24	58	79	36
VS Rugby	40	10	6	24	40	63	36
Weymouth	40	5	10	25	39	82	23

Bashley and Atherstone United both had 3 points deducted. Weymouth had 2 points deducted.

Midland Division

Team	P	W	D	L	F	A	Pts
Nuneaton Borough	42	29	5	8	102	45	92
Gresley Rovers	42	27	6	9	94	55	87
Rushden & Diamonds	42	25	10	7	85	41	85
Barri	42	26	5	11	82	49	83
Newport AFC	42	23	8	11	73	58	77
Bedworth United	42	22	8	12	72	55	74
Stourbridge	42	17	9	16	93	79	60
Sutton Coldfield Town	42	17	9	16	82	78	60
Redditch United	42	18	6	18	75	79	60
Tamworth	42	16	11	15	65	51	59
Weston-super-Mare	42	17	7	18	79	86	58
Leicester United	42	16	9	17	67	67	57
Grantham Town	42	16	9	17	60	73	57
Bilston Town	42	15	10	17	74	69	55
Evesham United	42	15	8	19	67	83	53
Bridgnorth Town	42	15	7	20	61	68	52
Dudley Town	42	14	8	20	60	75	50
Yate Town	42	15	5	22	63	81	50
Forest Green Rovers	42	12	6	24	61	97	42
Hinckley Town	42	9	11	22	56	89	37
King's Lynn	42	10	6	26	45	90	36
Racing Club Warwick	42	3	7	32	40	88	16

Hinckley Town had 1 point deducted.

Southern Division

Team	P	W	D	L	F	A	Pts
Sittingbourne	42	26	12	4	102	43	90
Salisbury City	42	27	7	8	87	50	88
Witney Town	42	25	9	8	77	37	84
Gravesend & Northfleet	42	25	4	13	99	63	79
Havant Town	42	23	6	13	78	55	75
Sudbury Town	42	20	11	11	89	54	71
Erith & Belvedere	42	22	5	15	73	66	71
Ashford Town	42	20	8	14	91	66	68
Braintree Town	42	20	6	16	95	65	66
Margate	42	19	7	16	65	58	64
Wealdstone	42	18	7	17	75	69	61
Buckingham Town	42	16	11	15	61	58	59
Baldock Town	42	15	9	18	59	63	54
Poole Town	42	15	7	20	61	69	52
Fareham Town	42	14	8	20	67	65	50
Burnham	42	14	8	20	53	77	50
Canterbury City	42	12	10	20	54	76	46
Newport IOW	42	9	16	17	44	56	43
Fisher Athletic	42	8	9	25	38	98	33
Andover	42	7	9	26	42	99	30
Dunstable	42	5	14	23	42	92	29
Bury Town	42	8	5	29	46	119	29

1993-94　Premier Division

Team	P	W	D	L	F	A	Pts
Farnborough Town	42	25	7	10	74	44	82
Cheltenham Town	42	21	12	9	67	38	75
Halesowen Town	42	21	11	10	69	46	74
Atherstone United	42	22	7	13	57	43	73
Crawley Town	42	21	10	11	56	42	73
Chelmsford City	42	21	7	14	74	59	70
Trowbridge Town	42	16	17	9	52	41	65
Sittingbourne	42	17	13	12	65	48	64
Corby Town	42	17	8	17	52	56	59
Gloucester City	42	17	6	19	55	60	57
Burton Albion	42	15	11	16	57	49	56
Hastings Town	42	16	7	19	51	60	55
Hednesford Town	42	15	9	18	67	66	54
Gresley Rovers	42	14	11	17	61	72	53
Worcester City	42	14	9	19	61	70	51
Solihull Borough	42	13	11	18	52	57	50
Cambridge City	42	13	11	18	50	60	50
Dorchester Town	42	12	11	19	38	51	47
Moor Green	42	11	10	21	49	66	43
Waterlooville	42	11	10	21	47	69	43
Bashley	42	11	10	21	47	80	43
Nuneaton Borough	42	11	8	23	42	66	41

Midland Division

Team	P	W	D	L	F	A	Pts
Rushden & Diamonds	42	29	11	2	109	37	98
VS Rugby	42	28	8	6	98	41	92
Weston-super-Mare	42	27	10	5	94	39	91
Newport AFC	42	26	9	7	84	37	87
Clevedon Town	42	24	10	8	75	46	82
Redditch United	42	19	11	12	79	62	68
Tamworth	42	19	7	16	82	68	64
Bilston Town	42	16	10	16	65	73	58
Stourbridge	42	17	6	19	71	75	57
Evesham United	42	16	8	18	50	60	56
Grantham Town	42	16	6	20	77	73	54
Bridgnorth Town	42	15	6	21	56	68	51
Racing Club Warwick	42	13	12	17	53	66	51
Dudley Town	42	13	10	19	64	61	49
Forest Green Rovers	42	12	12	18	61	84	48
Sutton Coldfield Town	42	12	8	22	53	75	44
Bedworth United	42	12	7	23	62	81	43
Hinckley Town	42	11	10	21	44	71	43
Leicester United	42	11	9	22	34	73	42
King's Lynn	42	9	11	22	47	72	38
Yate Town	42	10	6	26	48	86	36
Armitage	42	8	11	23	45	103	35

Southern Division

Team	P	W	D	L	F	A	Pts
Gravesend & Northfleet	42	27	11	4	87	24	92
Sudbury Town	42	27	8	7	98	47	89
Witney Town	42	27	7	8	69	36	89
Salisbury City	42	26	10	6	90	39	88
Havant Town	42	27	4	11	101	41	85
Ashford Town	42	24	13	5	93	46	85
Baldock Town	42	26	7	9	76	40	85
Newport IOW	42	22	8	12	74	51	74
Margate	42	20	8	14	76	58	68
Weymouth	42	18	9	15	71	65	63
Tonbridge	42	19	5	18	59	62	62
Buckingham Town	42	14	14	14	43	42	56
Braintree Town	42	16	7	19	72	84	55
Fareham Town	42	12	12	18	54	75	48
Poole Town	42	13	6	23	54	86	45
Burnham	42	10	9	23	53	92	39
Fisher 93	42	9	10	23	52	81	37
Dunstable	42	9	7	26	50	91	34
Erith & Belvedere	42	9	5	28	40	72	32
Canterbury City	42	8	7	27	35	80	31
Wealdstone	42	6	7	29	45	95	25
Bury Town	42	3	5	34	36	121	14

1994-95 Premier Division

Hednesford Town	42	28	9	5	99	49	93
Cheltenham Town	42	25	11	6	87	39	86
Burton Albion	42	20	15	7	55	39	75
Gloucester City	42	22	8	12	76	48	74
Rushden & Diamonds	42	19	11	12	99	65	68
Dorchester Town	42	19	10	13	84	61	67
Leek Town	42	19	10	13	72	60	67
Gresley Rovers	42	17	12	13	70	63	63
Cambridge City	42	18	8	16	60	55	62
Worcester City	42	14	15	13	46	34	57
Crawley Town	42	15	10	17	64	71	55
Hastings Town	42	13	14	15	55	57	53
Halesowen Town	42	14	10	18	81	80	52
Gravesend & Northfleet	42	13	13	16	38	55	52
Chelmsford City	42	14	6	22	56	60	48
Atherstone United	42	12	12	18	51	67	48
VS Rugby	42	11	14	17	49	61	47
Sudbury Town	42	12	10	20	50	77	46
Solihull Borough	42	10	15	17	39	65	45
Sittingbourne	42	11	10	21	51	73	43
Trowbridge Town	42	9	13	20	43	69	40
Corby Town	42	4	10	28	36	113	21

Corby Town had 1 point deducted for fielding ineligible players

Midland Division

Newport AFC	42	29	8	5	106	39	95
Ilkeston Town	42	25	6	11	101	75	81
Tamworth	42	24	8	10	98	70	80
Moor Green	42	23	8	11	105	63	77
Bridgnorth Town	42	22	10	10	75	49	76
Buckingham Town	42	20	14	8	55	37	74
Nuneaton Borough	42	19	11	12	76	55	68
Rothwell Town	42	19	7	16	71	71	64
King's Lynn	42	18	8	16	76	64	62
Racing Club Warwick	42	17	11	14	68	63	62
Dudley Town	42	17	10	15	65	69	61
Bilston Town	42	17	8	17	73	64	59
Bedworth United	42	17	7	18	64	68	58
Evesham United	42	14	10	18	57	56	52
Hinckley Town	42	14	10	18	61	76	52
Stourbridge	42	15	7	20	59	77	52
Sutton Coldfield Town	42	12	10	20	62	72	46
Forest Green Rovers	42	11	13	18	56	76	46
Redditch United	42	8	14	20	47	64	38
Leicester United	42	10	8	24	51	99	38
Grantham Town	42	8	9	25	55	93	33
Armitage	42	2	5	35	35	116	11

Southern Division

Salisbury City	42	30	7	5	88	37	97
Baldock Town	42	28	10	4	92	44	94
Havant Town	42	25	10	7	81	34	85
Waterlooville	42	24	8	10	77	36	80
Ashford Town	42	21	12	9	106	72	75
Weston-super-Mare	42	18	13	11	82	54	67
Bashley	42	18	11	13	62	49	65
Weymouth	42	16	13	13	60	55	61
Newport IOW	42	17	10	15	67	67	61
Witney Town	42	14	14	14	57	57	56
Clevedon Town	42	14	13	15	73	64	55
Tonbridge Angels	42	14	12	16	74	87	54
Margate	42	15	7	20	60	72	52
Braintree Town	42	12	13	17	64	71	49
Wealdstone	42	13	8	21	76	94	47
Yate Town	42	11	13	18	57	75	46
Fisher 93	42	9	16	17	54	70	43
Bury Town	42	11	8	23	59	86	41
Erith & Belvedere	42	10	9	23	49	94	39
Poole Town	42	10	8	24	53	79	38
Fareham Town	42	10	8	24	46	91	38
Burnham	42	7	7	28	40	89	28

1995-96 Premier Division

Rushden & Diamonds	42	29	7	6	99	41	94
Halesowen Town	42	27	11	4	70	36	92
Cheltenham Town	42	21	11	10	76	57	74
Gloucester City	42	21	8	13	65	47	71
Gresley Rovers	42	20	10	12	70	58	70
Worcester City	42	19	12	11	61	43	69
Merthyr Tydfil	42	19	6	17	67	59	63
Hastings Town	42	16	13	13	68	56	61
Crawley Town	42	15	13	14	57	56	58
Sudbury Town	42	15	10	17	69	71	55
Gravesend & Northfleet	42	15	10	17	60	62	55
Chelmsford City	42	13	16	13	46	53	55
Dorchester Town	42	15	8	19	62	57	53
Newport AFC	42	13	13	16	53	59	52
Salisbury City	42	14	10	18	57	69	52
Burton Albion	42	13	12	17	55	56	51
Atherstone United	42	12	12	18	58	75	48
Baldock Town	42	11	14	17	51	56	47
Cambridge City	42	12	10	20	56	68	46
Ilkeston Town	42	11	10	21	53	87	43
Stafford Rangers	42	11	4	27	58	90	37
VS Rugby	42	5	10	27	37	92	25

Midland Division

Nuneaton Borough	42	30	5	7	82	35	95
King's Lynn	42	27	5	10	85	43	84
Bedworth United	42	24	10	8	76	42	81
Moor Green	42	22	8	12	81	47	74
Paget Rangers	42	21	9	12	70	45	72
Tamworth	42	22	3	17	97	64	69
Solihull Borough	42	19	9	14	77	64	66
Rothwell Town	42	17	14	11	79	62	65
Buckingham Town	42	18	9	15	74	62	63
Dudley Town	42	15	16	11	83	66	61
Stourbridge	42	17	8	17	60	63	59
Bilston Town	42	16	9	17	61	62	57
Sutton Coldfield Town	42	16	9	17	62	67	57
Grantham Town	42	17	5	20	71	83	56
Redditch United	42	14	11	17	57	77	53
Leicester United	42	13	13	16	58	72	52
Hinckley Town	42	14	7	21	62	83	49
Racing Club Warwick	42	10	13	19	67	90	43
Evesham United	42	11	6	25	59	94	39
Corby Town	42	9	7	26	52	95	34
Bury Town	42	8	8	26	57	95	32
Bridgnorth Town	42	7	6	29	53	112	27

Bedworth United 1 point deducted, King's Lynn had 2 points deducted

Southern Division

Sittingbourne	42	28	4	10	102	44	88
Ashford Town	42	25	9	8	75	44	84
Waterlooville	42	24	8	10	87	44	80
Newport IOW	42	24	6	12	75	58	78
Braintree Town	42	24	8	10	93	70	77
Weymouth	42	24	4	14	75	55	76
Havant Town	42	23	11	8	73	42	74
Forest Green Rovers	42	22	8	12	85	55	74
Trowbridge Town	42	18	8	16	86	51	62
Yate Town	42	17	8	17	85	71	59
Margate	42	18	5	19	68	62	59
Witney Town	42	16	11	15	60	54	59
Weston-super-Mare	42	16	9	17	78	68	57
Cinderford Town	42	16	8	18	74	77	56
Fisher 93	42	14	13	15	58	59	55
Bashley	42	14	11	17	63	61	53
Clevedon Town	42	15	6	21	70	80	51
Tonbridge Angels	42	13	10	19	58	79	49
Fleet Town	42	14	5	23	58	79	47
Fareham Town	42	12	5	25	71	97	41
Erith & Belvedere	42	4	4	34	38	111	16
Poole Town	42	0	1	41	17	188	1

Braintree Town 3 points deducted, Havant Town had 6 points deducted

1996-97   Premier Division

Team	P	W	D	L	F	A	Pts
Gresley Rovers	42	25	10	7	75	40	85
Cheltenham Town	42	21	11	10	76	44	74
Gloucester City	42	21	10	11	81	56	73
Halesowen Town	42	21	10	11	77	54	73
King's Lynn	42	20	8	14	65	61	68
Burton Albion	42	18	12	12	70	53	66
Nuneaton Borough	42	19	9	14	61	52	66
Sittingbourne	42	19	7	16	76	65	64
Merthyr Tydfil	42	17	9	16	69	61	60
Worcester City	42	15	14	13	52	50	59
Atherstone United	42	15	13	14	46	47	58
Salisbury City	42	15	13	14	57	66	58
Sudbury Town	42	16	7	19	72	72	55
Gravesend & Northfleet	42	16	7	19	63	73	55
Dorchester Town	42	14	9	19	62	66	51
Hastings Town	42	12	15	15	49	60	51
Crawley Town	42	13	8	21	49	67	47
Cambridge City	42	11	13	18	57	65	46
Ashford Town	42	9	18	15	53	79	45
Baldock Town	42	11	8	23	52	90	41
Newport AFC	42	9	13	20	40	60	40
Chelmsford City	42	6	14	22	49	70	32

Midland Division

Team	P	W	D	L	F	A	Pts
Tamworth	40	30	7	3	90	28	97
Rothwell Town	40	20	11	9	82	54	71
Ilkeston Town	40	19	13	8	76	50	70
Grantham Town	40	22	4	14	65	46	70
Bedworth United	40	18	11	11	77	41	65
Solihull Borough	40	19	8	13	84	62	65
Bilston Town	40	18	10	12	74	57	64
Moor Green	40	18	7	15	88	68	61
Stafford Rangers	40	17	9	14	68	62	60
Raunds Town	40	16	11	13	61	66	59
Racing Club Warwick	40	16	10	14	70	72	58
Shepshed Dynamo	40	14	12	14	64	65	54
Redditch United	40	15	8	17	56	59	53
Paget Rangers	40	13	9	18	42	55	48
Dudley Town	40	12	10	18	70	89	46
Hinckley Town	40	11	11	18	39	63	44
Stourbridge	40	10	9	21	61	81	39
Evesham United	40	9	12	19	55	77	39
VS Rugby	40	9	9	22	49	81	36
Corby Town	40	8	8	24	49	88	32
Sutton Coldfield Town	40	7	9	24	29	85	30

Leicester United FC closed down and their record was expunged from the League table.

Southern Division

Team	P	W	D	L	F	A	Pts
Forest Green Rovers	42	27	10	5	87	40	91
St Leonards Stamcroft	42	26	9	7	95	48	87
Havant Town	42	23	10	9	81	49	79
Weston-super-Mare	42	21	13	8	82	43	76
Margate	42	21	9	12	70	47	72
Witney Town	42	20	11	11	71	42	71
Weymouth	42	20	10	12	82	51	70
Tonbridge Angels	42	17	15	10	56	44	66
Newport IOW	42	15	15	12	73	58	60
Fisher Athletic (London)	42	18	6	18	77	77	60
Clevedon Town	42	17	9	16	75	76	60
Fareham Town	42	14	12	16	53	70	54
Bashley	42	15	8	19	73	84	53
Dartford	42	14	10	18	59	64	52
Waterlooville	42	14	9	19	58	67	51
Cirencester Town	42	12	12	18	50	68	48
Cinderford Town	42	13	7	22	64	76	46
Trowbridge Town	42	11	11	20	50	61	44
Yate Town	42	12	8	22	55	87	44
Fleet Town	42	12	6	24	47	91	42
Erith & Belvedere	42	9	10	23	60	95	37
Buckingham Town	42	2	8	32	27	107	14

1997-98

Premier Division

Team	P	W	D	L	F	A	Pts
Forest Green Rovers	42	27	8	7	93	55	89
Merthyr Tydfil	42	24	12	6	80	42	84
Burton Albion	42	21	8	13	64	43	71
Dorchester Town	42	19	13	10	63	38	70
Halesowen Town	42	18	15	9	70	38	69
Bath City	42	19	12	11	72	51	69
Worcester City	42	19	12	11	54	44	69
King's Lynn	42	18	11	13	64	65	65
Atherstone United	42	17	12	13	55	49	63
Crawley Town	42	17	8	17	63	60	59
Gloucester City	42	16	11	15	57	57	59
Nuneaton Borough	42	17	6	19	68	61	57
Cambridge City	42	16	8	18	62	70	56
Hastings Town	42	14	12	16	67	70	54
Tamworth	42	14	11	17	68	65	53
Rothwell Town	42	11	16	15	55	73	49
Gresley Rovers	42	14	6	22	59	77	48
Salisbury City	42	12	12	18	53	72	48
Bromsgrove Rovers	42	13	6	23	67	85	45
Sittingbourne	42	12	8	22	47	66	44
Ashford Town	42	8	5	29	34	85	29
St Leonards Stamcroft	42	5	10	27	48	97	25

Midland Division

Team	P	W	D	L	F	A	Pts
Grantham Town	40	30	4	6	87	39	94
Ilkeston Town	40	29	6	5	123	39	93
Solihull Borough	40	22	9	9	81	48	75
Raunds Town	40	20	8	12	73	44	68
Wisbech Town	40	20	7	13	79	57	67
Moor Green	40	20	7	13	72	55	67
Bilston Town	40	20	5	15	69	57	65
Blakenall	40	17	13	10	66	55	64
Stafford Rangers	40	18	6	16	57	56	60
Redditch United	40	16	11	13	59	41	59
Stourbridge	40	16	9	15	57	55	57
Hinckley United	40	15	11	14	59	56	56
Brackley Town	40	15	7	18	45	57	52
Bedworth United	40	15	5	20	50	73	50
Racing Club Warwick	40	11	9	20	49	56	42
Shepshed Dynamo	40	9	14	17	55	74	41
Sutton Coldfield Town	40	9	12	19	42	68	39
Paget Rangers	40	9	12	19	40	75	39
VS Rugby	40	8	12	20	53	93	36
Evesham United	40	7	9	24	47	94	30
Corby Town	40	2	8	30	41	112	14

Southern Division

Team	P	W	D	L	F	A	Pts
Weymouth	42	32	2	8	107	48	98
Chelmsford City	42	29	8	5	86	39	95
Bashley	42	29	4	9	101	59	91
Newport IOW	42	25	9	8	72	34	84
Fisher Athletic (London)	42	25	5	12	87	50	80
Margate	42	23	8	11	71	42	77
Newport AFC	42	21	6	15	83	65	69
Witney Town	42	20	9	13	74	58	69
Clevedon Town	42	20	7	15	57	55	67
Waterlooville	42	17	7	18	69	64	58
Dartford	42	17	7	18	60	60	58
Havant Town	42	13	14	15	65	70	53
Fleet Town	42	16	5	21	63	83	53
Tonbridge Angels	42	14	10	18	49	55	52
Trowbridge Town	42	14	6	22	55	69	48
Erith & Belvedere	42	11	13	18	47	68	46
Fareham Town	42	12	9	21	75	87	45
Cirencester Town	42	12	7	23	63	88	43
Weston-super-Mare	42	12	5	25	49	86	41
Baldock Town	42	10	5	27	53	81	35
Cinderford Town	42	6	5	31	40	112	23
Yate Town	42	5	7	30	44	97	22

1998-99 Premier Division

Team	P	W	D	L	F	A	Pts
Nuneaton Borough	42	27	9	6	91	33	90
Boston United	42	17	16	9	69	51	67
Ilkeston Town	42	18	13	11	72	59	67
Bath City	42	18	11	13	70	44	65
Hastings Town	42	18	11	13	57	49	65
Gloucester City	42	18	11	13	57	52	65
Worcester City	42	18	9	15	58	54	63
Halesowen Town	42	17	11	14	72	60	62
Tamworth	42	19	5	18	62	67	62
King's Lynn	42	17	10	15	53	46	61
Crawley Town	42	17	10	15	57	58	61
Salisbury City	42	16	12	14	56	61	60
Burton Albion	42	17	7	18	58	52	58
Weymouth	42	14	14	14	56	55	56
Merthyr Tydfil	42	15	8	19	52	62	53
Atherstone United	42	12	14	16	47	52	50
Grantham Town	42	14	8	20	51	58	50
Dorchester Town	42	11	15	16	49	63	48
Rothwell Town	42	13	9	20	47	67	48
Cambridge City	42	11	12	19	47	68	45
Gresley Rovers	42	12	8	22	49	73	44
Bromsgrove Rovers	42	8	7	27	38	84	31

Hastings Town resigned from the League

Midland Division

Team	P	W	D	L	F	A	Pts
Clevedon Town	42	28	8	6	83	35	92
Newport AFC	42	26	7	9	92	51	85
Redditch United	42	22	12	8	81	45	75
Hinckley United	42	20	12	10	58	40	72
Stafford Rangers	42	21	8	13	92	60	71
Bilston Town	42	20	11	11	79	69	71
Solihull Borough	42	19	12	11	76	53	69
Moor Green	42	20	7	15	71	61	67
Blakenall	42	17	14	11	65	54	65
Shepshed Dynamo	42	17	12	13	62	54	63
Sutton Coldfield Town	42	17	8	17	46	57	59
Stourbridge	42	16	10	16	60	55	58
Evesham United	42	16	9	17	63	63	57
Wisbech Town	42	16	9	17	59	66	57
Weston-super-Mare	42	15	10	17	59	56	55
Bedworth United	42	15	9	18	63	52	54
Cinderford Town	42	13	8	21	61	74	47
Stamford AFC	42	13	7	22	60	75	46
Paget Rangers	42	11	12	19	49	58	45
VS Rugby	42	12	9	21	53	74	45
Racing Club Warwick	42	5	8	29	38	93	23
Bloxwich Town	42	1	2	39	26	151	5

Southern Division

Team	P	W	D	L	F	A	Pts
Havant & Waterlooville	42	29	7	6	85	32	94
Margate	42	27	8	7	84	33	89
Folkestone Invicta	42	26	8	8	92	47	86
Newport IOW	42	23	7	12	68	40	76
Chelmsford City	42	20	12	10	91	51	72
Raunds Town	42	19	13	10	87	50	70
Ashford Town	42	17	12	13	59	54	63
Baldock Town	42	17	9	16	60	59	60
Fisher Athletic (London)	42	16	11	15	58	54	59
Bashley	42	17	7	18	74	77	58
Witney Town	42	15	12	15	56	48	57
Cirencester Town	42	16	8	18	61	66	56
Sittingbourne	42	12	18	12	53	56	54
Dartford	42	14	10	18	48	53	52
Erith & Belvedere	42	15	7	20	48	64	52
Tonbridge Angels	42	12	15	15	48	59	51
St Leonards	42	14	8	20	57	72	50
Fleet Town	42	12	11	19	54	72	47
Corby Town	42	10	10	22	48	73	40
Yate Town	42	10	7	25	37	79	37
Andover	42	6	10	26	50	115	28
Brackley Town	42	6	8	28	41	105	26

1999-2000 Premier Division

Team	P	W	D	L	F	A	Pts
Boston United	42	27	11	4	102	39	92
Burton Albion	42	23	9	10	73	43	78
Margate	42	23	8	11	64	43	77
Bath City	42	19	15	8	70	49	72
King's Lynn	42	19	14	9	59	43	71
Tamworth	42	20	10	12	80	51	70
Newport County	42	16	18	8	67	50	66
Clevedon Town	42	18	9	15	52	52	63
Ilkeston Town	42	16	12	14	77	69	60
Weymouth	42	14	16	12	60	51	58
Halesowen Town	42	14	14	14	52	54	56
Crawley Town	42	15	8	19	68	82	53
Havant & Waterlooville	42	13	13	16	63	68	52
Cambridge City	42	14	10	18	52	66	52
Worcester City	42	13	11	18	60	66	50
Salisbury City	42	14	8	20	70	84	50
Merthyr Tydfil	42	13	9	20	51	63	48
Dorchester Town	42	10	17	15	56	65	47
Grantham Town	42	14	5	23	63	76	47
Gloucester City	42	8	14	20	40	82	38
Rothwell Town	42	5	14	23	48	85	29
Atherstone United	42	5	13	24	30	76	28

Eastern Division

Team	P	W	D	L	F	A	Pts
Fisher Athletic (London)	42	31	5	6	107	42	98
Folkestone Invicta	42	30	7	5	101	39	97
Newport IOW	42	25	7	10	74	40	82
Chelmsford City	42	24	8	10	74	38	80
Hastings Town	42	22	9	11	76	56	75
Ashford Town	42	21	9	12	70	49	72
Tonbridge Angels	42	20	10	12	82	60	70
Dartford	42	17	6	19	52	58	57
Burnham	42	15	9	18	55	64	54
Baldock Town	42	14	10	18	57	69	52
Erith & Belvedere	42	14	9	19	62	68	51
Witney Town	42	13	11	18	48	60	50
VS Rugby	42	13	11	18	58	79	50
Wisbech Town	42	14	7	21	58	66	49
Spalding United	42	14	6	22	52	71	48
Sittingbourne	42	13	7	22	48	75	46
Stamford	42	9	18	15	50	62	45
St Leonards	42	11	12	19	67	81	45
Raunds Town	42	11	12	19	44	63	45
Bashley	42	12	7	23	56	95	43
Corby Town	42	11	12	19	56	62	42
Fleet Town	42	8	8	26	54	104	32

Corby Town had 3 points deducted for fielding an ineligible player
Raunds Town gave notice to withdraw and take the place of the 2nd relegated Club. They then unsuccessfully sought re-election

Western Division

Team	P	W	D	L	F	A	Pts
Stafford Rangers	42	29	6	7	107	47	93
Moor Green	42	26	12	4	85	33	90
Hinckley United	42	25	12	5	89	47	87
Tiverton Town	42	26	7	9	91	44	85
Solihull Borough	42	20	11	11	85	66	71
Blakenall	42	19	12	11	70	46	69
Cirencester Town	42	20	8	14	72	64	68
Bilston Town	42	16	18	8	66	52	66
Cinderford Town	42	17	11	14	62	64	62
Redditch United	42	17	10	15	73	65	61
Gresley Rovers	42	14	15	13	54	49	57
Weston-super-Mare	42	16	9	17	55	55	57
Sutton Coldfield Town	42	13	17	12	49	52	56
Evesham United	42	13	12	17	69	61	51
Bedworth United	42	13	10	19	52	71	49
Rocester	42	12	12	18	63	78	48
Bromsgrove Rovers	42	13	7	22	59	72	46
Shepshed Dynamo	42	12	7	23	46	66	43
Paget Rangers	42	11	4	27	44	82	37
Racing Club Warwick	42	7	14	21	41	82	35
Stourbridge	42	10	3	29	45	101	33
Yate Town	42	3	3	36	28	108	12

2000-2001 **Premier Division**

Margate	42	28	7	7	75	27	91
Burton Albion	42	25	13	4	76	36	88
King's Lynn	42	18	11	13	67	58	65
Welling United	42	17	13	12	59	55	64
Weymouth	42	17	12	13	69	51	63
Havant & Waterlooville	42	18	9	15	65	53	63
Stafford Rangers	42	18	9	15	70	59	63
Worcester City	42	18	8	16	52	53	62
Moor Green	42	18	8	16	49	53	62
Newport County	42	17	10	15	70	61	61
Crawley Town	42	17	10	15	61	54	61
Tamworth	42	17	8	17	58	55	59
Salisbury City	42	17	8	17	64	69	59
Ilkeston Town	42	16	11	15	51	61	59
Bath City	42	15	13	14	67	68	55
Cambridge City	42	13	11	18	56	59	50
Folkestone Invicta	42	14	6	22	49	74	48
Merthyr Tydfil	42	11	13	18	49	62	46
Clevedon Town	42	11	7	24	61	74	40
Fisher Athletic (London)	42	12	6	24	51	85	39
Dorchester Town	42	10	8	24	40	70	38
Halesowen Town	42	8	13	21	47	69	37

Bath City and Fisher Athletic (London) both had 3 points deducted

Eastern Division

Newport IOW	42	28	10	4	91	30	94
Chelmsford City	42	27	9	6	102	45	90
Grantham Town	42	25	11	6	100	47	86
Histon	42	23	11	8	84	53	80
Baldock Town	42	23	10	9	81	44	79
Hastings Town	42	22	10	10	72	50	76
Stamford	42	20	11	11	69	59	71
Tonbridge Angels	42	18	11	13	79	58	65
Langney Sports	42	19	8	15	75	55	65
Rothwell Town	42	20	5	17	86	74	62
Corby Town	42	14	10	18	64	92	52
Ashford Town	42	15	4	23	53	83	49
Banbury United	42	12	11	19	57	54	47
Witney Town	42	12	11	19	55	71	47
Bashley	42	10	14	18	57	71	44
Dartford	42	11	11	20	49	67	44
Burnham	42	10	14	18	39	65	43
Wisbech Town	42	10	9	23	45	89	39
St Leonards	42	9	10	23	55	87	37
Erith & Belvedere	42	10	7	25	49	92	37
Sittingbourne	42	8	9	25	41	79	33
Spalding United	42	7	12	23	35	73	33

Burnham had 1 point deducted, Rothwell Town had 3 points deducted

Western Division

Hinckley United	42	30	8	4	102	38	98
Tiverton Town	42	28	7	7	97	36	91
Bilston Town	42	27	9	6	88	48	90
Evesham United	42	27	5	10	86	46	86
Mangotsfield United	42	25	9	8	91	45	84
Solihull Borough	42	22	12	8	73	43	78
Redditch United	42	17	13	12	76	69	64
Weston-super-Mare	42	17	10	15	68	58	61
Atherstone United	42	16	11	15	64	58	59
Rocester	42	18	5	19	57	77	59
Cirencester Town	42	14	15	13	65	74	57
Rugby United	42	13	10	19	51	68	49
Gloucester City	42	12	11	19	76	86	47
Blakenall	42	13	10	19	54	64	46
Shepshed Dynamo	42	12	9	21	56	73	45
Bedworth United	42	12	9	21	38	60	45
Racing Club Warwick	42	13	6	23	46	77	45
Gresley Rovers	42	11	8	23	46	65	41
Cinderford Town	42	11	8	23	56	84	41
Sutton Coldfield Town	42	7	14	21	45	66	35
Paget Rangers	42	9	4	29	38	93	31
Bromsgrove Rovers	42	7	9	26	47	92	30

Blakenall had 3 points deducted

2001-2002

Premier Division

Kettering Town	42	27	6	9	80	41	87
Tamworth	42	24	13	5	81	41	85
Havant & Waterlooville	42	22	9	11	74	50	75
Crawley Town	42	21	10	11	67	48	73
Newport County	42	19	9	14	61	48	66
Tiverton Town	42	17	10	15	70	63	61
Moor Green	42	18	7	17	64	62	61
Worcester City	42	16	12	14	65	54	60
Stafford Rangers	42	17	9	16	70	62	60
Ilkeston Town	42	14	16	12	58	61	58
Weymouth	42	15	11	16	59	67	56
Hinckley United	42	14	13	15	64	62	55
Folkestone Invicta	42	14	12	16	51	61	54
Cambridge City	42	12	16	14	60	70	52
Welling United	42	13	12	17	69	66	51
Hednesford Town	42	15	6	21	59	70	51
Bath City	42	13	11	18	56	65	50
Chelmsford City	42	13	11	18	63	75	50
Newport IOW	42	12	12	18	38	61	48
King's Lynn	42	11	13	18	44	57	46
Merthyr Tydfil	42	12	8	22	53	71	44
Salisbury City	42	6	8	28	36	87	26

Eastern Division

Hastings Town	42	29	8	5	85	38	95
Grantham Town	42	29	6	7	99	43	93
Dorchester Town	42	26	10	6	81	36	88
Histon	42	23	8	11	83	49	77
Stamford	42	24	4	14	76	61	76
Fisher Athletic (London)	42	20	10	12	83	56	70
Eastbourne Borough	42	21	6	15	63	46	69
Dartford	42	18	5	19	62	66	59
Erith & Belvedere	42	18	3	21	75	79	57
Bashley	42	15	11	16	71	64	56
Burnham	42	15	10	17	52	54	55
Rugby United	42	16	6	20	56	67	54
Rothwell Town	42	14	8	20	45	66	50
Ashford Town	42	14	6	22	58	78	48
Banbury United	42	13	9	20	53	66	47
Chatham Town	42	13	8	21	56	87	47
Sittingbourne	42	14	4	24	46	69	46
Spalding United	42	13	6	23	72	84	45
Tonbridge Angels	42	13	6	23	65	80	45
St Leonards	42	14	3	25	52	88	45
Corby Town	42	10	13	19	54	82	43
Wisbech Town	42	11	8	23	56	84	41

Banbury United had 1 point deducted.

Western Division

Halesowen Town	40	27	9	4	85	24	90
Chippenham Town	40	26	9	5	81	28	87
Weston-super-Mare	40	22	10	8	70	38	76
Solihull Borough	40	20	11	9	75	42	71
Gresley Rovers	40	19	9	12	59	50	66
Sutton Coldfield Town	40	17	11	12	53	46	62
Mangotsfield United	40	17	10	13	74	54	61
Stourport Swifts	40	18	6	16	59	59	60
Atherstone United	40	16	8	16	61	59	56
Clevedon Town	40	15	11	14	57	58	56
Bedworth United	40	16	7	17	59	63	55
Evesham United	40	16	7	17	54	70	55
Cirencester Town	40	17	3	20	64	69	54
Gloucester City	40	14	10	16	48	63	52
Cinderford Town	40	14	9	17	54	67	51
Shepshed Dynamo	40	10	10	20	64	84	40
Bilston Town	40	11	7	22	50	72	40
Redditch United	40	11	6	23	47	77	39
Swindon Supermarine	40	11	4	25	52	76	37
Racing Club Warwick	40	8	11	21	38	63	35
Rocester	40	5	12	23	33	75	27

2002-2003

Premier Division

Team	P	W	D	L	F	A	Pts
Tamworth	42	26	10	6	73	32	88
Stafford Rangers	42	21	12	9	76	40	75
Dover Athletic	42	19	14	9	42	35	71
Tiverton Town	42	19	12	11	60	43	69
Chippenham Town	42	17	17	8	59	37	68
Worcester City	42	18	13	11	60	39	67
Crawley Town	42	17	13	12	64	51	64
Havant & Waterlooville	42	15	15	12	67	64	60
Chelmsford City	42	15	12	15	65	63	57
Newport County	42	15	11	16	53	52	56
Hednesford Town	42	14	13	15	59	60	55
Moor Green	42	13	14	15	49	58	53
Hinckley United	42	12	16	14	61	64	52
Bath City	42	13	13	16	50	61	52
Welling United	42	13	12	17	55	58	51
Grantham Town	42	14	9	19	59	65	51
Weymouth	42	12	15	15	44	62	51
Cambridge City	42	13	10	19	54	56	49
Halesowen Town	42	12	13	17	52	63	49
Hastings United	42	10	13	19	44	57	43
Ilkeston Town	42	10	10	22	54	92	40
Folkestone Invicta	42	7	7	28	57	105	28

Eastern Division

Team	P	W	D	L	F	A	Pts
Dorchester Town	42	28	9	5	114	40	93
Eastbourne Borough	42	29	6	7	92	33	93
Stamford	42	27	6	9	80	39	87
Salisbury City	42	27	8	7	81	42	86
Bashley	42	23	12	7	90	44	81
King's Lynn	42	24	7	11	98	62	79
Rothwell Town	42	22	10	10	77	52	76
Banbury United	42	21	11	10	75	50	74
Tonbridge Angels	42	20	11	11	71	55	71
Histon	42	20	7	15	99	62	67
Ashford Town	42	18	9	15	63	57	63
Sittingbourne	42	15	8	19	57	69	53
Burnham	42	15	7	20	62	79	52
Fisher Athletic	42	15	5	22	57	80	50
Chatham Town	42	14	5	23	54	84	47
Newport IOW	42	12	6	24	53	87	42
Dartford	42	11	8	23	48	78	41
Erith & Belvedere	42	11	6	25	65	96	39
Corby Town	42	9	11	22	49	84	38
Fleet Town	42	8	8	26	34	80	32
Spalding United	42	4	6	32	40	108	18
St. Leonards	42	4	4	34	38	116	16

Salisbury City had 3 points deducted.

Western Division

Team	P	W	D	L	F	A	Pts
Merthyr Tydfil	42	28	8	6	78	32	92
Weston-super-Mare	42	26	7	9	77	42	85
Bromsgrove Rovers	42	23	7	12	73	41	76
Solihull Borough	42	21	13	8	77	48	76
Gloucester City	42	22	9	11	87	58	75
Mangotsfield United	42	21	10	11	106	53	73
Redditch United	42	22	6	14	76	42	72
Rugby United	42	20	9	13	58	43	69
Gresley Rovers	42	19	10	13	63	54	67
Taunton Town	42	20	7	15	76	78	67
Sutton Coldfield Town	42	18	10	14	63	53	64
Evesham United	42	19	6	17	76	72	63
Clevedon Town	42	14	13	15	54	60	55
Cirencester Town	42	15	7	20	62	82	52
Cinderford Town	42	13	12	17	50	67	51
Shepshed Dynamo	42	12	6	24	48	76	42
Stourport Swifts	42	10	11	21	48	66	41
Bedworth United	42	11	7	24	46	74	40
Swindon Supermarine	42	11	5	26	52	85	38
Atherstone United	42	9	10	23	45	78	37
Rocester	42	9	10	23	34	74	37
Racing Club Warwick	42	3	9	30	33	104	18

2003-2004

Premier Division

Team	P	W	D	L	F	A	Pts
Crawley Town	42	25	9	8	77	43	84
Weymouth	42	20	12	10	76	47	72
Stafford Rangers	42	19	11	12	55	43	68
Nuneaton Borough	42	17	15	10	65	49	66
Worcester City	42	18	9	15	71	50	63
Hinckley United	42	15	14	13	55	46	59
Newport County	42	15	14	13	52	50	59
Cambridge City	42	14	15	13	54	53	57
Welling United	42	16	8	18	56	58	56
Weston-super-Mare	42	14	13	15	52	52	55
Eastbourne Borough	42	14	13	15	48	56	55
Havant & Waterlooville	42	15	10	17	59	70	55
Moor Green	42	14	12	16	42	54	54
Merthyr Tydfil	42	13	14	15	60	66	53
Tiverton Town	42	12	15	15	63	64	51
Bath City	42	13	12	17	49	57	51
Dorchester Town	42	14	9	19	56	69	51
Chelmsford City	42	11	16	15	46	53	49
Dover Athletic	42	12	13	17	50	59	49
Hednesford Town	42	12	12	18	56	69	48
Chippenham Town	42	10	17	15	51	63	47
Grantham Town	42	10	15	17	45	67	45

Eastern Division

Team	P	W	D	L	F	A	Pts
King's Lynn	42	28	7	7	90	35	91
Histon	42	26	10	6	96	41	88
Tonbridge Angels	42	27	7	8	82	46	88
Eastleigh	42	27	4	11	88	40	82
Folkestone Invicta	42	20	15	7	91	45	75
Salisbury City	42	21	11	10	73	45	74
Stamford	42	20	11	11	63	45	71
Banbury United	42	19	10	13	65	57	67
Burgess Hill Town	42	19	7	16	67	54	64
Sittingbourne	42	18	8	16	61	55	62
Bashley	42	18	7	17	66	58	61
Ashford Town	42	15	9	18	51	53	54
Chatham Town	42	13	10	19	49	67	49
Fisher Athletic	42	13	10	19	61	81	49
Corby Town	42	12	9	21	44	75	45
Dartford	42	13	6	23	48	81	45
Burnham	42	12	11	19	52	76	44
Hastings United	42	12	7	23	60	91	43
Newport IOW	42	11	7	24	42	69	40
Rothwell Town	42	9	11	22	30	47	38
Erith & Belvedere	42	7	10	25	45	84	31
Fleet Town	42	5	7	30	35	114	22

Eastleigh and Burnham both had 3 points deducted.

Western Division

Team	P	W	D	L	F	A	Pts
Redditch United	40	25	9	6	75	30	84
Gloucester City	40	24	7	9	77	46	79
Cirencester Town	40	24	4	12	73	40	76
Halesowen Town	40	20	13	7	64	40	73
Rugby United	40	21	8	11	57	40	71
Team Bath	40	21	6	13	62	41	69
Solihull Borough	40	19	9	12	50	31	66
Sutton Coldfield Town	40	16	15	9	52	38	63
Bromsgrove Rovers	40	16	11	13	60	48	59
Ilkeston Town	40	16	10	14	58	59	58
Clevedon Town	40	16	5	19	55	59	53
Gresley Rovers	40	15	7	18	52	60	52
Mangotsfield United	40	14	8	18	70	70	50
Evesham United	40	15	5	20	56	57	50
Taunton Town	40	14	8	18	50	55	50
Yate Town	40	11	9	20	51	79	42
Swindon Supermarine	40	10	9	21	41	69	39
Stourport Swifts	40	9	11	20	43	62	38
Bedworth United	40	8	12	20	39	61	36
Cinderford Town	40	7	9	24	50	94	30
Shepshed Dynamo	40	5	13	22	31	87	28

2004-2005 Premier Division

Team	P	W	D	L	F	A	Pts
Histon	42	24	6	12	93	57	78
Chippenham Town	42	22	9	11	81	55	75
Merthyr Tydfil	42	19	14	9	62	47	71
Hednesford Town	42	20	10	12	68	40	70
Bedford Town	42	19	12	11	70	52	69
Bath City	42	19	12	11	57	43	69
Cirencester Town	42	19	11	12	63	52	68
Tiverton Town	42	18	13	11	70	55	67
Halesowen Town	42	19	9	14	64	52	66
Aylesbury United	42	20	3	19	67	66	63
King's Lynn	42	19	4	19	78	69	61
Chesham United	42	18	5	19	84	82	59
Grantham Town	42	17	7	18	57	55	58
Team Bath	42	14	12	16	54	68	54
Gloucester City	42	12	17	13	63	61	53
Rugby United	42	13	12	17	48	60	51
Banbury United	42	13	9	20	56	69	48
Hitchin Town	42	13	9	20	55	77	48
Hemel Hempstead Town	42	11	10	21	60	88	43
Dunstable Town	42	11	6	25	56	98	39
Stamford	42	6	18	18	40	60	36
Solihull Borough	42	10	4	28	45	85	34

Eastern Division

Team	P	W	D	L	F	A	Pts
Fisher Athletic	42	30	6	6	96	41	96
East Thurrock United	42	25	12	5	92	38	87
Maldon Town	42	27	6	9	92	51	87
Uxbridge	42	26	7	9	87	37	85
Wivenhoe Town	42	21	11	10	74	49	74
Barking & East Ham United	42	20	10	12	63	37	70
Boreham Wood	42	19	9	14	80	61	66
Barton Rovers	42	20	4	18	76	72	64
Waltham Forest	42	16	9	17	68	61	57
Leighton Town	42	13	15	14	57	59	54
Chatham Town	42	15	9	18	53	63	54
Wingate & Finchley	42	15	8	19	60	75	53
Arlesey Town	42	14	10	18	53	67	52
Beaconsfield SYCOB	42	12	12	18	54	65	48
Harlow Town	42	13	8	21	53	65	47
Dartford	42	11	13	18	58	75	46
Aveley	42	12	9	21	57	69	45
Berkhamsted Town	42	15	7	20	66	101	45
Sittingbourne	42	10	12	20	53	70	42
Great Wakering Rovers	42	9	11	22	45	78	38
Erith & Belvedere	42	11	7	24	56	92	37
Tilbury	42	6	9	27	41	108	27

Berkhamsted Town had 7 points deducted.
Erith & Belvedere had 3 points deducted.

Western Division

Team	P	W	D	L	F	A	Pts
Mangotsfield United	42	24	11	7	89	49	83
Yate Town	42	24	9	9	83	40	81
Evesham United	42	23	10	9	66	31	79
Clevedon Town	42	24	6	12	82	49	78
Bromsgrove Rovers	42	19	15	8	60	42	72
Ashford Town (Middlesex)	42	17	13	12	63	46	64
Brackley Town	42	18	10	14	69	53	64
Paulton Rovers	42	18	7	17	62	61	61
Burnham	42	17	7	18	64	64	58
Rothwell Town	42	16	10	16	57	57	58
Thame United	42	17	6	19	58	69	57
Corby Town	42	14	12	16	52	62	54
Marlow	42	13	14	15	58	67	53
Stourport Swifts	42	15	7	20	62	63	52
Bedworth United	42	15	7	20	51	60	52
Cinderford Town	42	13	12	17	50	64	51
Taunton Town	42	14	8	20	66	75	50
Sutton Coldfield Town	42	16	11	15	54	61	48
Swindon Supermarine	42	12	12	18	43	60	48
Bracknell Town	42	10	13	19	53	75	43
Oxford City	42	11	8	23	49	71	41
Egham Town	42	6	4	32	25	97	22

Sutton Coldfield Town had 11 points deducted.

2005-2006

Premier Division

Team	P	W	D	L	F	A	Pts
Salisbury City	42	30	5	7	83	27	95
Bath City	42	25	8	9	66	33	83
King's Lynn	42	25	7	10	73	41	82
Chippenham Town	42	22	11	9	69	45	77
Bedford Town	42	22	10	10	69	53	76
Yate Town	42	21	5	16	78	74	68
Banbury United	42	17	11	14	66	61	62
Halesowen Town	42	15	15	12	54	45	60
Merthyr Tydfil	42	17	9	16	62	58	60
Mangotsfield United	42	15	13	14	67	67	58
Grantham Town	42	15	11	16	49	49	56
Tiverton Town	42	14	10	18	69	65	52
Gloucester City	42	14	10	18	57	60	52
Hitchin Town	42	13	12	17	59	76	51
Rugby Town	42	13	11	18	58	66	50
Cheshunt	42	13	9	20	57	70	48
Team Bath	42	14	6	22	55	68	48
Cirencester Town	42	14	4	24	49	68	46
Northwood	42	12	6	24	53	88	42
Evesham United	42	9	14	19	46	58	41
Aylesbury United	42	9	12	21	43	69	39
Chesham United	42	9	9	24	43	84	36

Eastern Division

Team	P	W	D	L	F	A	Pts
Boreham Wood	42	24	12	6	84	41	84
Corby Town	42	25	9	8	63	33	84
Enfield Town	42	24	9	9	75	43	81
Stamford	42	20	10	12	73	53	70
Barking & East Ham United	42	20	10	12	63	47	70
Wivenhoe Town	42	17	11	14	56	54	62
Dartford	42	16	13	13	65	57	61
Waltham Forest	42	17	8	17	64	66	59
Harlow Town	42	14	16	12	57	56	58
Arlesey Town	42	15	11	16	58	65	56
Rothwell Town	42	13	14	15	48	53	53
Wingate & Finchley	42	13	14	15	57	64	53
Great Wakering Rovers	42	13	12	17	65	67	51
Uxbridge	42	13	11	18	62	64	50
Potters Bar Town	42	13	11	18	60	66	50
Enfield	42	13	11	18	52	64	50
Chatham Town	42	13	10	19	51	57	49
Sittingbourne	42	12	12	18	53	69	48
Barton Rovers	42	13	8	21	59	73	47
Aveley	42	11	13	18	51	70	46
Ilford	42	8	17	17	35	59	41
Berkhamsted Town	42	8	12	22	51	81	36

Western Division

Team	P	W	D	L	F	A	Pts
Clevedon Town	42	28	6	8	86	45	90
Ashford Town (Middlesex)	42	24	8	10	84	50	80
Brackley Town	42	23	9	10	71	34	78
Hemel Hempstead Town	42	22	9	11	86	47	75
Swindon Supermarine	42	22	9	11	70	47	75
Marlow	42	22	6	14	62	59	72
Sutton Coldfield Town	42	21	6	15	91	62	69
Leighton Town	42	19	8	15	55	48	65
Willenhall Town	42	17	12	13	78	61	63
Rushall Olympic	42	17	11	14	73	57	62
Bromsgrove Rovers	42	17	11	14	65	50	62
Solihull Borough	42	15	13	14	50	51	58
Beaconsfield SYCOB	42	14	13	15	60	66	55
Burnham	42	16	5	21	58	71	53
Cinderford Town	42	14	9	19	71	79	51
Bedworth United	42	14	9	19	46	57	51
Paulton Rovers	42	12	10	20	55	76	46
Taunton Town	42	12	9	21	67	81	45
Bracknell Town	42	12	6	24	53	77	42
Stourport Swifts	42	9	14	19	55	80	41
Dunstable Town	42	8	12	22	45	91	36
Thame United	42	4	5	33	30	122	17

2006-2007 Premier Division

	P	W	D	L	F	A	Pts
Bath City	42	27	10	5	84	29	91
Team Bath	42	23	9	10	66	42	78
King's Lynn	42	22	10	10	69	40	76
Maidenhead United	42	20	10	12	58	36	70
Hemel Hempstead Town	42	19	12	11	79	60	69
Halesowen Town	42	18	13	11	66	53	67
Chippenham Town	42	19	9	14	61	56	66
Stamford	42	16	11	15	65	62	59
Mangotsfield United	42	13	19	10	44	45	58
Gloucester City	42	15	13	14	67	70	58
Hitchin Town	42	16	9	17	55	68	57
Merthyr Tydfil	42	14	14	14	47	46	56
Banbury United	42	15	10	17	60	64	55
Yate Town	42	14	12	16	59	71	54
Tiverton Town	42	14	8	20	56	67	50
Cheshunt	42	14	7	21	56	71	49
Rugby Town	42	15	4	23	58	79	49
Clevedon Town	42	12	12	18	60	61	48
Wealdstone	42	13	9	20	69	82	48
Corby Town	42	10	9	23	52	69	39
Cirencester Town	42	9	12	21	46	76	39
Northwood	42	8	10	24	44	74	34

Division One Midlands

	P	W	D	L	F	A	Pts
Brackley Town	42	29	4	9	95	53	91
Bromsgrove Rovers	42	23	7	12	86	62	76
Chasetown	42	23	6	13	59	39	75
Willenhall Town	42	20	12	10	67	47	72
Evesham United	42	19	15	8	66	51	72
Aylesbury United	42	20	11	11	58	42	71
Stourbridge	42	17	15	10	70	53	66
Woodford United	42	18	11	13	71	54	65
Cinderford Town	42	18	10	14	70	60	64
Rothwell Town	42	18	7	17	72	61	61
Dunstable Town	42	16	12	14	64	53	60
Sutton Coldfield Town	42	16	9	17	62	63	57
Bishop's Cleeve	42	17	5	20	68	66	56
Solihull Borough	42	17	5	20	72	84	56
Rushall Olympic	42	15	9	18	56	55	54
Bedworth United	42	13	8	21	73	83	47
Malvern Town	42	12	11	19	46	66	47
Leighton Town	42	12	8	22	44	60	44
Spalding United	42	12	6	24	45	62	42
Barton Rovers	42	11	9	22	51	93	42
Berkhamsted Town	42	10	7	25	53	97	37
Stourport Swifts	42	9	7	26	43	87	34

Division One South & West

	P	W	D	L	F	A	Pts
Bashley	42	32	6	4	111	35	102
Paulton Rovers	42	20	14	8	66	42	74
Burnham	42	23	4	15	74	60	73
Swindon Supermarine	42	20	11	11	68	40	71
Taunton Town	42	19	14	9	68	50	71
Thatcham Town	42	21	7	14	70	60	70
Marlow	42	19	12	11	74	49	69
Uxbridge	42	20	8	14	68	58	68
Andover	42	19	9	14	70	59	66
Didcot Town	42	16	13	13	86	67	61
Abingdon United	42	16	11	15	68	67	59
Oxford City	42	17	8	17	62	75	59
Winchester City	42	16	10	16	67	65	58
Windsor & Eton	42	16	10	16	76	75	58
Chesham United	42	17	6	19	68	79	57
Hillingdon Borough	42	13	13	16	80	85	52
Lymington & New Milton	42	16	3	23	81	79	51
Brook House	42	14	6	22	71	92	48
Bracknell Town	42	11	13	18	51	62	46
Newport IOW	42	9	3	30	44	106	30
Hanwell Town	42	6	7	29	52	102	24
Beaconsfield SYCOB	42	5	6	31	36	104	21

Hanwell Town had one point deducted.

2007-2008 Premier Division

	P	W	D	L	F	A	Pts
King's Lynn	42	24	13	5	91	36	85
Team Bath	42	25	8	9	71	41	83
Halesowen Town	42	22	13	7	80	46	79
Chippenham Town	42	20	13	9	73	44	73
Bashley	42	19	12	11	60	46	69
Gloucester City	42	19	11	12	81	50	68
Hemel Hempstead Town	42	19	11	12	67	50	68
Brackley Town	42	16	12	14	57	53	60
Banbury United	42	14	16	12	55	57	58
Yate Town	42	16	10	16	71	76	58
Clevedon Town	42	13	18	11	49	46	57
Swindon Supermarine	42	14	12	16	51	67	54
Merthyr Tydfil	42	13	14	15	65	70	53
Mangotsfield United	42	12	16	14	38	42	52
Rugby Town	42	13	12	17	55	66	51
Corby Town	42	14	8	20	60	67	50
Tiverton Town	42	13	11	18	45	60	50
Hitchin Town	42	12	11	19	46	61	47
Bedford Town	42	12	9	21	54	73	45
Bromsgrove Rovers	42	10	12	20	46	67	42
Cirencester Town	42	8	8	26	44	80	32
Cheshunt	42	5	8	29	42	103	23

Division One Midlands

	P	W	D	L	F	A	Pts
Evesham United	40	28	7	5	68	24	91
Leamington	40	27	8	5	74	27	89
Stourbridge	40	25	3	12	97	48	78
Sutton Coldfield Town	40	23	8	9	93	52	77
Rushall Olympic	40	23	7	10	68	23	76
Chesham United	40	23	7	10	78	40	76
Chasetown	40	23	6	11	71	38	75
Aylesbury United	40	19	9	12	64	49	66
Leighton Town	40	17	12	11	59	42	63
Romulus	40	18	8	14	60	53	62
Barton Rovers	40	14	16	10	54	45	58
Bishop's Cleeve	40	17	7	16	63	61	58
Dunstable Town	40	14	5	21	63	65	47
Willenhall Town	40	12	13	15	53	58	46
Bedworth United	40	12	10	18	40	51	46
Cinderford Town	40	12	6	22	47	82	42
Stourport Swifts	40	10	8	22	40	81	38
Rothwell Town	40	9	5	26	34	69	32
Woodford United	40	7	6	27	30	88	27
Malvern Town	40	3	9	28	34	95	18
Berkhamsted Town	40	2	4	34	27	126	10

Willenhall Town had 3 points deducted.

Division One South & West

	P	W	D	L	F	A	Pts
Farnborough	42	27	8	7	120	48	89
Fleet Town	42	26	7	9	78	48	85
Didcot Town	42	24	11	7	99	42	83
Oxford City	42	24	9	9	82	41	81
Uxbridge	42	22	9	11	72	50	75
Bridgwater Town	42	19	13	10	74	45	70
Paulton Rovers	42	20	10	12	77	57	70
Windsor & Eton	42	20	9	13	75	66	69
Marlow	42	20	6	16	74	54	66
Burnham	42	18	9	15	67	55	63
Gosport Borough	42	18	8	16	69	67	62
Godalming Town	42	17	9	16	70	70	60
Hillingdon Borough	42	16	8	18	68	70	56
AFC Hayes	42	17	4	21	75	99	55
Thatcham Town	42	13	10	19	59	62	49
Abingdon United	42	13	9	20	64	75	48
Winchester City	42	13	9	20	58	71	48
Taunton Town	42	12	11	19	66	79	47
Andover	42	11	7	24	62	101	40
Bracknell Town	42	8	10	24	45	93	34
Slough Town	42	9	5	28	44	87	32
Newport IOW	42	2	5	35	25	143	11

2008-2009 Premier Division

Team	P	W	D	L	F	A	Pts
Corby Town	42	25	9	8	85	38	84
Farnborough	42	23	14	5	67	36	83
Gloucester City	42	21	12	9	80	45	75
Cambridge City	42	21	10	11	62	40	73
Hemel Hempstead Town	42	21	7	14	71	48	70
Oxford City	42	19	10	13	76	55	67
Merthyr Tydfil	42	19	10	13	66	55	67
Chippenham Town	42	20	8	14	64	51	65
Evesham United	42	16	13	13	48	39	61
Halesowen Town	42	19	6	17	65	73	60
Brackley Town	42	15	12	15	69	62	57
Tiverton Town	42	16	9	17	51	50	57
Swindon Supermarine	42	15	12	15	59	61	57
Bashley	42	15	12	15	52	58	57
Bedford Town	42	14	8	20	44	55	50
Stourbridge	42	13	11	18	62	78	50
Rugby Town	42	11	10	21	63	71	43
Clevedon Town	42	11	10	21	51	80	43
Banbury United	42	11	8	23	43	83	41
Hitchin Town	42	10	10	22	57	79	40
Yate Town	42	9	9	24	54	91	36
Mangotsfield United	42	10	6	26	39	80	36

Chippenham Town and Halesowen town both had 3 points deducted.

Division One Midlands

Team	P	W	D	L	F	A	Pts
Leamington	42	32	5	5	114	44	101
Nuneaton Town	42	28	8	6	85	31	92
Atherstone Town	42	24	13	5	82	45	85
Chasetown	42	25	9	8	67	31	84
Chesham United	42	22	10	10	70	38	76
Sutton Coldfield Town	42	24	4	14	79	62	76
Bury Town	42	22	9	11	88	41	75
Leighton Town	42	18	13	11	57	46	67
Marlow	42	19	9	14	65	53	66
Aylesbury United	42	19	7	16	65	58	64
Romulus	42	17	10	15	60	42	61
AFC Sudbury	42	17	10	15	66	65	61
Bromsgrove Rovers	42	15	8	19	58	53	53
Bedworth United	42	14	7	21	50	66	49
Soham Town Rangers	42	13	7	22	48	79	46
Stourport Swifts	42	10	10	22	46	74	40
Barton Rovers	42	12	4	26	50	79	40
Arlesey Town	42	11	5	26	40	70	38
Rothwell Town	42	8	12	22	35	79	36
Woodford United	42	9	7	26	38	80	34
Dunstable Town	42	11	3	28	54	89	23
Malvern Town	42	2	10	30	27	119	16

Dunstable Town had 13 points deducted.

Division One South & West

Team	P	W	D	L	F	A	Pts
Truro City	42	29	8	5	120	49	95
Windsor & Eton	42	26	7	9	77	44	85
AFC Totton	42	23	13	6	89	39	82
Beaconsfield SYCOB	42	24	9	9	77	44	81
Didcot Town	42	21	10	11	91	52	73
Thatcham Town	42	20	8	14	74	58	68
Bridgwater Town	42	19	8	15	69	56	65
North Leigh	42	17	10	15	68	64	61
AFC Hayes	42	18	7	17	80	92	61
Paulton Rovers	42	16	10	16	65	62	58
Cinderford Town	42	15	11	16	71	75	56
Gosport Borough	42	15	10	17	64	67	55
Uxbridge	42	15	9	18	76	72	54
Cirencester Town	42	14	10	18	78	79	52
Abingdon United	42	15	7	20	63	77	52
Slough Town	42	11	12	19	62	91	45
Burnham	42	12	9	21	52	83	45
Bishop's Cleeve	42	10	13	19	51	71	43
Andover	42	10	12	20	58	102	42
Taunton Town	42	9	9	24	50	85	36
Bracknell Town	42	9	8	25	39	75	35
Winchester City	42	10	8	24	47	84	35

Winchester City had 3 points deducted.

2009-2010 Premier Division

Team	P	W	D	L	F	A	Pts
Farnborough	42	28	9	5	100	44	93
Nuneaton Town	42	26	10	6	91	37	88
Chippenham Town	42	21	11	10	67	43	74
Hednesford Town	42	20	13	9	79	51	73
Brackley Town	42	21	9	12	83	61	72
Cambridge City	42	18	17	7	73	44	71
Bashley	42	20	11	11	79	61	71
Halesowen Town	42	21	17	4	84	53	70
Stourbridge	42	19	13	10	80	65	70
Leamington	42	19	8	15	84	75	65
Truro City	42	17	11	14	78	65	62
Banbury United	42	14	13	15	53	67	55
Oxford City	42	13	15	14	63	66	54
Swindon Supermarine	42	10	14	18	48	76	44
Didcot Town	42	10	11	21	56	70	41
Evesham United	42	9	14	19	35	52	41
Merthyr Tydfil	42	12	11	19	62	72	37
Bedford Town	42	9	10	23	50	88	37
Tiverton Town	42	8	12	22	35	61	36
Hemel Hempstead Town	42	8	10	24	50	81	34
Clevedon Town	42	6	11	25	48	92	29
Rugby Town	42	4	8	30	41	114	20

Halesowen Town and Merthyr Tydfil both had 10 points deducted.

Division One Midlands

Team	P	W	D	L	F	A	Pts
Bury Town	42	32	6	4	115	40	102
Hitchin Town	42	31	7	4	91	36	100
Burnham	42	26	9	7	67	43	87
Chesham United	42	24	8	10	76	41	80
Slough Town	42	23	8	11	87	54	77
Sutton Coldfield Town	42	22	11	9	93	61	77
Woodford United	42	18	8	16	70	68	62
Romulus	42	16	13	13	66	48	61
Arlesey Town	42	17	10	15	58	48	61
Leighton Town	42	18	6	18	63	66	60
Soham Town Rangers	42	17	7	18	73	80	58
Biggleswade Town	42	14	13	15	56	63	55
Atherstone Town	42	15	9	18	65	82	54
AFC Sudbury	42	13	12	17	55	54	51
Marlow	42	12	14	16	64	65	50
Bedworth United	42	12	11	19	59	72	47
Stourport Swifts	42	11	10	21	63	69	43
Rothwell Town	42	11	8	23	53	80	41
Beaconsfield SYCOB	42	8	8	26	46	96	32
Bromsgrove Rovers	42	8	15	19	45	68	29
Barton Rovers	42	6	9	27	49	95	27
Aylesbury United	42	4	6	32	48	133	18

Bromsgrove Rovers had 10 points deducted.
Rothwell Town resigned from the League at the end of the season.

Division One South & West

Team	P	W	D	L	F	A	Pts
Windsor & Eton	42	31	8	3	84	20	101
AFC Totton	42	32	4	6	105	36	100
Bridgwater Town	42	26	11	5	83	30	89
VT	42	25	7	10	90	52	82
Cirencester Town	42	23	9	10	91	46	78
Frome Town	42	20	15	7	68	44	75
Paulton Rovers	42	20	10	12	73	58	70
Gosport Borough	42	19	10	13	80	59	66
Mangotsfield United	42	19	5	18	77	66	62
North Leigh	42	18	7	17	83	72	61
Bishop's Cleeve	42	15	13	14	64	64	58
Thatcham Town	42	17	6	19	76	72	57
Yate Town	42	15	10	17	58	64	55
Abingdon United	42	15	7	20	65	84	52
Uxbridge	42	14	6	22	70	85	48
Cinderford Town	42	13	8	21	66	78	47
Hungerford Town	42	13	6	23	53	68	45
Bedfont Green	42	12	8	22	77	90	44
Taunton Town	42	11	7	24	50	85	40
Andover	42	9	11	22	54	85	38
AFC Hayes	42	7	4	31	55	105	25
Bracknell Town	42	2	0	40	29	187	6

Gosport Borough had 1 point deducted.

2010-2011

Premier Division

Truro City	40	27	6	7	91	35	87
Hednesford Town	40	26	5	9	82	38	83
Salisbury City	40	23	10	7	82	45	79
Cambridge City	40	24	7	9	74	40	79
Leamington	40	24	6	10	68	39	78
Chesham United	40	20	11	9	64	35	71
Chippenham Town	40	18	14	8	54	41	68
Stourbridge	40	18	8	14	72	61	62
Brackley Town	40	16	10	14	67	47	58
Swindon Supermarine	40	17	7	16	56	58	58
Bashley	40	14	10	16	55	63	52
Evesham United	40	14	9	17	54	49	51
Cirencester Town	40	13	8	19	59	67	47
Oxford City	40	11	12	17	48	54	45
Hemel Hempstead Town	40	13	6	21	50	59	45
Banbury United	40	11	8	21	44	67	40
Bedford Town	40	10	7	23	41	76	37
Weymouth	40	12	8	20	55	85	34
Didcot Town	40	7	11	22	39	69	32
Tiverton Town	40	7	8	25	33	77	29
Halesowen Town	40	5	9	26	24	107	24

Weymouth had 10 points deducted.
Banbury United had 1 point deducted.
Windsor & Eton was wound up in the High Court on 2nd February 2011,
due to unpaid taxes. Their record was expunged on 8th February 2011
when it stood as: 26   8   12   6   33   35   36

Division One Central

Arlesey Town	42	30	7	5	108	34	88
Hitchin Town	42	26	9	7	107	44	87
Daventry Town	42	26	9	7	95	47	81
Biggleswade Town	42	24	9	9	89	51	81
Slough Town	42	24	4	14	91	66	76
Rugby Town	42	20	11	11	74	56	71
Leighton Town	42	19	12	11	72	50	69
Aylesbury	42	19	11	12	73	62	68
Woodford United	42	18	9	15	61	59	63
Bedfont Town	42	17	12	13	66	66	63
Marlow	42	15	9	18	68	65	54
Barton Rovers	42	14	9	19	59	64	51
Uxbridge	42	14	8	20	76	87	50
Burnham	42	14	7	21	61	87	49
Bedworth United	42	12	12	18	49	62	48
Ashford Town	42	13	8	21	69	85	47
Soham Town Rangers	42	10	10	22	55	81	40
North Greenford United	42	10	10	22	51	86	40
AFC Hayes	42	11	6	25	54	96	39
Northwood	42	11	6	25	59	106	39
Atherstone Town	42	10	6	26	61	118	36
Beaconsfield SYCOB	42	7	12	23	49	75	33

Arlesey Town had 9 points deducted.
Daventry Town had 6 points deducted.
Atherstone Town resigned from the League at the end of the season.

Division One South & West

AFC Totton	40	31	4	5	121	35	97
Sholing	40	30	5	5	90	27	95
Mangotsfield United	40	26	7	7	79	48	85
Frome Town	40	24	7	9	77	31	79
Thatcham Town	40	20	7	13	70	43	67
North Leigh	40	19	8	13	81	81	65
Hungerford Town	40	17	12	11	58	43	63
Almondsbury Town	40	17	12	11	62	54	63
Taunton Town	40	16	10	14	49	49	58
Bideford	40	17	7	16	68	73	58
Paulton Rovers	40	15	12	13	64	63	57
Cinderford Town	40	16	8	16	63	61	56
Gosport Borough	40	16	7	17	58	65	55
Yate Town	40	12	8	20	43	48	44
Bishop's Cleeve	40	10	12	18	47	59	42
Abingdon United	40	11	7	22	56	85	40
Stourport Swifts	40	10	10	20	52	81	40
Bridgwater Town	40	9	11	20	47	86	38
Wimborne Town	40	10	5	25	45	81	35
Clevedon Town	40	6	8	26	46	86	26
Andover	40	2	5	33	32	109	11

Almondsbury Town resigned from the League at the end of the season.

2011-2012

Premier Division

Brackley Town	42	25	10	7	92	48	85
Oxford City	42	22	11	9	68	41	77
AFC Totton	42	21	11	10	81	43	74
Chesham United	42	21	10	11	76	53	73
Cambridge City	42	21	9	12	78	52	72
Stourbridge	42	20	12	10	67	45	72
Leamington	42	18	15	9	60	47	69
St Albans City	42	17	11	14	72	77	62
Barwell	42	17	10	15	70	61	61
Bedford Town	42	15	10	17	60	69	55
Chippenham Town	42	14	11	17	55	53	53
Frome Town	42	12	16	14	44	49	52
Bashley	42	13	13	16	58	74	52
Hitchin Town	42	13	12	17	54	57	51
Redditch United	42	14	9	19	45	50	51
Banbury United	42	13	10	19	54	61	49
Weymouth	42	13	9	20	54	75	48
Arlesey Town	42	12	11	19	43	60	47
Hemel Hempstead Town	42	10	14	18	46	66	44
Evesham United	42	12	8	22	49	71	44
Swindon Supermarine	42	11	11	20	50	86	44
Cirencester Town	42	7	9	26	40	78	30

Division One Central

St Neots Town	42	29	6	7	115	36	93
Slough Town	42	26	9	7	74	42	87
Bedworth United	42	23	9	10	90	57	78
Uxbridge	42	22	8	12	79	59	74
Beaconsfield SYCOB	42	20	9	13	65	55	69
Rugby Town	42	19	10	13	67	65	67
Northwood	42	19	9	14	74	62	66
Biggleswade Town	42	19	7	16	75	54	64
Ashford Town	42	16	11	15	62	61	59
AFC Hayes	42	14	16	12	58	59	58
Barton Rovers	42	16	8	18	64	63	56
Chalfont St Peter	42	14	14	14	65	68	56
Leighton Town	42	15	10	17	60	67	55
Bedfont Town	42	15	9	18	53	64	54
Burnham	42	13	13	16	64	67	52
Daventry Town	42	15	5	22	52	72	50
Chertsey Town	42	15	5	22	65	93	50
North Greenford United	42	13	10	19	56	72	49
Woodford United	42	12	8	22	56	70	44
Aylesbury	42	12	8	22	50	82	44
Fleet Town	42	8	8	26	43	83	32
Marlow	42	6	10	26	50	86	28

Bedfont Town resigned from the League at the end of the season.

Division One South & West

Bideford	40	28	8	4	77	41	92
Poole Town	40	25	6	9	78	39	81
Gosport Borough	40	22	14	4	73	44	80
Sholing	40	22	8	10	71	43	74
Hungerford Town	40	21	8	11	65	44	71
North Leigh	40	21	5	14	90	63	68
Paulton Rovers	40	18	10	12	60	39	64
Thatcham Town	40	16	14	10	51	42	62
Tiverton Town	40	16	11	13	52	42	59
Cinderford Town	40	17	8	15	49	39	59
Bishop's Cleeve	40	16	11	13	40	42	59
Halesowen Town	40	15	6	19	55	56	51
Yate Town	40	13	11	16	58	59	50
Mangotsfield United	40	14	7	19	62	66	49
Bridgwater Town	40	13	4	23	47	77	43
Didcot Town	40	11	9	20	39	68	42
Taunton Town	40	10	10	20	47	76	40
Abingdon United	40	9	10	21	35	69	37
Wimborne Town	40	8	11	21	50	77	35
Clevedon Town	40	9	6	25	51	75	33
Stourport Swifts	40	5	5	30	39	88	20

Andover resigned from the League and were wound up during July 2011.
Thatcham Town transferred to the Southern League Central Division at the end of the Season.
Halesowen Town transferred to the Northern Premier League Division One South at the end of the Season.

2012-2013

Premier Division

Leamington	42	30	5	7	85	46	95
Stourbridge	42	25	8	9	94	42	83
Chesham United	42	21	12	9	69	48	75
Hemel Hempstead Town	42	22	6	14	95	71	72
Gosport Borough	42	19	13	10	78	43	70
Arlesey Town	42	21	6	15	70	51	69
Barwell	42	19	12	11	67	50	69
Cambridge City	42	20	6	16	63	57	66
Weymouth	42	18	8	16	59	71	62
Bedford Town	42	18	7	17	61	56	61
St Albans City	42	18	6	18	81	71	60
St Neots Town	42	15	7	20	77	77	52
Hitchin Town	42	15	7	20	62	68	52
AFC Totton	42	15	7	20	62	84	52
Chippenham Town	42	13	12	17	63	67	51
Banbury United	42	14	9	19	60	75	51
Bashley	42	13	10	19	47	63	49
Frome Town	42	11	12	19	40	55	45
Redditch United	42	12	7	23	32	65	43
Bideford	42	11	9	22	58	73	42
Bedworth United	42	11	9	22	39	73	42
Kettering Town	42	8	8	26	47	102	22

Kettering Town had 10 points deducted for financial irregularities.

Division One Central

Burnham	42	31	6	5	108	39	99
Rugby Town	42	31	3	8	103	45	96
Godalming Town	42	28	8	6	94	39	92
Biggleswade Town	42	26	7	9	97	50	85
Beaconsfield SYCOB	42	26	6	10	81	47	84
Slough Town	42	26	5	11	103	50	83
Royston Town	42	24	10	8	86	49	82
Daventry Town	42	22	10	10	81	47	76
Guildford City	42	20	6	16	86	75	66
Ashford Town	42	17	10	15	85	79	61
Uxbridge	42	19	4	19	78	85	61
Aylesbury	42	16	10	16	76	73	58
Northwood	42	17	6	19	80	73	57
Barton Rovers	42	16	5	21	62	78	53
AFC Hayes	42	13	8	21	73	81	47
Chalfont St. Peter	42	18	7	17	76	74	46
Thatcham Town	42	10	5	27	59	86	35
Fleet Town	42	10	5	27	47	76	35
North Greenford United	42	9	6	27	56	95	33
Chertsey Town	42	9	4	29	50	98	31
Leighton Town	42	6	5	31	43	121	23
Woodford United	42	0	0	42	21	185	0

Chalfont St. Peter had 15 points deducted for fielding an ineligible player.

Division One South & West

Poole Town	42	30	8	4	82	36	98
Hungerford Town	42	26	6	10	71	44	84
Merthyr Town	42	24	11	7	84	38	83
Swindon Supermarine	42	25	6	11	79	51	81
Paulton Rovers	42	23	6	13	64	54	75
Yate Town	42	21	6	15	69	63	69
Sholing	42	20	8	14	87	56	68
Shortwood United	42	20	7	15	62	45	67
North Leigh	42	19	4	19	70	69	61
Cinderford Town	42	17	8	17	61	66	59
Cirencester Town	42	15	13	14	54	57	57
Wimborne Town	42	15	10	17	59	60	55
Mangotsfield United	42	15	10	17	53	61	55
Evesham United	42	14	9	19	49	58	51
Clevedon Town	42	12	13	17	61	67	49
Tiverton Town	42	11	14	17	51	58	47
Didcot Town	42	12	10	20	59	76	46
Taunton Town	42	12	8	22	59	85	44
Bridgwater Town	42	10	10	22	52	78	40
Abingdon United	42	10	8	24	42	66	38
Bishop's Cleeve	42	10	7	25	49	66	37
Winchester City	42	9	2	31	42	105	26

Winchester City had 3 points deducted for fielding an ineligible player.
Cirencester Town had 1 point deducted for fielding an ineligible player.
Sholing resigned from the League at the end of the season.

Division One Central

Dunstable Town	42	28	6	8	94	44	90
Rugby Town	42	27	8	7	100	45	89
Kettering Town	42	27	7	8	86	41	88
Daventry Town	42	27	5	10	82	40	86
Slough Town	42	26	5	11	101	51	83
Barton Rovers	42	24	8	10	79	48	80
Royston Town	42	21	10	11	80	58	73
Beaconsfield SYCOB	42	22	7	13	79	60	73
Northwood	42	21	6	15	72	62	69
Uxbridge	42	18	7	17	84	70	61
Egham Town	42	17	9	16	80	58	60
Aylesbury United	42	16	9	17	64	72	57
St. Ives Town	42	16	8	18	68	77	56
Chalfont St. Peter	42	14	8	20	49	60	50
Potters Bar Town	42	13	10	19	61	86	49
Aylesbury	42	14	6	22	56	73	48
Marlow	42	12	11	19	73	84	47
AFC Hayes	42	12	8	22	51	74	44
Leighton Town	42	6	13	23	45	85	31
North Greenford United	42	7	5	30	52	114	26
Chertsey Town	42	6	4	32	38	117	22
Ashford Town	42	5	6	31	32	107	21

2013-2014

Premier Division

Hemel Hempstead Town	44	32	6	6	128	38	102
Chesham United	44	29	5	10	102	47	92
Cambridge City	44	27	7	10	95	49	88
St. Albans City	44	25	10	9	89	49	85
Stourbridge	44	26	6	12	114	54	84
Hungerford Town	44	26	6	12	83	45	84
Poole Town	44	25	10	9	82	48	82
Bideford	44	18	13	13	75	64	67
Biggleswade Town	44	16	16	12	85	61	64
Redditch United	44	20	3	21	68	85	63
Corby Town	44	18	6	20	65	68	60
Weymouth	44	18	6	20	69	80	60
Hitchin Town	44	16	11	17	63	52	59
Frome Town	44	16	9	19	63	74	57
Arlesey Town	44	15	10	19	68	79	55
St Neots Town	44	15	9	20	74	76	54
Truro City	44	15	9	20	68	84	54
Chippenham Town	44	14	6	24	59	87	48
Banbury United	44	14	5	25	64	116	47
Burnham	44	12	8	24	60	91	44
AFC Totton	44	10	7	27	58	119	37
Bedford Town	44	6	6	32	46	114	24
Bashley	44	4	4	36	33	131	16

Poole Town had 3 points deducted for fielding an ineligible player.
Hinckley United folded on 7th October 2013 and their record was officially expunged from the league table on 21st October 2013 when it stood as:

	10	1	3	6	9	20	6

Division One South & West

Cirencester Town	42	29	5	8	95	45	92
Merthyr Town	42	28	5	9	111	58	89
Tiverton Town	42	26	8	8	80	51	86
Paulton Rovers	42	24	9	9	102	54	81
Swindon Supermarine	42	24	7	11	91	52	79
Shortwood United	42	23	9	10	91	44	78
North Leigh	42	22	6	14	83	46	72
Taunton Town	42	21	7	14	71	58	69
Yate Town	42	20	8	14	81	69	68
Stratford Town	42	19	5	18	103	85	62
Mangotsfield United	42	18	7	17	65	62	61
Didcot Town	42	17	6	19	70	85	57
Wimborne Town	42	16	7	19	78	70	55
Bridgwater Town	42	14	11	17	62	64	53
Cinderford Town	42	13	10	19	69	79	49
Evesham United	42	12	11	19	66	80	47
Clevedon Town	42	12	5	25	48	96	41
Godalming Town	42	10	9	23	47	79	39
Thatcham Town	42	11	6	25	41	99	39
Bishop's Cleeve	42	11	1	30	52	93	34
Fleet Town	42	7	8	27	43	90	29
Guildford City	42	7	6	29	45	134	27

Taunton Town had 1 point deducted for fielding an ineligible player.
Thatcham Town resigned from the League at the end of the season.

FOOTBALL CONFERENCE

1979-80

Altrincham	38	24	8	6	79	35	56
Weymouth	38	22	10	6	73	37	54
Worcester City	38	19	11	8	53	36	49
Boston United	38	16	13	9	52	43	45
Gravesend & Northfleet	38	17	10	11	49	44	44
Maidstone United	38	16	11	11	54	37	43
Kettering Town	38	15	13	10	55	50	43
Northwich Victoria	38	16	10	12	50	38	42
Bangor City	38	14	14	10	41	46	42
Nuneaton Borough	38	13	13	12	58	44	39
Scarborough	38	12	15	11	47	38	39
Yeovil Town	38	13	10	15	46	49	36
Telford United	38	13	8	17	52	60	34
Barrow	38	14	6	18	47	55	34
Wealdstone	38	9	15	14	42	54	33
Bath City	38	10	12	16	43	69	32
Barnet	38	10	10	18	32	48	30
AP Leamington	38	7	11	20	32	63	25
Stafford Rangers	38	6	10	22	41	57	22
Redditch United	38	5	8	25	26	69	18

1980-81

Altrincham	38	23	8	7	72	41	54
Kettering Town	38	21	9	8	66	37	51
Scarborough	38	17	13	8	49	29	47
Northwich Victoria	38	17	11	10	53	40	45
Weymouth	38	19	6	13	54	40	44
Bath City	38	16	10	12	51	32	42
Maidstone United	38	16	9	13	64	53	41
Boston United	38	16	9	13	63	58	41
Barrow	38	15	8	15	50	49	38
Frickley Athletic	38	15	8	15	61	62	38
Stafford Rangers	38	11	15	12	56	56	37
Worcester City	38	14	7	17	47	54	35
Telford United	38	13	9	16	47	59	35
Yeovil Town	38	14	6	18	60	64	34
Gravesend & Northfleet	38	13	8	17	48	55	34
AP Leamington	38	10	11	17	47	66	31
Barnet	38	12	7	19	39	64	31
Nuneaton Borough	38	10	9	19	49	65	29
Wealdstone	38	9	11	18	37	56	29
Bangor City	38	6	12	20	35	68	24

1981-82

Runcorn	42	28	9	5	75	37	93
Enfield	42	26	8	8	90	46	86
Telford United	42	23	8	11	70	51	77
Worcester City	42	21	8	13	70	60	71
Dagenham	42	19	12	11	69	51	69
Northwich Victoria	42	20	9	13	56	46	69
Scarborough	42	19	11	12	65	52	68
Barrow	42	18	11	13	59	50	65
Weymouth	42	18	9	15	56	47	63
Boston United	42	17	11	14	61	57	62
Altrincham	42	14	13	15	66	56	55
Bath City	42	15	10	17	50	57	55
Yeovil Town	42	14	11	17	56	68	53
Stafford Rangers	42	12	16	14	48	47	52
Frickley Athletic	42	14	10	18	47	60	52
Maidstone United	42	11	15	16	55	59	48
Trowbridge Town	42	12	11	19	38	54	47
Barnet	42	9	14	19	36	52	41
Kettering Town	42	9	13	20	64	76	40
Gravesend & Northfleet	42	10	10	22	51	69	40
Dartford	42	10	9	23	47	69	39
AP Leamington	42	4	10	28	40	105	22

1982-83

Enfield	42	25	9	8	95	48	84
Maidstone United	42	25	8	9	83	34	83
Wealdstone	42	22	13	7	80	41	79
Runcorn	42	22	8	12	73	53	74
Boston United	42	20	12	10	77	57	72
Telford United	42	20	11	11	69	48	71
Weymouth	42	20	10	12	63	48	70
Northwich Victoria	42	18	10	14	68	63	64
Scarborough	42	17	12	13	71	58	63
Bath City	42	17	9	16	58	55	60
Nuneaton Borough	42	15	13	14	57	60	58
Altrincham	42	15	10	17	62	56	55
Bangor City	42	14	13	15	71	77	55
Dagenham	42	12	15	15	60	65	51
Barnet	42	16	3	23	55	78	51
Frickley Athletic	42	12	13	17	66	77	49
Worcester City	42	12	10	20	58	87	46
Trowbridge Town	42	12	7	23	56	88	43
Kettering Town	42	11	7	24	69	99	40
Yeovil Town	42	11	7	24	63	99	40
Barrow	42	8	12	22	46	74	36
Stafford Rangers	42	5	14	23	40	75	29

1983-84

Maidstone United	42	23	13	6	71	34	70
Nuneaton Borough	42	24	11	7	70	40	69
Altrincham	42	23	9	10	64	39	65
Wealdstone	42	21	14	7	75	36	62
Runcorn	42	20	13	9	61	45	62
Bath City	42	17	12	13	60	48	53
Northwich Victoria	42	16	14	12	54	47	51
Worcester City	42	15	13	14	64	55	49
Barnet	42	16	10	16	55	58	49
Kidderminster Harriers	42	14	14	14	54	61	49
Telford United	42	17	11	14	50	58	49
Frickley Athletic	42	17	10	15	68	56	48
Scarborough	42	14	16	12	52	55	48
Enfield	42	14	9	19	61	58	43
Weymouth	42	13	8	21	54	65	42
Gateshead	42	12	13	17	59	73	42
Boston United	42	13	12	17	66	80	41
Dagenham	42	14	8	20	57	69	40
Kettering Town	42	12	9	21	53	67	37
Yeovil Town	42	12	8	22	55	77	35
Bangor City	42	10	6	26	54	82	29
Trowbridge Town	42	5	7	30	33	87	19

2 points for a Home win, 3 points for an Away win, 1 point for any Draw

1984-85

Wealdstone	42	20	10	12	64	54	62
Nuneaton Borough	42	19	14	9	85	53	58
Dartford	42	17	13	12	57	48	57
Bath City	42	21	9	12	52	49	57
Altrincham	42	21	6	15	63	47	56
Scarborough	42	17	13	12	69	62	54
Enfield	42	17	13	12	84	61	53
Kidderminster Harriers	42	17	8	17	79	77	51
Northwich Victoria	42	16	11	15	50	46	50
Telford United	42	15	14	13	59	54	49
Frickley Athletic	42	18	7	17	65	71	49
Kettering Town	42	15	12	15	68	59	48
Maidstone United	42	15	13	14	58	51	48
Runcorn	42	13	15	14	48	47	48
Barnet	42	15	11	16	59	52	47
Weymouth	42	15	13	14	70	66	45
Boston United	42	15	10	17	69	69	45
Barrow	42	11	16	15	47	57	43
Dagenham	42	13	10	19	47	67	41
Worcester City	42	12	9	21	55	84	38
Gateshead	42	9	12	21	51	82	33
Yeovil Town	42	6	11	25	44	87	25

Gateshead had 1 point deducted

2 points awarded for a Home win, 3 points awarded for an Away win,
1 point awarded for any Draw.

1985-86

Enfield	42	27	10	5	94	47	76
Frickley Athletic	42	25	10	7	78	50	69
Kidderminster Harriers	42	24	7	11	99	62	67
Altrincham	42	22	11	9	70	49	63
Weymouth	42	19	15	8	75	60	61
Runcorn	42	19	14	9	70	44	60
Stafford Rangers	42	19	13	10	61	54	60
Telford United	42	18	10	14	68	66	51
Kettering Town	42	15	15	12	55	53	49
Wealdstone	42	16	9	17	57	56	47
Cheltenham Town	42	16	11	15	69	69	46
Bath City	42	13	11	18	53	54	45
Boston United	42	16	7	19	66	76	44
Barnet	42	13	11	18	56	60	41
Scarborough	42	13	11	18	54	66	40
Northwich Victoria	42	10	12	20	42	54	37
Maidstone United	42	9	16	17	57	66	36
Nuneaton Borough	42	13	5	24	58	73	36
Dagenham	42	10	12	20	48	66	36
Wycombe Wanderers	42	10	13	19	55	84	36
Dartford	42	8	9	25	51	82	26
Barrow	42	7	8	27	41	86	24

2 points awarded for a Home win, 3 points awarded for an Away win,
1 point awarded for any Draw

1986-87

Scarborough	42	27	10	5	64	33	91
Barnet	42	25	10	7	86	39	85
Maidstone United	42	21	10	11	71	48	73
Enfield	42	21	7	14	66	47	70
Altrincham	42	18	15	9	66	53	69
Boston United	42	21	6	15	82	74	69
Sutton United	42	19	11	12	81	51	68
Runcorn	42	18	13	11	71	58	67
Telford United	42	18	10	14	69	59	64
Bath City	42	17	12	13	63	62	63
Cheltenham Town	42	16	13	13	64	50	61
Kidderminster Harriers	42	17	4	21	77	81	55
Stafford Rangers	42	14	11	17	58	60	53
Weymouth	42	13	12	17	68	77	51
Dagenham	42	14	7	21	56	72	49
Kettering Town	42	12	11	19	54	66	47
Northwich Victoria	42	10	14	18	53	69	44
Nuneaton Borough	42	10	14	18	48	73	44
Wealdstone	42	11	10	21	50	70	43
Welling United	42	10	10	22	61	84	40
Frickley Athletic	42	7	11	24	47	82	32
Gateshead	42	6	13	23	48	95	31

Nuneaton Borough were expelled at the end of the season after their main
stand was closed for fire safety reasons.

1987-88

Lincoln City	42	24	10	8	86	48	82
Barnet	42	23	11	8	93	45	80
Kettering Town	42	22	9	11	68	48	75
Runcorn	42	21	11	10	68	47	74
Telford United	42	20	10	12	65	50	70
Stafford Rangers	42	20	9	13	79	58	69
Kidderminster Harriers	42	18	15	9	75	66	69
Sutton United	42	16	18	8	77	54	66
Maidstone United	42	18	9	15	79	64	63
Weymouth	42	18	9	15	53	43	63
Macclesfield Town	42	18	9	15	64	62	63
Enfield	42	15	10	17	68	78	55
Cheltenham Town	42	11	20	11	64	67	53
Altrincham	42	14	10	18	59	59	52
Fisher Athletic	42	13	13	16	58	61	52
Boston United	42	14	7	21	60	75	49
Northwich Victoria	42	10	17	15	46	57	47
Wycombe Wanderers	42	11	13	18	50	76	46
Welling United	42	11	9	22	50	72	42
Bath City	42	9	10	23	48	76	37
Wealdstone	42	5	17	20	39	76	32
Dagenham	42	5	6	31	37	104	21

1988-89

Maidstone United	40	25	9	6	92	46	84
Kettering Town	40	23	7	10	56	39	76
Boston United	40	22	8	10	61	51	74
Wycombe Wanderers	40	20	11	9	68	52	71
Kidderminster Harriers	40	21	6	13	68	57	69
Runcorn	40	19	8	13	77	53	65
Macclesfield Town	40	17	10	13	63	57	61
Barnet	40	18	7	15	64	69	61
Yeovil Town	40	15	11	14	68	67	56
Northwich Victoria	40	14	11	15	64	65	53
Welling United	40	14	11	15	45	46	53
Sutton United	40	12	15	13	64	54	51
Enfield	40	14	8	18	62	67	50
Altrincham	40	13	10	17	51	61	49
Cheltenham Town	40	12	12	16	55	58	48
Telford United	40	13	9	18	37	43	48
Chorley	40	13	6	21	57	71	45
Fisher Athletic	40	10	11	19	55	65	41
Stafford Rangers	40	11	7	22	49	74	40
Aylesbury United	40	9	9	22	43	71	36
Weymouth	40	7	10	23	37	70	31
Newport County	29	4	7	18	31	62	19

Newport County were expelled from League and their record was deleted.

1989-90

Darlington	42	26	9	7	76	25	87
Barnet	42	26	7	9	81	41	85
Runcorn	42	19	13	10	79	62	70
Macclesfield Town	42	17	15	10	56	41	66
Kettering Town	42	18	12	12	66	53	66
Welling United	42	18	10	14	62	50	64
Yeovil Town	42	17	12	13	62	54	63
Sutton United	42	19	6	17	68	64	63
Merthyr Tydfil	42	16	14	12	67	63	62
Wycombe Wanderers	42	17	10	15	64	56	61
Cheltenham Town	42	16	11	15	58	60	59
Telford United	42	15	13	14	56	63	58
Kidderminster Harriers	42	15	9	18	64	67	54
Barrow	42	12	16	14	51	67	52
Northwich Victoria	42	15	5	22	51	67	50
Altrincham	42	12	13	17	49	48	49
Stafford Rangers	42	12	12	18	50	62	48
Boston United	42	13	8	21	48	67	47
Fisher Athletic	42	13	7	22	55	78	46
Chorley	42	13	6	23	42	67	45
Farnborough Town	42	10	12	20	60	73	42
Enfield	42	10	6	26	52	89	36

1990-91

Barnet	42	26	9	7	103	52	87
Colchester United	42	25	10	7	68	35	85
Altrincham	42	23	13	6	87	46	82
Kettering Town	42	23	11	8	67	45	80
Wycombe Wanderers	42	21	11	10	75	46	74
Telford United	42	20	7	15	62	52	67
Macclesfield Town	42	17	12	13	63	52	63
Runcorn	42	16	10	16	69	67	58
Merthyr Tydfil	42	16	9	17	62	61	57
Barrow	42	15	12	15	59	65	57
Welling United	42	13	15	14	55	57	54
Northwich Victoria	42	13	13	16	65	75	52
Kidderminster Harriers	42	14	10	18	56	67	52
Yeovil Town	42	13	11	18	58	58	50
Stafford Rangers	42	12	14	16	48	51	50
Cheltenham Town	42	12	12	18	54	72	48
Gateshead	42	14	6	22	52	92	48
Boston United	42	12	11	19	55	69	47
Slough Town	42	13	6	23	51	80	45
Bath City	42	10	12	20	55	61	42
Sutton United	42	10	9	23	62	82	39
Fisher Athletic	42	5	15	22	38	79	30

1991-92

Colchester United	42	28	10	4	98	40	94
Wycombe Wanderers	42	30	4	8	84	35	94
Kettering Town	42	20	13	9	72	50	73
Merthyr Tydfil	42	18	14	10	59	56	68
Farnborough Town	42	18	12	12	68	53	66
Telford United	42	19	7	16	62	66	64
Redbridge Forest	42	18	9	15	69	56	63
Boston United	42	18	9	15	71	66	63
Bath City	42	16	12	14	54	51	60
Witton Albion	42	16	10	16	63	60	58
Northwich Victoria	42	16	6	20	63	58	54
Welling United	42	14	12	16	69	79	54
Macclesfield Town	42	13	13	16	50	50	52
Gateshead	42	12	12	18	49	57	48
Yeovil Town	42	11	14	17	40	49	47
Runcorn	42	11	13	18	50	63	46
Stafford Rangers	42	10	16	16	41	59	46
Altrincham	42	11	12	19	61	82	45
Kidderminster Harriers	42	12	9	21	56	77	45
Slough Town	42	13	6	23	56	82	45
Cheltenham Town	42	10	13	19	56	82	43
Barrow	42	8	14	20	52	72	38

1992-93

Wycombe Wanderers	42	24	11	7	84	37	83
Bromsgrove Rovers	42	18	14	10	67	49	68
Dagenham & Redbridge	42	19	11	12	75	47	67
Yeovil Town	42	18	12	12	59	49	66
Slough Town	42	18	11	13	60	55	65
Stafford Rangers	42	18	10	14	55	47	64
Bath City	42	15	14	13	53	46	59
Woking	42	17	8	17	58	62	59
Kidderminster Harriers	42	14	16	12	60	60	58
Altrincham	42	15	13	14	49	52	58
Northwich Victoria	42	16	8	18	68	55	56
Stalybridge Celtic	42	13	17	12	48	55	56
Kettering Town	42	14	13	15	61	63	55
Gateshead	42	14	10	18	53	56	52
Telford United	42	14	10	18	55	60	52
Merthyr Tydfil	42	14	10	18	51	79	52
Witton Albion	42	11	17	14	62	65	50
Macclesfield Town	42	12	13	17	40	50	49
Runcorn	42	13	10	19	58	76	49
Welling United	42	12	12	18	57	72	48
Farnborough Town	42	12	11	19	68	87	47
Boston United	42	9	13	20	50	69	40
Dagenham & Redbridge had 1 point deducted							

1993-94

Kidderminster Harriers	42	22	9	11	63	35	75
Kettering Town	42	19	15	8	46	24	72
Woking	42	18	13	11	58	58	67
Southport	42	18	12	12	57	51	66
Runcorn	42	14	19	9	63	57	61
Dagenham & Redbridge	42	15	14	13	62	54	59
Macclesfield Town	42	16	11	15	48	49	59
Dover Athletic	42	17	7	18	48	49	58
Stafford Rangers	42	14	15	13	56	52	57
Altrincham	42	16	9	17	41	42	57
Gateshead	42	15	12	15	45	53	57
Bath City	42	13	17	12	47	38	56
Halifax Town	42	13	16	13	55	49	55
Stalybridge Celtic	42	14	12	16	54	55	54
Northwich Victoria	42	11	19	12	44	45	52
Welling United	42	13	12	17	47	49	51
Telford United	42	13	12	17	41	49	51
Bromsgrove Rovers	42	12	15	15	54	66	51
Yeovil Town	42	14	9	19	49	62	51
Merthyr Tydfil	42	12	15	15	60	61	49
Slough Town	42	11	14	17	44	58	47
Witton Albion	42	7	13	22	37	63	34
Merthyr Tydfil had 2 points deducted							

1994-95

Macclesfield Town	42	24	8	10	70	40	80
Woking	42	21	12	9	76	54	75
Southport	42	21	9	12	68	50	72
Altrincham	42	20	8	14	77	60	68
Stevenage Borough	42	20	7	15	68	49	67
Kettering Town	42	19	10	13	73	56	67
Gateshead	42	19	10	13	61	53	67
Halifax Town	42	17	12	13	68	54	63
Runcorn	42	16	10	16	59	71	58
Northwich Victoria	42	14	15	13	77	66	57
Kidderminster Harriers	42	16	9	17	63	61	57
Bath City	42	15	12	15	55	56	57
Bromsgrove Rovers	42	14	13	15	66	69	55
Farnborough Town	42	15	10	17	45	64	55
Dagenham & Redbridge	42	13	13	16	56	69	52
Dover Athletic	42	11	16	15	48	55	49
Welling United	42	13	10	19	57	74	49
Stalybridge Celtic	42	11	14	17	52	72	47
Telford United	42	10	16	16	53	62	46
Merthyr Tydfil	42	11	11	20	53	63	44
Stafford Rangers	42	9	11	22	53	79	38
Yeovil Town	42	8	14	20	50	71	37
Yeovil Town had 1 point deducted for fielding an ineligible player							

1995-96

	P	W	D	L	F	A	Pts
Stevenage Borough	42	27	10	5	101	44	91
Woking	42	25	8	9	83	54	83
Hednesford Town	42	23	7	12	71	46	76
Macclesfield Town	42	22	9	11	66	49	75
Gateshead	42	18	13	11	58	46	67
Southport	42	18	12	12	77	64	66
Kidderminster Harriers	42	18	10	14	78	66	64
Northwich Victoria	42	16	12	14	72	64	60
Morecambe	42	17	8	17	78	72	59
Farnborough Town	42	15	14	13	63	58	59
Bromsgrove Rovers	42	15	14	13	59	57	59
Altrincham	42	15	13	14	59	64	58
Telford United	42	15	10	17	51	56	55
Stalybridge Celtic	42	16	7	19	59	68	55
Halifax Town	42	13	13	16	49	63	52
Kettering Town	42	13	9	20	68	84	48
Slough Town	42	13	8	21	63	76	47
Bath City	42	13	7	22	45	66	46
Welling United	42	10	15	17	42	53	45
Dover Athletic	42	11	7	24	51	74	40
Runcorn	42	9	8	25	48	87	35
Dagenham & Redbridge	42	7	12	23	43	73	33

1996-97

	P	W	D	L	F	A	Pts
Macclesfield Town	42	27	9	6	80	30	90
Kidderminster Harriers	42	26	7	9	84	42	85
Stevenage Borough	42	24	10	8	87	53	82
Morecambe	42	19	9	14	69	56	66
Woking	42	18	10	14	71	63	64
Northwich Victoria	42	17	12	13	61	54	63
Farnborough Town	42	16	13	13	58	53	61
Hednesford Town	42	16	12	14	52	50	60
Telford United	42	16	10	16	46	56	58
Gateshead	42	15	11	16	59	63	56
Southport	42	15	10	17	51	61	55
Rushden & Diamonds	42	14	11	17	61	63	53
Stalybridge Celtic	42	14	10	18	53	58	52
Kettering Town	42	14	9	19	53	62	51
Hayes	42	12	14	16	54	55	50
Slough Town	42	12	14	16	62	65	50
Dover Athletic	42	12	14	16	57	68	50
Welling United	42	13	9	20	50	60	48
Halifax Town	42	12	12	18	55	74	48
Bath City	42	12	11	19	53	80	47
Bromsgrove Rovers	42	12	5	25	41	67	41
Altrincham	42	9	12	21	49	73	39

1997-98

	P	W	D	L	F	A	Pts
Halifax Town	42	25	12	5	74	43	87
Cheltenham Town	42	23	9	10	63	43	78
Woking	42	22	8	12	72	46	74
Rushden & Diamonds	42	23	5	14	79	57	74
Morecambe	42	21	10	11	77	64	73
Hereford United	42	18	13	11	56	49	67
Hednesford Town	42	18	12	12	59	50	66
Slough Town	42	18	10	14	58	49	64
Northwich Victoria	42	15	15	12	63	59	60
Welling United	42	17	9	16	64	62	60
Yeovil Town	42	17	8	17	73	63	59
Hayes	42	16	10	16	62	52	58
Dover Athletic	42	15	10	17	60	70	55
Kettering Town	42	13	13	16	53	60	52
Stevenage Borough	42	13	12	17	59	63	51
Southport	42	13	11	18	56	58	50
Kidderminster Harriers	42	11	14	17	56	63	47
Farnborough Town	42	12	8	22	56	70	44
Leek Town	42	10	14	18	52	67	44
Telford United	42	10	12	20	53	76	42
Gateshead	42	8	11	23	51	87	35
Stalybridge Celtic	42	7	8	27	48	93	29

1998-99

	P	W	D	L	F	A	Pts
Cheltenham Town	42	22	14	6	71	36	80
Kettering Town	42	22	10	10	58	37	76
Hayes	42	22	8	12	63	50	74
Rushden & Diamonds	42	20	12	10	71	42	72
Yeovil Town	42	20	11	11	68	54	71
Stevenage Borough	42	17	17	8	62	45	68
Northwich Victoria	42	19	9	14	60	51	66
Kingstonian	42	17	13	12	50	49	64
Woking	42	18	9	15	51	45	63
Hednesford Town	42	15	16	11	49	44	61
Dover Athletic	42	15	13	14	54	48	58
Forest Green Rovers	42	15	13	14	55	50	58
Hereford United	42	15	10	17	49	46	55
Morecambe	42	15	8	19	60	76	53
Kidderminster Harriers	42	14	9	19	56	52	51
Doncaster Rovers	42	12	12	18	51	55	48
Telford United	42	10	16	16	44	60	46
Southport	42	10	15	17	47	59	45
Barrow	42	11	10	21	40	63	43
Welling United	42	9	14	19	44	65	41
Leek Town	42	8	8	26	48	76	32
Farnborough Town	42	7	11	24	41	89	32

1999-2000

	P	W	D	L	F	A	Pts
Kidderminster Harriers	42	26	7	9	75	40	85
Rushden & Diamonds	42	21	13	8	71	42	76
Morecambe	42	18	16	8	70	48	70
Scarborough	42	19	12	11	60	35	69
Kingstonian	42	20	7	15	58	44	67
Dover Athletic	42	18	12	12	65	56	66
Yeovil Town	42	18	10	14	60	63	64
Hereford United	42	15	14	13	61	52	59
Southport	42	15	13	14	55	58	58
Stevenage Borough	42	16	9	17	60	54	57
Hayes	42	16	8	18	57	58	56
Doncaster Rovers	42	15	9	18	46	48	54
Kettering Town	42	12	16	14	44	50	52
Woking	42	13	13	16	45	53	52
Nuneaton Borough	42	12	15	15	49	53	51
Telford United	42	14	9	19	56	66	51
Hednesford Town	42	15	6	21	45	68	51
Northwich Victoria	42	13	12	17	53	78	51
Forest Green Rovers	42	13	8	21	54	63	47
Welling United	42	13	8	21	54	66	47
Altrincham	42	9	19	14	51	60	46
Sutton United	42	8	10	24	39	75	34

2000-2001

	P	W	D	L	F	A	Pts
Rushden & Diamonds	42	25	11	6	78	36	86
Yeovil Town	42	24	8	10	73	50	80
Dagenham & Redbridge	42	23	8	11	71	54	77
Southport	42	20	9	13	58	46	69
Leigh RMI	42	19	11	12	63	57	68
Telford United	42	19	8	15	51	51	65
Stevenage Borough	42	15	18	9	71	61	63
Chester City	42	16	14	12	49	43	62
Doncaster Rovers	42	15	13	14	47	43	58
Scarborough	42	14	16	12	56	54	58
Hereford United	42	14	15	13	60	46	57
Boston United	42	13	17	12	74	63	56
Nuneaton Borough	42	13	15	14	60	60	54
Woking	42	13	15	14	52	57	54
Dover Athletic	42	14	11	17	54	56	53
Forest Green Rovers	42	11	15	16	43	54	48
Northwich Victoria	42	11	13	18	49	67	46
Hayes	42	12	10	20	44	71	46
Morecambe	42	11	12	19	64	66	45
Kettering Town	42	11	10	21	46	62	43
Kingstonian	42	8	10	24	47	73	34
Hednesford Town	42	5	13	24	46	86	28

2001-2002

Boston United	42	25	9	8	84	42	84
Dagenham & Redbridge	42	24	12	6	70	47	84
Yeovil Town	42	19	13	10	66	53	70
Doncaster Rovers	42	18	13	11	68	46	67
Barnet	42	19	10	13	64	48	67
Morecambe	42	17	11	14	63	67	62
Farnborough Town	42	18	7	17	66	54	61
Margate	42	14	16	12	59	53	58
Telford United	42	14	15	13	63	58	57
Nuneaton Borough	42	16	9	17	57	57	57
Stevenage Borough	42	15	10	17	57	60	55
Scarborough	42	14	14	14	55	63	55
Northwich Victoria	42	16	7	19	57	70	55
Chester City	42	15	9	18	54	51	54
Southport	42	13	14	15	53	49	53
Leigh RMI	42	15	8	19	56	58	53
Hereford United	42	14	10	18	50	53	52
Forest Green Rovers	42	12	15	15	54	76	51
Woking	42	13	9	20	59	70	48
Hayes	42	13	5	24	53	80	44
Stalybridge Celtic	42	11	10	21	40	69	43
Dover Athletic	42	11	6	25	41	65	39

Scarborough had 1 point deducted.

2002-2003

Yeovil Town	42	28	11	3	100	37	95
Morecambe	42	23	9	10	86	42	78
Doncaster Rovers	42	22	12	8	73	47	78
Chester City	42	21	12	9	59	31	75
Dagenham & Redbridge	42	21	9	12	71	59	72
Hereford United	42	19	7	16	64	51	64
Scarborough	42	18	10	14	63	54	64
Halifax Town	42	18	10	14	50	51	64
Forest Green Rovers	42	17	8	17	61	62	59
Margate	42	15	11	16	60	66	56
Barnet	42	13	14	15	65	68	53
Stevenage Borough	42	14	10	18	61	55	52
Farnborough Town	42	13	12	17	57	56	51
Northwich Victoria	42	13	12	17	66	72	51
Telford United	42	14	7	21	54	69	49
Burton Albion	42	13	10	19	52	77	49
Gravesend & Northfleet	42	12	12	18	62	73	48
Leigh RMI	42	14	6	22	44	71	48
Woking	42	11	14	17	52	81	47
Nuneaton Borough	42	13	7	22	51	78	46
Southport	42	11	12	19	54	69	45
Kettering Town	42	8	7	27	37	73	31

2003-2004

Chester City	42	27	11	4	85	34	92
Hereford United	42	28	7	7	103	44	91
Shrewsbury Town	42	20	14	8	67	42	74
Barnet	42	19	14	9	60	46	71
Aldershot Town	42	20	10	12	80	67	70
Exeter City	42	19	12	11	71	57	69
Morecambe	42	20	7	15	66	66	67
Stevenage Borough	42	18	9	15	58	52	63
Woking	42	15	16	11	65	52	61
Accrington Stanley	42	15	13	14	68	61	58
Gravesend & Northfleet	42	14	15	13	69	66	57
Telford United	42	15	10	17	49	51	55
Dagenham & Redbridge	42	15	9	18	59	64	54
Burton Albion	42	15	7	20	57	59	51
Scarborough	42	12	15	15	51	54	51
Margate	42	14	9	19	56	64	51
Tamworth	42	13	10	19	49	68	49
Forest Green Rovers	42	12	12	18	58	80	48
Halifax Town	42	12	8	22	43	65	44
Farnborough Town	42	10	9	23	53	74	39
Leigh RMI	42	7	8	27	46	97	29
Northwich Victoria	42	4	11	27	30	80	23

Burton Albion had 1 point deducted.

2004-2005

Conference National

Barnet	42	26	8	8	90	44	86
Hereford United	42	21	11	10	68	41	74
Carlisle United	42	20	13	9	74	37	73
Aldershot Town	42	21	10	11	68	52	73
Stevenage Borough	42	22	6	14	65	52	72
Exeter City	42	20	11	11	71	50	71
Morecambe	42	19	14	9	69	50	71
Woking	42	18	14	10	58	45	68
Halifax Town	42	19	9	14	74	56	66
Accrington Stanley	42	18	11	13	72	58	65
Dagenham & Redbridge	42	19	8	15	68	60	65
Crawley Town	42	16	9	17	50	50	57
Scarborough	42	14	14	14	60	46	56
Gravesend & Northfleet	42	13	11	18	58	64	50
Tamworth	42	14	11	17	53	63	50
Burton Albion	42	13	11	18	50	66	50
York City	42	11	10	21	39	66	43
Canvey Island	42	9	15	18	53	65	42
Northwich Victoria	42	14	10	18	58	72	42
Forest Green Rovers	42	6	15	21	41	81	33
Farnborough Town	42	6	11	25	35	89	29
Leigh RMI	42	4	6	32	31	98	18

Northwich Victoria had 10 points deducted.
Tamworth had 3 points deducted.
Northwich Victoria were relegated after their new owners could not re-register the club in the required time-frame.

Conference North

Southport	42	25	9	8	83	45	84
Nuneaton Borough	42	25	6	11	68	45	81
Droylsden	42	24	7	11	82	52	79
Kettering Town	42	21	7	14	56	50	70
Altrincham	42	19	12	11	66	46	69
Harrogate Town	42	19	11	12	62	49	68
Worcester City	42	16	12	14	59	53	60
Stafford Rangers	42	14	17	11	52	44	59
Redditch United	42	18	8	16	65	59	59
Hucknall Town	42	15	14	13	59	57	59
Gainsborough Trinity	42	16	9	17	55	55	57
Hinckley United	42	15	11	16	55	62	56
Lancaster City	42	14	12	16	51	59	54
Alfreton Town	42	15	8	19	53	55	53
Vauxhall Motors	42	14	11	17	48	57	53
Barrow	42	14	10	18	50	64	52
Worksop Town	42	16	12	14	59	59	50
Moor Green	42	13	10	19	55	64	49
Stalybridge Celtic	42	12	12	18	52	70	48
Runcorn FC Halton	42	10	12	20	44	63	42
Ashton United	42	8	9	25	46	79	33
Bradford Park Avenue	42	5	9	28	37	70	24

Worksop Town had 10 points deducted.
Redditch United had 3 points deducted.

Conference South

Grays Athletic	42	30	8	4	118	31	98
Cambridge City	42	23	6	13	60	44	75
Thurrock	42	21	6	15	61	56	69
Lewes	42	18	11	13	73	64	65
Eastbourne Borough	42	18	10	14	65	47	64
Basingstoke Town	42	19	6	17	57	52	63
Weymouth	42	17	11	14	62	59	62
Dorchester Town	42	17	11	14	77	81	62
Bognor Regis Town	42	17	9	16	70	65	60
Bishop's Stortford	42	17	8	17	70	66	59
Weston-super-Mare	42	15	13	14	55	60	58
Hayes	42	15	11	16	55	57	56
Havant & Waterlooville	42	16	7	19	64	69	55
St. Albans City	42	16	6	20	64	76	54
Sutton United	42	14	11	17	60	71	53
Welling United	42	15	7	20	64	68	52
Hornchurch	42	17	10	15	71	63	51
Newport County	42	13	11	18	56	61	50
Carshalton Athletic	42	13	9	20	44	72	48
Maidenhead United	42	12	10	20	54	81	46
Margate	42	12	8	22	54	75	34
Redbridge	42	11	3	28	50	86	33

Horchurch and Margate had 10 points deducted.
Redbridge had 3 points deducted.
Hornchurch disbanded at the end of the season. A new club was formed as AFC Hornchurch and joined the Essex Senior League for the next season.

Conference North

Northwich Victoria	42	29	5	8	97	49	92
Stafford Rangers	42	25	10	7	68	34	85
Nuneaton Borough	42	22	11	9	68	43	77
Droylsden	42	20	12	10	80	56	72
Harrogate Town	42	22	5	15	66	56	71
Kettering Town	42	19	10	13	63	49	67
Stalybridge Celtic	42	19	9	14	74	54	66
Worcester City	42	16	14	12	58	46	62
Moor Green	42	15	16	11	67	64	61
Hinckley United	42	14	16	12	60	55	58
Hyde United (P)	42	15	11	16	68	61	56
Hucknall Town	42	14	13	15	56	55	55
Workington (P)	42	14	13	15	60	62	55
Barrow	42	12	11	19	62	67	47
Lancaster City	42	12	11	19	52	66	47
Gainsborough Trinity	42	11	13	18	45	65	46
Alfreton Town	42	10	15	17	46	58	45
Vauxhall Motors	42	12	7	23	50	71	43
Worksop Town	42	10	11	21	46	71	41
Redditch United	42	9	12	21	53	78	39
Leigh RMI	42	9	13	20	45	79	39
Hednesford Town	42	7	14	21	42	87	35

Leigh RMI had 1 point deducted.

2005-2006

Conference National

Accrington Stanley	42	28	7	7	76	45	91
Hereford United	42	22	14	6	59	33	80
Grays Athletic	42	21	13	8	94	55	76
Halifax Town	42	21	12	9	55	40	75
Morecambe	42	22	8	12	68	41	74
Stevenage Borough	42	19	12	11	62	47	69
Exeter City	42	18	9	15	65	48	63
York City	42	17	12	13	63	48	63
Burton Albion	42	16	12	14	50	52	60
Dagenham & Redbridge	42	16	10	16	63	59	58
Woking	42	14	14	14	58	47	56
Cambridge United	42	15	10	17	51	57	55
Aldershot Town	42	16	6	20	61	74	54
Canvey Island	42	13	12	17	47	58	51
Kidderminster Harriers	42	13	11	18	39	55	50
Gravesend & Northfleet	42	13	10	19	45	57	49
Crawley Town	42	12	11	19	48	55	47
Southport	42	10	10	22	36	68	40
Forest Green Rovers	42	8	14	20	49	62	38
Tamworth	42	8	14	20	32	63	38
Scarborough	42	9	10	23	40	66	37
Altrincham	42	10	11	21	40	71	23

Altrincham had 18 points deducted for fielding an ineligible player but were not relegated after Canvey Island withdrew from the League and Scarborough were relegated for a breach of the rules.

Conference South

Weymouth	42	30	4	8	80	34	90
St. Albans City	42	27	5	10	94	47	86
Farnborough Town	42	23	9	10	65	41	78
Lewes	42	21	10	11	78	57	73
Histon	42	21	8	13	70	56	71
Havant & Waterlooville	42	21	10	11	64	48	70
Cambridge City	42	20	10	12	78	46	67
Eastleigh	42	21	3	18	65	58	66
Welling United	42	16	17	9	58	44	65
Thurrock	42	16	10	16	60	60	58
Dorchester Town	42	16	7	19	60	72	55
Bognor Regis Town	42	12	13	17	54	55	49
Sutton United	42	13	10	19	48	61	49
Weston-super-Mare	42	14	7	21	57	88	49
Bishop's Stortford	42	11	15	16	55	63	48
Yeading	42	13	8	21	47	62	47
Eastbourne Borough	42	10	16	16	51	61	46
Newport County	42	12	8	22	50	67	44
Basingstoke Town	42	12	8	22	47	72	44
Hayes	42	11	9	22	47	60	42
Carshalton Athletic	42	8	16	18	42	68	40
Maidenhead United	42	8	9	25	49	99	31

Weymouth had 4 points deducted.
Havant & Waterlooville and Cambridge City had 3 points deducted.
Maidenhead United had 2 points deducted.

2006-2007

Conference National

Dagenham & Redbridge	46	28	11	7	93	48	95
Oxford United	46	22	15	9	66	33	81
Morecambe	46	23	12	11	64	46	81
York City	46	23	11	12	65	45	80
Exeter City	46	22	12	12	67	48	78
Burton Albion	46	22	9	15	52	47	75
Gravesend & Northfleet	46	21	11	14	63	56	74
Stevenage Borough	46	20	10	16	76	66	70
Aldershot Town	46	18	11	17	64	62	65
Kidderminster Harriers	46	17	12	17	43	50	63
Weymouth	46	18	9	19	56	73	63
Rushden & Diamonds	46	17	11	18	58	54	62
Northwich Victoria	46	18	4	24	51	69	58
Forest Green Rovers	46	13	18	15	59	64	57
Woking	46	15	12	19	56	61	57
Halifax Town	46	15	10	21	55	62	55
Cambridge United	46	15	10	21	57	66	55
Crawley Town	46	17	12	17	52	52	53
Grays Athletic	46	13	13	20	56	55	52
Stafford Rangers	46	14	10	22	49	71	52
Altrincham	46	13	12	21	53	67	51
Tamworth	46	13	9	24	43	61	48
Southport	46	11	14	21	57	67	47
St. Alban's City	46	10	10	26	57	89	40

Crawley Town had 10 points deducted.
Gravesend & Northfleet changed their name to Ebbsfleet United.

Conference North

Droylsden	42	23	9	10	85	55	78
Kettering Town	42	20	13	9	75	58	73
Workington	42	20	10	12	61	46	70
Hinckley United	42	19	12	11	68	54	69
Farsley Celtic	42	19	11	12	58	51	68
Harrogate Town	42	18	13	11	58	41	67
Blyth Spartans	42	19	9	14	57	49	66
Hyde United	42	18	11	13	79	62	65
Worcester City	42	16	14	12	67	54	62
Nuneaton Borough	42	15	15	12	54	45	60
Moor Green	42	16	11	15	53	51	59
Gainsborough Trinity	42	15	11	16	51	57	56
Hucknall Town	42	15	9	18	69	69	54
Alfreton Town	42	14	12	16	44	50	54
Vauxhall Motors	42	12	15	15	62	64	51
Barrow	42	12	14	16	47	48	50
Leigh RMI	42	13	10	19	47	61	49
Stalybridge Celtic	42	13	10	19	64	81	49
Redditch United	42	11	15	16	61	68	48
Scarborough	42	13	16	13	50	45	45
Worksop Town	42	12	9	21	44	62	45
Lancaster City	42	2	5	35	27	110	1

Scarborough and Lancaster City each had 10 points deducted.
Moor Green merged with Solihull Borough of the Southern League to form Solihull Moors who continued in the Football Conference – North.
Scarborough disbanded and a new club – Scarborough Athletic – was formed which joined the Northern Counties (East) League.

Conference South

Histon	42	30	4	8	85	44	94
Salisbury City	42	21	12	9	65	37	75
Braintree Town	42	21	11	10	51	38	74
Havant & Waterlooville	42	20	13	9	75	46	73
Bishop's Stortford	42	21	10	11	72	61	73
Newport County	42	21	7	14	83	57	70
Eastbourne Borough	42	18	15	9	58	42	69
Welling United	42	21	6	15	65	51	69
Lewes	42	15	17	10	67	52	62
Fisher Athletic	42	15	11	16	77	77	56
Farnborough Town	42	19	8	15	59	52	55
Bognor Regis Town	42	13	13	16	56	62	52
Cambridge City	42	15	7	20	44	52	52
Sutton United	42	14	9	19	58	63	51
Eastleigh	42	11	15	16	48	53	48
Yeading	42	12	9	21	56	78	45
Dorchester Town	42	11	12	19	49	77	45
Thurrock	42	11	11	20	58	79	44
Basingstoke Town	42	9	16	17	46	58	43
Hayes	42	11	10	21	47	73	43
Weston-super-Mare	42	8	11	23	49	77	35
Bedford Town	42	8	7	27	43	82	31

Farnborough Town had 10 points deducted.
Hayes and Yeading merged and continued in the Football Conference – South as Hayes & Yeading United.
Farnborough Town disbanded and a new club – Farnborough – was formed which joined the Southern League.

2007-2008

Conference National (Blue Square Premier)

Aldershot Town	46	31	8	7	82	48	101
Cambridge United	46	25	11	10	68	41	86
Torquay United	46	26	8	12	83	57	86
Exeter City	46	22	17	7	83	58	83
Burton Albion	46	23	12	11	79	56	81
Stevenage Borough	46	24	7	15	82	55	79
Histon	46	20	12	14	76	67	72
Forest Green Rovers	46	19	14	13	76	59	71
Oxford United	46	20	11	15	56	48	71
Grays Athletic	46	19	13	14	58	47	70
Ebbsfleet United	46	19	12	15	65	61	69
Salisbury City	46	18	14	14	70	60	68
Kidderminster Harriers	46	19	10	17	74	57	67
York City	46	17	11	18	71	74	62
Crawley Town	46	19	9	18	73	67	60
Rushden & Diamonds	46	15	14	17	55	55	59
Woking	46	12	17	17	53	61	53
Weymouth	46	11	13	22	53	73	46
Northwich Victoria	46	11	11	24	52	78	44
Halifax Town	46	12	16	18	61	70	42
Altrincham	46	9	14	23	56	82	41
Farsley Celtic	46	10	9	27	48	86	39
Stafford Rangers	46	5	10	31	42	99	25
Droylsden	46	5	9	32	46	103	24

Halifax Town had 10 points deducted.
Crawley Town had 6 points deducted.
Halifax Town disbanded and a new club – F.C. Halifax Town – was formed which joined the Northern Premier League.

Conference North (Blue Square North)

Kettering Town	42	30	7	5	93	34	97
AFC Telford United	42	24	8	10	70	43	80
Stalybridge Celtic	42	25	4	13	88	51	79
Southport	42	22	11	9	77	50	77
Barrow	42	21	13	8	70	39	76
Harrogate Town	42	21	11	10	55	41	74
Nuneaton Borough	42	19	14	9	58	40	71
Burscough	42	19	8	15	62	58	65
Hyde United	42	20	3	19	84	66	63
Boston United	42	17	8	17	65	57	59
Gainsborough Trinity	42	15	12	15	62	65	57
Worcester City	42	14	12	16	48	68	54
Redditch United	42	15	8	19	41	58	53
Workington	42	13	11	18	52	56	50
Tamworth (R)	42	13	11	18	53	59	50
Alfreton Town	42	12	11	19	49	54	47
Solihull Moors	42	12	11	19	50	76	47
Blyth Spartans	42	12	10	20	52	62	46
Hinckley United	42	11	12	19	48	69	45
Hucknall Town	42	11	6	25	53	75	39
Vauxhall Motors	42	7	7	28	42	100	28
Leigh RMI	42	6	8	28	36	87	26

Boston United were relegated for being in administration.
Nuneaton Borough disbanded and new club – Nuneaton Town – was formed which joined the Southern League.

2008-2009

Conference National (Blue Square Premier)

Burton Albion	46	27	7	12	81	52	88
Cambridge United	46	24	14	8	65	39	86
Histon	46	23	14	9	78	48	83
Torquay United	46	23	14	9	72	47	83
Stevenage Borough	46	23	12	11	73	54	81
Kidderminster Harriers	46	23	10	13	69	48	79
Oxford United	46	24	10	12	72	51	77
Kettering Town	46	21	13	12	50	37	76
Crawley Town	46	19	14	13	77	55	70
Wrexham	46	18	12	16	64	48	66
Rushden & Diamonds	46	16	15	15	61	50	63
Mansfield Town	46	19	9	18	57	55	62
Eastbourne Borough	46	18	6	22	58	70	60
Ebbsfleet United	46	16	10	20	52	60	58
Altrincham	46	15	11	20	49	66	56
Salisbury City	46	14	13	19	54	64	55
York City	46	11	19	16	47	51	52
Forest Green Rovers	46	12	16	18	70	76	52
Grays Athletic	46	14	10	22	44	64	52
Barrow	46	12	15	19	51	65	51
Woking	46	10	14	22	37	60	44
Northwich Victoria	46	11	10	25	56	75	43
Weymouth	46	11	10	25	45	86	43
Lewes	46	6	6	34	28	89	24

Oxford United had 5 points deducted.
Crawley Town had 1 point deducted.
Mansfield Town had 4 points deducted.

Conference South (Blue Square South)

Lewes	42	27	8	7	81	39	89
Eastbourne Borough	42	23	11	8	83	38	80
Hampton & Richmond	42	21	14	7	87	49	77
Fisher Athletic	42	22	5	15	65	61	71
Braintree Town	42	19	12	11	52	42	69
Eastleigh	42	19	10	13	76	62	67
Havant & Waterlooville	42	19	10	13	59	53	67
Bath City	42	17	15	10	59	36	66
Newport County	42	18	12	12	64	49	66
Bishop's Stortford	42	18	10	14	72	60	64
Bromley	42	19	7	16	77	66	64
Thurrock	42	18	9	15	63	64	63
Hayes & Yeading United	42	14	12	16	67	73	54
Cambridge City	42	14	10	18	71	72	52
Basingstoke Town	42	12	14	16	54	75	50
Welling United	42	13	7	22	41	64	46
Maidenhead United	42	11	12	19	56	59	45
Bognor Regis Town	42	11	11	20	49	67	44
St. Alban's City	42	10	12	20	43	69	42
Weston Super Mare	42	9	10	23	52	85	37
Dorchester Town	42	8	10	24	36	70	34
Sutton United	42	5	9	28	32	86	24

Cambridge City were relegated as they were unable to meet ground requirements.

Conference North (Blue Square North)

Tamworth	42	24	13	5	70	41	85
Gateshead	42	24	8	10	81	48	80
Alfreton Town	42	20	17	5	81	48	77
AFC Telford United	42	22	10	10	65	34	76
Southport	42	21	13	8	63	36	76
Stalybridge Celtic	42	20	10	12	71	50	70
Droylsden	42	18	14	10	64	44	68
Fleetwood Town	42	17	11	14	70	66	62
Harrogate Town	42	17	10	15	66	57	61
Hinckley United	42	16	9	17	56	59	57
Vauxhall Motors	42	14	11	17	51	67	53
Workington	42	13	12	17	54	55	51
Gainsborough Trinity	42	12	14	16	57	63	50
Redditch United	42	12	14	16	49	61	50
Blyth Spartans	42	14	7	21	50	58	49
Solihull Moors	42	13	10	19	49	73	49
Kings Lynn	42	10	18	14	50	60	48
Stafford Rangers	42	12	12	18	41	56	48
Farsley Celtic	42	14	5	23	58	65	47
Hyde United	42	11	9	22	57	80	42
Burscough	42	10	6	26	43	80	36
Hucknall Town	42	5	13	24	39	84	28

King's Lynn were relegated as they were unable to meet ground requirements.

Conference South (Blue Square South)

AFC Wimbledon	42	26	10	6	86	36	88
Hampton & Richmond Borough	42	25	10	7	74	37	85
Eastleigh	42	25	8	9	69	49	83
Hayes & Yeading United	42	24	9	9	74	43	81
Chelmsford City	42	23	8	11	72	52	77
Maidenhead United	42	21	8	13	57	46	71
Welling United	42	19	11	12	61	44	68
Bath City	42	20	8	14	56	45	68
Bishop's Stortford	42	17	8	17	60	60	59
Newport County	42	16	11	15	50	51	59
Team Bath	42	16	7	19	62	64	55
St. Alban's City	42	14	12	16	56	50	54
Bromley	42	15	9	18	60	64	54
Braintree Town	42	14	10	18	57	54	52
Havant & Waterlooville	42	11	15	16	59	58	48
Worcester City	42	12	11	19	38	53	47
Weston Super Mare	42	12	11	19	43	68	47
Basingstoke Town	42	10	16	16	36	55	46
Dorchester Town	42	10	12	20	39	61	42
Thurrock	42	9	13	20	54	60	40
Bognor Regis Town	42	7	12	23	33	68	26
Fisher Athletic	42	5	3	34	22	100	18

Bognor Regis Town had 7 points deducted.
Team Bath disbanded at the end of the season.

Conference North (Blue Square North)

Southport	40	25	11	4	91	45	86
Fleetwood Town	40	26	7	7	86	44	85
Alfreton Town	40	21	11	8	77	45	74
Workington	40	20	10	10	46	37	70
Droylsden	40	18	10	12	82	62	64
Corby Town	40	18	9	13	73	62	63
Hinckley United	40	16	14	10	60	52	62
Ilkeston Town	40	16	13	11	53	45	61
Stalybridge Celtic	40	16	7	17	71	64	55
Eastwood Town	40	15	9	16	50	55	54
AFC Telford United	40	14	9	17	52	55	51
Northwich Victoria	40	15	13	12	62	55	48
Blyth Spartans	40	13	9	18	67	72	48
Gainsborough Trinity	40	12	11	17	50	57	47
Hyde United	40	11	12	17	45	72	45
Stafford Rangers	40	10	14	16	59	70	44
Solihull Moors	40	11	9	20	47	58	42
Gloucester City	40	12	6	22	47	59	42
Redditch United	40	10	8	22	49	83	38
Vauxhall Motors	40	7	14	19	45	81	35
Harrogate Town	40	8	6	26	41	80	30

Farsley started the season with a 10 point deduction for entering administration. They later resigned from the Conference and their record was expunged.
Northwich Victoria were initially thrown out of the Conference for entering administration but, after a successful appeal, started the season with a 10 point deduction. They were subsequently demoted at the end of the season.

2009-2010

Conference National (Blue Square Premier)

Stevenage Borough	44	30	9	5	79	24	99
Luton Town	44	26	10	8	84	40	88
Oxford United	44	25	11	8	64	31	86
Rushden & Diamonds	44	22	13	9	77	39	79
York City	44	22	12	10	62	35	78
Kettering Town	44	18	12	14	51	41	66
Crawley Town	44	19	9	16	50	57	66
AFC Wimbledon	44	18	10	16	61	47	64
Mansfield Town	44	17	11	16	69	60	62
Cambridge United	44	15	14	15	65	53	59
Wrexham	44	15	13	16	45	39	58
Salisbury City	44	21	5	18	58	63	58
Kidderminster Harriers	44	15	12	17	57	52	57
Altrincham	44	13	15	16	53	51	54
Barrow	44	13	13	18	50	67	52
Tamworth	44	11	16	17	42	52	49
Hayes & Yeading United	44	12	12	20	59	85	48
Histon	44	11	13	20	44	67	46
Eastbourne Borough	44	11	13	20	42	72	46
Gateshead	44	13	7	24	46	69	45
Forest Green Rovers	44	12	9	23	50	76	45
Ebbsfleet United	44	12	8	24	50	82	44
Grays Athletic	44	5	13	26	35	91	26

Chester City were initially deducted 25 points for entering administration and insolvency but were then later expelled from the Conference and their record was expunged.
Salisbury City had 10 points deducted and were subsequently demoted from the Conference at the end of the season.
Grays Athletic had 2 points deducted and withdrew from the Conference at the end of the season.
Gateshead had 1 point deducted.

Conference South (Blue Square South)

Newport County	42	32	7	3	93	26	103
Dover Athletic	42	22	9	11	66	47	75
Chelmsford City	42	22	9	11	62	48	75
Bath City	42	20	12	10	66	46	72
Woking	42	21	9	12	57	44	72
Havant & Waterlooville	42	19	14	9	65	44	71
Braintree Town	42	18	17	7	56	41	71
Staines Town	42	18	13	11	59	40	67
Welling United	42	18	9	15	66	51	63
Thurrock	42	16	13	13	66	60	61
Eastleigh	42	17	9	16	71	66	60
Bromley	42	15	10	17	68	64	55
St. Albans City	42	15	10	17	45	55	55
Hampton & Richmond Borough	42	14	9	19	56	66	51
Basingstoke Town	42	13	10	19	49	68	49
Maidenhead United	42	12	12	18	52	59	48
Dorchester Town	42	13	9	20	56	74	48
Bishop's Stortford	42	12	11	19	48	59	47
Lewes	42	9	15	18	49	63	42
Worcester City	42	10	10	22	48	60	40
Weston-super-Mare	42	5	8	29	48	93	23
Weymouth	42	5	7	30	31	103	22

2010-2011

Conference National (Blue Square Premier)

Crawley Town	46	31	12	3	93	30	105
AFC Wimbledon	46	27	9	10	83	47	90
Luton Town	46	23	15	8	85	37	84
Wrexham	46	22	15	9	66	49	81
Fleetwood Town	46	22	12	12	68	42	78
Kidderminster Harriers	46	20	17	9	74	60	72
Darlington	46	18	17	11	61	42	71
York City	46	19	14	13	55	50	71
Newport County	46	18	15	13	78	60	69
Bath City	46	16	15	15	64	68	63
Grimsby Town	46	15	17	14	72	62	62
Mansfield Town	46	17	10	19	73	75	61
Rushden & Diamonds	46	16	14	16	65	62	57
Gateshead	46	14	15	17	65	68	57
Kettering Town	46	15	13	18	64	75	56
Hayes & Yeading United	46	15	6	25	57	81	51
Cambridge United	46	11	17	18	53	61	50
Barrow	46	12	14	20	52	67	50
Tamworth	46	12	13	21	62	83	49
Forest Green Rovers	46	10	16	20	53	72	46
Southport	46	11	13	22	56	77	46
Altrincham	46	11	11	24	47	87	44
Eastbourne Borough	46	10	9	27	62	104	39
Histon	46	8	9	29	41	90	28

Kidderminster Harriers, Histon and Rushden & Diamonds each had 5 points deducted.
Kettering Town had two points deducted.
Rushden & Diamonds were expelled from the Football Conference on 11th June 2011.

Conference North (Blue Square North)

Alfreton Town	40	29	5	6	97	33	92
AFC Telford United	40	23	13	4	71	29	82
Boston United	40	23	10	7	72	33	79
Eastwood Town	40	22	7	11	82	50	73
Guiseley	40	20	13	7	56	41	73
Nuneaton Town	40	21	9	10	66	44	72
Solihull Moors	40	18	10	12	66	49	64
Droylsden	40	17	9	14	69	67	60
Blyth Spartans	40	16	10	14	61	54	58
Stalybridge Celtic	40	16	9	15	64	55	57
Workington	40	16	6	18	52	60	54
Harrogate Town	40	13	11	16	53	66	50
Corby Town	40	13	10	17	58	80	49
Gloucester City	40	14	5	21	49	63	47
Hinckley United	40	13	7	20	76	76	46
Worcester City	40	12	10	18	49	55	46
Vauxhall Motors	40	12	9	19	52	71	45
Gainsborough Trinity	40	12	5	23	50	74	41
Hyde	40	10	6	24	44	73	36
Stafford Rangers	40	8	8	24	39	78	32
Redditch United	40	2	8	30	30	105	9

Redditch United had 5 points deducted.
Ilkeston Town were wound-up on 8th September 2010 and the club was expelled from the league on 15th September 2010. Their record was expunged when it stood as: 7   1   3   3   7   13   7

Conference South (Blue Square South)

Braintree Town	42	27	8	7	78	33	89
Farnborough	42	25	7	10	83	47	82
Ebbsfleet United	42	22	12	8	75	51	78
Chelmsford City	42	23	8	11	82	50	77
Woking	42	22	10	10	63	42	76
Welling United	42	24	8	10	81	47	75
Dover Athletic	42	22	8	12	80	51	74
Eastleigh	42	22	6	14	74	53	72
Havant & Waterlooville	42	16	10	16	56	51	58
Dartford	42	15	12	15	60	59	57
Bromley	42	15	12	15	49	61	57
Weston-super-Mare	42	15	8	19	56	67	53
Basingstoke Town	42	13	10	19	50	63	49
Boreham Wood	42	12	11	19	56	67	47
Staines Town	42	11	14	17	48	63	47
Bishop's Stortford	42	13	6	23	48	79	45
Dorchester Town	42	10	14	18	49	59	44
Hampton & Richmond Borough	42	9	15	18	43	61	42
Maidenhead United	42	10	10	22	43	70	40
Thurrock	42	8	13	21	50	77	37
Lewes	42	9	9	24	34	70	36
St. Albans City	42	7	13	22	39	75	24

St. Albans City had 10 points deducted.
Welling United had 5 points deducted.

2011-2012

Conference National (Blue Square Premier)

Fleetwood Town	46	31	10	5	102	48	103
Wrexham	46	30	8	8	85	33	98
Mansfield Town	46	25	14	7	87	48	89
York City	46	23	14	9	81	45	83
Luton Town	46	22	15	9	78	42	81
Kidderminster Harriers	46	22	10	14	82	63	76
Southport	46	21	13	12	72	69	76
Gateshead	46	21	11	14	69	62	74
Cambridge United	46	19	14	13	57	41	71
Forest Green Rovers	46	19	13	14	66	45	70
Grimsby Town	46	19	13	14	79	60	70
Braintree Town	46	17	11	18	76	80	62
Barrow	46	17	9	20	62	76	60
Ebbsfleet United	46	14	12	20	69	84	54
Alfreton Town	46	15	9	22	62	86	54
Stockport County	46	12	15	19	58	74	51
Lincoln City	46	13	10	23	56	66	49
Tamworth	46	11	15	20	47	70	48
Newport County	46	11	14	21	53	65	47
AFC Telford United	46	10	16	20	45	65	46
Hayes & Yeading United	46	11	8	27	58	90	41
Darlington	46	11	13	22	47	73	36
Bath City	46	7	10	29	43	89	31
Kettering Town	46	8	9	29	40	100	30

Darlington had 10 points deducted for entering administration. At the end of the season they were relegated four divisions for exiting administration without a CVA.
Kettering Town had 3 points deducted for failing to pay football creditors. At the end of the season they resigned from the Football Conference, dropping down two divisions.

Conference North (Blue Square North)

Hyde	42	27	9	6	90	36	90
Guiseley	42	25	10	7	87	50	85
FC Halifax Town	42	21	11	10	80	59	74
Gainsborough Trinity	42	23	5	14	74	61	74
Nuneaton Town	42	22	12	8	74	41	72
Stalybridge Celtic	42	20	11	11	83	64	71
Worcester City	42	18	11	13	63	58	65
Altrincham	42	17	10	15	90	71	61
Droylsden	42	16	11	15	83	86	59
Bishop's Stortford	42	17	7	18	70	75	58
Boston United	42	15	9	18	60	67	54
Colwyn Bay	42	15	8	19	55	71	53
Workington	42	14	10	18	56	61	52
Gloucester City	42	15	7	20	53	60	52
Harrogate Town	42	14	10	18	59	69	52
Histon	42	12	15	15	67	72	51
Corby Town	42	14	8	20	69	71	50
Vauxhall Motors	42	14	8	20	63	78	50
Solihull Moors	42	13	10	19	44	54	49
Hinckley United	42	13	9	20	75	90	48
Blyth Spartans	42	7	13	22	50	80	34
Eastwood Town	42	4	8	30	37	105	20

Nuneaton Town had 6 points deducted for fielding an ineligible player.

2012-2013

Conference National (Blue Square Premier)

Mansfield Town	46	30	5	11	92	52	95
Kidderminster Harriers	46	28	9	9	82	40	93
Newport County	46	25	10	11	85	60	85
Grimsby Town	46	23	14	9	70	38	83
Wrexham	46	22	14	10	74	45	80
Hereford United	46	19	13	14	73	63	70
Luton Town	46	18	13	15	70	62	67
Dartford	46	19	9	18	67	63	66
Braintree Town	46	19	9	18	63	72	66
Forest Green Rovers	46	18	11	17	63	49	65
Macclesfield Town	46	17	12	17	65	70	63
Woking	46	18	8	20	73	81	62
Alfreton Town	46	16	12	18	69	74	60
Cambridge United	46	15	14	17	68	69	59
Nuneaton Town	46	14	15	17	55	63	57
Lincoln City	46	15	11	20	66	73	56
Gateshead	46	13	16	17	58	61	55
Hyde	46	16	7	23	63	75	55
Tamworth	46	15	10	21	55	69	55
Southport	46	14	12	20	72	86	54
Stockport County	46	13	11	22	57	80	50
Barrow	46	11	13	22	45	83	46
Ebbsfleet United	46	8	15	23	55	89	39
AFC Telford United	46	6	17	23	52	79	35

Conference South (Blue Square South)

Woking	42	30	7	5	92	41	97
Dartford	42	26	10	6	89	40	88
Welling United	42	24	9	9	79	47	81
Sutton United	42	20	14	8	68	53	74
Basingstoke Town	42	20	11	11	65	50	71
Chelmsford City	42	18	13	11	67	44	67
Dover Athletic	42	17	15	10	62	49	66
Boreham Wood	42	17	10	15	66	58	61
Tonbridge Angels	42	15	12	15	70	67	57
Salisbury City	42	15	12	15	55	54	57
Dorchester Town	42	16	8	18	58	65	56
Eastleigh	42	15	9	18	57	63	54
Weston-super-Mare	42	14	9	19	58	71	51
Truro City	42	13	9	20	65	80	48
Staines Town	42	12	10	20	53	64	46
Farnborough	42	15	6	21	52	79	46
Bromley	42	10	15	17	52	66	45
Eastbourne Borough	42	12	9	21	54	69	45
Havant & Waterlooville	42	11	11	20	64	75	44
Maidenhead United	42	11	10	21	49	74	43
Hampton & Richmond	42	10	12	20	53	69	42
Thurrock	42	5	11	26	33	84	26

Farnborough had 5 points deducted for a breach of the League's financial rules.

Conference North (Blue Square North)

Chester	42	34	5	3	103	32	107
Guiseley	42	28	7	7	83	45	91
Brackley Town	42	26	7	9	76	44	85
Altrincham	42	24	8	10	100	51	80
FC Halifax Town	42	21	12	9	86	38	75
Harrogate Town	42	20	9	13	72	50	69
Bradford Park Avenue	42	19	9	14	75	52	66
Gainsborough Trinity	42	18	12	12	68	45	66
Solihull Moors	42	17	9	16	57	53	60
Oxford City	42	13	16	13	62	57	55
Gloucester City	42	16	6	20	54	63	54
Vauxhall Motors	42	15	8	19	58	64	53
Stalybridge Celtic	42	13	13	16	55	62	52
Workington	42	16	8	18	60	68	52
Worcester City	42	14	8	20	57	62	50
Boston United	42	14	7	21	68	73	49
Bishop's Stortford	42	12	13	17	58	74	49
Colwyn Bay	42	14	7	21	57	78	49
Histon	42	11	11	20	48	73	44
Corby Town	42	12	8	22	66	92	44
Droylsden	42	5	7	30	43	124	22
Hinckley United	42	3	4	35	37	143	7

Workington had 4 points deducted for fielding an ineligible player.
Hinckley United had 3 points deducted for failing to pay football creditors then a further 3 points deducted for failing to fulfil their fixture against Bishop's Stortford.

Conference South (Blue Square South)

Welling United	42	26	8	8	90	44	86
Salisbury City	42	25	8	9	80	47	82
Dover Athletic	42	22	10	10	69	44	76
Eastleigh	42	22	6	14	79	61	72
Chelmsford City	42	22	6	14	70	56	72
Sutton United	42	20	10	12	66	49	70
Weston-super-Mare	42	19	10	13	61	55	67
Dorchester Town	42	19	8	15	59	62	65
Boreham Wood	42	15	17	10	59	46	62
Havant & Waterlooville	42	14	16	12	68	60	58
Bath City	42	15	10	17	60	58	55
Eastbourne Borough	42	14	9	19	42	52	51
Farnborough	42	19	7	16	76	75	50
Basingstoke Town	42	12	12	18	63	73	48
Bromley	42	14	6	22	54	69	48
Tonbridge Angels	42	12	12	18	56	77	48
Hayes & Yeading United	42	13	9	20	64	89	48
Staines Town	42	13	8	21	61	78	47
Maidenhead United	42	13	6	23	64	68	45
AFC Hornchurch	42	11	11	20	47	64	44
Billericay Town	42	11	7	24	62	90	40
Truro City	42	9	8	25	57	90	25

Truro had 10 points deducted for entering administration.
Farnborough had 4 points deducted for fielding an ineligible player then a
further 10 points deducted for entering administration.
Salisbury City had 1 point deducted for fielding an ineligible player.

Conference North (Blue Square North)

AFC Telford United	42	25	10	7	82	53	85
North Ferriby United	42	24	10	8	80	51	82
Altrincham	42	24	9	9	95	51	81
Hednesford Town	42	24	6	12	87	65	78
Guiseley	42	23	9	10	78	56	78
Boston United	42	20	12	10	85	60	72
Brackley Town	42	18	15	9	66	45	69
Solihull Moors	42	17	14	11	63	52	65
Harrogate Town	42	19	9	14	75	59	63
Bradford Park Avenue	42	15	12	15	66	70	57
Barrow	42	14	14	14	50	56	56
Colwyn Bay	42	14	12	16	63	67	54
Leamington	42	13	13	16	54	53	52
Stockport County	42	12	14	16	58	57	50
Worcester City	42	13	11	18	40	53	50
Gainsborough Trinity	42	13	6	23	67	86	45
Gloucester City	42	11	11	20	64	77	44
Vauxhall Motors	42	12	8	22	43	74	44
Stalybridge Celtic	42	10	9	23	57	88	39
Oxford City	42	9	13	20	50	70	37
Histon	42	7	11	24	42	76	32
Workington	42	6	10	26	39	85	28

Harrogate Town had 3 points deducted for fielding an ineligible player.
Oxford City had 3 points deducted for fielding an ineligible player.
Vauxhall Motors resigned from the League at the end of the season.

2013-2014

Conference National (Blue Square Premier)

Luton Town	46	30	11	5	102	35	101
Cambridge United	46	23	13	10	72	35	82
Gateshead	46	22	13	11	72	50	79
Grimsby Town	46	22	12	12	65	46	78
FC Halifax Town	46	22	11	13	85	58	77
Braintree Town	46	21	11	14	57	39	74
Kidderminster Harriers	46	20	12	14	66	59	72
Barnet	46	19	13	14	58	53	70
Woking	46	20	8	18	66	69	68
Forest Green Rovers	46	19	10	17	80	66	67
Alfreton Town	46	21	7	18	69	74	67
Salisbury City	46	19	10	17	58	63	67
Nuneaton Town	46	18	12	16	54	60	66
Lincoln City	46	17	14	15	60	59	65
Macclesfield Town	46	18	7	21	62	63	61
Welling United	46	16	12	18	59	61	60
Wrexham	46	16	11	19	61	61	59
Southport	46	14	11	21	53	71	53
Aldershot Town	46	16	13	17	69	62	51
Hereford United	46	13	12	21	44	63	51
Chester	46	12	15	19	49	70	51
Dartford	46	12	8	26	49	74	44
Tamworth	46	10	9	27	43	81	39
Hyde	46	1	7	38	38	119	10

Aldershot Town had 10 points deducted after entering administration.
Alfreton Town had 3 points deducted for fielding an ineligible player.

Conference South (Blue Square South)

Eastleigh	42	26	8	8	71	40	86
Sutton United	42	23	12	7	77	39	81
Bromley	42	25	5	12	82	50	80
Ebbsfleet United	42	21	11	10	67	40	74
Dover Athletic	42	20	9	13	63	38	69
Havant & Waterlooville	42	19	12	11	57	43	69
Bath City	42	18	12	12	64	52	66
Staines Town	42	18	9	15	56	57	63
Concord Rangers	42	17	10	15	58	58	61
Eastbourne Borough	42	16	10	16	54	58	58
Weston-super-Mare	42	16	9	17	50	55	57
Gosport Borough	42	16	7	19	46	51	55
Boreham Wood	42	14	11	17	65	55	53
Basingstoke Town	42	15	8	19	55	56	53
Bishop's Stortford	42	13	13	16	63	68	52
Farnborough	42	16	4	22	62	77	52
Chelmsford City	42	14	7	21	57	77	49
Maidenhead United	42	12	10	20	55	69	46
Whitehawk	42	12	10	20	56	71	46
Hayes & Yeading United	42	13	6	23	45	52	45
Tonbridge Angels	42	9	13	20	43	77	40
Dorchester Town	42	8	7	27	33	94	31

ISTHMIAN LEAGUE

1905-06

London Caledonians	10	7	1	2	25	8	15
Clapton	10	6	1	3	11	13	13
Casuals	10	3	4	3	14	14	10
Civil Service	10	4	1	5	16	20	9
Ealing Association	10	3	2	5	15	19	8
Ilford	10	1	3	6	5	12	5

1906-07

Ilford	10	8	2	0	26	9	18
London Caledonians	10	6	0	4	19	14	12
Clapton	10	4	3	3	18	11	11
Civil Service	10	3	1	6	11	19	7
Ealing Association	10	3	1	6	12	22	7
Casuals	10	2	1	7	15	26	5

1907-08

London Caledonians	10	5	2	3	20	15	12
Clapton	10	4	3	3	24	14	11
Ilford	10	5	1	4	28	22	11
Oxford City	10	5	1	4	20	20	11
Dulwich Hamlet	10	3	2	5	15	18	8
West Norwood	10	3	1	6	13	31	7

1908-09

Bromley	18	11	1	6	42	29	23
Leytonstone	18	9	4	5	43	31	22
Ilford	18	9	4	5	37	36	22
Dulwich Hamlet	18	9	2	7	39	30	20
Clapton	18	8	4	6	34	32	20
Oxford City	18	6	4	8	29	32	16
Nunhead	18	7	2	9	31	35	16
Shepherd's Bush	18	6	3	9	26	44	15
London Caledonians	18	4	6	8	25	34	14
West Norwood	18	5	2	11	40	43	12

1909-10

Bromley	18	11	4	3	32	10	26
Clapton	18	10	4	4	56	19	24
Nunhead	18	10	4	4	49	26	24
Ilford	18	10	3	5	31	17	23
Dulwich Hamlet	18	8	4	6	26	26	20
Leytonstone	18	7	3	8	44	46	17
Oxford City	18	5	4	9	28	45	14
London Caledonians	18	5	3	10	19	40	13
West Norwood	18	5	2	11	28	54	12
Shepherd's Bush	18	2	3	13	23	55	7

1910-11

Clapton	18	11	4	3	39	19	26
Leytonstone	18	12	1	5	47	30	25
Dulwich Hamlet	18	8	5	5	28	22	21
Oxford City	18	7	4	7	32	43	18
Ilford	18	8	1	9	41	32	17
Shepherd's Bush	18	7	3	8	31	27	17
Bromley	18	8	4	6	32	27	16
Nunhead	18	5	4	9	32	36	14
West Norwood	18	4	5	9	24	43	13
London Caledonians	18	3	3	12	18	45	9

Bromley had 4 points deducted

1911-12

London Caledonians	20	11	7	2	39	25	29
Ilford	20	11	3	6	37	24	25
Nunhead	20	10	5	5	36	30	25
Dulwich Hamlet	20	8	5	7	33	23	21
West Norwood	20	9	3	8	38	38	21
Clapton	20	7	5	8	37	37	19
Woking	20	7	5	8	38	41	19
Shepherd's Bush	20	5	6	9	39	49	16
Leytonstone	20	5	6	9	28	38	16
Oxford City	20	5	5	10	33	36	15
Tunbridge Wells	20	5	4	11	23	40	14

1912-13

London Caledonians	20	14	5	1	38	12	33
Leytonstone	20	12	3	5	45	20	27
Nunhead	20	12	3	5	36	23	27
Clapton	20	7	7	6	23	20	21
Dulwich Hamlet	20	8	4	8	34	28	20
Woking	20	7	5	8	33	40	19
Oxford City	20	6	6	8	23	39	18
Ilford	20	6	5	9	27	37	17
Shepherd's Bush	20	5	5	10	26	38	15
Tunbridge Wells	20	5	4	11	22	36	14
West Norwood	20	3	3	14	23	37	9

1913-14

London Caledonians	20	12	6	2	55	23	30
Nunhead	20	11	6	3	49	27	28
Ilford	20	11	4	5	52	35	26
Dulwich Hamlet	20	10	4	6	34	22	24
New Crusaders	20	10	3	7	40	30	23
Oxford City	20	10	0	10	42	42	20
Leytonstone	20	8	4	8	29	32	20
Clapton	20	8	3	9	29	27	19
Shepherd's Bush	20	7	2	11	24	46	16
West Norwood	20	4	3	13	27	47	11
Woking	20	1	1	18	11	61	3

1919

Leytonstone	8	5	1	2	21	7	11
Ilford	8	4	2	2	22	16	10
Dulwich Hamlet	8	3	2	3	19	17	8
Nunhead	8	3	2	3	18	19	8
Clapton	8	0	3	5	14	35	3

1919-20

Dulwich Hamlet	22	15	3	4	58	16	33
Nunhead	22	14	5	3	48	26	33
Tufnell Park	22	12	4	6	45	32	28
Ilford	22	13	1	8	63	42	27
Oxford City	22	12	3	7	63	51	27
London Caledonians	22	10	3	9	32	30	23
Leytonstone	22	8	3	11	50	43	19
Clapton	22	8	3	11	38	44	19
Civil Service	22	7	4	11	35	40	18
Woking	22	6	3	13	36	42	15
West Norwood	22	5	4	13	19	53	14
Casuals	22	3	2	17	20	88	8

1920-21

	P	W	D	L	F	A	Pts
Ilford	22	16	4	2	70	24	36
London Caledonians	22	13	5	4	45	17	31
Tufnell Park	22	14	3	5	43	24	31
Nunhead	22	12	5	5	53	33	29
Dulwich Hamlet	22	11	6	5	60	30	28
Oxford City	22	12	3	7	56	38	27
Leytonstone	22	8	6	8	36	29	22
Clapton	22	7	7	8	33	52	21
Civil Service	22	3	7	12	28	45	13
Woking	22	3	5	14	16	43	11
Casuals	22	3	3	16	31	87	9
West Norwood	22	2	2	18	18	67	6

1921-22

	P	W	D	L	F	A	Pts
Ilford	26	17	4	5	66	34	38
Dulwich Hamlet	26	14	8	4	65	24	36
London Caledonians	26	16	4	6	41	21	36
Nunhead	26	12	5	9	65	41	29
Clapton	26	13	3	10	51	46	29
Tufnell Park	26	10	7	9	44	39	27
Oxford City	26	12	2	12	48	47	26
Wycombe Wanderers	26	12	2	12	61	64	26
Civil Service	26	9	8	9	60	48	26
Woking	26	10	6	10	39	49	26
Leytonstone	26	9	6	11	41	48	24
West Norwood	26	8	5	13	43	57	21
Wimbledon	26	7	4	15	52	56	18
Casuals	26	0	2	24	25	107	2

1922-23

	P	W	D	L	F	A	Pts
Clapton	26	15	7	4	51	33	37
Nunhead	26	15	5	6	52	32	35
London Caledonians	26	13	7	6	43	26	33
Ilford	26	11	7	8	57	38	29
Casuals	26	12	5	9	68	51	29
Civil Service	26	9	10	7	39	36	28
Wycombe Wanderers	26	11	4	11	61	61	26
Dulwich Hamlet	26	9	7	10	60	44	25
Leytonstone	26	9	7	10	45	56	25
Tufnell Park	26	9	5	12	41	45	23
Wimbledon	26	10	2	14	49	50	22
Woking	26	7	6	13	42	67	20
Oxford City	26	6	5	15	45	68	17
West Norwood	26	5	5	16	25	71	15

1923-24

	P	W	D	L	F	A	Pts
St Albans City	26	17	5	4	72	38	39
Dulwich Hamlet	26	15	6	5	49	28	36
Clapton	26	14	5	7	73	50	33
Wycombe Wanderers	26	14	5	7	88	65	33
London Caledonians	26	14	3	9	53	49	31
Civil Service	26	12	5	9	52	47	29
Casuals	26	13	1	12	65	54	27
Ilford	26	9	6	11	56	59	24
Nunhead	26	8	8	10	41	46	24
Wimbledon	26	8	4	14	43	62	20
Tufnell Park	26	8	2	16	38	53	18
Woking	26	5	8	13	31	62	18
Oxford City	26	7	2	17	53	74	16
Leytonstone	26	6	4	16	41	68	16

1924-25

	P	W	D	L	F	A	Pts
London Caledonians	26	18	5	3	76	36	41
Clapton	26	19	1	6	64	34	39
St Albans City	26	16	2	8	69	39	34
Tufnell Park	26	11	4	11	47	41	26
Ilford	26	11	4	11	46	42	26
Leytonstone	26	12	2	12	55	63	26
The Casuals	26	12	1	13	55	58	25
Wycombe Wanderers	26	11	2	13	58	61	24
Civil Service	26	10	4	12	52	64	24
Nunhead	26	9	5	12	45	43	23
Wimbledon	26	10	2	14	50	54	22
Dulwich Hamlet	26	8	5	13	42	57	21
Oxford City	26	9	2	15	38	71	20
Woking	26	5	3	18	33	67	13

1925-26

	P	W	D	L	F	A	Pts
Dulwich Hamlet	26	20	1	5	80	49	41
London Caledonians	26	18	1	7	81	44	37
Clapton	26	14	4	8	64	50	32
Wycombe Wanderers	26	14	3	9	97	83	31
St Albans City	26	12	6	8	76	54	30
Nunhead	26	13	4	9	49	43	30
Ilford	26	13	2	11	81	70	28
Leytonstone	26	12	1	13	75	63	25
Woking	26	8	6	12	56	73	22
Tufnell Park	26	8	5	13	36	53	21
The Casuals	26	8	4	14	48	61	20
Wimbledon	26	9	1	16	61	77	19
Oxford City	26	8	1	17	48	76	17
Civil Service	26	5	1	20	43	99	11

1926-27

	P	W	D	L	F	A	Pts
St Albans City	26	20	1	5	96	34	41
Ilford	26	18	0	9	76	57	34
Wimbledon	26	15	3	8	72	45	33
Nunhead	26	11	8	7	51	33	30
Woking	26	12	6	8	68	60	30
London Caledonians	26	11	7	8	58	47	29
Clapton	26	11	4	11	58	60	26
Leytonstone	26	11	1	14	54	78	23
Dulwich Hamlet	26	9	4	13	60	58	22
Wycombe Wanderers	26	10	2	14	59	86	22
Tufnell Park	26	8	4	14	45	55	20
Oxford City	26	7	5	14	46	72	19
The Casuals	26	8	3	15	37	78	19
Civil Service	26	6	4	16	48	65	16

1927-28

	P	W	D	L	F	A	Pts
St Albans City	26	15	5	6	86	50	35
London Caledonians	26	12	9	5	63	38	33
Ilford	26	14	4	8	72	54	32
Woking	26	13	5	8	72	56	31
Nunhead	26	13	2	11	57	54	28
Wimbledon	26	12	3	11	57	48	27
Leytonstone	26	13	1	12	53	56	27
Clapton	26	8	10	8	52	47	26
Dulwich Hamlet	26	8	9	9	56	49	25
The Casuals	26	8	8	10	54	58	24
Wycombe Wanderers	26	9	5	12	60	69	23
Oxford City	26	7	7	12	36	57	21
Civil Service	26	8	4	14	38	76	20
Tufnell Park	26	4	4	18	38	82	12

1928-29

Nunhead	26	15	6	5	47	35	36
London Caledonians	26	15	4	7	65	33	34
Dulwich Hamlet	26	14	6	6	65	34	34
Wimbledon	26	9	10	7	66	54	28
Ilford	26	12	3	11	67	52	27
Clapton	26	11	5	10	60	55	27
Tufnell Park	26	11	5	10	58	55	27
St Albans City	26	12	3	11	63	69	27
Leytonstone	26	11	3	12	56	79	25
Wycombe Wanderers	26	10	3	13	58	60	23
Oxford City	26	10	3	13	61	71	23
The Casuals	26	8	5	13	49	60	21
Woking	26	8	3	15	39	65	19
Civil Service	26	4	5	17	39	71	13

1929-30

Nunhead	26	19	3	4	69	36	41
Dulwich Hamlet	26	15	6	5	74	39	36
Kingstonian	26	15	4	7	57	37	34
Ilford	26	16	1	9	84	60	33
Woking	26	11	5	10	66	65	27
Wimbledon	26	11	2	13	64	66	24
Wycombe Wanderers	26	10	4	12	49	52	24
The Casuals	26	8	7	11	50	51	23
Oxford City	26	10	3	13	45	60	23
St Albans City	26	9	4	13	54	77	22
Clapton	26	8	4	14	47	57	20
London Caledonians	26	8	3	15	49	69	19
Leytonstone	26	8	3	15	48	68	19
Tufnell Park	26	6	7	13	35	54	19

1930-31

Wimbledon	26	18	6	2	69	37	42
Dulwich Hamlet	26	12	9	5	51	39	33
Wycombe Wanderers	26	12	6	8	67	45	30
The Casuals	26	12	6	8	71	56	30
St Albans City	26	11	7	8	67	66	29
Ilford	26	10	6	10	70	62	26
Oxford City	26	10	5	11	43	48	25
London Caledonians	26	8	8	10	43	53	24
Kingstonian	26	10	4	12	49	64	24
Tufnell Park	26	9	5	12	45	61	23
Nunhead	26	9	4	13	49	54	22
Woking	26	9	4	13	56	63	22
Clapton	26	7	4	15	62	75	18
Leytonstone	26	6	4	16	46	65	16

1931-32

Wimbledon	26	17	2	7	60	35	36
Ilford	26	13	9	4	71	45	35
Dulwich Hamlet	26	15	3	8	69	43	33
Wycombe Wanderers	26	14	5	7	72	50	33
Oxford City	26	15	2	9	63	49	32
Kingstonian	26	13	3	10	71	50	29
Tufnell Park	26	9	7	10	50	48	25
Nunhead	26	9	7	10	54	61	25
The Casuals	26	10	4	12	59	65	24
Clapton	26	9	5	12	50	57	23
Leytonstone	26	9	3	14	36	61	21
St Albans City	26	8	4	14	57	78	20
Woking	26	6	5	15	44	64	17
London Caledonians	26	2	7	17	24	74	11

1932-33

Dulwich Hamlet	26	15	6	5	71	45	36
Leytonstone	26	16	4	6	66	43	36
Kingstonian	26	15	2	9	77	49	32
Ilford	26	14	0	12	60	58	28
The Casuals	26	12	2	12	48	36	26
Tufnell Park	26	11	3	12	51	51	25
St Albans City	26	12	1	13	57	63	25
Clapton	26	10	5	11	51	65	25
Oxford City	26	9	6	11	49	54	24
Woking	26	10	4	12	53	61	24
Wycombe Wanderers	26	10	4	12	47	56	24
Nunhead	26	8	6	12	42	50	22
Wimbledon	26	8	5	13	55	67	21
London Caledonians	26	5	6	15	35	64	16

1933-34

Kingstonian	26	15	7	4	80	42	37
Dulwich Hamlet	26	15	5	6	68	36	35
Wimbledon	26	13	7	6	62	35	33
Tufnell Park	26	14	5	7	55	50	33
Ilford	26	15	2	9	60	56	32
The Casuals	26	13	5	8	47	32	31
Leytonstone	26	13	3	10	55	48	29
Nunhead	26	10	5	11	48	44	25
London Caledonians	26	7	8	11	29	51	22
Wycombe Wanderers	26	9	2	15	57	60	20
St Albans City	26	8	4	14	44	75	20
Oxford City	26	7	4	15	45	57	18
Clapton	26	5	6	15	35	62	16
Woking	26	6	1	19	43	81	13

1934-35

Wimbledon	26	14	7	5	63	30	35
Oxford City	26	14	4	8	69	50	32
Leytonstone	26	15	2	9	49	36	32
Dulwich Hamlet	26	11	7	8	66	45	29
Tufnell Park	26	11	7	8	53	44	29
Kingstonian	26	11	6	9	44	40	28
Nunhead	26	10	7	9	35	34	27
London Caledonians	26	9	7	10	40	41	25
St Albans City	26	9	6	11	61	80	24
Ilford	26	9	6	11	40	56	24
Clapton	26	7	7	12	46	48	21
Woking	26	9	3	14	44	68	21
Wycombe Wanderers	26	7	6	13	51	69	20
The Casuals	26	6	5	15	37	57	17

1935-36

Wimbledon	26	19	2	5	82	29	40
The Casuals	26	14	5	7	60	45	33
Ilford	26	13	3	10	67	47	29
Dulwich Hamlet	26	10	8	8	64	47	28
Nunhead	26	11	6	9	51	40	28
Wycombe Wanderers	26	13	2	11	60	68	28
Clapton	26	11	5	10	42	46	27
Oxford City	26	11	4	11	60	58	26
St Albans City	26	11	2	13	59	64	24
Woking	26	9	4	13	43	62	22
Tufnell Park	26	9	3	14	42	61	21
London Caledonians	26	9	3	14	35	52	21
Kingstonian	26	9	2	15	43	56	20
Leytonstone	26	7	3	16	34	67	17

1936-37

Kingstonian	26	18	3	5	63	43	39
Nunhead	26	17	3	6	77	32	37
Leytonstone	26	16	4	6	71	42	36
Ilford	26	14	5	7	86	39	33
Dulwich Hamlet	26	12	6	8	64	48	30
Wycombe Wanderers	26	10	5	11	55	52	25
Wimbledon	26	9	7	10	52	53	25
Clapton	26	10	5	11	42	51	25
The Casuals	26	10	3	13	46	58	23
Woking	26	9	4	13	53	69	22
Oxford City	26	8	5	13	56	89	21
St Albans City	26	7	5	14	44	62	19
Tufnell Park	26	4	7	15	43	74	15
London Caledonians	26	5	4	17	26	66	14

1937-38

Leytonstone	26	17	6	3	72	34	40
Ilford	26	17	3	6	70	39	37
Tufnell Park	26	15	2	9	62	47	32
Nunhead	26	14	3	9	52	44	31
Wycombe Wanderers	26	12	5	9	69	55	29
Dulwich Hamlet	26	13	3	10	57	46	29
Kingstonian	26	12	4	10	51	48	28
Clapton	26	9	6	11	49	53	24
Wimbledon	26	10	3	13	62	49	23
London Caledonians	26	9	4	13	44	55	22
Oxford City	26	7	7	12	35	71	21
The Casuals	26	8	3	15	51	74	19
Woking	26	7	2	17	41	72	16
St Albans City	26	4	5	17	31	60	13

1938-39

Leytonstone	26	18	4	4	68	32	40
Ilford	26	17	4	5	68	32	38
Kingstonian	26	17	3	6	62	39	37
Dulwich Hamlet	26	15	5	6	60	32	35
Wimbledon	26	14	3	9	88	56	31
Nunhead	26	11	6	9	54	44	28
The Casuals	26	11	6	9	54	51	28
Clapton	26	12	2	12	69	61	26
Wycombe Wanderers	26	10	6	10	62	62	26
St Albans City	26	8	5	13	44	50	21
Woking	26	9	2	15	35	56	20
Oxford City	26	4	4	18	44	84	12
Tufnell Park	26	4	4	18	33	87	12
London Caledonians	26	3	4	19	26	81	10

1945-46

Walthamstow Avenue	26	21	0	5	100	31	42
Oxford City	26	17	6	3	91	40	40
Romford	26	15	3	8	83	59	33
Dulwich Hamlet	26	14	2	10	63	59	30
Tufnell Park	26	12	4	10	70	55	28
Woking	26	10	7	9	56	54	27
Ilford	26	12	2	12	56	71	26
Leytonstone	26	11	3	12	61	75	25
Wycombe Wanderers	26	9	3	14	80	88	21
Wimbledon	26	7	6	13	52	72	20
Corinthian Casuals	26	8	4	14	58	83	20
Clapton	26	8	3	15	51	62	19
St Albans City	26	6	6	14	48	85	18
Kingstonian	26	6	3	17	48	86	15

1946-47

Leytonstone	26	19	2	5	92	36	40
Dulwich Hamlet	26	17	3	6	78	46	37
Romford	26	13	8	5	76	52	34
Walthamstow Avenue	26	13	4	9	64	37	30
Oxford City	26	12	6	8	70	51	30
Kingstonian	26	12	4	10	54	57	28
Wycombe Wanderers	26	9	8	9	62	62	26
Wimbledon	26	10	5	11	68	64	25
Ilford	26	7	7	12	66	78	21
Tufnell Park	26	8	5	13	45	69	21
Woking	26	7	7	12	34	62	21
Clapton	26	6	8	12	41	59	20
St Albans City	26	7	5	14	47	79	19
Corinthian Casuals	26	4	4	18	36	80	12

1947-48

Leytonstone	26	19	1	6	87	38	39
Kingstonian	26	16	6	4	74	39	38
Walthamstow Avenue	26	17	3	6	61	37	37
Dulwich Hamlet	26	17	2	7	71	39	36
Wimbledon	26	13	6	7	66	40	32
Romford	26	14	1	11	53	47	29
Oxford City	26	10	5	11	50	68	25
Woking	26	10	3	13	63	55	23
Ilford	26	7	8	11	51	59	22
St Albans City	26	9	2	15	43	56	20
Wycombe Wanderers	26	7	5	14	51	65	19
Tufnell Park	26	7	4	15	38	83	18
Clapton	26	5	4	17	35	69	14
Corinthian Casuals	26	5	2	19	33	81	12

1948-49

Dulwich Hamlet	26	15	6	5	60	31	36
Walthamstow Avenue	26	16	4	6	65	38	36
Wimbledon	26	15	4	7	64	41	34
Ilford	26	14	3	9	56	36	31
Oxford City	26	13	5	8	48	34	31
Leytonstone	26	12	6	8	49	44	30
Woking	26	14	1	11	64	59	29
Romford	26	11	3	12	47	54	25
Kingstonian	26	10	4	12	43	47	24
Corinthian Casuals	26	11	2	13	47	59	24
Wycombe Wanderers	26	11	2	13	49	61	24
St Albans City	26	6	6	14	40	60	16
Clapton	26	5	5	16	32	61	15
Tufnell Park	26	1	5	20	28	70	7

St Albans City had 2 points deducted

1949-50

Leytonstone	26	17	5	4	77	31	39
Wimbledon	26	18	2	6	72	51	38
Kingstonian	26	16	3	7	59	39	35
Walthamstow Avenue	26	14	6	6	73	42	34
Dulwich Hamlet	26	14	3	9	60	47	31
St Albans City	26	12	3	11	59	45	27
Woking	26	10	6	10	60	71	26
Wycombe Wanderers	26	9	7	10	51	52	25
Romford	26	10	4	12	45	49	24
Ilford	26	10	4	12	46	53	24
Clapton	26	8	6	12	51	59	22
Oxford City	26	6	6	14	35	54	18
Corinthian Casuals	26	4	5	17	41	69	13
Tufnell Park	26	3	2	21	24	91	8

1950-51

Leytonstone	26	20	3	3	72	26	43
Walthamstow Avenue	26	15	4	7	57	37	34
Romford	26	15	3	8	58	49	33
Wimbledon	26	13	5	8	58	39	31
Dulwich Hamlet	26	14	2	10	54	43	30
Woking	26	11	6	9	65	55	28
Ilford	26	12	4	10	44	45	28
Corinthian Casuals	26	13	0	13	62	60	26
St Albans City	26	11	4	11	32	36	26
Kingstonian	26	9	4	13	46	54	22
Wycombe Wanderers	26	8	3	15	46	64	19
Oxford City	26	7	4	15	47	65	18
Clapton	26	6	5	15	29	50	17
Tufnell Park Edmonton	26	4	1	21	24	73	9

1951-52

Leytonstone	26	13	9	4	63	36	35
Wimbledon	26	16	3	7	65	44	35
Walthamstow Avenue	26	15	4	7	71	43	34
Romford	26	14	4	8	64	42	32
Kingstonian	26	11	7	8	62	48	29
Wycombe Wanderers	26	12	5	9	64	59	29
Woking	26	11	5	10	60	71	27
Dulwich Hamlet	26	11	4	11	60	53	26
Corinthian Casuals	26	11	4	11	55	66	26
St Albans City	26	9	7	10	48	53	25
Ilford	26	8	5	13	32	47	21
Clapton	26	9	2	15	50	59	20
Oxford City	26	6	3	17	50	72	15
Tufnell Park Edmonton	26	2	6	18	25	73	10

1952-53

Walthamstow Avenue	28	19	6	3	53	25	44
Bromley	28	17	4	7	71	35	38
Leytonstone	28	14	6	8	60	38	34
Wimbledon	28	14	5	9	68	37	33
Kingstonian	28	13	6	9	62	50	32
Dulwich Hamlet	28	15	2	11	62	52	32
Romford	28	12	8	8	62	52	32
Wycombe Wanderers	28	14	2	12	54	62	30
St Albans City	28	11	6	11	43	57	28
Barking	28	9	7	12	42	51	25
Ilford	28	10	4	14	59	57	24
Woking	28	10	4	14	57	72	24
Corinthian Casuals	28	7	9	12	45	56	23
Oxford City	28	5	2	21	37	87	12
Clapton	28	2	5	21	27	71	9

1953-54

Bromley	28	18	3	7	76	45	39
Walthamstow Avenue	28	13	7	8	55	30	33
Wycombe Wanderers	28	15	3	10	65	44	33
Ilford	28	11	10	7	48	44	32
Corinthian Casuals	28	12	7	9	59	44	31
Woking	28	13	4	11	54	58	30
Leytonstone	28	12	5	11	58	48	29
St Albans City	28	11	6	11	54	55	28
Dulwich Hamlet	28	11	6	11	55	57	28
Romford	28	11	5	12	57	54	27
Clapton	28	11	5	12	42	56	27
Barking	28	11	2	15	59	84	24
Kingstonian	28	8	7	13	59	71	23
Wimbledon	28	7	8	13	43	59	22
Oxford City	28	4	6	18	49	84	14

1954-55

Walthamstow Avenue	28	21	1	6	80	38	43
St Albans City	28	18	3	7	61	41	39
Bromley	28	18	2	8	66	34	38
Wycombe Wanderers	28	16	3	9	68	43	35
Ilford	28	13	5	10	64	46	31
Barking	28	15	1	12	55	51	31
Woking	28	12	3	13	75	79	27
Kingstonian	28	10	7	11	47	57	27
Leytonstone	28	10	4	14	35	51	24
Oxford City	28	10	3	15	43	74	23
Clapton	28	9	4	15	41	50	22
Wimbledon	28	10	2	16	48	62	22
Corinthian Casuals	28	9	3	16	50	65	21
Dulwich Hamlet	28	7	5	16	48	60	19
Romford	28	4	10	14	43	73	18

1955-56

Wycombe Wanderers	28	19	5	4	82	36	43
Bromley	28	12	7	9	54	43	31
Leytonstone	28	12	7	9	50	44	31
Woking	28	14	3	11	62	60	31
Barking	28	12	7	9	41	45	31
Kingstonian	28	12	6	10	67	64	30
Walthamstow Avenue	28	13	3	12	61	45	29
Ilford	28	10	8	10	44	52	28
Oxford City	28	10	7	11	48	55	27
Clapton	28	9	8	11	45	48	26
Wimbledon	28	12	2	14	51	62	26
Corinthian Casuals	28	9	7	12	56	56	25
Dulwich Hamlet	28	9	6	13	55	67	24
Romford	28	9	6	13	42	55	24
St Albans City	28	2	10	16	36	62	14

1956-57

Wycombe Wanderers	30	18	6	6	86	53	42
Woking	30	20	1	9	104	47	41
Bromley	30	16	5	9	78	60	37
Oxford City	30	16	3	11	65	57	35
Ilford	30	12	8	10	59	65	32
Tooting & Mitcham United	30	10	11	9	53	48	31
Kingstonian	30	11	9	10	72	77	31
Walthamstow Avenue	30	11	8	11	48	46	30
Dulwich Hamlet	30	13	3	14	65	54	29
St Albans City	30	13	3	14	62	71	29
Leytonstone	30	11	6	13	50	50	28
Clapton	30	9	9	12	48	59	27
Wimbledon	30	10	5	15	47	66	25
Romford	30	10	5	15	53	81	25
Barking	30	7	6	17	48	72	20
Corinthian Casuals	30	7	4	19	46	78	18

1957-58

Tooting & Mitcham United	30	20	6	4	79	33	46
Wycombe Wanderers	30	19	4	7	78	42	42
Walthamstow Avenue	30	17	5	8	63	35	39
Bromley	30	13	9	8	66	51	35
Oxford City	30	13	6	11	59	48	32
Leytonstone	30	13	6	11	49	48	32
Wimbledon	30	15	2	13	64	66	32
Corinthian Casuals	30	12	8	10	62	68	32
Woking	30	12	7	11	70	58	31
Barking	30	10	6	14	49	61	26
St Albans City	30	11	3	16	56	76	25
Clapton	30	8	9	13	42	65	25
Kingstonian	30	7	8	15	45	66	22
Dulwich Hamlet	30	7	7	16	49	64	21
Ilford	30	8	4	18	46	70	20
Romford	30	6	8	16	45	71	20

1958-59

Wimbledon	30	22	3	5	91	38	47
Dulwich Hamlet	30	18	5	7	68	44	41
Wycombe Wanderers	30	18	4	8	93	50	40
Oxford City	30	17	4	9	87	58	38
Walthamstow Avenue	30	16	5	9	59	40	37
Tooting & Mitcham United	30	15	4	11	84	55	34
Barking	30	14	2	14	59	53	30
Woking	30	12	6	12	66	66	30
Bromley	30	11	7	12	56	55	29
Clapton	30	10	6	14	55	67	26
Ilford	30	10	6	14	46	67	26
Kingstonian	30	9	4	17	54	72	22
St Albans City	30	8	6	16	53	89	22
Leytonstone	30	7	6	17	40	87	20
Romford	30	7	5	18	54	76	19
Corinthian Casuals	30	7	5	18	44	92	19

1959-60

Tooting & Mitcham United	30	17	8	5	75	43	42
Wycombe Wanderers	30	19	3	8	84	46	41
Wimbledon	30	18	3	9	66	36	39
Kingstonian	30	18	3	9	76	51	39
Corinthian Casuals	30	18	1	11	69	61	37
Bromley	30	15	6	9	75	46	36
Dulwich Hamlet	30	14	6	10	65	47	34
Walthamstow Avenue	30	11	11	8	48	38	33
Oxford City	30	10	10	10	57	57	30
Leytonstone	30	10	8	12	43	46	28
Woking	30	10	6	14	54	61	26
St Albans City	30	10	6	14	50	65	26
Maidstone United	30	10	5	15	53	60	25
Barking	30	7	4	19	30	75	18
Ilford	30	5	6	19	34	86	16
Clapton	30	3	4	23	32	92	10

1960-61

Bromley	30	20	6	4	89	42	46
Walthamstow Avenue	30	20	5	5	87	38	45
Wimbledon	30	18	6	6	72	43	42
Dulwich Hamlet	30	17	4	9	71	59	35
Maidstone United	30	14	8	8	63	39	36
Leytonstone	30	15	6	9	46	34	36
Tooting & Mitcham United	30	14	3	13	69	51	31
Wycombe Wanderers	30	12	5	13	63	61	29
St Albans City	30	12	4	14	45	72	28
Oxford City	30	10	7	13	59	59	27
Corinthian Casuals	30	9	9	12	49	59	27
Kingstonian	30	10	6	14	55	61	26
Woking	30	10	6	14	58	71	26
Ilford	30	5	8	17	30	69	18
Barking	30	3	8	19	30	76	14
Clapton	30	3	5	22	25	77	11

1961-62

Wimbledon	30	19	6	5	68	24	44
Leytonstone	30	17	7	6	61	44	41
Walthamstow Avenue	30	14	8	8	51	31	36
Kingstonian	30	15	5	10	65	48	35
Tooting & Mitcham United	30	12	10	8	62	47	34
Oxford City	30	12	9	9	56	49	33
Wycombe Wanderers	30	12	7	11	57	51	31
Corinthian Casuals	30	12	7	11	45	51	31
St Albans City	30	10	9	11	55	55	29
Woking	30	9	9	12	51	60	27
Dulwich Hamlet	30	11	4	15	55	66	26
Barking	30	9	8	13	40	64	26
Ilford	30	7	10	13	50	59	24
Bromley	30	10	4	16	49	69	24
Clapton	30	6	8	16	45	67	20
Maidstone United	30	6	7	17	34	59	19

1962-63

Wimbledon	30	19	8	3	84	33	46
Kingstonian	30	18	8	4	79	37	44
Tooting & Mitcham United	30	17	8	5	65	37	42
Ilford	30	19	3	8	70	44	41
Walthamstow Avenue	30	14	7	9	51	44	35
Maidstone United	30	13	8	9	56	45	34
Bromley	30	12	10	8	57	51	34
Leytonstone	30	12	7	11	48	50	31
Wycombe Wanderers	30	10	10	10	56	61	30
St Albans City	30	11	5	14	54	49	27
Barking	30	8	10	12	39	50	26
Oxford City	30	8	9	13	55	64	25
Woking	30	8	6	16	42	66	22
Clapton	30	7	4	19	30	71	18
Dulwich Hamlet	30	4	5	21	30	71	13
Corinthian Casuals	30	4	4	22	28	71	12

1963-64

Wimbledon	38	27	6	5	87	44	60
Hendon	38	25	4	9	124	38	54
Kingstonian	38	24	4	10	100	62	52
Sutton United	38	23	5	10	99	64	51
Enfield	38	20	10	8	96	56	50
Oxford City	38	20	8	10	90	55	48
Tooting & Mitcham United	38	19	8	11	78	51	46
St Albans City	38	14	12	12	62	63	40
Ilford	38	16	8	14	75	79	40
Maidstone United	38	15	8	15	65	71	38
Walthamstow Avenue	38	15	6	17	70	66	36
Leytonstone	38	14	8	16	66	71	36
Wycombe Wanderers	38	13	6	19	74	80	32
Hitchin Town	38	14	4	20	67	100	32
Bromley	38	11	8	19	64	75	30
Barking	38	10	9	19	46	69	29
Woking	38	10	9	19	48	88	29
Corinthian Casuals	38	10	4	24	52	92	24
Dulwich Hamlet	38	6	12	20	47	97	24
Clapton	38	2	5	31	31	120	9

1964-65

Hendon	38	28	7	3	123	49	63
Enfield	38	29	5	4	98	35	63
Kingstonian	38	24	8	6	86	44	56
Leytonstone	38	24	5	9	115	62	53
Oxford City	38	20	7	11	76	51	47
St Albans City	38	18	9	11	63	43	45
Sutton United	38	17	11	10	74	57	45
Wealdstone	38	19	6	13	93	68	44
Bromley	38	14	11	13	71	80	39
Tooting & Mitcham United	38	15	7	16	71	66	37
Hitchin Town	38	13	9	16	61	66	35
Walthamstow Avenue	38	15	5	18	63	82	35
Wycombe Wanderers	38	13	7	18	70	85	33
Corinthian Casuals	38	13	7	18	56	77	33
Barking	38	10	8	20	58	80	28
Ilford	38	8	8	22	43	89	24
Maidstone United	38	8	6	24	49	86	22
Dulwich Hamlet	38	8	5	25	45	79	21
Clapton	38	8	3	27	43	91	19
Woking	38	7	4	27	45	113	18

Hendon beat Enfield in a play-off to decide the Championship

1965-66

	P	W	D	L	F	A	Pts
Leytonstone	38	27	7	4	98	33	63
Hendon	38	27	5	6	111	55	59
Enfield	38	24	8	6	104	54	56
Wycombe Wanderers	38	25	6	7	100	65	56
Kingstonian	38	24	5	9	94	55	53
Wealdstone	38	20	6	12	90	64	46
Maidstone United	38	19	6	13	74	61	44
St Albans City	38	19	5	14	57	56	43
Sutton United	38	17	7	14	83	72	41
Tooting & Mitcham United	38	16	7	15	65	58	39
Corinthian Casuals	38	17	5	16	74	67	39
Woking	38	12	10	16	60	83	34
Walthamstow Avenue	38	12	9	17	81	75	33
Oxford City	38	10	9	19	49	72	29
Barking	38	10	7	21	51	72	27
Bromley	38	10	5	23	69	101	25
Ilford	38	7	10	21	50	84	24
Hitchin Town	38	6	8	24	57	118	20
Clapton	38	5	6	27	46	103	16
Dulwich Hamlet	38	5	5	28	30	95	15

1966-67

	P	W	D	L	F	A	Pts
Sutton United	38	26	7	5	89	33	59
Walthamstow Avenue	38	22	12	4	89	47	56
Wycombe Wanderers	38	23	8	7	92	54	54
Enfield	38	25	2	11	87	33	52
Hendon	38	20	9	9	64	37	49
Tooting & Mitcham United	38	19	10	9	76	60	48
Leytonstone	38	19	9	10	67	38	47
St Albans City	38	16	12	10	59	45	44
Kingstonian	38	18	8	12	60	49	44
Oxford City	38	15	9	14	74	61	39
Woking	38	13	10	15	65	71	36
Wealdstone	38	13	8	17	72	73	34
Barking	38	11	12	15	56	61	34
Bromley	38	12	7	19	50	67	31
Clapton	38	10	8	20	49	92	28
Ilford	38	8	10	20	43	77	26
Corinthian Casuals	38	9	7	22	45	68	25
Maidstone United	38	6	10	22	43	90	22
Hitchin Town	38	8	6	24	39	89	22
Dulwich Hamlet	38	3	4	31	33	107	10

1967-68

	P	W	D	L	F	A	Pts
Enfield	38	28	8	2	85	22	64
Sutton United	38	22	11	5	89	27	55
Hendon	38	23	6	9	90	36	52
Leytonstone	38	21	10	7	78	41	52
St Albans City	38	20	8	10	78	41	48
Walthamstow Avenue	38	19	9	10	81	64	47
Wealdstone	38	19	8	11	80	45	46
Tooting & Mitcham United	38	19	5	14	57	45	43
Barking	38	17	8	13	75	57	42
Oxford City	38	17	4	17	59	58	38
Kingstonian	38	14	10	14	56	61	38
Hitchin Town	38	14	9	15	61	73	37
Bromley	38	12	10	16	58	80	34
Wycombe Wanderers	38	13	5	20	73	85	31
Dulwich Hamlet	38	10	7	21	39	66	27
Clapton	38	10	7	21	51	88	27
Woking	38	8	8	22	50	90	24
Corinthian Casuals	38	7	10	21	40	80	24
Ilford	38	7	7	24	41	77	21
Maidstone United	38	3	4	31	26	131	10

1968-69

	P	W	D	L	F	A	Pts
Enfield	38	27	7	4	103	28	61
Hitchin Town	38	23	10	5	67	41	56
Sutton United	38	22	9	7	83	29	53
Wycombe Wanderers	38	23	6	9	70	37	52
Wealdstone	38	20	11	7	73	48	51
Hendon	38	22	5	11	69	47	49
St Albans City	38	17	13	8	75	44	47
Barking	38	20	7	11	69	46	47
Oxford City	38	18	8	12	76	64	44
Tooting & Mitcham United	38	16	10	12	68	55	42
Leytonstone	38	18	4	16	71	53	40
Kingstonian	38	15	8	15	62	56	38
Walthamstow Avenue	38	10	10	18	47	71	30
Maidstone United	38	10	8	20	47	75	28
Clapton	38	10	7	21	52	76	27
Woking	38	8	7	23	45	77	23
Bromley	38	8	7	23	52	95	23
Dulwich Hamlet	38	6	9	23	31	77	21
Ilford	38	6	8	24	33	77	20
Corinthian Casuals	38	2	4	32	23	120	8

1969-70

	P	W	D	L	F	A	Pts
Enfield	38	27	8	3	91	26	62
Wycombe Wanderers	38	25	11	2	85	24	61
Sutton United	38	24	9	5	75	35	57
Barking	38	21	9	8	93	47	51
Hendon	38	19	12	7	77	44	50
St Albans City	38	21	8	9	69	40	50
Hitchin Town	38	19	10	9	71	40	48
Tooting & Mitcham United	38	19	5	14	88	62	43
Leytonstone	38	17	7	14	57	41	41
Wealdstone	38	15	10	13	53	48	40
Oxford City	38	15	7	16	61	78	37
Kingstonian	38	13	9	16	55	57	35
Ilford	38	8	15	15	42	73	31
Dulwich Hamlet	38	8	12	18	46	66	28
Woking	38	10	7	21	46	69	27
Walthamstow Avenue	38	11	5	22	52	81	27
Clapton	38	9	7	22	45	87	25
Maidstone United	38	7	8	23	48	84	22
Corinthian Casuals	38	6	3	29	30	99	15
Bromley	38	3	4	31	28	111	10

1970-71

	P	W	D	L	F	A	Pts
Wycombe Wanderers	38	28	6	4	93	32	62
Sutton United	38	29	3	6	76	35	61
St Albans City	38	23	10	5	87	26	56
Enfield	38	24	7	7	67	24	55
Ilford	38	21	7	10	74	51	49
Hendon	38	18	11	9	81	37	47
Barking	38	20	4	14	89	59	44
Leytonstone	38	17	10	11	68	50	44
Woking	38	18	6	14	57	50	42
Walthamstow Avenue	38	14	11	13	63	52	39
Oxford City	38	13	10	15	51	48	36
Hitchin Town	38	12	9	17	46	60	33
Wealdstone	38	12	8	18	45	64	32
Tooting & Mitcham United	38	11	9	18	44	66	31
Kingstonian	38	11	8	19	53	71	30
Bromley	38	10	6	22	34	77	26
Dulwich Hamlet	38	7	10	21	30	66	24
Maidstone United	38	7	6	25	42	84	20
Clapton	38	5	7	26	33	101	17
Corinthian Casuals	38	2	8	28	23	103	12

1971-72

	P	W	D	L	F	A	Pts
Wycombe Wanderers	40	31	3	6	102	20	65
Enfield	40	26	8	6	90	41	60
Walton & Hersham	40	24	8	8	69	25	56
Hendon	40	23	10	7	79	35	56
Bishop's Stortford	40	24	5	11	61	37	53
Sutton United	40	21	10	9	77	43	52
St Albans City	40	23	4	13	74	47	50
Ilford	40	17	11	12	62	52	45
Barking	40	20	4	16	65	61	44
Hitchin Town	40	17	10	13	68	66	44
Bromley	40	16	10	14	67	64	42
Hayes	40	14	12	14	50	48	40
Oxford City	40	13	9	18	67	74	35
Woking	40	11	10	19	52	58	32
Kingstonian	40	10	12	18	49	59	32
Walthamstow Avenue	40	12	8	20	58	71	32
Leytonstone	40	11	8	21	48	68	30
Tooting & Mitcham United	40	6	9	25	38	93	21
Clapton	40	7	7	26	45	118	21
Dulwich Hamlet	40	4	12	24	35	81	20
Corinthian Casuals	40	3	4	33	21	116	10

1972-73

	P	W	D	L	F	A	Pts
Hendon	42	34	6	2	88	18	74
Walton & Hersham	42	25	11	6	60	25	61
Leatherhead	42	23	10	9	76	32	56
Wycombe Wanderers	42	25	6	11	66	32	56
Walthamstow Avenue	42	20	12	10	66	48	52
Tooting & Mitcham United	42	20	11	11	73	39	51
Sutton United	42	21	9	12	69	48	51
Kingstonian	42	20	10	12	60	49	50
Enfield	42	20	8	14	90	54	48
Bishop's Stortford	42	18	12	12	58	51	48
Hayes	42	19	8	15	69	42	46
Dulwich Hamlet	42	18	9	15	59	52	45
Ilford	42	18	9	15	61	59	45
Leytonstone	42	17	11	14	55	54	45
Woking	42	18	8	16	61	56	44
Hitchin Town	42	15	9	18	52	64	39
Barking	42	8	7	27	45	88	23
St Albans City	42	5	12	25	34	76	22
Oxford City	42	6	7	29	30	101	19
Bromley	42	4	10	28	31	70	18
Clapton	42	3	11	28	31	100	17
Corinthian Casuals	42	3	8	31	30	106	14

1973-74 First Division

	P	W	D	L	F	A	Pts
Wycombe Wanderers	42	27	9	6	96	34	90
Hendon	42	25	13	4	63	20	88
Bishop's Stortford	42	26	9	7	78	26	87
Dulwich Hamlet	42	22	11	9	71	38	77
Leatherhead	42	23	6	13	81	44	75
Walton & Hersham	42	20	12	10	68	50	72
Woking	42	22	6	14	63	55	72
Leytonstone	42	20	9	13	63	44	69
Ilford	42	20	8	14	60	44	68
Hayes	42	17	14	11	65	43	65
Oxford City	42	15	16	11	45	47	61
Sutton United	42	13	16	13	51	52	55
Hitchin Town	42	15	10	17	68	73	55
Barking	42	14	12	16	57	58	54
Kingstonian	42	12	15	15	47	46	51
Tooting & Mitcham United	42	14	9	19	57	62	51
Enfield	42	13	11	18	50	57	50
Walthamstow Avenue	42	11	13	18	46	62	46
Bromley	42	7	9	26	37	81	30
Clapton	42	8	3	31	36	128	27
St Albans City	42	4	7	31	30	92	19
Corinthian Casuals	42	3	4	35	31	107	13

Second Division

	P	W	D	L	F	A	Pts
Dagenham	30	22	4	4	68	23	70
Slough Town	30	18	6	6	46	23	60
Hertford Town	30	17	5	8	46	29	56
Chesham Town	30	16	6	8	61	43	54
Aveley	30	16	5	9	50	28	53
Tilbury	30	14	5	11	47	36	47
Maidenhead United	30	12	11	7	36	30	47
Horsham	30	12	9	9	47	35	45
Harwich & Parkeston	30	11	9	10	46	41	42
Staines Town	30	10	8	12	34	41	38
Carshalton Athletic	30	8	8	14	34	51	32
Hampton	30	6	10	14	33	51	28
Harlow Town	30	6	9	15	33	48	27
Finchley	30	6	7	17	29	52	25
Southall	30	3	10	17	17	52	19
Wokingham Town	30	3	8	19	30	74	17

1974-75

First Division

	P	W	D	L	F	A	Pts
Wycombe Wanderers	42	28	11	3	93	30	95
Enfield	42	29	8	5	78	26	95
Dagenham	42	28	5	9	95	44	89
Tooting & Mitcham United	42	25	9	8	78	46	84
Dulwich Hamlet	42	24	10	8	75	38	82
Leatherhead	42	23	10	9	83	42	79
Ilford	42	23	10	9	98	51	79
Oxford City	42	17	9	16	63	56	60
Slough Town	42	17	6	19	68	52	57
Sutton United	42	17	6	19	68	63	57
Bishop's Stortford	42	17	6	19	56	64	57
Hitchin Town	42	15	10	17	57	71	55
Hendon	42	15	7	20	59	74	52
Walthamstow Avenue	42	13	9	20	56	62	48
Woking	42	12	10	20	53	73	46
Hayes	42	10	14	18	52	66	44
Barking	42	12	8	22	57	81	44
Leytonstone	42	12	7	23	42	61	43
Kingstonian	42	13	4	25	48	73	43
Clapton	42	12	4	26	46	96	40
Walton & Hersham	42	9	4	29	37	108	31
Bromley	42	6	3	33	25	110	21

Second Division

	P	W	D	L	F	A	Pts
Staines Town	34	23	2	9	65	23	71
Southall	34	20	3	11	55	41	63
Tilbury	34	19	5	10	64	36	60
Harwich & Parkeston	34	18	4	12	52	44	58
Chesham United	34	17	6	11	59	39	57
St Albans City	34	15	11	8	42	37	56
Harlow Town	34	16	6	12	53	47	54
Horsham	34	16	5	13	59	49	53
Maidenhead United	34	13	7	14	38	40	46
Hampton	34	12	7	15	44	42	43
Croydon	34	11	10	13	48	55	43
Hertford Town	34	10	7	17	35	52	37
Boreham Wood	34	7	15	12	41	49	36
Wokingham Town	34	10	6	18	32	43	36
Finchley	34	9	9	16	36	53	36
Carshalton Athletic	34	9	9	16	38	58	36
Aveley	34	9	7	18	34	63	34
Corinthian Casuals	34	8	9	17	35	59	33

Tilbury had 2 points deducted

1975-76 First Division

Enfield	42	26	9	7	83	38	87
Wycombe Wanderers	42	24	10	8	71	41	82
Dagenham	42	25	6	11	89	55	81
Ilford	42	22	10	10	58	39	76
Dulwich Hamlet	42	22	5	15	67	41	71
Hendon	42	20	11	11	60	41	71
Tooting & Mitcham United	42	19	11	12	73	49	68
Leatherhead	42	19	10	13	63	53	67
Staines Town	42	19	9	14	46	37	66
Slough Town	42	17	12	13	58	45	63
Sutton United	42	17	11	14	71	60	62
Bishop's Stortford	42	15	12	15	51	47	57
Walthamstow Avenue	42	14	11	17	47	60	53
Woking	42	14	9	19	58	62	51
Barking	42	15	6	21	57	70	51
Hitchin Town	42	13	11	18	45	57	50
Hayes	42	10	19	13	44	48	49
Kingstonian	42	13	8	21	53	87	47
Southall & Ealing Borough	42	11	9	22	56	69	42
Leytonstone	42	10	10	22	41	63	40
Oxford City	42	9	8	25	29	65	35
Clapton	42	3	3	36	19	112	12

Second Division

Tilbury	42	32	6	4	97	30	102
Croydon	42	28	14	0	81	27	98
Carshalton Athletic	42	28	6	8	75	37	90
Chesham United	42	21	12	9	91	51	75
Harwich & Parkeston	42	21	11	10	78	56	74
Hampton	42	21	9	12	72	52	72
St Albans City	42	18	12	12	59	48	66
Boreham Wood	42	17	12	13	68	50	63
Harrow Borough	42	15	12	15	71	74	57
Hornchurch	42	15	11	16	61	61	56
Horsham	42	14	13	15	60	55	55
Wembley	42	14	13	15	51	54	55
Wokingham Town	42	13	16	13	45	52	55
Walton & Hersham	42	14	12	16	61	56	54
Finchley	42	14	11	17	52	53	53
Bromley	42	11	11	20	64	86	44
Aveley	42	11	9	22	34	51	42
Harlow Town	42	11	9	22	50	73	42
Maidenhead United	42	6	17	19	32	65	35
Ware	42	7	12	23	50	95	33
Hertford Town	42	5	9	28	32	87	24
Corinthian Casuals	42	4	7	31	42	113	19

1976-77 First Division

Enfield	42	24	12	6	63	34	84
Wycombe Wanderers	42	25	8	9	71	34	83
Dagenham	42	23	10	9	80	39	79
Hendon	42	19	10	13	60	48	67
Tilbury	42	18	13	11	57	49	67
Tooting & Mitcham	42	18	10	14	85	72	64
Walthamstow Avenue	42	19	7	16	61	55	64
Slough Town	42	18	9	15	51	46	63
Hitchin Town	42	19	6	17	60	66	63
Leatherhead	42	18	7	17	61	47	61
Staines Town	42	16	13	13	52	48	61
Leytonstone	42	16	11	15	59	57	59
Barking	42	16	9	17	63	61	57
Southall & Ealing Borough	42	15	8	19	52	64	53
Croydon	42	13	10	19	38	52	49
Sutton United	42	14	7	21	40	55	49
Kingstonian	42	13	7	22	45	60	46
Hayes	42	12	10	20	49	69	46
Woking	42	11	12	19	47	61	45
Bishop's Stortford	42	11	11	20	51	71	44
Dulwich Hamlet	42	11	8	23	52	68	41
Ilford	42	10	8	24	32	73	38

Second Division

Boreham Wood	42	35	4	5	80	26	103
Carshalton Athletic	42	25	12	5	80	33	87
Harwich & Parkeston	42	23	8	11	93	61	77
Wembley	42	23	8	11	82	58	77
Harrow Borough	42	21	12	9	78	44	75
Horsham	42	23	5	14	67	56	74
Bromley	42	20	10	12	71	46	70
Oxford City	42	20	8	14	73	55	68
Hampton	42	20	8	14	62	45	68
Wokingham Town	42	16	14	12	60	44	62
Hornchurch	42	18	7	17	62	53	61
Chesham United	42	17	10	15	63	66	61
St Albans City	42	16	12	14	59	53	60
Walton & Hersham	42	17	9	16	57	56	60
Aveley	42	14	8	20	49	62	50
Corinthian Casuals	42	13	6	23	52	75	45
Harlow Town	42	11	8	23	39	77	41
Hertford Town	42	9	9	24	45	80	36
Maidenhead United	42	8	8	26	36	73	32
Clapton	42	7	9	28	43	87	30
Finchley	42	5	13	24	36	82	28
Ware	42	5	8	29	43	98	23

1977-78 Premier Division

Enfield	42	35	5	2	96	27	110
Dagenham	42	24	7	11	78	55	79
Wycombe Wanderers	42	22	9	11	66	41	75
Tooting & Mitcham United	42	22	8	12	64	49	74
Hitchin Town	42	20	9	13	69	53	69
Sutton United	42	18	12	12	66	57	66
Leatherhead	42	18	11	13	62	48	65
Croydon	42	18	10	14	61	52	64
Walthamstow Avenue	42	17	12	13	64	61	63
Barking	42	17	7	18	76	66	58
Carshalton Athletic	42	15	11	16	60	62	56
Hayes	42	15	11	16	46	53	56
Hendon	42	16	7	19	57	55	55
Woking	42	14	11	17	62	62	53
Boreham Wood	42	15	8	19	48	65	53
Slough Town	42	14	8	20	52	69	0
Staines Town	42	12	13	17	46	60	49
Tilbury	42	11	12	19	57	68	45
Kingstonian	42	8	13	21	43	65	37
Leytonstone	42	7	15	20	44	71	36
Southall & Ealing Borough	42	6	15	21	43	74	33
Bishop's Stortford	42	7	8	27	36	83	29

First Division

Dulwich Hamlet	42	28	9	5	91	25	93
Oxford City	42	26	5	11	85	44	83
Bromley	42	23	13	6	74	41	82
Walton & Hersham	42	22	11	9	69	41	77
Ilford	42	21	14	7	57	47	77
St Albans City	42	22	10	10	83	46	76
Wokingham Town	42	19	12	11	69	48	69
Harlow Town	42	19	8	15	63	49	65
Harrow Borough	42	17	10	15	59	54	61
Maidenhead United	42	16	13	13	55	54	61
Hertford Town	42	15	14	13	57	51	59
Chesham United	42	14	13	15	69	70	55
Hampton	42	13	13	16	49	53	52
Harwich & Parkeston	42	12	13	17	68	79	49
Wembley	42	15	3	24	56	82	48
Horsham	42	12	10	20	41	57	46
Finchley	42	11	13	18	41	68	46
Aveley	42	13	7	22	47	75	46
Ware	42	8	13	21	61	95	37
Clapton	42	10	6	26	46	78	36
Hornchurch	42	8	10	24	47	81	34
Corinthian Casuals	42	3	10	29	40	88	19

Second Division

	P	W	D	L	F	A	Pts
Epsom & Ewell	32	21	5	6	65	34	68
Metropolitan Police	32	19	6	7	53	30	63
Farnborough Town	32	19	4	9	68	40	61
Molesey	32	17	8	7	47	27	59
Egham Town	32	15	9	8	52	34	54
Tring Town	32	14	11	7	62	32	53
Letchworth Garden City	32	14	11	7	67	48	53
Lewes	32	13	7	12	52	51	46
Rainham Town	32	13	6	13	42	50	45
Worthing	32	11	9	12	40	45	42
Eastbourne United	32	10	8	14	40	50	38
Cheshunt	32	9	6	17	43	60	33
Feltham	32	7	9	16	30	49	30
Camberley Town	32	6	11	15	32	49	29
Hemel Hempstead	32	6	9	17	33	50	27
Epping Town	32	7	6	19	37	64	27
Willesden	32	7	3	22	38	88	24

Second Division

	P	W	D	L	F	A	Pts
Farnborough Town	34	26	3	5	77	34	81
Camberley Town	34	21	8	5	71	32	71
Molesey	34	19	11	4	55	33	68
Lewes	34	19	6	9	66	50	63
Feltham	34	16	7	11	47	36	55
Letchworth Garden City	34	14	10	10	56	48	52
Eastbourne United	34	16	4	14	47	45	52
Hemel Hempstead	34	13	11	10	46	37	50
Epping Town	34	14	7	13	49	44	49
Rainham Town	34	13	10	11	42	41	49
Cheshunt	34	11	8	15	43	49	41
Hungerford Town	34	11	8	15	48	58	41
Worthing	34	9	8	17	40	50	35
Hornchurch	34	9	8	17	39	62	35
Egham Town	34	7	12	15	48	54	33
Tring Town	34	6	8	20	33	56	26
Willesden	34	6	8	20	41	77	26
Corinthian Casuals	34	4	7	23	23	65	19

1978-79

Premier Division

	P	W	D	L	F	A	Pts
Barking	42	28	9	5	92	50	93
Dagenham	42	25	6	11	83	63	81
Enfield	42	22	11	9	69	37	77
Dulwich Hamlet	42	21	13	8	69	39	76
Slough Town	42	20	12	10	61	44	72
Wycombe Wanderers	42	20	9	13	59	44	69
Woking	42	18	14	10	79	59	68
Croydon	42	19	9	14	61	51	66
Hendon	42	16	14	12	55	48	62
Leatherhead	42	17	9	16	57	45	60
Sutton United	42	17	9	16	62	51	60
Tooting & Mitcham United	42	15	14	13	52	52	59
Walthamstow Avenue	42	15	6	21	61	69	51
Tilbury	42	13	1	18	60	76	50
Boreham Wood	42	13	10	19	50	67	49
Hitchin Town	42	12	11	19	59	71	47
Carshalton Athletic	42	10	16	16	49	69	46
Hayes	42	9	18	15	45	58	45
Oxford City	42	12	7	23	50	80	43
Staines Town	42	6	16	20	40	64	34
Leytonstone	42	8	7	27	36	75	31
Kingstonian	42	3	15	24	35	72	24

First Division

	P	W	D	L	F	A	Pts
Harlow Town	42	31	7	4	93	32	100
Harrow Borough	42	26	8	8	85	49	86
Maidenhead United	42	25	6	11	72	50	81
Bishop's Stortford	42	22	11	9	68	40	77
Horsham	42	23	7	12	63	47	76
Hertford Town	42	21	11	10	62	41	74
Harwich & Parkeston	42	22	5	15	90	57	71
Bromley	42	18	12	12	76	50	66
Hampton	42	17	11	14	59	47	62
Epsom & Ewell	42	18	7	17	69	57	61
Wembley	42	15	14	13	57	50	59
Aveley	42	17	6	19	57	67	57
Wokingham Town	42	17	8	17	64	68	56
Clapton	42	15	8	19	67	80	53
Metropolitan Police	42	12	13	17	58	55	49
Walton & Hersham	42	12	9	21	47	71	45
Ilford	42	13	5	24	48	80	44
Ware	42	11	10	21	46	69	43
Chesham United	42	11	9	22	46	66	42
Finchley	42	7	15	20	43	74	36
St Albans City	42	7	7	28	43	90	28
Southall & Ealing Borough	42	5	5	32	41	114	20

Wokingham Town had 3 points deducted

1979-80

Premier Division

	P	W	D	L	F	A	Pts
Enfield	42	25	9	8	74	32	84
Walthamstow Avenue	42	24	9	9	87	48	81
Dulwich Hamlet	42	21	16	5	66	37	79
Sutton United	42	20	13	9	67	40	73
Dagenham	42	20	13	9	82	56	73
Tooting & Mitcham United	42	21	6	15	62	59	69
Barking	42	19	10	13	72	51	67
Harrow Borough	42	17	15	10	64	51	66
Woking	42	17	13	12	78	59	64
Wycombe Wanderers	42	17	13	12	72	53	64
Harlow Town	42	14	12	16	55	61	54
Hitchin Town	42	13	15	14	55	69	54
Hendon	42	12	13	17	50	57	49
Slough Town	42	13	10	19	54	71	49
Boreham Wood	42	13	10	19	50	69	49
Staines Town	42	14	6	22	46	67	48
Hayes	42	12	9	21	48	68	45
Leatherhead	42	11	11	20	51	60	44
Carshalton Athletic	42	12	7	23	48	78	43
Croydon	42	10	10	22	51	59	40
Oxford City	42	10	9	23	49	87	39
Tilbury	42	7	11	24	41	90	30

Tilbury had 2 points deducted

First Division

	P	W	D	L	F	A	Pts
Leytonstone & Ilford	42	31	6	5	83	35	99
Bromley	42	24	10	8	93	44	82
Maidenhead United	42	24	8	10	81	46	80
Bishop's Stortford	42	24	8	10	74	47	80
Kingstonian	42	22	8	12	59	44	74
Chesham United	42	18	13	11	68	56	67
St Albans City	42	17	13	12	65	47	64
Farnborough Town	42	19	7	16	70	57	64
Epsom & Ewell	42	18	7	17	62	57	61
Camberley Town	42	16	10	16	43	38	58
Walton & Hersham	42	15	12	15	61	50	57
Wembley	42	16	8	18	46	52	56
Wokingham Town	42	14	11	17	45	49	53
Hertford Town	42	13	11	18	71	74	50
Aveley	42	12	13	17	45	55	49
Hampton	42	14	7	21	57	74	49
Finchley	42	13	9	20	44	59	48
Metropolitan Police	42	13	8	21	46	67	47
Ware	42	11	12	19	45	61	45
Clapton	42	14	3	25	48	77	45
Harwich & Parkeston	42	11	6	25	51	84	38
Horsham	42	6	4	32	29	113	22

Harwich & Parkeston had 1 point deducted

Second Division

Billericay Town	36	31	3	2	100	18	96
Lewes	36	24	7	5	82	33	79
Hungerford Town	36	21	8	7	78	36	71
Eastbourne United	36	21	6	9	77	45	69
Letchworth Garden City	36	21	6	9	63	32	69
Hornchurch	36	21	6	9	66	39	69
Molesey	36	15	9	12	67	60	54
Barton Rovers	36	15	7	14	49	49	52
Worthing	36	14	9	13	58	54	51
Cheshunt	36	13	7	16	47	52	46
Rainham Town	36	12	7	17	54	65	43
Egham Town	36	11	9	16	47	53	42
Southall & Ealing Borough	36	11	6	19	43	69	39
Feltham	36	8	11	17	23	49	35
Tring Town	36	7	13	16	38	55	34
Epping Town	36	10	4	22	44	69	34
Willesden	36	9	6	21	32	83	33
Hemel Hempstead	36	4	9	23	33	72	21
Corinthian Casuals	36	6	3	27	24	92	21

Second Division

Feltham	38	24	10	4	65	30	82
Hornchurch	38	25	6	7	74	35	81
Hungerford Town	38	23	10	5	84	29	79
Barton Rovers	38	19	11	8	61	25	68
Worthing	38	19	11	8	74	43	68
Cheshunt	38	19	11	8	57	33	68
Letchworth Garden City	38	18	7	13	49	40	61
Southall	38	14	11	13	48	52	53
Dorking Town	38	13	12	13	47	45	51
Horsham	38	16	3	19	47	47	51
Hemel Hempstead	38	14	7	17	47	54	49
Egham Town	38	13	9	16	45	62	48
Harwich & Parkeston	38	12	11	15	57	58	47
Rainham Town	38	11	13	14	44	45	46
Epping Town	38	12	7	19	37	50	43
Eastbourne United	38	11	10	17	59	75	43
Willesden	38	11	8	19	57	68	41
Tring Town	38	11	6	21	40	71	39
Molesey	38	4	9	25	31	83	21
Corinthian Casuals	38	1	8	29	17	95	11

1980-81   Premier Division

Slough Town	42	23	13	6	73	34	82
Enfield	42	23	11	8	81	43	80
Wycombe Wanderers	42	22	9	11	76	49	75
Leytonstone & Ilford	42	19	12	11	78	57	69
Sutton United	42	19	12	11	82	65	69
Hendon	42	18	10	14	66	58	64
Dagenham	42	17	11	14	79	66	62
Hayes	42	18	8	16	45	50	62
Harrow Borough	42	16	11	15	57	52	59
Bromley	42	16	9	17	63	69	57
Staines Town	42	15	9	18	60	61	54
Tooting & Mitcham United	42	15	8	19	49	53	53
Hitchin Town	42	14	10	18	64	62	52
Croydon	42	12	15	15	51	51	51
Dulwich Hamlet	42	13	12	17	62	67	51
Leatherhead	42	12	14	16	36	50	50
Carshalton Athletic	42	14	8	20	57	82	50
Barking	42	13	12	17	58	72	49
Harlow Town	42	11	15	16	53	66	48
Walthamstow Avenue	42	13	7	22	50	81	46
Boreham Wood	42	10	13	19	46	69	43
Woking	42	11	7	24	40	69	37

Barking had 1 point deducted
Woking had 3 points deducted

First Division

Bishop's Stortford	42	30	6	6	84	28	96
Billericay Town	42	29	6	7	67	34	93
Epsom & Ewell	42	24	12	6	80	36	84
Farnborough Town	42	23	11	8	75	39	80
St Albans City	42	24	5	13	85	61	77
Kingstonian	42	20	9	13	63	52	66
Oxford City	42	18	9	15	71	48	63
Wokingham Town	42	16	15	11	70	56	63
Metropolitan Police	42	18	7	17	61	58	61
Chesham United	42	17	7	18	64	64	58
Lewes	42	17	7	18	72	83	58
Maidenhead United	42	16	7	19	58	62	55
Walton & Hersham	42	12	15	15	46	53	51
Hertford Town	42	13	11	18	46	65	50
Hampton	42	12	13	17	46	53	49
Aveley	42	13	9	20	54	55	48
Wembley	42	13	8	21	47	61	47
Clapton	42	12	8	22	53	86	44
Ware	42	9	13	20	50	69	40
Tilbury	42	10	8	24	42	84	35
Camberley Town	42	8	7	27	42	88	31
Finchley	42	6	11	25	36	77	29

Kingstonian and Tilbury both had 3 points deducted

1981-82

Premier Division

Leytonstone & Ilford	42	26	5	11	91	52	83
Sutton United	42	22	9	11	72	49	75
Wycombe Wanderers	42	21	10	11	63	48	73
Staines Town	42	21	9	12	58	45	72
Walthamstow Avenue	42	21	7	14	81	62	70
Harrow Borough	42	18	13	11	77	55	67
Tooting & Mitcham United	42	19	10	13	58	47	67
Slough Town	42	17	13	12	64	54	64
Leatherhead	42	16	12	14	57	52	60
Hayes	42	16	10	16	58	52	58
Croydon	42	16	9	17	59	57	57
Barking	42	14	14	14	53	51	56
Hendon	42	13	13	16	56	65	52
Dulwich Hamlet	42	14	10	18	47	59	52
Bishop's Stortford	42	15	5	22	50	70	50
Carshalton Athletic	42	14	8	20	58	86	50
Billericay Town	42	11	16	15	41	50	49
Hitchin Town	42	12	11	19	56	77	47
Bromley	42	13	7	22	63	79	46
Woking	42	11	13	18	57	75	46
Harlow Town	42	10	11	21	50	73	41
Boreham Wood	42	8	13	21	47	58	37

First Division

Wokingham Town	40	29	5	6	86	30	92
Bognor Regis Town	40	23	10	7	65	34	79
Metropolitan Police	40	22	11	7	75	48	77
Oxford City	40	21	11	8	82	47	74
Feltham	40	20	8	12	65	49	68
Lewes	40	19	7	14	73	66	64
Hertford Town	40	16	10	14	62	54	58
Wembley	40	14	15	11	69	55	57
Farnborough Town	40	15	11	14	71	57	56
Epsom & Ewell	40	16	8	16	52	44	56
Kingstonian	40	16	7	17	57	56	55
Hampton	40	15	9	16	52	52	54
Hornchurch	40	13	15	12	42	50	54
Aveley	40	14	10	16	46	58	52
St Albans City	40	14	9	17	55	55	51
Maidenhead United	40	11	10	19	49	70	43
Tilbury	40	9	15	16	49	66	42
Walton & Hersham	40	10	11	19	43	65	41
Chesham United	40	9	9	22	41	71	36
Clapton	40	9	7	24	44	75	34
Ware	40	5	2	33	29	105	17

Second Division

Worthing	40	29	6	5	95	25	93
Cheshunt	40	25	7	8	79	33	82
Hungerford Town	40	22	10	8	89	42	74
Barton Rovers	40	22	8	10	65	32	74
Windsor & Eton	40	22	6	12	69	49	72
Corinthian Casuals	40	19	12	9	67	50	69
Harwich & Parkeston	40	19	12	9	64	47	69
Letchworth Garden City	40	15	11	14	67	55	56
Dorking Town	40	13	17	10	52	44	56
Hemel Hempstead	40	15	9	16	54	49	54
Basildon United	40	16	5	19	64	51	53
Finchley	40	14	9	17	57	68	51
Southall	40	12	14	14	36	42	50
Epping Town	40	12	11	17	48	62	47
Molesey	40	13	7	20	61	73	46
Egham Town	40	11	9	20	56	64	42
Rainham Town	40	11	9	20	53	83	42
Tring Town	40	9	13	18	49	78	40
Eastbourne United	40	9	12	19	51	73	39
Horsham	40	10	9	21	42	79	39
Camberley Town	40	3	2	35	21	140	11

Hungerford Town had 2 points deducted

1982-83   Premier Division

Wycombe Wanderers	42	26	7	9	79	47	85
Leytonstone & Ilford	42	24	9	9	71	39	81
Harrow Borough	42	24	7	11	91	58	79
Hayes	42	23	9	10	63	41	78
Sutton United	42	20	8	14	96	71	68
Dulwich Hamlet	42	18	14	10	59	52	68
Slough Town	42	18	13	11	73	36	67
Bognor Regis Town	42	19	8	15	53	48	65
Tooting & Mitcham United	42	18	9	15	65	62	63
Billericay Town	42	17	10	15	54	51	61
Croydon	42	17	9	16	68	58	60
Hendon	42	18	6	18	68	61	60
Bishop's Stortford	42	17	9	16	61	58	60
Barking	42	14	14	14	47	55	56
Bromley	42	14	12	16	51	50	54
Carshalton Athletic	42	15	9	18	58	60	54
Wokingham Town	42	13	9	20	37	51	48
Walthamstow Avenue	42	12	11	19	48	64	47
Staines Town	42	12	11	19	62	79	47
Hitchin Town	42	11	9	22	49	77	42
Woking	42	6	6	30	30	79	24
Leatherhead	42	4	5	33	35	121	17

First Division

Worthing	40	25	6	9	76	39	81
Harlow Town	40	21	11	8	84	55	74
Farnborough Town	40	20	13	7	69	39	73
Hertford Town	40	20	11	9	70	61	71
Oxford City	40	19	13	8	70	49	70
Boreham Wood	40	21	6	13	62	42	69
Metropolitan Police	40	19	9	12	77	57	66
Walton & Hersham	40	17	6	17	65	59	57
Hampton	40	15	10	15	62	60	55
Wembley	40	14	10	16	62	61	52
Aveley	40	15	7	18	52	62	52
Kingstonian	40	13	12	15	53	53	51
Tilbury	40	12	10	18	41	47	46
Feltham	40	11	12	17	45	54	45
Chesham United	40	13	6	21	43	70	45
Epsom & Ewell	40	10	14	16	44	49	44
Lewes	40	12	8	20	47	71	44
Cheshunt	40	10	13	17	41	49	43
Hornchurch	40	11	8	21	45	74	41
Maidenhead United	40	10	10	20	57	87	40
St Albans City	40	10	9	21	52	79	37

St Albans City had 2 points deducted

Second Division

Clapton	42	30	4	8	96	46	94
Windsor & Eton	42	27	7	8	98	43	88
Barton Rovers	42	26	6	10	86	48	84
Leyton Wingate	42	25	8	9	111	41	83
Basildon United	42	23	13	6	92	42	82
Uxbridge	42	22	12	8	80	42	78
Hungerford Town	42	22	10	10	82	39	76
Corinthian Casuals	42	23	6	13	95	48	75
Egham Town	42	21	8	13	77	67	71
Tring Town	42	20	10	12	86	59	70
Letchworth Garden City	42	18	13	11	68	53	66
Southall	42	18	7	17	81	80	61
Molesey	42	17	9	16	73	56	60
Dorking Town	42	15	9	18	56	75	54
Hemel Hempstead	42	12	14	16	53	59	50
Rainham Town	42	14	4	24	57	94	46
Eastbourne United	42	10	6	26	54	104	36
Epping Town	42	6	8	28	29	89	26
Ware	42	6	6	30	34	97	24
Finchley	42	4	12	26	28	92	24
Horsham	42	5	7	30	32	106	22
Harwich & Parkeston	42	5	7	30	42	130	22

Letchworth Garden City had 1 point deducted

1983-84   Premier Division

Harrow Borough	42	25	13	4	73	42	88
Worthing	42	20	11	11	89	72	71
Slough Town	42	20	9	13	73	56	69
Sutton United	42	18	12	12	67	45	66
Hayes	42	17	13	12	56	41	64
Hitchin Town	42	16	15	11	58	57	63
Wycombe Wanderers	42	16	14	12	63	52	62
Wokingham Town	42	18	10	14	78	55	61
Hendon	42	17	10	15	62	51	61
Dulwich Hamlet	42	16	11	15	61	64	59
Bishop's Stortford	42	15	13	14	56	57	58
Harlow Town	42	15	11	16	64	64	56
Bognor Regis Town	42	14	13	15	62	69	55
Staines Town	42	15	9	18	63	72	54
Billericay Town	42	15	8	19	53	73	53
Barking	42	13	13	16	60	64	52
Croydon	42	14	10	18	52	58	52
Walthamstow Avenue	42	13	10	19	53	67	49
Leytonstone & Ilford	42	13	9	20	54	67	48
Carshalton Athletic	42	11	10	21	59	72	43
Tooting & Mitcham United	42	10	13	19	50	63	43
Bromley	42	7	11	24	33	72	32

Wokingham Town had 3 points deducted

First Division

Windsor & Eton	42	26	7	9	89	44	85
Epsom & Ewell	42	23	9	10	73	51	78
Wembley	42	21	11	10	65	32	74
Maidenhead United	42	22	8	12	67	42	74
Boreham Wood	42	22	7	13	74	43	73
Farnborough Town	42	18	12	12	78	60	66
Hampton	42	18	12	12	65	49	66
Metropolitan Police	42	20	5	17	79	64	65
Chesham United	42	18	8	16	64	57	62
Tilbury	42	17	10	15	54	64	61
Leatherhead	42	15	10	17	67	56	55
Aveley	42	15	10	17	49	53	55
Woking	42	16	7	19	66	73	55
Hertford Town	42	15	9	18	56	73	54
Oxford City	42	14	9	19	57	56	51
Lewes	42	13	12	17	49	65	51
Walton & Hersham	42	13	10	19	52	70	49
Hornchurch	42	13	10	19	43	63	49
Kingstonian	42	13	9	20	47	67	48
Clapton	42	12	11	19	49	67	47
Cheshunt	42	12	8	22	45	64	44
Feltham	42	7	4	31	31	106	25

Second Division

Basildon United	42	30	7	5	88	27	97
St Albans City	42	29	9	5	100	46	96
Leyton Wingate	42	29	4	9	97	41	91
Tring Town	42	23	11	8	89	44	80
Corinthian Casuals	42	23	11	8	75	47	80
Hungerford Town	42	21	12	9	94	47	75
Uxbridge	42	18	15	9	61	36	69
Grays Athletic	42	20	9	13	72	57	69
Dorking	42	21	5	16	66	54	68
Southall	42	20	8	14	79	60	65
Egham Town	42	16	15	11	59	49	63
Epping Town	42	15	16	11	61	50	61
Molesey	42	13	14	15	59	68	53
Barton Rovers	42	15	8	19	54	64	53
Letchworth Garden City	42	15	7	20	48	66	52
Newbury Town	42	14	5	23	60	82	47
Hemel Hempstead	42	12	9	21	63	69	45
Rainham Town	42	7	5	30	38	114	26
Finchley	42	5	9	28	28	78	24
Eastbourne United	42	7	3	32	36	98	24
Ware	42	6	6	30	48	114	24
Horsham	42	7	4	31	40	104	23

Southall had 2 points deducted
Horsham had 3 points deducted

1984-85

Premier Division

Sutton United	42	23	15	4	115	55	84
Worthing	42	24	8	10	89	59	80
Wycombe Wanderers	42	24	6	12	68	46	78
Wokingham Town	42	20	13	9	74	54	73
Windsor & Eton	42	19	10	13	65	55	67
Bognor Regis Town	42	20	6	16	67	58	66
Dulwich Hamlet	42	16	17	9	82	57	65
Harrow Borough	42	18	8	16	70	56	62
Hayes	42	17	8	17	60	56	59
Tooting & Mitcham United	42	16	11	15	64	66	59
Walthamstow Avenue	42	15	11	16	64	65	56
Croydon	42	15	12	15	62	63	54
Epsom & Ewell	42	13	14	15	65	62	53
Slough Town	42	13	12	17	69	74	51
Carshalton Athletic	42	14	8	20	55	68	50
Bishop's Stortford	42	12	12	18	48	67	48
Hendon	42	9	19	14	62	65	46
Billericay Town	42	11	14	17	53	74	46
Barking	42	13	7	22	43	75	46
Hitchin Town	42	10	15	17	55	70	45
Leytonstone & Ilford	42	11	10	21	37	72	43
Harlow Town	42	5	12	25	45	95	27

Billericay Town had 1 point deducted
Croydon had 3 points deducted

First Division

Farnborough Town	42	26	8	8	101	45	86
Kingstonian	42	23	10	9	67	39	79
Leatherhead	42	23	10	9	109	61	76
Chesham United	42	22	8	12	78	46	74
Wembley	42	20	10	12	59	40	70
St Albans City	42	19	10	13	79	60	67
Tilbury	42	18	13	11	86	68	67
Bromley	42	18	9	15	71	64	63
Hampton	42	17	11	14	75	62	62
Staines Town	42	16	11	15	59	53	59
Maidenhead United	42	17	8	17	65	64	59
Walton & Hersham	42	16	8	18	60	69	55
Aveley	42	16	7	19	62	78	55
Oxford City	42	14	12	16	62	53	54
Lewes	42	15	9	18	70	72	54
Basildon United	42	15	8	19	55	61	53
Boreham Wood	42	15	7	20	72	83	52
Hornchurch	42	15	6	21	55	74	51
Woking	42	15	6	21	60	91	51
Metropolitan Police	42	10	12	20	65	92	42
Clapton	42	5	11	26	50	124	26
Hertford Town	42	5	10	27	36	97	25

Walton & Hersham had 1 point deducted
Leatherhead had 3 points deducted

Second Division North

Leyton Wingate	38	24	9	5	98	50	81
Finchley	38	24	8	6	66	31	79
Heybridge Swifts	38	22	9	7	71	33	75
Stevenage Borough	38	23	6	9	79	49	75
Saffron Walden Town	38	22	8	8	73	31	74
Tring Town	38	19	11	8	76	41	68
Chalfont St Peter	38	17	10	11	72	41	61
Flackwell Heath	38	16	11	11	54	40	59
Berkhamsted Town	38	15	12	11	50	42	57
Letchworth Garden City	38	17	6	15	66	69	57
Royston Town	38	13	9	16	47	77	48
Cheshunt	38	14	5	19	52	57	47
Marlow	38	13	6	19	64	81	45
Hemel Hempstead	38	11	7	20	49	65	40
Barton Rovers	38	9	8	21	40	62	35
Wolverton Town	38	9	8	21	38	77	35
Kingsbury Town	38	9	7	22	53	72	34
Harefield United	38	7	9	22	51	81	30
Haringey Borough	38	6	12	20	38	79	30
Ware	38	7	5	26	40	100	26

Finchley had 1 point deducted
The record of Epping Town was expunged

Second Division South

Grays Athletic	36	24	9	3	84	25	81
Uxbridge	36	22	10	4	81	20	76
Molesey	36	20	5	11	62	42	65
Hungerford Town	36	18	9	9	71	49	63
Whyteleafe	36	17	10	9	66	34	61
Egham Town	36	17	7	12	54	42	58
Southall	36	18	3	15	54	57	57
Bracknell Town	36	15	7	14	54	48	52
Banstead Athletic	36	14	8	14	63	70	50
Horsham	36	13	10	13	44	39	49
Ruislip Manor	36	13	10	13	48	49	49
Dorking	36	12	11	13	45	50	47
Rainham Town	36	12	8	16	58	61	44
Feltham	36	10	13	13	44	58	43
Camberley Town	36	10	12	14	44	54	42
Eastbourne United	36	10	9	17	66	72	39
Petersfield Town	36	9	5	22	41	80	32
Newbury Town	36	8	7	21	35	69	16
Chertsey Town	36	2	3	31	23	118	6

Chertsey Town had 3 points deducted
Newbury Town had 15 points deducted

1985-86

Premier Division

Sutton United	42	29	8	5	109	39	95
Yeovil Town	42	28	7	7	92	48	91
Farnborough Town	42	23	8	11	90	50	77
Croydon	42	23	7	12	70	50	76
Harrow Borough	42	21	8	13	76	66	71
Slough Town	42	18	8	16	66	68	62
Bishop's Stortford	42	17	10	15	55	61	61
Kingstonian	42	15	15	12	57	56	60
Dulwich Hamlet	42	17	9	16	64	79	60
Wokingham Town	42	16	10	16	67	64	58
Windsor & Eton	42	17	7	18	58	75	58
Tooting & Mitcham United	42	14	11	17	65	76	53
Walthamstow Avenue	42	12	14	16	69	70	50
Worthing	42	13	10	19	72	82	49
Bognor Regis Town	42	15	6	21	63	70	48
Hayes	42	10	17	15	36	42	47
Hitchin Town	42	11	14	17	53	69	47
Barking	42	11	13	18	45	55	46
Hendon	42	10	13	19	59	77	43
Carshalton Athletic	42	9	13	20	56	79	40
Billericay Town	42	9	12	21	59	78	39
Epsom & Ewell	42	8	12	22	63	90	36

Bognor Regis Town had 3 points deducted

First Division

St Albans City	42	23	11	8	92	61	80
Bromley	42	24	8	10	68	41	80
Wembley	42	22	12	8	59	30	78
Oxford City	42	22	11	9	75	51	77
Hampton	42	21	11	10	63	45	74
Leyton Wingate	42	21	10	11	77	56	73
Uxbridge	42	20	8	14	64	49	68
Staines Town	42	18	10	14	69	66	64
Boreham Wood	42	15	16	11	62	54	61
Walton & Hersham	42	16	10	16	68	71	58
Lewes	42	16	8	18	61	75	56
Leytonstone & Ilford	42	13	15	14	57	67	54
Finchley	42	12	17	13	61	59	53
Grays Athletic	42	13	11	18	69	75	50
Leatherhead	42	14	8	20	62	68	50
Tilbury	42	13	11	18	60	66	50
Maidenhead United	42	13	7	22	61	67	46
Basildon United	42	12	9	21	52	72	45
Hornchurch	42	11	11	20	44	59	44
Chesham United	42	12	6	24	51	87	42
Harlow Town	42	8	14	20	53	70	38
Aveley	42	8	6	28	59	98	30

Second Division North

Stevenage Borough	38	26	6	6	71	24	84
Kingsbury Town	38	25	8	5	84	35	83
Heybridge Swifts	38	20	8	10	65	46	68
Cheshunt	38	18	10	10	60	40	64
Hertford Town	38	17	7	14	60	50	58
Chalfont St Peter	38	15	11	12	53	50	56
Tring Town	38	14	13	11	58	46	55
Royston Town	38	13	13	12	59	57	52
Saffron Walden Town	38	13	12	13	61	65	51
Berkhamsted Town	38	14	8	16	45	52	50
Haringey Borough	38	14	7	17	49	51	49
Letchworth Garden City	38	13	8	17	46	52	47
Rainham Town	38	14	4	20	54	91	46
Hemel Hempstead	38	12	9	17	50	66	45
Ware	38	11	11	16	56	61	44
Vauxhall Motors	38	11	10	17	58	62	43
Barton Rovers	38	12	7	19	50	60	43
Harefield United	38	9	12	17	56	72	39
Clapton	38	10	7	21	51	90	37
Wolverton Town	38	8	11	19	42	58	35

Second Division South

Southwick	38	25	8	5	86	34	83
Bracknell Town	38	24	9	5	80	23	81
Woking	38	23	9	6	94	45	78
Newbury Town	38	22	7	9	86	53	73
Whyteleafe	38	21	10	7	61	41	73
Molesey	38	21	8	9	59	39	71
Metropolitan Police	38	20	6	12	72	48	66
Southall	38	19	7	12	76	58	64
Dorking	38	18	10	10	70	57	64
Feltham	38	16	7	15	65	60	55
Banstead Athletic	38	15	8	15	60	66	53
Petersfield United	38	12	9	17	61	71	45
Hungerford Town	38	11	6	21	57	78	39
Flackwell Heath	38	11	6	21	46	72	39
Eastbourne United	38	9	8	21	51	81	35
Camberley Town	38	9	7	22	53	64	34
Egham Town	38	7	8	23	41	83	29
Horsham	38	6	10	22	33	74	28
Ruislip Manor	38	5	12	21	44	87	27
Marlow	38	6	5	27	47	108	23

1986-87

Premier Division

Wycombe Wanderers	42	32	5	5	103	32	101
Yeovil Town	42	28	8	6	71	27	92
Slough Town	42	23	8	11	70	44	77
Hendon	42	22	7	13	67	53	73
Bognor Regis Town	42	20	10	12	85	61	70
Harrow Borough	42	20	10	12	68	44	70
Croydon	42	18	10	14	51	48	64
Barking	42	16	14	12	76	56	62
Farnborough Town	42	17	11	14	66	72	62
Bishop's Stortford	42	15	15	12	62	57	60
Bromley	42	16	11	15	63	72	59
Kingstonian	42	16	9	17	58	50	57
Windsor & Eton	42	13	15	14	47	52	54
St Albans City	42	14	9	19	61	70	51
Carshalton Athletic	42	13	9	20	55	68	48
Wokingham Town	42	14	6	22	47	61	48
Hayes	42	12	12	18	45	68	48
Dulwich Hamlet	42	12	10	20	62	71	46
Tooting & Mitcham United	42	12	9	21	41	53	45
Hitchin Town	42	13	5	24	56	69	44
Worthing	42	8	9	25	58	107	33
Walthamstow Avenue	42	4	6	32	36	113	18

First Division

Leytonstone & Ilford	42	30	5	7	78	29	95
Leyton Wingate	42	23	13	6	68	31	82
Bracknell Town	42	24	9	9	92	48	81
Southwick	42	23	7	12	80	66	76
Wembley	42	21	9	12	61	47	72
Grays Athletic	42	19	10	13	76	64	67
Kingsbury Town	42	20	7	15	69	67	67
Boreham Wood	42	20	6	16	59	52	66
Uxbridge	42	18	9	15	60	59	63
Leatherhead	42	17	11	14	45	48	62
Hampton	42	18	5	19	57	55	59
Basildon United	42	16	10	16	58	68	58
Billericay Town	42	14	12	16	57	52	54
Staines Town	42	13	13	16	40	51	52
Lewes	42	15	6	21	55	65	51
Stevenage Borough	42	12	11	19	61	67	47
Oxford City	42	11	10	21	64	72	43
Walton & Hersham	42	11	10	21	53	74	43
Tilbury	42	12	7	23	46	70	43
Epsom & Ewell	42	12	7	23	44	68	43
Maidenhead United	42	11	4	27	44	76	37
Finchley	42	6	11	25	44	90	29

Second Division North

	P	W	D	L	F	A	Pts
Chesham United	42	28	6	8	81	48	90
Wolverton Town	42	23	14	5	74	32	83
Haringey Borough	42	22	13	7	86	40	79
Heybridge Swifts	42	21	11	10	81	54	74
Aveley	42	19	13	10	68	50	70
Letchworth Garden City	42	19	11	12	77	62	68
Barton Rovers	42	18	11	13	49	39	65
Tring Town	42	19	7	16	69	49	64
Collier Row	42	19	5	18	67	65	62
Ware	42	17	8	17	51	50	59
Saffron Walden Town	42	14	14	14	56	54	56
Wivenhoe Town	42	15	11	16	61	61	56
Vauxhall Motors	42	15	10	17	61	57	55
Hornchurch	42	13	16	13	60	60	55
Hertford Town	42	14	13	15	52	53	55
Berkhamsted Town	42	12	16	14	62	64	52
Harlow Town	42	13	11	18	45	55	50
Rainham Town	42	12	11	19	53	70	47
Clapton	42	10	11	21	45	63	41
Hemel Hempstead	42	9	12	21	48	77	39
Royston Town	42	4	12	26	37	109	24
Cheshunt	42	5	6	31	43	114	21

Second Division South

	P	W	D	L	F	A	Pts
Woking	40	27	7	6	110	32	88
Marlow	40	28	4	8	78	36	88
Dorking	40	24	12	4	78	30	84
Feltham	40	25	3	12	79	34	78
Ruislip Manor	40	22	10	8	85	47	76
Chertsey Town	40	18	11	11	56	44	65
Metropolitan Police	40	16	13	11	70	61	61
Chalfont St Peter	40	17	10	13	60	55	61
Hungerford Town	40	14	14	12	55	48	56
Harefield United	40	14	14	12	53	47	56
Eastbourne United	40	15	10	15	72	59	55
Whyteleafe	40	12	15	13	52	63	51
Horsham	40	14	8	18	54	61	50
Egham Town	40	14	6	20	45	77	48
Camberley Town	40	13	3	24	62	89	42
Flackwell Heath	40	9	11	20	34	63	38
Banstead Athletic	40	7	15	18	44	61	36
Petersfield United	40	9	8	23	45	84	34
Molesey	40	7	12	21	37	89	33
Newbury Town	40	6	14	20	51	83	32
Southall	40	6	6	28	28	85	24

1987-88   Premier Division

	P	W	D	L	F	A	Pts
Yeovil Town	42	24	9	9	66	34	81
Bromley	42	23	7	12	68	40	76
Slough Town	42	21	9	12	67	41	72
Leytonstone & Ilford	42	20	11	11	59	43	71
Wokingham Town	42	21	7	14	62	52	70
Hayes	42	20	9	13	62	48	69
Windsor & Eton	42	16	17	9	59	43	65
Farnborough Town	42	17	11	14	63	60	62
Carshalton Athletic	42	16	13	13	49	41	61
Hendon	42	16	12	14	62	58	60
Tooting & Mitcham United	42	15	14	13	57	59	59
Harrow Borough	42	15	11	16	53	58	56
Bishop's Stortford	42	15	10	17	55	58	55
Kingstonian	42	14	12	16	47	53	54
St Albans City	42	15	6	21	60	69	51
Bognor Regis Town	42	14	9	19	41	57	51
Leyton Wingate	42	14	8	20	58	64	50
Croydon	42	11	13	18	40	52	46
Barking	42	11	12	19	44	57	45
Dulwich Hamlet	42	10	11	21	46	64	41
Hitchin Town	42	10	8	24	46	79	38
Basingstoke Town	42	6	17	19	37	71	35

First Division

	P	W	D	L	F	A	Pts
Marlow	42	32	5	5	100	44	101
Grays Athletic	42	30	10	2	74	25	100
Woking	42	25	7	10	91	52	82
Boreham Wood	42	21	9	12	65	45	72
Staines Town	42	19	11	12	71	48	68
Wembley	42	18	11	13	54	46	65
Basildon United	42	18	9	15	65	58	63
Walton & Hersham	42	15	16	11	53	44	61
Hampton	42	17	10	15	59	54	61
Leatherhead	42	16	11	15	64	53	59
Southwick	42	13	12	17	59	63	51
Oxford City	42	13	12	17	70	77	51
Worthing	42	14	8	20	67	73	50
Kingsbury Town	42	11	17	14	62	69	50
Walthamstow Avenue	42	13	11	18	53	66	50
Lewes	42	12	13	17	83	77	49
Uxbridge	42	11	16	15	41	47	49
Chesham United	42	12	10	20	69	77	46
Bracknell Town	42	12	9	21	54	80	45
Billericay Town	42	11	11	20	58	88	44
Stevenage Borough	42	11	9	22	36	64	42
Wolverton Town	42	3	3	36	23	124	12

Second Division North

	P	W	D	L	F	A	Pts
Wivenhoe Town	42	26	10	6	105	42	88
Collier Row	42	22	13	7	71	39	79
Tilbury	42	18	15	9	61	40	69
Berkhamsted Town	42	19	12	11	71	53	69
Harlow Town	42	17	16	9	67	36	67
Ware	42	17	15	10	63	58	66
Witham Town	42	17	14	11	69	47	65
Vauxhall Motors	42	16	17	9	56	42	65
Heybridge Swifts	42	17	13	12	56	50	64
Tring Town	42	18	6	18	69	67	60
Letchworth Garden City	42	18	5	19	59	64	59
Finchley	42	16	10	16	67	54	58
Clapton	42	14	15	13	50	62	57
Hornchurch	42	13	15	14	56	65	54
Barton Rovers	42	13	10	19	43	60	49
Rainham Town	42	12	12	18	63	66	48
Royston Town	42	13	8	21	49	70	47
Saffron Walden Town	42	13	7	22	34	67	46
Hemel Hempstead	42	11	12	19	38	71	45
Haringey Borough	42	11	8	23	54	78	41
Aveley	42	8	13	21	42	65	37
Hertford Town	42	8	4	30	45	92	28

Second Division South

	P	W	D	L	F	A	Pts
Chalfont St Peter	42	26	9	7	81	35	87
Metropolitan Police	42	23	17	2	80	32	86
Dorking	42	25	11	6	86	39	86
Feltham	42	21	12	9	74	41	75
Epsom & Ewell	42	21	11	10	71	49	74
Chertsey Town	42	22	7	13	63	47	73
Whyteleafe	42	20	11	11	84	55	71
Hungerford Town	42	21	7	14	66	54	70
Ruislip Manor	42	21	5	16	74	57	68
Yeading	42	19	10	13	83	56	67
Maidenhead United	42	18	12	12	69	54	66
Eastbourne United	42	18	10	14	67	57	64
Harefield Town	42	18	6	18	59	60	60
Egham Town	42	12	12	18	45	55	48
Horsham	42	12	10	20	45	66	46
Southall	42	13	7	22	45	72	46
Molesey	42	11	11	20	42	63	44
Newbury Town	42	8	13	21	40	81	37
Camberley Town	42	9	9	24	51	94	36
Flackwell Heath	42	6	8	28	42	96	26
Banstead Athletic	42	6	7	29	34	81	25
Petersfield United	42	6	7	29	45	102	25

1988-89   Premier Division

Leytonstone & Ilford	42	26	11	5	76	36	89
Farnborough Town	42	24	9	9	85	61	81
Slough Town	42	24	6	12	72	42	78
Carshalton Athletic	42	19	15	8	59	36	72
Grays Athletic	42	19	13	10	62	47	70
Kingstonian	42	19	11	12	54	37	68
Bishop's Stortford	42	20	6	16	70	56	66
Hayes	42	18	12	12	61	47	66
Bognor Regis Town	42	17	11	14	38	49	62
Barking	42	16	13	13	49	45	61
Wokingham Town	42	15	11	16	60	54	56
Hendon	42	13	17	12	51	68	56
Windsor & Eton	42	14	13	15	52	50	55
Bromley	42	13	15	14	61	48	54
Leyton Wingate	42	13	15	14	55	56	54
Dulwich Hamlet	42	12	12	18	58	57	48
St Albans City	42	12	9	21	51	59	45
Dagenham	42	11	12	19	53	68	45
Harrow Borough	42	9	13	20	53	75	40
Marlow	42	9	11	22	48	83	38
Tooting & Mitcham United	42	10	6	26	41	81	36
Croydon	42	4	9	29	27	81	21

First Division

Staines Town	40	26	9	5	79	29	87
Basingstoke Town	40	25	8	7	85	36	83
Woking	40	24	10	6	72	30	82
Hitchin Town	40	21	11	8	60	32	74
Wivenhoe Town	40	22	6	12	62	44	72
Lewes	40	21	8	11	72	54	71
Walton & Hersham	40	21	7	12	56	36	70
Kingsbury Town	40	20	7	13	65	41	67
Uxbridge	40	19	7	14	60	54	64
Wembley	40	18	6	16	45	58	60
Boreham Wood	40	16	9	15	57	52	57
Leatherhead	40	14	8	18	56	58	50
Metropolitan Police	40	13	9	18	52	68	48
Chesham United	40	12	9	19	54	67	45
Southwick	40	9	15	16	44	58	42
Chalfont St Peter	40	11	9	20	56	82	42
Hampton	40	7	14	19	37	62	35
Worthing	40	8	10	22	49	80	32
Collier Row	40	8	7	25	37	82	31
Bracknell Town	40	8	6	26	38	70	30
Basildon United	40	6	7	27	34	77	25

Worthing had 2 points deducted.

Second Division North

Harlow Town	42	27	9	6	83	38	90
Purfleet	42	22	12	8	60	42	78
Tring Town	42	22	10	10	65	44	76
Stevenage Borough	42	20	13	9	84	55	73
Heybridge Swifts	42	21	9	12	64	43	72
Billericay Town	42	19	11	12	65	52	68
Clapton	42	18	11	13	65	56	65
Barton Rovers	42	18	11	13	58	50	65
Aveley	42	18	10	14	54	52	64
Hertford Town	42	16	13	13	62	49	59
Ware	42	17	8	17	60	65	59
Hemel Hempstead	42	16	10	16	55	58	58
Witham Town	42	16	7	19	69	67	55
Vauxhall Motors	42	15	9	18	53	57	54
Berkhamsted Town	42	14	10	18	57	70	52
Hornchurch	42	11	16	15	59	61	49
Tilbury	42	13	10	19	53	60	49
Royston Town	42	12	7	23	46	72	43
Rainham Town	42	9	15	18	49	62	42
Saffron Walden Town	42	8	16	18	54	72	40
Letchworth Garden City	42	4	18	20	34	71	30
Wolverton Town	42	5	7	30	42	95	13

Hertford Town 2 points deducted, Wolverton Town 9 points deducted.

Second Division South

Dorking	40	32	4	4	109	35	100
Whyteleafe	40	25	9	6	86	41	84
Finchley	40	21	9	10	70	45	72
Molesey	40	19	13	8	58	42	70
Harefield United	40	19	7	14	56	45	64
Hungerford Town	40	17	13	10	55	45	64
Ruislip Manor	40	16	9	15	56	43	57
Feltham	40	16	9	15	58	53	57
Epsom & Ewell	40	16	8	16	55	55	56
Egham Town	40	16	7	17	54	58	55
Eastbourne United	40	15	9	16	68	61	54
Chertsey Town	40	13	14	13	55	58	53
Flackwell Heath	40	13	11	16	51	49	50
Camberley Town	40	15	5	20	51	71	50
Yeading	40	13	9	18	47	63	46
Banstead Athletic	40	12	8	20	50	65	44
Maidenhead United	40	10	13	17	44	61	43
Southall	40	11	10	19	41	73	43
Newbury Town	40	11	8	21	47	65	41
Horsham	40	7	14	19	36	68	35
Petersfield United	40	5	7	28	36	87	22

Yeading had 2 points deducted.

1989-90   Premier Division

Slough Town	42	27	11	4	85	38	92
Wokingham Town	42	26	11	5	67	34	89
Aylesbury United	42	25	9	8	86	30	84
Kingstonian	42	24	9	9	87	51	81
Grays Athletic	42	19	13	10	59	44	70
Dagenham	42	17	15	10	54	43	66
Leyton Wingate	42	20	6	16	54	48	66
Basingstoke Town	42	18	9	15	65	55	63
Bishop's Stortford	42	19	6	17	60	59	63
Carshalton Athletic	42	19	5	18	63	59	59
Redbridge Forest	42	16	11	15	65	62	59
Hendon	42	15	10	17	54	63	55
Windsor & Eton	42	13	15	14	51	47	54
Hayes	42	14	11	17	61	59	53
St Albans City	42	13	10	19	49	59	49
Staines Town	42	14	6	22	53	69	48
Marlow	42	11	13	18	42	59	46
Harrow Borough	42	11	10	21	51	79	43
Bognor Regis Town	42	9	14	19	37	67	41
Barking	42	7	11	24	53	86	32
Bromley	42	7	11	24	32	69	32
Dulwich Hamlet	42	6	8	28	32	80	26

Carshalton Athletic had 3 points deducted.

First Division

Wivenhoe Town	42	31	7	4	94	36	100
Woking	42	30	8	4	102	29	98
Southwick	42	23	15	4	68	30	84
Hitchin Town	42	22	13	7	60	30	79
Walton & Hersham	42	20	10	12	68	50	70
Dorking	42	19	12	11	66	41	69
Boreham Wood	42	17	13	12	60	59	64
Harlow Town	42	16	13	13	60	53	61
Metropolitan Police	42	16	11	15	54	59	59
Chesham United	42	15	12	15	46	49	57
Chalfont St Peter	42	14	13	15	50	59	55
Tooting & Mitcham United	42	14	13	15	42	51	55
Worthing	42	15	8	19	56	63	53
Whyteleafe	42	11	16	15	50	65	49
Lewes	42	12	11	19	55	65	47
Wembley	42	11	10	21	57	68	43
Croydon	42	9	16	17	43	57	43
Uxbridge	42	11	10	21	52	75	43
Hampton	42	8	13	21	28	51	37
Leatherhead	42	7	10	25	34	77	31
Purfleet	42	7	8	27	33	78	29
Kingsbury Town	42	8	10	24	45	78	25

Kingsbury Town had 9 points deducted

Second Division North

Heybridge Swifts	42	26	9	7	79	29	87
Aveley	42	23	16	3	68	24	85
Hertford Town	42	24	11	7	92	51	83
Stevenage Borough	42	21	16	5	70	31	79
Barton Rovers	42	22	6	14	60	45	72
Tilbury	42	20	9	13	68	54	69
Basildon United	42	13	20	9	50	44	59
Collier Row	42	15	13	14	43	45	58
Royston Town	42	15	11	16	63	72	56
Saffron Walden Town	42	15	11	16	60	73	56
Vauxhall Motors	42	14	13	15	55	54	55
Clapton	42	13	16	13	50	46	54
Ware	42	14	11	17	53	59	53
Hemel Hempstead	42	12	15	15	58	70	51
Billericay Town	42	13	11	18	49	58	50
Hornchurch	42	12	12	18	49	64	48
Berkhamsted Town	42	9	16	17	44	68	43
Finchley	42	11	10	21	50	75	43
Tring Town	42	10	9	23	48	70	39
Witham Town	42	8	14	20	44	56	38
Rainham Town	42	9	11	22	48	75	38
Letchworth Garden City	42	7	12	23	30	68	33

Clapton had 1 point deducted

Second Division South

Yeading	40	29	4	7	86	37	91
Molesey	40	24	11	5	76	30	83
Abingdon Town	40	22	9	9	64	39	75
Ruislip Manor	40	20	12	8	60	32	72
Maidenhead United	40	20	12	8	66	39	72
Southall	40	22	5	13	56	33	71
Newbury Town	40	21	7	12	50	36	70
Flackwell Heath	40	16	11	13	69	65	59
Hungerford Town	40	14	16	10	54	51	58
Egham Town	40	12	14	14	39	38	50
Banstead Athletic	40	14	8	18	46	47	50
Harefield United	40	13	9	18	44	46	48
Chertsey Town	40	13	9	18	53	58	48
Epsom & Ewell	40	13	9	18	49	54	48
Malden Vale	40	13	7	20	36	67	46
Eastbourne United	40	11	10	19	47	65	43
Camberley Town	40	11	9	20	44	66	42
Feltham	40	11	7	22	47	80	40
Bracknell Town	40	10	9	21	40	57	39
Petersfield United	40	10	8	22	48	93	38
Horsham	40	4	8	28	29	70	20

1990-91   Premier Division

Redbridge Forest	42	29	6	7	74	43	93
Enfield	42	26	11	5	83	30	89
Aylesbury United	42	24	11	7	90	47	83
Woking	42	24	10	8	84	39	82
Kingstonian	42	21	12	9	86	57	75
Grays Athletic	42	20	8	14	66	53	68
Marlow	42	18	13	11	72	49	67
Hayes	42	20	5	17	60	57	65
Carshalton Athletic	42	19	7	16	80	67	64
Wivenhoe Town	42	16	11	15	69	66	59
Wokingham Town	42	15	13	14	58	54	58
Windsor & Eton	42	15	10	17	48	63	55
Bishop's Stortford	42	14	12	16	54	49	54
Dagenham	42	13	11	18	62	68	50
Hendon	42	12	10	20	48	62	46
St Albans City	42	11	12	19	60	74	45
Bognor Regis Town	42	12	8	22	44	71	44
Basingstoke Town	42	12	7	23	57	95	43
Staines Town	42	10	10	22	46	79	39
Harrow Borough	42	10	8	24	57	84	38
Barking	42	8	10	24	41	85	34
Leyton Wingate	42	7	7	28	44	91	28

Staines Town had 1 point deducted

First Division

Chesham United	42	27	8	7	102	37	89
Bromley	42	22	14	6	62	37	80
Yeading	42	23	8	11	75	45	77
Aveley	42	21	9	12	76	43	72
Hitchin Town	42	21	9	12	78	50	72
Tooting & Mitcham United	42	20	12	10	71	48	72
Walton & Hersham	42	21	8	13	73	48	71
Molesey	42	22	5	15	65	46	71
Whyteleafe	42	21	6	15	62	53	69
Dorking	42	20	5	17	78	67	65
Chalfont St Peter	42	19	5	18	56	63	62
Dulwich Hamlet	42	16	11	15	67	54	59
Harlow Town	42	17	8	17	73	64	59
Boreham Wood	42	15	8	19	46	53	53
Wembley	42	13	12	17	62	59	51
Uxbridge	42	15	5	22	45	61	50
Croydon	42	15	5	22	44	85	50
Heybridge Swifts	42	13	10	19	46	59	49
Southwick	42	13	8	21	49	75	47
Lewes	42	10	8	24	49	82	38
Metropolitan Police	42	9	6	27	55	76	33
Worthing	42	2	4	36	28	157	10

Second Division North

Stevenage Borough	42	34	5	3	122	29	107
Vauxhall Motors	42	24	10	8	82	50	82
Billericay Town	42	22	8	12	70	41	74
Ware	42	22	8	12	78	51	74
Berkhamsted Town	42	19	11	12	60	51	68
Witham Town	42	19	10	13	70	59	67
Purfleet	42	17	14	11	68	57	65
Rainham Town	42	19	7	16	57	46	64
Hemel Hempstead	42	16	14	12	62	56	62
Barton Rovers	42	17	10	15	61	58	61
Saffron Walden Town	42	16	13	13	72	77	61
Collier Row	42	16	11	15	63	63	59
Kingsbury Town	42	17	8	17	64	72	59
Edgware Town	42	17	7	18	73	65	58
Hertford Town	42	16	10	16	69	70	58
Royston Town	42	14	15	13	78	62	57
Tilbury	42	14	6	22	70	79	48
Basildon United	42	11	10	21	61	90	43
Hornchurch	42	10	9	23	53	87	39
Clapton	42	9	10	23	54	93	34
Finchley	42	6	7	29	50	112	24
Tring Town	42	1	9	32	30	99	12

Finchley had 1 point deducted. Clapton had 3 points deducted

Second Division South

Abingdon Town	42	29	7	6	95	28	94
Maidenhead United	42	28	8	6	85	33	92
Egham Town	42	27	6	9	100	46	87
Malden Vale	42	26	5	11	72	44	83
Ruislip Manor	42	25	5	12	93	44	80
Southall	42	23	10	9	84	43	79
Harefield United	42	23	10	9	81	56	79
Newbury Town	42	23	8	11	71	45	77
Hungerford Town	42	16	13	13	84	69	61
Leatherhead	42	17	9	16	82	55	60
Banstead Athletic	42	15	13	14	58	62	58
Hampton	42	14	15	13	62	43	57
Epsom & Ewell	42	15	12	15	49	50	57
Chertsey Town	42	15	9	18	76	72	54
Horsham	42	14	7	21	58	67	49
Flackwell Heath	42	11	11	20	56	78	44
Bracknell Town	42	11	7	24	60	97	40
Feltham	42	10	8	24	45	80	38
Cove	42	10	7	25	51	94	37
Eastbourne United	42	10	7	25	53	109	37
Petersfield United	42	6	3	33	35	119	21
Camberley Town	42	1	6	35	27	143	9

1991-92
Premier Division

Woking	42	30	7	5	96	25	97
Enfield	42	24	7	11	59	45	79
Sutton United	42	19	13	10	88	51	70
Chesham United	42	20	10	12	67	48	70
Wokingham Town	42	19	10	13	73	58	67
Marlow	42	20	7	15	56	50	67
Aylesbury United	42	16	17	9	69	46	65
Carshalton Athletic	42	18	8	16	64	67	62
Dagenham	42	15	16	11	70	59	61
Kingstonian	42	17	8	17	71	65	59
Windsor & Eton	42	15	11	16	56	56	56
Bromley	42	14	12	16	51	57	54
St Albans City	42	14	11	17	66	70	53
Basingstoke Town	42	14	11	17	56	65	53
Grays Athletic	42	14	11	17	53	68	53
Wivenhoe Town	42	16	4	22	56	81	52
Hendon	42	13	9	20	59	73	48
Harrow Borough	42	11	13	18	58	78	46
Hayes	42	10	14	18	52	63	44
Staines Town	42	11	10	21	43	73	43
Bognor Regis Town	42	9	11	22	51	89	38
Bishop's Stortford	42	7	12	23	41	68	33

First Division

Stevenage Borough	40	30	6	4	95	37	96
Yeading	40	24	10	6	83	34	82
Dulwich Hamlet	40	22	9	9	71	40	75
Boreham Wood	40	22	7	11	65	40	73
Wembley	40	21	6	13	54	43	69
Abingdon Town	40	19	8	13	60	47	65
Tooting & Mitcham United	40	16	13	11	57	45	61
Hitchin Town	40	17	10	13	55	45	61
Walton & Hersham	40	15	13	12	62	50	58
Molesey	40	16	9	15	55	61	57
Dorking	40	16	7	17	68	65	55
Barking	40	14	11	15	51	54	53
Chalfont St Peter	40	15	6	19	62	70	51
Leyton Wingate	40	13	11	16	53	56	50
Uxbridge	40	13	8	19	47	62	47
Maidenhead United	40	13	7	20	52	61	46
Harlow Town	40	11	9	20	50	70	42
Croydon	40	11	6	23	44	68	39
Heybridge Swifts	40	8	9	23	33	71	33
Whyteleafe	40	7	10	23	42	78	31
Aveley	40	8	3	29	33	95	27

Second Division

Purfleet	42	27	8	7	97	48	89
Lewes	42	23	14	5	74	36	83
Billericay Town	42	24	8	10	75	44	80
Leatherhead	42	23	6	13	68	40	75
Ruislip Manor	42	20	9	13	74	51	69
Egham Town	42	19	12	11	81	62	69
Metropolitan Police	42	20	9	13	76	58	69
Saffron Walden Town	42	19	11	12	86	67	68
Hemel Hempstead	42	18	10	14	63	50	64
Hungerford Town	42	18	7	17	53	58	61
Barton Rovers	42	17	8	17	61	64	59
Worthing	42	17	8	17	67	72	59
Witham Town	42	16	11	15	56	61	59
Banstead Athletic	42	16	10	16	69	58	58
Malden Vale	42	15	12	15	63	48	57
Rainham Town	42	14	13	15	53	48	55
Ware	42	14	9	19	58	62	51
Berkhamsted Town	42	13	11	18	56	57	50
Harefield United	42	11	7	24	47	66	40
Southall	42	8	7	27	39	93	31
Southwick	42	6	2	34	29	115	20
Newbury Town	42	4	8	30	30	117	20

Third Division

Edgware Town	40	30	3	7	106	44	93
Chertsey Town	40	29	4	7	115	44	91
Tilbury	40	26	9	5	84	40	87
Hampton	40	26	5	9	93	35	83
Horsham	40	23	8	9	92	51	77
Cove	40	21	9	10	74	49	72
Flackwell Heath	40	19	12	9	78	50	69
Thame United	40	19	7	14	73	46	64
Epsom & Ewell	40	17	11	12	55	50	62
Collier Row	40	17	9	14	67	59	60
Royston Town	40	17	7	16	59	58	58
Kingsbury Town	40	12	10	18	54	61	46
Hertford Town	40	12	10	18	55	73	46
Petersfield United	40	12	9	19	45	67	45
Camberley Town	40	11	8	21	52	69	41
Feltham & Hounslow	40	11	2	22	53	78	40
Bracknell Town	40	10	7	23	48	90	37
Hornchurch	40	8	7	25	40	87	31
Tring Town	40	9	4	27	35	94	31
Clapton	40	9	3	28	47	92	30
Eastbourne United	40	5	5	30	34	121	20

1992-93
Premier Division

Chesham United	42	30	8	4	104	34	98
St Albans City	42	28	9	5	103	50	93
Enfield	42	25	6	11	94	48	81
Carshalton Athletic	42	22	10	10	96	56	76
Sutton United	42	18	14	10	74	57	68
Grays Athletic	42	18	11	13	61	64	65
Stevenage Borough	42	18	8	16	62	60	62
Harrow Borough	42	16	14	12	59	60	62
Hayes	42	16	13	13	64	59	61
Aylesbury United	42	18	6	18	70	77	60
Hendon	42	12	18	12	52	54	54
Basingstoke Town	42	12	17	13	49	45	53
Kingstonian	42	14	10	18	59	58	52
Dulwich Hamlet	42	12	14	16	52	66	50
Marlow	42	12	11	19	72	73	47
Wokingham Town	42	11	13	18	62	81	46
Bromley	42	11	13	18	51	72	46
Wivenhoe Town	42	13	7	22	41	75	46
Yeading	42	11	12	19	58	66	45
Staines Town	42	10	13	19	59	77	43
Windsor & Eton	42	8	7	27	40	90	31
Bognor Regis Town	42	5	10	27	46	106	25

First Division

Hitchin Town	40	25	7	8	67	29	82
Molesey	40	23	11	6	81	38	80
Dorking	40	23	9	8	73	40	78
Purfleet	40	19	12	9	67	42	69
Bishop's Stortford	40	19	10	11	63	42	67
Abingdon Town	40	17	13	10	65	47	64
Tooting & Mitcham United	40	17	12	11	68	46	63
Billericay Town	40	18	6	16	67	61	60
Wembley	40	14	15	11	44	34	57
Walton & Hersham	40	14	12	14	58	54	54
Boreham Wood	40	12	14	14	44	43	50
Maidenhead United	40	10	18	12	45	50	48
Leyton	40	11	14	15	56	61	47
Whyteleafe	40	12	10	18	63	71	46
Uxbridge	40	11	13	16	50	59	46
Heybridge Swifts	40	11	9	20	47	65	42
Croydon	40	11	9	20	54	82	42
Chalfont St Peter	40	7	17	16	48	70	38
Barking	40	10	8	22	42	80	38
Lewes	40	9	10	21	34	80	37
Aveley	40	9	7	24	45	87	34

Second Division

Worthing	42	28	7	7	105	50	91
Ruislip Manor	42	25	12	5	78	33	87
Berkhamsted Town	42	24	8	10	77	55	80
Hemel Hempstead	42	22	12	8	84	52	78
Metropolitan Police	42	22	6	14	84	51	72
Malden Vale	42	20	9	13	78	54	69
Chertsey Town	42	20	7	15	84	60	67
Saffron Walden Town	42	19	10	13	63	49	67
Newbury Town	42	14	18	10	53	51	60
Hampton	42	16	11	15	59	59	59
Edgware Town	42	16	10	16	84	75	58
Egham Town	42	16	9	17	60	71	57
Banstead Athletic	42	14	13	15	67	52	55
Leatherhead	42	14	11	17	66	61	53
Ware	42	12	11	19	68	76	47
Witham Town	42	10	16	16	54	65	46
Tilbury	42	12	8	22	55	101	44
Barton Rovers	42	9	14	19	40	66	41
Hungerford Town	42	11	8	23	37	93	41
Rainham Town	42	9	10	23	56	80	37
Harefield United	42	10	7	25	37	72	37
Southall	42	7	7	28	43	106	28

Third Division

Aldershot Town	38	28	8	2	90	35	92
Thame United	38	21	11	6	84	38	74
Collier Row	38	21	11	6	68	30	74
Leighton Town	38	21	10	7	89	47	73
Cove	38	21	8	9	69	42	71
Northwood	38	19	11	8	84	68	68
Royston Town	38	17	8	13	59	42	59
East Thurrock United	38	17	7	14	69	58	58
Kingsbury Town	38	15	9	14	62	59	54
Hertford Town	38	14	10	14	61	64	52
Flackwell Heath	38	15	6	17	82	76	51
Tring Town	38	12	11	15	59	63	47
Hornchurch	38	11	13	14	53	52	46
Horsham	38	12	7	19	63	72	43
Epsom & Ewell	38	10	11	17	52	67	41
Bracknell Town	38	7	13	18	52	94	34
Clapton	38	8	7	23	46	74	31
Camberley Town	38	8	7	23	37	72	31
Petersfield United	38	6	12	20	36	90	30
Feltham & Hounslow	38	5	4	29	47	119	19

1993-94

Premier Division

Stevenage Borough	42	31	4	7	88	39	97
Enfield	42	28	8	6	80	28	92
Marlow	42	25	7	10	90	67	82
Chesham United	42	24	8	10	73	45	80
Sutton United	42	23	10	9	77	31	79
Carshalton Athletic	42	22	7	13	81	53	73
St Albans City	42	21	10	11	81	54	73
Hitchin Town	42	21	7	14	81	56	70
Harrow Borough	42	18	11	13	54	56	65
Kingstonian	42	18	9	15	101	64	63
Hendon	42	18	9	15	61	51	63
Aylesbury United	42	17	7	18	64	67	58
Hayes	42	15	8	19	63	72	53
Grays Athletic	42	15	5	22	56	69	50
Bromley	42	14	7	21	56	69	49
Dulwich Hamlet	42	13	8	21	52	74	47
Yeading	42	11	13	18	58	66	46
Molesey	42	11	11	20	44	62	44
Wokingham Town	42	11	6	25	38	67	39
Dorking	42	9	4	29	58	104	31
Basingstoke Town	42	5	12	25	38	86	27
Wivenhoe Town	42	5	3	34	38	152	18

First Division

Bishop's Stortford	42	24	13	5	83	31	85
Purfleet	42	22	12	8	70	44	78
Walton & Hersham	42	22	11	9	81	53	77
Tooting & Mitcham United	42	21	12	9	66	37	75
Heybridge Swifts	42	20	11	11	72	45	71
Billericay Town	42	20	11	11	70	51	71
Abingdon Town	42	20	10	12	61	50	70
Worthing	42	19	11	12	79	46	68
Leyton	42	20	8	14	88	66	68
Boreham Wood	42	17	15	10	69	50	66
Staines Town	42	18	9	15	85	56	63
Bognor Regis Town	42	15	14	13	57	48	59
Wembley	42	16	10	16	66	52	58
Barking	42	15	11	16	63	69	56
Uxbridge	42	15	8	19	57	58	53
Whyteleafe	42	15	6	21	71	90	51
Maidenhead United	42	12	13	17	52	48	49
Berkhamsted Town	42	12	9	21	65	77	45
Ruislip Manor	42	10	8	24	42	79	38
Chalfont St Peter	42	7	10	25	40	79	31
Windsor & Eton	42	8	7	27	47	94	31
Croydon	42	3	3	36	37	198	12

Second Division

Newbury Town	42	32	7	3	115	36	103
Chertsey Town	42	33	3	6	121	48	102
Aldershot Town	42	30	7	5	78	27	97
Barton Rovers	42	25	8	9	68	37	83
Witham Town	42	21	10	11	68	51	73
Malden Vale	42	20	10	12	70	49	70
Thame United	42	19	12	11	87	51	69
Metropolitan Police	42	20	9	13	75	54	69
Banstead Athletic	42	19	9	14	56	53	66
Aveley	42	19	5	18	60	66	62
Edgware Town	42	16	10	16	88	75	58
Saffron Walden Town	42	17	7	18	61	62	58
Hemel Hempstead	42	14	11	17	47	43	53
Egham Town	42	14	8	20	48	65	50
Ware	42	14	7	21	48	76	49
Hungerford Town	42	13	7	22	56	66	46
Tilbury	42	13	3	26	59	81	42
Hampton	42	12	5	25	42	70	41
Leatherhead	42	10	6	26	46	92	36
Lewes	42	8	11	24	38	85	34
Collier Row	42	7	8	27	37	88	29
Rainham Town	42	4	2	36	24	116	14

Third Division

Bracknell Town	40	25	8	7	78	29	83
Cheshunt	40	23	12	5	62	34	81
Oxford City	40	24	6	10	94	55	78
Harlow Town	40	22	11	7	61	36	77
Southall	40	17	12	11	66	53	63
Camberley Town	40	18	7	15	56	50	61
Hertford Town	40	18	6	16	67	65	60
Royston Town	40	15	11	14	44	41	56
Northwood	40	15	11	14	78	77	56
Epsom & Ewell	40	15	9	16	63	62	54
Harefield United	40	12	15	13	45	55	51
Cove	40	15	6	19	59	74	51
Kingsbury Town	40	12	14	14	57	54	50
Feltham & Hounslow	40	14	7	19	60	63	49
Leighton Town	40	12	11	17	51	64	47
East Thurrock Town	40	10	15	15	65	64	45
Clapton	40	12	9	19	51	65	45
Hornchurch	40	12	8	20	42	60	44
Tring Town	40	10	11	19	48	64	41
Flackwell Heath	40	9	11	20	44	83	38
Horsham	40	6	8	26	43	86	26

1994-95 Premier Division

Enfield	42	28	9	5	106	43	93
Slough Town	42	22	13	7	82	56	79
Hayes	42	20	14	8	66	47	74
Aylesbury United	42	21	6	15	86	59	69
Hitchin Town	42	18	12	12	68	59	66
Bromley	42	18	11	13	76	67	65
St Albans City	42	17	13	12	96	81	64
Molesey	42	18	8	16	65	61	62
Yeading	42	14	15	13	60	59	57
Harrow Borough	42	17	6	19	64	67	57
Dulwich Hamlet	42	16	9	17	70	82	57
Carshalton Athletic	42	16	9	17	69	84	57
Kingstonian	42	16	8	18	62	57	56
Walton & Hersham	42	14	11	17	75	73	53
Sutton United	42	13	12	17	74	69	51
Purfleet	42	13	12	17	76	90	51
Hendon	42	12	14	16	57	65	50
Grays Athletic	42	11	16	15	57	61	49
Bishop's Stortford	42	12	11	19	53	76	47
Chesham United	42	12	9	21	60	87	45
Marlow	42	10	9	23	52	84	39
Wokingham Town	42	6	9	27	39	86	27

First Division

Boreham Wood	42	31	5	6	90	38	98
Worthing	42	21	13	8	93	49	76
Chertsey Town	42	21	11	10	109	57	74
Aldershot Town	42	23	5	14	80	53	74
Billericay Town	42	20	9	13	68	52	69
Staines Town	42	17	12	13	83	65	63
Basingstoke Town	42	17	10	15	81	71	61
Tooting & Mitcham United	42	15	14	13	58	48	59
Wembley	42	16	11	15	70	61	59
Abingdon Town	42	16	11	15	67	69	59
Whyteleafe	42	17	7	18	70	78	58
Maidenhead United	42	15	12	15	73	76	57
Uxbridge	42	15	11	16	54	62	56
Leyton	42	15	10	17	67	66	55
Barking	42	16	7	19	74	77	55
Heybridge Swifts	42	16	6	20	73	78	54
Ruislip Manor	42	14	11	17	70	75	53
Bognor Regis Town	42	13	14	15	57	63	53
Berkhamsted Town	42	14	10	18	54	70	52
Newbury Town	42	12	15	15	58	71	51
Wivenhoe Town	42	8	7	27	47	94	31
Dorking	42	3	3	36	40	163	12

Second Division

Thame United	42	30	3	9	97	49	93
Barton Rovers	42	25	7	10	93	51	82
Oxford City	42	24	8	10	86	47	80
Bracknell Town	42	23	9	10	86	47	78
Metropolitan Police	42	19	12	11	81	65	69
Hampton	42	20	9	13	79	74	69
Croydon	42	20	5	17	85	65	65
Banstead Athletic	42	18	10	14	73	59	64
Saffron Walden Town	42	17	13	12	64	59	64
Chalfont St Peter	42	17	12	13	67	54	63
Witham Town	42	18	9	15	75	64	63
Leatherhead	42	16	12	14	71	75	60
Edgware Town	42	16	10	16	70	66	58
Tilbury	42	15	9	18	62	82	54
Cheshunt	42	13	13	16	66	81	52
Ware	42	14	7	21	61	81	49
Egham Town	42	11	14	17	60	65	47
Hemel Hempstead	42	10	11	21	45	76	41
Hungerford Town	42	11	7	24	55	81	40
Windsor & Eton	42	10	8	24	58	84	38
Aveley	42	9	5	28	48	95	32
Malden Vale	42	5	9	28	46	108	24

Third Division

Collier Row	40	30	5	5	86	23	95
Canvey Island	40	28	4	8	88	42	88
Bedford Town	40	22	11	7	90	50	77
Northwood	40	22	8	10	80	47	74
Horsham	40	22	6	12	84	61	72
Southall	40	21	8	11	87	59	71
Leighton Town	40	20	8	12	66	43	68
Camberley Town	40	19	8	13	59	39	65
Kingsbury Town	40	18	11	1	72	54	65
Hornchurch	40	17	8	15	64	63	59
Clapton	40	14	11	15	69	61	53
Tring Town	40	13	12	15	68	69	51
East Thurrock United	40	14	8	18	60	79	50
Epsom & Ewell	40	13	10	17	58	62	49
Harlow Town	40	13	8	19	53	83	47
Harefield United	40	12	8	20	51	79	44
Hertford Town	40	11	10	19	56	78	43
Feltham & Hounslow	40	13	4	23	64	87	43
Flackwell Heath	40	8	4	28	50	99	28
Lewes	40	6	5	29	34	104	23
Cove	40	3	5	32	37	94	14

1995-96

Premier Division

Hayes	42	24	14	4	76	32	86
Enfield	42	26	8	8	78	35	86
Boreham Wood	42	24	11	7	69	29	83
Yeovil Town	42	23	11	8	83	51	80
Dulwich Hamlet	42	23	11	8	85	59	80
Carshalton Athletic	42	22	8	12	68	49	74
St Albans City	42	20	12	10	70	41	72
Kingstonian	42	20	11	11	62	38	71
Harrow Borough	42	19	10	13	70	56	67
Sutton United	42	17	14	11	71	56	65
Aylesbury United	42	17	12	13	71	58	63
Bishop's Stortford	42	16	9	17	61	62	57
Yeading	42	11	14	17	48	60	47
Hendon	42	12	10	20	52	65	46
Chertsey Town	42	13	6	23	45	71	45
Purfleet	42	12	8	22	48	67	44
Grays Athletic	42	11	11	20	43	63	44
Hitchin Town	42	10	10	22	41	74	40
Bromley	42	10	7	25	52	91	37
Molesey	42	9	9	24	46	81	36
Walton & Hersham	42	9	7	26	42	79	34
Worthing	42	4	7	31	42	106	19

First Division

Oxford City	42	28	7	7	98	60	91
Heybridge Swifts	42	27	7	8	97	43	88
Staines Town	42	23	11	8	82	59	80
Leyton Pennant	42	22	7	13	77	57	73
Aldershot Town	42	21	9	12	81	46	72
Billericay Town	42	19	9	14	58	58	66
Bognor Regis Town	42	18	11	13	71	53	65
Marlow	42	19	5	18	72	75	62
Basingstoke Town	42	16	13	13	70	60	61
Uxbridge	42	16	12	14	46	49	60
Wokingham Town	42	16	10	16	62	65	58
Chesham United	42	15	12	15	51	44	57
Thame United	42	14	13	15	64	73	55
Maidenhead United	42	12	14	16	50	63	50
Whyteleafe	42	12	13	17	71	81	49
Abingdon Town	42	13	9	20	63	80	48
Barton Rovers	42	12	10	20	69	87	46
Berkhamsted Town	42	11	11	20	52	68	44
Tooting & Mitcham United	42	11	10	21	45	64	43
Ruislip Manor	42	11	9	22	55	77	42
Wembley	42	11	8	23	49	66	41
Barking	42	4	12	26	35	90	24

Second Division

Canvey Island	40	25	12	3	91	36	87
Croydon	40	25	6	9	78	42	81
Hampton	40	23	10	7	74	44	79
Banstead Athletic	40	21	11	8	72	36	74
Collier Row	40	21	11	8	73	41	74
Wivenhoe Town	40	21	8	11	82	57	71
Metropolitan Police	40	18	10	12	57	45	64
Bedford Town	40	18	10	12	69	59	64
Bracknell Town	40	18	8	14	69	50	62
Edgware Town	40	16	9	15	72	67	57
Tilbury	40	12	11	17	52	62	47
Ware	40	13	8	19	55	80	47
Chalfont St Peter	40	11	13	16	58	63	46
Leatherhead	40	12	10	18	71	77	46
Saffron Walden Town	40	11	12	17	56	58	45
Cheshunt	40	10	12	18	56	90	42
Hemel Hempstead	40	10	10	20	46	62	40
Egham Town	40	12	3	25	42	74	39
Witham Town	40	8	10	22	35	68	34
Hungerford Town	40	9	7	24	44	79	34
Dorking	40	8	5	27	44	104	29

Third Division

Horsham	40	29	5	6	95	40	92
Leighton Town	40	28	5	7	95	34	89
Windsor & Eton	40	27	6	7	117	46	87
Wealdstone	40	23	8	9	104	39	77
Harlow Town	40	22	10	8	85	62	76
Northwood	40	20	9	11	76	56	69
Epsom & Ewell	40	18	14	8	95	57	68
Kingsbury Town	40	15	16	9	61	48	61
East Thurrock United	40	17	8	15	61	50	59
Aveley	40	16	10	14	62	53	58
Wingate & Finchley	40	16	7	17	74	70	55
Lewes	40	14	7	19	56	72	49
Flackwell Heath	40	14	5	21	60	84	47
Hornchurch	40	11	8	21	55	77	41
Harefield United	40	11	7	22	49	89	40
Tring Town	40	10	8	22	40	78	38
Camberley Town	40	9	9	22	45	81	36
Hertford Town	40	10	5	25	72	103	35
Cove	40	8	10	22	37	89	34
Clapton	40	9	6	25	48	89	33
Southall	40	9	5	26	34	104	32

1996-97

Premier Division

Yeovil Town	42	31	8	3	83	34	101
Enfield	42	28	11	3	91	29	98
Sutton United	42	18	13	11	87	70	67
Dagenham & Redbridge	42	18	11	13	57	43	65
Yeading	42	17	14	11	58	47	65
St Albans City	42	18	11	13	65	55	65
Aylesbury United	42	18	11	13	64	54	65
Purfleet	42	17	11	14	67	63	62
Heybridge Swifts	42	16	14	12	62	62	62
Boreham Wood	42	15	13	14	56	52	58
Kingstonian	42	16	8	18	79	79	56
Dulwich Hamlet	42	14	13	15	57	57	55
Carshalton Athletic	42	14	11	17	51	56	53
Hitchin Town	42	15	7	20	67	73	52
Oxford City	42	14	10	18	67	83	52
Hendon	42	13	12	17	53	59	51
Harrow Borough	42	12	14	16	58	62	50
Bromley	42	13	9	20	67	72	48
Bishop's Stortford	42	10	13	19	43	64	43
Staines Town	42	10	8	24	46	71	38
Grays Athletic	42	8	9	25	43	78	33
Chertsey Town	42	8	7	27	40	98	31

First Division

Chesham United	42	27	6	9	80	46	87
Basingstoke Town	42	22	13	7	81	38	79
Walton & Hersham	42	21	13	8	67	41	76
Hampton	42	21	12	9	62	39	75
Billericay Town	42	21	12	9	69	49	75
Bognor Regis Town	42	21	9	12	63	44	72
Aldershot Town	42	19	14	9	67	45	71
Uxbridge	42	15	17	10	65	48	62
Whyteleafe	42	18	7	17	71	68	61
Molesey	42	17	9	16	50	53	60
Abingdon Town	42	15	11	16	44	42	56
Leyton Pennant	42	14	12	16	71	72	54
Maidenhead United	42	15	10	17	57	57	52
Wokingham Town	42	14	10	18	41	45	52
Thame United	42	13	10	19	57	69	49
Worthing	42	11	11	20	58	77	44
Barton Rovers	42	11	11	20	31	58	44
Croydon	42	11	10	21	44	57	43
Berkhamsted Town	42	11	9	22	47	66	42
Canvey Island	42	9	14	19	52	71	41
Marlow	42	11	6	25	41	84	39
Tooting & Mitcham United	42	8	8	26	40	85	32

Maidenhead United had 3 points deducted

Second Division

Collier Row & Romford	42	28	12	2	93	33	96
Leatherhead	42	30	5	7	116	45	95
Wembley	42	23	11	8	92	45	80
Barking	42	22	13	7	69	40	79
Horsham	42	22	11	9	78	48	77
Edgware Town	42	20	14	8	74	50	74
Bedford Town	42	21	8	13	77	43	71
Banstead Athletic	42	21	5	16	75	52	68
Windsor & Eton	42	17	13	12	65	62	64
Leighton Town	42	17	12	13	64	52	63
Bracknell Town	42	17	9	16	78	71	60
Wivenhoe Town	42	17	9	16	69	62	60
Chalfont St Peter	42	14	13	15	53	61	55
Hungerford Town	42	14	13	15	68	77	55
Metropolitan Police	42	14	7	21	72	75	49
Tilbury	42	14	7	21	68	77	49
Witham Town	42	11	10	21	39	67	43
Egham Town	42	10	9	23	47	86	39
Cheshunt	42	9	3	30	37	101	30
Ware	42	7	8	27	44	80	29
Dorking	42	7	6	29	40	100	27
Hemel Hempstead	42	5	6	31	34	125	21

Third Division

Wealdstone	32	24	3	5	72	24	75
Braintree Town	32	23	5	4	99	29	74
Northwood	32	18	10	4	60	31	64
Harlow Town	32	19	4	9	60	41	61
Aveley	32	17	6	9	64	39	57
East Thurrock United	32	16	6	10	58	51	54
Camberley Town	32	15	6	11	55	44	51
Wingate & Finchley	32	11	7	14	52	63	40
Hornchurch	32	11	6	15	35	51	39
Clapton	32	11	6	15	31	49	39
Lewes	32	10	8	14	45	53	38
Kingsbury Town	32	11	4	17	41	54	37
Hertford Town	32	10	6	16	55	65	36
Epsom & Ewell	32	8	5	19	62	78	29
Flackwell Heath	32	8	5	19	36	71	29
Tring Town	32	7	3	22	33	74	24
Southall	32	6	4	22	28	69	22

1997-98 Premier Division

Kingstonian	42	25	12	5	84	35	87
Boreham Wood	42	23	11	8	81	42	80
Sutton United	42	22	12	8	83	56	78
Dagenham & Redbridge	42	21	10	11	73	50	73
Hendon	42	21	10	11	69	50	73
Heybridge Swifts	42	18	11	13	74	62	65
Enfield	42	18	8	16	66	58	62
Basingstoke Town	42	17	11	14	56	60	62
Walton & Hersham	42	18	6	18	50	70	60
Purfleet	42	15	13	14	57	58	58
St Albans City	42	17	7	18	54	59	58
Harrow Borough	42	15	10	17	60	67	55
Gravesend & Northfleet	42	15	8	19	65	67	53
Chesham United	42	14	10	18	71	70	52
Bromley	42	13	13	16	53	53	52
Dulwich Hamlet	42	13	11	18	56	67	50
Carshalton Athletic	42	13	9	20	54	77	48
Aylesbury United	42	13	8	21	55	70	47
Bishop's Stortford	42	14	5	23	53	69	47
Yeading	42	12	11	19	49	65	47
Hitchin Town	42	8	15	19	45	62	39
Oxford City	42	7	9	26	35	76	30

First Division

Aldershot Town	42	28	8	6	89	36	92
Billericay Town	42	25	6	11	78	44	81
Hampton	42	22	15	5	75	47	81
Maidenhead United	42	25	5	12	76	37	80
Uxbridge	42	23	6	13	66	59	75
Grays Athletic	42	21	10	11	79	49	73
Romford	42	21	8	13	92	59	71
Bognor Regis Town	42	20	9	13	77	45	69
Leatherhead	42	18	11	13	70	51	65
Leyton Pennant	42	17	11	14	66	58	62
Chertsey Town	42	16	13	13	83	70	61
Worthing	42	17	6	19	64	71	57
Berkhamsted Town	42	15	8	19	59	69	53
Staines Town	42	13	10	19	54	71	49
Croydon	42	13	10	19	47	64	49
Barton Rovers	42	11	13	18	53	72	46
Wembley	42	10	15	17	38	61	45
Molesey	42	10	11	21	47	65	41
Whyteleafe	42	10	10	22	48	83	40
Wokingham Town	42	7	10	25	41	74	31
Abingdon Town	42	9	4	29	47	101	31
Thame United	42	7	9	26	33	96	30

Second Division

Canvey Island	42	30	8	4	116	41	98
Braintree Town	42	29	11	2	117	45	98
Wealdstone	42	24	11	7	81	46	83
Bedford Town	42	22	12	8	55	25	78
Metropolitan Police	42	21	8	13	80	65	71
Wivenhoe Town	42	18	12	12	84	66	66
Edgware Town	42	18	10	14	81	65	64
Chalfont St Peter	42	17	13	12	63	60	64
Northwood	42	17	11	14	65	69	62
Windsor & Eton	42	17	7	18	75	72	58
Tooting & Mitcham United	42	16	9	17	58	56	57
Barking	42	15	12	15	62	75	57
Banstead Athletic	42	15	9	18	60	63	54
Marlow	42	16	5	21	64	78	53
Horsham	42	13	9	20	67	75	48
Bracknell Town	42	13	8	21	68	93	47
Leighton Town	42	13	6	23	45	78	45
Hungerford Town	42	11	11	20	66	77	44
Witham Town	42	9	13	20	55	68	40
Tilbury	42	9	12	21	57	88	39
Egham Town	42	9	5	28	47	101	32
Cheshunt	42	4	10	28	31	90	32

Third Division

Hemel Hempstead	38	27	6	5	86	28	87
Hertford Town	38	26	5	7	77	31	83
Harlow Town	38	24	11	3	81	43	83
Camberley Town	38	24	7	7	93	43	79
Ford United	38	23	9	6	90	34	78
East Thurrock United	38	23	7	8	70	40	76
Epsom & Ewell	38	17	6	15	69	57	57
Ware	38	17	6	15	69	57	57
Aveley	38	16	7	15	65	57	55
Corinthian Casuals	38	16	6	16	59	57	54
Hornchurch	38	12	9	17	55	68	45
Clapton	38	13	6	19	46	61	45
Flackwell Heath	38	12	9	17	50	76	45
Croydon Athletic	38	12	7	19	58	63	43
Tring Town	38	12	7	19	51	69	43
Southall	38	10	6	22	41	85	46
Dorking	38	9	6	23	49	94	33
Wingate & Finchley	38	7	8	23	46	80	29
Lewes	38	7	5	26	34	88	26
Kingsbury Town	38	5	3	30	35	93	18

1998-99

Premier Division

Sutton United	42	27	7	8	89	39	88
Aylesbury United	42	23	8	11	67	38	77
Dagenham & Redbridge	42	20	13	9	71	44	73
Purfleet	42	22	7	13	71	52	73
Enfield	42	21	9	12	73	49	72
St Albans City	42	17	17	8	71	52	68
Aldershot Town	42	16	14	12	83	48	62
Basingstoke Town	42	17	10	15	63	53	61
Harrow Borough	42	17	9	16	72	66	60
Gravesend & Northfleet	42	18	6	18	54	53	60
Slough Town	42	16	11	15	60	53	59
Billericay Town	42	15	13	14	54	56	58
Hendon	42	16	9	17	70	71	57
Boreham Wood	42	14	15	13	59	63	57
Chesham United	42	15	9	18	58	79	54
Dulwich Hamlet	42	14	8	20	53	63	50
Heybridge Swifts	42	13	9	20	51	85	48
Walton & Hersham	42	12	7	23	50	77	43
Hampton	42	10	12	20	41	71	42
Carshalton Athletic	42	10	10	22	47	82	40
Bishop's Stortford	42	9	10	23	49	90	37
Bromley	42	8	11	23	50	72	35

First Division

Canvey Island	42	28	6	8	76	41	90
Hitchin Town	42	25	10	7	75	38	85
Wealdstone	42	26	6	10	75	48	84
Braintree Town	42	20	10	12	75	48	70
Bognor Regis Town	42	20	8	14	63	44	68
Grays Athletic	42	19	11	12	56	42	68
Oxford City	42	16	14	12	58	51	62
Croydon	42	16	13	13	53	53	61
Chertsey Town	42	14	16	12	57	57	58
Romford	42	14	15	13	58	63	57
Maidenhead United	42	13	15	14	50	46	54
Worthing	42	13	13	16	47	61	52
Leyton Pennant	42	13	12	17	62	70	51
Uxbridge	42	13	11	18	54	51	50
Barton Rovers	42	11	15	16	43	49	48
Yeading	42	12	10	20	51	55	46
Leatherhead	42	12	9	21	48	59	45
Whyteleafe	42	13	6	23	51	72	45
Staines Town	42	10	15	17	33	57	45
Molesey	42	8	20	14	35	52	44
Wembley	42	10	10	22	36	71	40
Berkhamsted Town	42	10	7	25	53	81	37

Second Division

Bedford Town	42	29	7	6	89	31	94
Harlow Town	42	27	8	7	100	47	89
Thame United	42	26	8	8	89	50	86
Hemel Hempstead	42	21	12	9	90	50	75
Windsor & Eton	42	22	6	14	87	55	72
Banstead Athletic	42	21	8	13	83	62	71
Northwood	42	20	7	15	67	68	67
Tooting & Mitcham United	42	19	9	14	63	62	66
Chalfont St Peter	42	16	12	14	70	71	60
Metropolitan Police	42	17	8	17	61	58	59
Leighton Town	42	16	10	16	60	64	58
Horsham	42	17	6	19	74	67	57
Marlow	42	16	9	17	72	68	57
Edgware Town	42	14	10	18	65	68	52
Witham Town	42	12	15	15	64	64	51
Hungerford Town	42	13	12	17	59	61	51
Wivenhoe Town	42	14	8	20	71	83	50
Wokingham Town	42	14	4	24	44	79	46
Barking	42	10	11	21	50	75	41
Hertford Town	42	11	2	29	44	96	35
Bracknell Town	42	7	10	25	48	92	31
Abingdon Town	42	6	6	30	48	124	24

Third Division

Ford United	38	27	5	6	110	42	86
Wingate & Finchley	38	25	5	8	79	38	80
Cheshunt	38	23	10	5	70	41	79
Lewes	38	25	3	10	86	45	78
Epsom & Ewell	38	19	5	14	61	51	62
Ware	38	19	4	15	79	60	61
Tilbury	38	17	8	13	74	52	59
Croydon Athletic	38	16	10	12	82	59	58
East Thurrock United	38	15	13	10	74	56	58
Egham Town	38	16	8	14	65	58	56
Corinthian Casuals	38	16	7	15	70	71	55
Southall	38	14	9	15	68	66	51
Camberley Town	38	14	8	16	66	77	50
Aveley	38	12	7	19	50	67	43
Flackwell Heath	38	11	9	18	59	70	42
Hornchurch	38	10	9	19	48	73	39
Clapton	38	11	6	21	48	89	39
Dorking	38	8	7	23	52	98	31
Kingsbury Town	38	6	3	29	40	98	21
Tring Town	38	5	6	27	38	108	21

1999-2000

Premier Division

Dagenham & Redbridge	42	32	5	5	97	35	101
Aldershot Town	42	24	5	13	71	51	77
Chesham United	42	20	10	12	64	50	70
Purfleet	42	18	15	9	70	48	69
Canvey Island	42	21	6	15	70	53	69
St Albans City	42	19	10	13	75	55	67
Billericay Town	42	18	12	12	62	62	66
Hendon	42	18	8	16	61	64	62
Slough Town	42	17	9	16	61	59	60
Dulwich Hamlet	42	17	5	20	62	68	56
Gravesend & Northfleet	42	15	10	17	66	67	55
Farnborough Town	42	14	11	17	52	55	53
Hampton & Richmond Borough	42	13	13	16	49	57	52
Enfield	42	13	11	18	64	68	50
Heybridge Swifts	42	13	11	18	57	65	50
Hitchin Town	42	13	11	18	59	72	50
Carshalton Athletic	42	12	12	18	55	65	48
Basingstoke Town	42	13	9	20	56	71	48
Harrow Borough	42	14	6	22	54	70	48
Aylesbury United	42	13	9	20	64	81	48
Boreham Wood	42	11	10	21	44	71	43
Walton & Hersham	42	11	8	23	44	70	41

First Division

Croydon	42	25	9	8	85	47	84
Grays Athletic	42	21	12	9	80	44	75
Maidenhead United	42	20	15	7	72	45	75
Thame United	42	20	13	9	61	38	73
Worthing	42	19	12	11	80	60	69
Staines Town	42	19	12	11	63	52	69
Whyteleafe	42	20	9	13	60	49	69
Bedford Town	42	17	12	13	59	52	63
Bromley	42	17	9	16	62	65	60
Uxbridge	42	15	13	14	60	44	58
Bishop's Stortford	42	16	10	16	57	62	58
Barton Rovers	42	16	8	18	64	83	56
Oxford City	42	17	4	21	57	55	55
Braintree Town	42	15	10	17	65	74	55
Yeading	42	12	18	12	53	54	54
Wealdstone	42	13	12	17	51	58	51
Bognor Regis Town	42	12	13	17	47	53	49
Harlow Town	42	11	13	18	62	76	46
Romford	42	12	9	21	51	70	45
Leatherhead	42	9	13	20	47	70	40
Chertsey Town	42	9	5	28	50	84	32
Leyton Pennant	42	7	9	26	34	85	30

Second Division

Hemel Hempstead	42	31	8	3	98	27	101
Northwood	42	29	9	4	109	40	96
Ford United	42	28	8	6	108	41	92
Berkhamsted Town	42	22	8	12	75	52	74
Windsor & Eton	42	20	13	9	73	53	73
Wivenhoe Town	42	20	9	13	61	47	69
Barking	42	18	13	11	70	51	67
Marlow	42	20	4	18	86	66	64
Metropolitan Police	42	18	7	17	75	71	61
Banstead Athletic	42	16	11	15	55	56	59
Tooting & Mitcham United	42	16	7	19	72	74	55
Wokingham Town	42	15	9	18	58	80	54
Wembley	42	14	11	17	47	53	53
Edgware Town	42	13	11	18	72	71	50
Hungerford Town	42	13	10	19	61	78	49
Cheshunt	42	12	12	18	53	65	48
Horsham	42	13	8	21	66	81	47
Leighton Town	42	13	8	21	65	84	47
Molesey	42	10	12	20	54	69	42
Wingate & Finchley	42	11	7	24	54	97	40
Witham Town	42	7	9	26	39	110	30
Chalfont St Peter	42	2	8	32	39	124	14

Third Division

East Thurrock United	40	26	7	7	89	42	85
Great Wakering Rovers	40	25	7	8	81	41	82
Tilbury	40	21	12	7	67	39	75
Hornchurch	40	19	12	9	72	57	69
Croydon Athletic	40	19	11	10	85	52	68
Epsom & Ewell	40	18	12	10	67	46	66
Lewes	40	18	10	12	73	51	64
Bracknell Town	40	15	16	9	81	64	61
Aveley	40	17	10	13	73	64	61
Corinthian Casuals	40	16	10	14	59	51	58
Flackwell Heath	40	17	6	17	74	76	57
Ware	40	16	8	16	74	62	56
Egham Town	40	14	13	13	48	43	55
Hertford Town	40	15	10	15	63	60	55
Abingdon Town	40	10	12	18	48	64	42
Kingsbury Town	40	11	8	21	55	86	41
Camberley Town	40	11	7	22	44	79	40
Tring Town	40	10	9	21	37	64	39
Dorking	40	9	10	21	53	69	37
Clapton	40	9	7	24	50	93	34
Southall	40	3	5	32	33	123	14

2000-2001   Premier Division

Team	P	W	D	L	F	A	Pts
Farnborough Town	42	31	6	5	86	27	99
Canvey Island	42	27	8	7	79	41	89
Basingstoke Town	42	22	13	7	73	40	79
Aldershot Town	41	21	11	9	73	39	74
Chesham United	42	22	6	14	78	52	72
Gravesend & Northfleet	42	22	5	15	63	46	71
Heybridge Swifts	42	18	13	11	74	60	67
Billericay Town	41	18	13	10	62	54	67
Hampton & Richmond Borough	42	18	12	12	73	60	66
Hitchin Town	42	18	5	19	72	69	59
Purfleet	42	14	13	15	55	55	55
Hendon	40	16	6	18	62	62	54
Sutton United	41	14	11	16	74	70	53
St Albans City	42	15	5	22	50	69	50
Grays Athletic	42	14	8	20	49	68	50
Maidenhead United	42	15	2	25	47	63	47
Croydon	42	12	10	20	55	77	46
Enfield	42	12	9	21	48	74	45
Harrow Borough	41	10	11	20	62	91	41
Slough Town	42	10	9	23	40	62	39
Carshalton Athletic	42	10	6	26	40	85	36
Dulwich Hamlet	42	4	10	28	33	84	22

First Division

Team	P	W	D	L	F	A	Pts
Boreham Wood	42	26	7	9	82	49	85
Bedford Town	42	22	16	4	81	40	82
Braintree Town	42	25	6	11	112	60	81
Bishop's Stortford	42	24	6	12	103	76	78
Thame United	42	22	8	12	86	54	74
Ford United	42	19	12	11	70	58	69
Uxbridge	42	21	5	16	73	55	68
Northwood	42	20	8	14	89	81	68
Whyteleafe	42	20	6	16	62	69	66
Oxford City	42	16	13	13	64	49	61
Harlow Town	42	15	16	11	70	66	61
Worthing	42	16	9	17	69	69	57
Staines Town	42	16	8	18	60	66	56
Aylesbury United	42	17	4	21	65	55	55
Yeading	42	15	9	18	72	74	54
Bognor Regis Town	42	13	11	18	71	71	50
Walton & Hersham	42	14	8	20	59	80	50
Bromley	42	14	6	22	63	86	48
Wealdstone	42	12	9	21	54	73	45
Leatherhead	42	12	4	26	37	87	40
Romford	42	9	4	29	53	113	31
Barton Rovers	42	2	9	31	30	94	15

Second Division

Team	P	W	D	L	F	A	Pts
Tooting & Mitcham United	42	26	11	5	92	35	89
Windsor	42	24	10	8	70	40	82
Barking	42	23	13	6	82	54	82
Berkhamsted Town	42	24	8	10	99	49	80
Wivenhoe Town	42	23	11	8	78	52	80
Hemel Hempstead	42	22	10	10	74	44	76
Horsham	42	19	9	14	84	61	66
Chertsey Town	42	18	9	15	59	59	63
Great Wakering Rovers	42	16	13	13	69	59	61
Tilbury	42	18	6	18	61	67	60
Banstead Athletic	42	17	8	17	69	58	59
East Thurrock United	42	16	11	15	72	64	59
Metropolitan Police	42	18	4	20	64	77	58
Marlow	42	15	11	16	62	61	56
Molesey	42	14	9	19	53	61	51
Wembley	42	12	10	20	39	63	46
Hungerford Town	42	11	9	22	40	73	42
Leyton Pennant	42	10	11	21	47	74	41
Cheshunt	42	11	6	25	48	77	39
Edgware Town	42	9	9	24	41	77	36
Leighton Town	42	8	10	24	44	87	34
Wokingham Town	42	3	12	27	39	94	20

Wokingham Town had 1 point deducted

Third Division

Team	P	W	D	L	F	A	Pts
Arlesey Town	42	34	6	2	138	37	108
Lewes	41	25	11	5	104	34	86
Ashford Town	42	26	7	9	102	49	85
Flackwell Heath	42	24	10	8	93	51	82
Corinthian Casuals	42	24	10	8	83	50	82
Aveley	42	24	3	15	85	61	75
Epsom & Ewell	42	23	4	15	76	52	73
Witham Town	42	21	9	12	76	57	72
Bracknell Town	41	19	10	12	90	70	67
Croydon Athletic	41	15	12	14	78	63	57
Ware	42	17	6	19	75	76	57
Tring Town	42	16	9	17	60	71	57
Egham Town	42	15	11	16	60	60	56
Hornchurch	42	14	13	15	73	60	55
Wingate & Finchley	42	15	7	20	75	75	52
Kingsbury Town	42	11	8	23	74	100	41
Abingdon Town	42	12	7	23	53	102	40
Dorking	42	10	9	23	59	99	39
Hertford Town	41	9	8	24	57	97	35
Camberley Town	42	8	8	26	53	107	32
Clapton	42	5	9	28	48	121	24
Chalfont St Peter	42	4	1	37	30	150	13

Abingdon Town had 3 points deducted

2001-2002   Premier Division

Team	P	W	D	L	F	A	Pts
Gravesend & Northfleet	42	31	6	5	90	33	99
Canvey Island	42	30	5	7	107	41	95
Aldershot Town	42	22	7	13	76	51	73
Braintree Town	42	23	4	15	66	61	73
Purfleet	42	19	15	8	67	44	72
Grays Athletic	42	20	10	12	65	55	70
Chesham United	42	19	10	13	69	53	67
Hendon	42	19	5	18	66	54	62
Billericay Town	42	16	13	13	59	60	61
St Albans City	42	16	9	17	71	60	57
Hitchin Town	42	15	10	17	73	81	55
Sutton United	42	13	15	14	62	62	54
Heybridge Swifts	42	15	9	18	68	85	54
Kingstonian	42	13	13	16	50	56	52
Boreham Wood	42	15	6	21	49	62	51
Maidenhead United	42	15	5	22	51	63	50
Bedford Town	42	12	12	18	64	69	48
Basingstoke Town	42	11	15	16	50	68	48
Enfield	42	11	9	22	48	77	42
Hampton & Richmond Borough	42	9	13	20	51	71	40
Harrow Borough	42	8	10	24	50	89	34
Croydon	42	7	5	30	36	93	26

First Division

Team	P	W	D	L	F	A	Pts
Ford United	42	27	7	8	92	56	88
Bishop's Stortford	42	26	9	7	104	51	87
Aylesbury United	42	23	10	9	96	64	79
Bognor Regis Town	42	20	13	9	74	55	73
Northwood	42	19	11	12	92	64	68
Carshalton Athletic	42	17	16	9	64	53	67
Harlow Town	42	19	9	14	77	65	66
Slough Town	42	17	11	14	68	51	62
Uxbridge	42	18	6	18	68	65	60
Oxford City	42	17	9	16	59	66	60
Thame United	42	15	14	13	75	61	59
Tooting & Mitcham United	42	16	11	15	70	70	59
Walton & Hersham	42	16	10	16	75	70	58
Yeading	42	16	10	16	84	90	58
Worthing	42	15	8	19	69	65	53
Staines Town	42	12	11	19	45	60	47
Dulwich Hamlet	42	11	13	18	64	76	46
Wealdstone	42	11	12	19	60	82	45
Bromley	42	10	11	21	44	74	41
Whyteleafe	42	10	11	21	46	86	41
Barking & East Ham United	42	8	7	27	61	123	31
Windsor & Eton	42	7	5	30	53	93	26

2002-2003

Second Division

Lewes	42	29	9	4	108	31	96
Horsham	42	27	9	6	104	44	90
Berkhamstead Town	42	23	10	9	82	51	79
Arlesey Town	42	23	6	13	89	55	75
Banstead Athletic	42	22	8	12	83	54	74
Leyton Pennant	42	22	8	12	84	60	74
Great Wakering Rovers	42	21	8	13	64	37	71
East Thurrock United	42	21	8	13	67	59	71
Marlow	42	18	13	11	73	63	67
Hemel Hempstead Town	42	18	10	14	82	66	64
Leatherhead	42	17	6	19	72	62	57
Ashford Town	42	15	11	16	58	71	56
Metropolitan Police	42	16	7	19	84	84	55
Barton Rovers	42	15	9	18	54	60	54
Hungerford Town	42	14	9	19	56	75	51
Tilbury	42	15	6	21	55	74	51
Chertsey Town	42	10	14	18	79	112	44
Wembley	42	9	10	23	51	82	37
Molesey	42	10	6	26	40	93	36
Cheshunt	42	7	13	22	51	84	34
Wivenhoe Town	42	8	9	25	55	111	33
Romford	42	4	7	31	42	105	19

Third Division

Croydon Athletic	42	30	5	7	138	41	95
Hornchurch	42	25	11	6	96	46	86
Aveley	42	26	6	10	109	55	84
Bracknell Town	42	25	8	9	96	54	83
Epsom & Ewell	42	20	15	7	79	51	75
Egham Town	42	21	11	10	72	59	74
Wingate & Finchley	42	20	9	13	80	60	69
Dorking	42	18	14	10	77	66	68
Tring Town	42	19	11	12	64	62	68
Corinthian-Casuals	42	18	13	11	69	44	67
Hertford Town	42	20	7	15	88	74	67
Witham Town	42	15	10	17	66	72	55
Ware	42	14	10	18	74	76	52
Chalfont St Peter	42	15	4	23	69	92	49
Wokingham Town	42	14	6	22	79	105	48
Abingdon Town	42	13	7	22	61	75	46
Leighton Town	42	8	12	22	56	95	36
Kingsbury Town	42	8	11	23	58	91	35
Edgware Town	42	9	7	26	65	101	34
Flackwell Heath	42	9	8	25	53	99	32
Clapton	42	9	4	29	45	118	31
Camberley Town	42	7	9	26	37	95	30

Premier Division

Aldershot Town	46	33	6	7	81	36	105
Canvey Island	46	28	8	10	112	56	92
Hendon	46	22	13	11	70	56	79
St. Albans City	46	23	8	15	73	65	77
Basingstoke Town	46	23	7	16	80	60	76
Sutton United	46	22	9	15	77	62	75
Hayes	46	20	13	13	67	54	73
Purfleet	46	19	15	12	68	48	72
Bedford Town	46	21	9	16	66	58	72
Maidenhead United	46	16	17	13	75	63	65
Kingstonian	46	16	17	13	71	64	65
Billericay Town	46	17	11	18	46	44	62
Bishop's Stortford	46	16	11	19	74	72	59
Hitchin Town	46	15	13	18	69	67	58
Ford United	46	15	12	19	78	84	57
Braintree Town	46	14	12	20	59	71	54
Aylesbury United	46	13	15	18	62	75	54
Harrow Borough	46	15	9	22	54	75	54
Grays Athletic	46	14	11	21	53	59	53
Heybridge Swifts	46	13	14	19	52	80	53
Chesham United	46	14	10	22	56	81	52
Boreham Wood	46	11	15	20	50	58	48
Enfield	46	9	11	26	47	101	38
Hampton & Richmond Borough	46	3	14	29	35	86	23

Division One (North)

Northwood	46	28	7	11	109	56	91
Hornchurch	46	25	15	6	85	48	90
Hemel Hempstead Town	46	26	7	13	70	55	85
Slough Town	46	22	14	10	86	59	80
Uxbridge	46	23	10	13	62	41	79
Aveley	46	21	14	11	66	48	77
Berkhamsted Town	46	21	13	12	92	68	76
Thame United	46	20	12	14	84	51	72
Wealdstone	46	21	9	16	85	69	72
Harlow Town	46	20	12	14	66	53	72
Marlow	46	19	10	17	74	63	67
Barking & East Ham United	46	19	9	18	73	76	66
Yeading	46	18	11	17	77	69	65
Great Wakering Rovers	46	17	14	15	64	70	65
Oxford City	46	17	13	16	55	51	64
Arlesey Town	46	17	12	17	69	71	63
East Thurrock United	46	17	10	19	75	79	61
Wingate & Finchley	46	15	11	20	70	74	56
Barton Rovers	46	15	7	24	53	65	52
Tilbury	46	14	7	25	55	96	49
Wivenhoe Town	46	9	11	26	56	94	38
Leyton Pennant	46	9	7	30	38	81	34
Wembley	46	7	11	28	57	111	32
Hertford Town	46	6	6	34	46	119	24

Division One (South)

Carshalton Athletic	46	28	8	10	73	44	92
Bognor Regis Town	46	26	10	10	92	34	88
Lewes	46	24	16	6	106	50	88
Dulwich Hamlet	46	23	12	11	73	49	81
Whyteleafe	46	21	13	12	74	51	76
Bromley	46	21	13	12	70	53	76
Walton & Hersham	46	20	13	13	87	63	73
Horsham	46	21	9	16	80	58	72
Epsom & Ewell	46	19	12	15	67	66	69
Egham Town	46	19	10	17	62	71	67
Tooting & Mitcham United	46	18	9	19	83	78	63
Worthing	46	17	12	17	78	75	63
Windsor & Eton	46	18	9	19	66	65	63
Leatherhead	46	16	13	17	71	66	61
Staines Town	46	14	16	16	57	63	58
Banstead Athletic	46	14	15	17	58	59	57
Ashford Town (Middlesex)	46	14	11	21	47	70	53
Croydon	46	15	8	23	56	87	53
Croydon Athletic	46	13	13	20	52	66	52
Bracknell Town	46	12	16	18	57	74	52
Corinthian Casuals	46	12	14	20	50	68	50
Molesey	46	13	9	24	52	79	48
Metropolitan Police	46	12	10	24	50	76	46
Chertsey Town	46	3	7	36	43	139	16

Division Two

Cheshunt	30	25	3	2	91	29	78
Leyton	30	21	5	4	77	22	68
Flackwell Heath	30	17	3	10	52	44	54
Abingdon Town	30	14	11	5	65	42	53
Hungerford Town	30	12	12	6	49	36	48
Leighton Town	30	14	3	13	61	43	45
Witham Town	30	12	8	10	40	43	44
Ware	30	12	5	13	47	53	41
Clapton	30	12	5	13	40	47	41
Tring Town	30	11	5	14	49	58	38
Kingsbury Town	30	9	11	10	38	48	38
Edgware Town	30	10	3	17	49	65	33
Wokingham Town	30	7	7	16	34	81	28
Dorking	30	6	6	18	49	63	24
Chalfont St. Peter	30	6	5	19	34	63	23
Camberley Town	30	4	4	22	23	61	16

2003-2004

Premier Division

Canvey Island	46	32	8	6	106	42	104
Sutton United	46	25	10	11	94	56	85
Thurrock	46	24	11	11	87	45	83
Hendon	46	25	8	13	68	47	83
Hornchurch	46	24	11	11	63	35	82
Grays Athletic	46	22	15	9	82	39	81
Carshalton Athletic	46	24	9	13	66	55	81
Hayes	46	21	11	14	56	46	74
Kettering Town	46	20	11	15	63	63	71
Bognor Regis Town	46	20	10	16	69	67	70
Bishop's Stortford	46	20	9	17	78	61	69
Maidenhead United	46	18	9	19	60	68	63
Ford United	46	16	14	16	69	63	62
Basingstoke Town	46	17	9	20	58	64	60
Bedford Town	46	14	13	19	62	63	55
Heybridge Swifts	46	14	11	21	57	78	53
Harrow Borough	46	12	14	20	47	63	50
Kingstonian	46	12	13	21	40	56	49
St. Albans City	46	12	12	22	55	83	48
Hitchin Town	46	13	8	25	55	89	47
Northwood	46	12	9	25	65	95	45
Billericay Town	46	11	11	24	51	66	44
Braintree Town	46	11	6	29	41	88	39
Aylesbury United	46	5	14	27	41	101	29

Hornchurch had 1 point deducted.

Division One (North)

Yeading	46	32	7	7	112	54	103
Leyton	46	29	9	8	90	53	96
Cheshunt	46	27	10	9	119	54	91
Chesham United	46	24	9	13	104	60	81
Dunstable Town	46	23	9	14	86	61	78
Hemel Hempstead Town	46	22	12	12	75	72	78
Wealdstone	46	23	7	16	81	51	76
Arlesey Town	46	23	7	16	95	70	76
Boreham Wood	46	20	13	13	82	59	73
Harlow Town	46	20	10	16	75	51	70
Wingate & Finchley	46	19	13	14	68	63	70
East Thurrock United	46	19	11	16	62	54	68
Uxbridge	46	15	14	17	59	57	59
Aveley	46	15	14	17	67	71	59
Thame United	46	16	9	21	72	83	57
Waltham Forest	46	15	13	18	62	60	55
Wivenhoe Town	46	15	10	21	79	104	55
Barton Rovers	46	16	6	24	52	80	54
Oxford City	46	14	11	21	55	65	53
Berkhamsted Town	46	12	10	24	66	88	46
Great Wakering Rovers	46	10	13	23	47	97	43
Tilbury	46	10	9	27	56	100	39
Barking & East Ham United	46	8	7	31	37	100	31
Enfield	46	5	7	34	44	138	22

Waltham Forest had 3 points deducted.

Division One (South)

Lewes	46	29	7	10	113	61	94
Worthing	46	26	14	6	87	46	92
Windsor & Eton	46	26	13	7	75	39	91
Slough Town	46	28	6	12	103	63	90
Hampton & Richmond Borough	46	26	11	9	82	45	89
Staines Town	46	26	9	11	85	52	87
Dulwich Hamlet	46	23	15	8	77	57	84
Bromley	46	22	10	14	80	58	76
Walton & Hersham	46	20	14	12	76	55	74
Croydon Athletic	46	20	10	16	70	54	70
Tooting & Mitcham United	46	20	9	17	82	68	69
Ashford Town (Middlesex)	46	18	13	15	69	62	67
Leatherhead	46	19	9	18	83	88	66
Bracknell Town	46	19	6	21	81	87	63
Horsham	46	16	11	19	71	69	59
Marlow	46	16	11	19	50	64	59
Whyteleafe	46	17	4	25	66	93	55
Banstead Athletic	46	15	8	23	56	73	53
Molesey	46	12	6	28	45	84	42
Metropolitan Police	46	9	14	23	58	84	41
Croydon	46	10	10	26	57	88	40
Egham Town	46	8	8	30	55	92	32
Corinthian Casuals	46	6	6	34	48	110	24
Epsom & Ewell	46	5	8	33	40	117	23

Division Two

Leighton Town	42	28	7	7	111	36	91
Dorking	42	27	8	7	87	47	89
Hertford Town	42	24	9	9	74	35	81
Chertsey Town	42	22	9	11	75	53	75
Flackwell Heath	42	22	5	15	71	53	71
Witham Town	42	20	10	12	75	54	70
Kingsbury Town	42	14	11	17	60	64	53
Ware	42	14	10	18	67	60	52
Abingdon Town	42	15	6	21	83	81	51
Camberley Town	42	15	6	21	51	71	51
Wembley	42	13	9	20	46	67	48
Wokingham Town	42	12	7	23	55	94	43
Edgware Town	42	12	6	24	62	88	42
Chalfont St. Peter	42	12	6	24	57	89	42
Clapton	42	8	5	29	47	129	29

2004-2005

Premier Division

Yeading	42	25	11	6	74	48	86
Billericay Town	42	23	11	8	78	40	80
Eastleigh	42	22	13	7	84	49	79
Braintree Town	42	19	17	6	67	33	74
Leyton	42	21	8	13	71	57	71
Hampton & Richmond	42	21	8	13	64	53	71
Heybridge Swifts	42	18	9	15	76	65	63
Chelmsford City	42	17	11	14	63	58	62
Staines Town	42	17	9	16	59	53	60
Worthing	42	16	11	15	50	45	59
Hendon	42	17	7	18	48	60	58
Salisbury City	42	16	9	17	60	64	57
Slough Town	42	15	10	17	61	66	55
Folkestone Invicta	42	14	10	18	51	53	52
Windsor & Eton	42	12	14	16	48	62	50
Harrow Borough	42	13	10	19	41	54	49
Northwood	42	14	7	21	49	66	49
Wealdstone	42	13	8	21	60	73	47
Cheshunt	42	12	11	19	58	71	47
Tonbridge Angels	42	11	10	21	47	73	43
Dover Athletic	42	10	9	23	50	66	39
Kingstonian	42	7	5	30	43	93	26

Division One

AFC Wimbledon	42	29	10	3	91	33	97
Walton & Hersham	42	28	4	10	69	34	88
Horsham	42	24	6	12	90	61	78
Bromley	42	22	9	11	69	44	75
Metropolitan Police	42	22	8	12	72	51	74
Cray Wanderers	42	19	16	7	95	54	73
Leatherhead	42	20	13	9	73	55	73
Tooting & Mitcham United	42	18	15	9	92	60	69
Whyteleafe	42	20	6	16	60	59	66
Burgess Hill Town	42	19	6	17	73	62	63
Hastings United	42	15	11	16	55	57	56
Croydon Athletic	42	13	16	13	66	65	55
Corinthian-Casuals	42	15	9	18	56	64	54
Bashley	42	13	13	16	68	74	52
Dulwich Hamlet	42	10	14	18	61	64	44
Molesey	42	12	8	22	46	70	44
Banstead Athletic	42	10	10	22	50	64	40
Newport IOW	42	10	10	22	50	88	40
Fleet Town	42	11	5	26	47	86	38
Ashford Town	42	8	12	22	47	85	36
Dorking	42	8	11	23	43	89	35
Croydon	42	5	10	27	37	91	25

Division Two

Ilford	30	22	3	5	62	23	69
Enfield	30	21	3	6	64	33	66
Brook House	30	20	4	6	65	25	64
Hertford Town	30	17	7	6	65	40	58
Witham Town	30	16	3	11	67	53	51
Chertsey Town	30	15	6	9	55	48	51
Abingdon Town	30	13	9	8	65	42	48
Edgware Town	30	12	3	15	40	41	39
Flackwell Heath	30	11	5	14	50	55	38
Ware	30	9	10	11	41	55	37
Chalfont St Peter	30	9	7	14	41	52	34
Camberley Town	30	9	5	16	36	44	32
Wembley	30	8	5	17	41	55	29
Epsom & Ewell	30	8	4	18	41	64	28
Kingsbury Town	30	5	4	21	35	76	19
Clapton	30	3	6	21	20	82	15

2005-2006

Premier Division

Braintree Town	42	28	10	4	74	32	94
Heybridge Swifts	42	28	3	11	70	46	87
Fisher Athletic	42	26	7	9	84	46	85
AFC Wimbledon	42	22	11	9	67	36	77
Hampton & Richmond	42	24	3	15	73	54	75
Staines Town	42	20	10	12	74	56	70
Billericay Town	42	19	12	11	69	45	69
Worthing	42	19	10	13	71	60	67
Walton & Hersham	42	19	7	16	55	50	64
Chelmsford City	42	18	10	14	57	62	64
Bromley	42	16	14	12	57	49	62
East Thurrock United	42	18	5	19	60	60	59
Folkestone Invicta	42	16	10	16	47	51	58
Margate	42	11	17	14	49	55	50
Leyton	42	13	9	20	58	61	48
Harrow Borough	42	13	9	20	56	73	48
Slough Town	42	13	8	21	63	75	47
Wealdstone	42	13	5	24	68	82	44
Hendon	42	9	12	21	44	64	39
Maldon Town	42	8	11	23	41	73	35
Windsor & Eton	42	8	8	26	37	75	32
Redbridge	42	3	5	34	28	97	14

Division One

Ramsgate	44	24	14	6	84	38	86
Horsham	44	25	11	8	94	55	86
Tonbridge Angels	44	24	8	12	71	48	80
Metropolitan Police	44	24	7	13	72	46	79
Dover Athletic	44	21	14	9	69	46	77
Tooting & Mitcham United	44	22	9	13	93	62	75
Kingstonian	44	20	14	10	82	56	74
Croydon Athletic	44	20	13	11	56	41	73
Bashley	44	20	10	14	63	61	70
Leatherhead	44	18	14	12	64	50	68
Cray Wanderers	44	20	8	16	80	74	68
Hastings United	44	19	10	15	65	58	67
Dulwich Hamlet	44	19	8	17	55	43	65
Fleet Town	44	13	19	12	50	56	58
Walton Casuals	44	16	10	18	68	75	58
Lymington & New Milton	44	12	11	21	61	80	47
Molesey	44	12	10	22	56	79	46
Whyteleafe	44	10	14	20	50	66	44
Burgess Hill Town	44	10	10	24	57	83	40
Banstead Athletic	44	8	13	23	43	71	37
Ashford Town	44	8	11	25	41	81	35
Newport IOW	44	6	11	27	38	97	29
Corinthian Casuals	44	6	9	29	39	85	27

Division Two

Ware	30	19	4	7	77	36	61
Witham Town	30	17	7	6	61	30	58
Brook House	30	17	7	6	63	33	58
Flackwell Heath	30	15	7	8	54	49	52
Egham Town	30	15	5	10	39	36	50
Chertsey Town	30	14	7	9	47	37	49
Edgware Town	30	13	5	12	46	41	44
Chalfont St Peter	30	13	2	15	50	53	41
Dorking	30	11	8	11	48	51	41
Croydon	30	11	7	12	43	43	40
Wembley	30	11	6	13	44	43	39
Kingsbury Town	30	9	10	11	32	37	37
Hertford Town	30	7	10	13	35	54	31
Camberley Town	30	5	8	17	31	57	23
Epsom & Ewell	30	5	6	19	32	64	21
Clapton	30	4	9	17	33	71	16

Clapton had 5 points deducted.

2006-2007 Premier Division

Hampton & Richmond	42	24	10	8	77	53	82
Bromley	42	23	11	8	83	43	80
Chelmsford City	42	23	8	11	96	51	77
Billericay Town	42	22	11	9	71	42	77
AFC Wimbledon	42	21	15	6	76	37	75
Margate	42	20	11	11	79	48	71
Boreham Wood	42	19	12	11	71	49	69
Horsham	42	18	14	10	70	57	68
Ramsgate	42	20	5	17	63	63	65
Heybridge Swifts	42	17	13	12	57	40	64
Tonbridge Angels	42	20	4	18	74	72	64
Staines Town	42	15	12	15	64	64	57
Carshalton Athletic	42	14	12	16	54	59	54
Hendon	42	16	6	20	53	64	54
Leyton	42	13	10	19	55	77	49
East Thurrock United	42	14	6	22	56	70	48
Ashford Town (Middlesex)	42	11	13	18	59	71	46
Folkestone Invicta	42	12	10	20	45	66	46
Harrow Borough	42	13	6	23	61	71	45
Worthing	42	8	11	23	57	82	35
Walton & Hersham	42	9	6	27	38	83	33
Slough Town	42	4	6	32	26	123	18

AFC Wimbledon had 3 points deducted.

Division One North

AFC Hornchurch	42	32	7	3	96	27	103
Harlow Town	42	24	10	8	71	31	82
Enfield Town	42	24	7	11	74	39	79
Maldon Town	42	20	11	11	50	42	71
AFC Sudbury	42	19	13	10	67	41	70
Canvey Island	42	19	10	13	65	47	67
Ware	42	19	10	13	70	56	67
Waltham Forest	42	17	14	11	60	56	65
Wingate & Finchley	42	16	11	15	58	49	59
Waltham Abbey	42	15	13	14	65	51	58
Wivenhoe Town	42	16	9	17	50	52	57
Great Wakering Rovers	42	16	9	17	57	64	57
Enfield	42	16	6	20	65	63	54
Potters Bar Town	42	14	9	19	60	62	51
Aveley	42	14	9	19	47	57	51
Redbridge	42	15	5	22	42	48	50
Bury Town	42	13	11	18	57	69	50
Arlesey Town	42	13	11	18	44	63	50
Tilbury	42	11	10	21	43	72	43
Witham Town	42	10	7	25	52	90	37
Ilford	42	9	5	28	36	97	32
Flackwell Heath	42	7	9	26	37	90	30

Division One South

Maidstone United	42	23	11	8	79	47	80
Tooting & Mitcham	42	22	13	7	70	41	79
Dover Athletic	42	22	11	9	77	41	77
Hastings United	42	22	10	10	79	56	76
Fleet Town	42	21	12	9	65	52	75
Metropolitan Police	42	18	15	9	65	48	69
Dartford	42	19	11	12	86	65	68
Dulwich Hamlet	42	18	13	11	83	56	67
Horsham YMCA	42	17	7	18	59	69	58
Sittingbourne	42	14	15	13	68	63	57
Leatherhead	42	15	10	17	58	63	55
Cray Wanderers	42	14	12	16	67	69	54
Kingstonian	42	13	13	16	60	63	52
Burgess Hill Town	42	13	12	17	58	81	51
Molesey	42	12	13	17	52	63	49
Chatham Town	42	12	11	19	52	62	47
Walton Casuals	42	11	13	18	57	71	46
Ashford Town	42	10	14	18	52	65	44
Croydon Athletic	42	12	8	22	44	77	44
Whyteleafe	42	9	15	18	52	65	42
Corinthian-Casuals	42	8	10	24	53	88	34
Godalming Town	42	8	9	25	45	76	33

2007-2008

Premier Division

Chelmsford City	42	26	9	7	84	39	87
Staines Town	42	22	12	8	85	54	78
AFC Wimbledon	42	22	9	11	81	47	75
AFC Hornchurch	42	20	10	12	68	44	70
Ramsgate	42	19	11	12	67	53	68
Ashford Town (Middlesex)	42	20	6	16	79	65	66
Hendon	42	18	11	13	79	67	65
Tonbridge Angels	42	17	12	13	77	57	63
Margate	42	17	11	14	71	68	62
Billericay Town	42	16	12	14	66	57	60
Horsham	42	18	5	19	63	63	59
Heybridge Swifts	42	14	13	15	64	64	55
Wealdstone	42	15	9	18	68	75	54
Hastings United	42	15	8	19	58	67	53
Harlow Town	42	13	13	16	56	52	52
Harrow Borough	42	15	7	20	61	74	52
Maidstone United	42	16	4	22	56	79	52
Carshalton Athletic	42	14	8	20	52	65	50
Boreham Wood	42	15	5	22	56	73	50
East Thurrock United	42	14	9	19	48	67	50
Folkestone Invicta	42	13	10	19	49	70	49
Leyton	42	4	4	34	35	123	16

East Thurrock United had one point deducted.

Division One North

Dartford	42	27	8	7	107	42	89
AFC Sudbury	42	24	8	10	86	40	80
Redbridge	42	24	9	9	70	43	80
Ware	42	23	10	9	110	58	79
Canvey Island	42	23	10	9	82	39	79
Brentwood Town	42	22	11	9	70	49	77
Bury Town	42	22	9	11	76	53	75
Edgware Town	42	20	14	8	53	39	74
Maldon Town	42	19	10	13	78	63	67
Northwood	42	18	12	12	71	61	66
Aveley	42	18	12	12	68	65	66
Enfield Town	42	18	9	15	60	63	63
Great Wakering Rovers	42	13	9	20	64	66	48
Waltham Abbey	42	12	10	20	42	78	46
Arlesey Town	42	12	9	21	64	84	45
Witham Town	42	12	5	25	75	109	41
Potters Bar Town	42	10	9	23	45	77	39
Wingate & Finchley	42	8	11	23	45	72	35
Waltham Forest	42	7	12	23	44	74	33
Tilbury	42	7	12	23	49	96	32
Ilford	42	8	8	26	47	95	32
Wivenhoe Town	42	8	7	27	46	86	31

Redbridge and Tilbury both had one point deducted.

Division One South

Dover Athletic	42	30	8	4	84	29	98
Tooting & Mitcham	42	26	8	8	88	41	86
Cray Wanderers	42	25	11	6	87	42	86
Metropolitan Police	42	24	3	15	69	47	75
Worthing	42	22	7	13	77	49	73
Dulwich Hamlet	42	20	10	12	68	47	70
Kingstonian	42	20	10	12	66	52	70
Ashford Town	42	19	10	13	64	51	67
Sittingbourne	42	20	7	15	56	58	67
Walton & Hersham	42	15	12	15	65	62	57
Whyteleafe	42	17	5	20	57	62	56
Burgess Hill Town	42	18	8	16	61	57	54
Croydon Athletic	42	14	9	19	65	76	51
Whitstable Town	42	14	8	20	69	84	50
Chipstead	42	15	5	22	58	76	50
Walton Casuals	42	11	15	16	55	68	48
Leatherhead	42	13	7	22	52	63	46
Chatham Town	42	12	10	20	58	70	46
Eastbourne Town	42	11	11	20	58	84	44
Corinthian-Casuals	42	11	11	20	51	77	44
Horsham YMCA	42	7	6	29	36	85	27
Molesey	42	3	9	30	36	100	18

Burgess Hill Town had 8 points deducted.

Division One North

Aveley	42	29	9	4	81	40	96
East Thurrock United	42	30	5	7	112	50	95
Brentwood Town	42	26	10	6	77	32	88
Waltham Abbey	42	25	7	10	85	45	82
Concord Rangers	42	23	10	9	83	34	79
Northwood	42	22	12	8	65	39	78
Wingate & Finchley	42	19	10	13	67	51	67
Redbridge	42	18	10	14	61	50	64
Ware	42	19	4	19	69	75	61
Chatham Town	42	18	6	18	58	60	60
Tilbury	42	16	10	16	62	53	58
Enfield Town	42	17	7	18	71	68	58
Great Wakering Rovers	42	16	10	16	56	62	58
Cheshunt	42	17	5	20	60	71	56
Leyton	42	12	15	15	63	56	51
Maldon Town	42	13	9	20	48	63	45
Ilford	42	12	5	25	27	68	41
Thamesmead Town	42	10	10	22	46	73	40
Potters Bar Town	42	9	10	23	52	73	36
Waltham Forest	42	9	7	26	39	81	34
Witham Town	42	6	9	27	37	103	27
Hillingdon Borough	42	4	4	34	35	107	16

Maldon Town had 3 points deducted.
Potters Bar Town had 1 point deducted.

2008-2009

Premier Division

Dover Athletic	42	33	5	4	91	34	104
Staines Town	42	23	13	6	75	41	82
Tonbridge Angels	42	20	13	9	82	54	73
Carshalton Athletic	42	19	11	12	64	63	68
Sutton United	42	18	13	11	57	53	67
AFC Hornchurch	42	19	8	15	60	51	65
Wealdstone	42	18	8	16	70	56	62
Dartford	42	17	11	14	62	49	62
Tooting & Mitcham United	42	16	10	16	57	57	58
Ashford Town (Middlesex)	42	18	2	22	64	66	56
Billericay Town	42	15	11	16	54	66	56
Canvey Island	42	16	7	19	65	70	55
Horsham	42	16	7	19	49	60	55
Harrow Borough	42	14	12	16	56	73	54
Maidstone United	42	14	11	17	46	51	53
Hendon	42	15	6	21	69	65	51
Hastings United	42	14	7	21	52	68	49
Boreham Wood	42	12	12	18	48	61	48
Margate	42	13	7	22	51	64	46
Harlow Town	42	13	6	23	61	77	42
Heybridge Swifts	42	10	11	21	41	63	41
Ramsgate	42	8	11	23	47	79	31

Harlow town had 3 points deducted.
Ramsgate had 4 points deducted.

Division One South

Kingstonian	42	26	8	8	91	48	86
Cray Wanderers	42	24	7	11	87	54	79
Fleet Town	42	21	15	6	82	43	78
Metropolitan Police	42	21	14	7	72	45	77
Worthing	42	21	13	8	77	48	76
Sittingbourne	42	19	13	10	63	54	70
Ashford Town	42	16	15	11	68	54	63
Merstham	42	18	10	14	57	54	63
Godalming Town	42	17	11	14	71	50	62
Croydon Athletic	42	16	14	12	67	54	62
Folkestone Invicta	42	16	11	15	54	46	59
Dulwich Hamlet	42	15	15	12	64	50	57
Eastbourne Town	42	17	6	19	66	72	57
Walton & Hersham	42	13	11	18	46	55	50
Leatherhead	42	14	8	20	57	74	50
Whitstable Town	42	14	8	20	58	77	50
Walton Casuals	42	12	8	22	43	60	44
Whyteleafe	42	11	10	21	48	64	43
Burgess Hill Town	42	10	13	19	49	66	43
Corinthian-Casuals	42	11	10	21	61	91	43
Chipstead	42	8	12	22	57	96	36
Crowborough Athletic	42	4	4	34	42	125	13

Merstham had one point deducted.
Dulwich Hamlet and Crowborough Athletic had 3 points deducted.

2009-2010

Premier Division

Dartford	42	29	6	7	101	45	93
Sutton United	42	22	9	11	65	45	75
Aveley	42	21	7	14	83	62	70
Boreham Wood	42	20	8	14	54	44	68
Kingstonian	42	20	8	14	73	69	68
Wealdstone	42	17	14	11	65	65	65
Hastings United	42	18	9	15	68	56	63
Tonbridge Angels	42	18	8	16	69	67	62
AFC Hornchurch	42	16	13	13	51	47	61
Hendon	42	18	6	18	61	59	60
Horsham	42	16	8	18	65	67	56
Tooting & Mitcham United	42	15	10	17	60	64	55
Billericay Town	42	14	12	16	44	42	54
Harrow Borough	42	13	14	15	66	63	53
Cray Wanderers	42	14	9	19	54	70	51
Canvey Island	42	13	11	18	57	62	50
Carshalton Athletic	42	12	13	17	58	64	49
Maidstone United	42	13	10	19	39	57	49
Margate	42	11	12	19	50	72	45
Ashford Town (Middlesex)	42	11	11	20	62	80	44
Waltham Abbey	42	12	8	22	49	74	44
Bognor Regis Town	42	9	14	19	45	65	41

Division One North

Lowestoft Town	42	32	5	5	115	37	101
Concord Rangers	42	26	8	8	94	42	86
Wingate & Finchley	42	24	9	9	88	55	81
Enfield Town	42	23	11	8	81	47	80
East Thurrock United	42	23	8	11	102	59	77
Heybridge Swifts	42	21	8	13	67	56	71
Thamesmead Town	42	20	7	15	67	56	67
VCD Athletic (R)	42	19	10	13	61	53	67
Great Wakering Rovers	42	18	10	14	67	70	64
Northwood	42	17	10	15	65	61	61
Tilbury	42	15	11	16	61	60	56
Brentwood Town	42	15	7	20	53	53	52
Romford	42	15	7	20	71	88	52
Potters Bar Town	42	14	8	20	51	67	50
Cheshunt	42	16	2	24	57	83	50
Waltham Forest	42	13	9	20	51	75	48
Maldon Town	42	13	6	23	54	74	45
Ilford	42	11	10	21	47	72	43
Redbridge	42	9	15	18	42	62	42
Ware	42	11	9	22	57	84	42
Leyton	42	5	15	22	40	84	30
Harlow Town	42	6	7	29	46	98	15

VCD Athletic were relegated at the end of the season due to their failure to meet ground grading requirements.
Harlow Town had 10 points deducted for entering administration. They were reprieved from relegation but this was subject to a further appeal at the time of going to press.

Division One South

Croydon Athletic	42	27	8	7	92	39	89
Folkestone Invicta	42	28	8	6	54	23	82
Worthing	42	25	5	12	83	53	80
Godalming Town	42	26	5	11	71	44	80
Leatherhead	42	22	8	12	78	45	74
Fleet Town	42	22	6	14	74	49	72
Burgess Hill Town	42	19	10	13	64	50	67
Walton & Hersham	42	18	8	16	55	54	62
Sittingbourne	42	18	7	17	63	48	61
Metropolitan Police	42	17	9	16	59	50	60
Horsham YMCA	42	15	14	13	67	61	59
Dulwich Hamlet	42	14	12	16	57	64	54
Corinthian-Casuals	42	17	3	22	66	79	54
Ramsgate	42	13	14	15	55	61	53
Whyteleafe	42	15	6	21	60	64	51
Merstham	42	12	12	18	62	80	48
Chatham Town	42	14	4	24	55	75	46
Whitstable Town	42	14	3	25	41	85	45
Chipstead	42	11	10	21	47	65	43
Ashford Town (Kent)	42	9	11	22	49	90	38
Walton Casuals	42	8	10	24	41	66	34
Eastbourne Town	42	6	11	25	29	77	29

Folkestone Invicta had 10 points deducted.
Godalming Town had 3 points deducted.

2010-2011

Premier Division

Sutton United	42	26	9	7	76	33	87
Tonbridge Angels	42	22	10	10	71	45	76
Bury Town	42	22	10	10	67	49	76
Lowestoft Town	42	20	15	7	68	30	75
Harrow Borough	42	22	7	13	77	51	73
Canvey Island	42	21	10	11	69	51	73
Kingstonian	42	21	9	12	66	50	72
Concord Rangers	42	21	8	13	72	55	71
Cray Wanderers	42	20	9	13	72	46	69
AFC Hornchurch	42	19	12	11	60	46	69
Billericay Town	42	20	9	13	56	45	69
Wealdstone	42	16	10	16	58	54	58
Carshalton Athletic	42	14	10	18	49	57	52
Tooting & Mitcham United	42	13	10	19	63	85	49
Hendon	42	12	10	20	61	81	46
Margate	42	11	12	19	52	64	45
Horsham	42	11	11	20	43	77	44
Hastings United	42	9	11	22	50	65	38
Aveley	42	10	8	24	35	62	38
Maidstone United	42	9	10	23	45	75	37
Croydon Athletic	42	10	4	28	44	95	31
Folkestone Invicta	42	5	12	25	34	68	27

Croydon Athletic had 3 points deducted.

Division One North

East Thurrock United	40	30	5	5	92	38	95
Needham Market	40	26	9	5	95	49	87
Wingate & Finchley	40	21	9	10	72	54	72
Harlow Town	40	21	8	11	61	51	71
Brentwood Town	40	20	9	11	75	55	69
Enfield Town	40	21	5	14	76	44	68
AFC Sudbury	40	18	12	10	82	64	66
Maldon & Tiptree	40	18	9	13	70	67	63
Heybridge Swifts	40	17	10	13	81	59	61
Grays Athletic	40	17	10	13	69	51	61
Waltham Abbey	40	16	10	14	75	63	58
Romford	40	16	7	17	63	66	55
Potters Bar Town	40	14	9	17	60	68	51
Ware	40	13	6	21	57	77	45
Great Wakering Rovers	40	13	5	22	60	82	44
Redbridge	40	10	9	21	51	79	39
Thamesmead Town	40	11	6	23	42	71	39
Cheshunt	40	10	8	22	49	81	38
Tilbury	40	11	4	25	41	66	37
Ilford	40	8	8	24	42	81	32
Waltham Forest	40	6	8	26	43	90	26

Leyton withdrew from Division One North on 14th January 2011 and were subsequently expelled from the League. The club's record was expunged when it stood at: 19 1 6 12 13 45 9
Waltham Forest were reprieved from relegation due to this withdrawal.

2011-2012

Premier Division

Billericay Town	42	24	13	5	82	38	85
AFC Hornchurch	42	26	4	12	68	35	82
Lowestoft Town	42	25	7	10	80	53	82
Wealdstone	42	20	15	7	76	39	75
Bury Town	42	22	9	11	85	55	75
Lewes	42	21	10	11	55	47	73
Hendon	42	21	9	12	69	44	72
Canvey Island	42	22	5	15	66	55	71
Cray Wanderers	42	20	8	14	74	55	68
East Thurrock United	42	18	8	16	70	65	62
Kingstonian	42	18	7	17	58	64	61
Metropolitan Police	42	18	6	18	63	46	60
Wingate & Finchley	42	16	11	15	63	79	59
Concord Rangers	42	16	9	17	72	66	57
Margate	42	15	9	18	66	65	54
Carshalton Athletic	42	14	10	18	48	55	52
Harrow Borough	42	13	8	21	53	70	47
Hastings United	42	13	8	21	43	61	47
Leatherhead	42	11	8	23	46	62	41
Aveley	42	5	12	25	41	88	27
Tooting & Mitcham United	42	7	6	29	47	116	27
Horsham	42	3	6	33	38	105	14

Horsham had 1 point deducted for fielding an ineligible player.

Division One South

Metropolitan Police	42	30	6	6	102	41	96
Bognor Regis Town	42	29	9	4	103	43	96
Whitehawk	42	26	10	6	109	44	88
Leatherhead	42	27	7	8	100	41	88
Dulwich Hamlet	42	19	8	15	79	59	65
Walton & Hersham	42	18	8	16	69	58	62
Burgess Hill Town	42	16	14	12	69	60	62
Ramsgate	42	16	12	14	65	63	60
Faversham Town	42	14	17	11	55	48	59
Chipstead	42	15	12	15	63	67	57
Sittingbourne	42	16	8	18	52	66	56
Walton Casuals	42	15	8	19	65	71	53
Fleet Town	42	14	10	18	68	90	52
Worthing	42	12	14	16	76	72	50
Whitstable Town	42	12	13	17	58	75	49
Whyteleafe	42	14	3	25	65	94	45
Godalming Town	42	13	6	23	52	82	45
Eastbourne Town	42	11	11	20	60	78	44
Merstham	42	10	15	17	60	85	44
Corinthian-Casuals	42	11	9	22	53	80	42
Chatham Town	42	10	10	22	52	80	40
Horsham YMCA	42	5	8	29	41	119	23

Merstham had one point deducted.
Chatham Town were reprieved from relegation after transferring to the Isthmian League Division One North for the next season.

Division One North

Leiston	42	28	7	7	99	41	91
Enfield Town	42	27	9	6	96	46	90
Tilbury	42	23	11	8	82	62	80
Needham Market	42	23	8	11	104	56	77
Grays Athletic	42	24	8	10	80	47	77
Redbridge	42	21	10	11	79	59	73
Harlow Town	42	21	8	13	70	49	71
AFC Sudbury	42	20	9	13	65	57	69
Brentwood Town	42	18	8	16	58	42	62
Thamesmead Town	42	17	7	18	68	70	58
Maldon & Tiptree	42	16	10	16	62	66	58
Potters Bar Town	42	16	9	17	67	76	57
Romford	42	15	12	15	64	73	57
Waltham Abbey	42	15	10	17	79	76	55
Chatham Town	42	16	6	20	54	63	54
Heybridge Swifts	42	15	7	20	59	64	52
Waltham Forest	42	12	7	23	59	95	43
Cheshunt	42	9	12	21	42	83	39
Soham Town Rangers	42	7	13	22	55	93	34
Ilford	42	8	6	28	47	85	30
Ware	42	8	6	28	40	78	30
Great Wakering Rovers	42	6	11	25	43	91	29

Grays Athletic had 3 points deducted for fielding an ineligible player.

Division One South

Team	P	W	D	L	F	A	Pts
Whitehawk	40	29	6	5	82	26	90
Bognor Regis Town	40	26	10	4	105	37	88
Dulwich Hamlet	40	26	8	6	73	26	86
Folkestone Invicta	40	23	7	10	82	53	76
Godalming Town	40	22	7	11	77	53	73
Maidstone United	40	20	7	13	68	50	67
Worthing	40	18	10	12	69	45	64
Hythe Town	40	17	8	15	62	62	59
Merstham	40	17	8	15	63	69	59
Chipstead	40	16	8	16	59	57	56
Ramsgate	40	16	7	17	61	72	55
Walton & Hersham	40	14	8	18	54	52	50
Corinthian-Casuals	40	12	12	16	49	63	48
Eastbourne Town	40	11	13	16	49	63	46
Walton Casuals	40	12	6	22	51	74	42
Crawley Down	40	12	5	23	65	81	41
Faversham Town	40	10	10	20	43	67	40
Whitstable Town	40	12	4	24	46	87	40
Sittingbourne	40	6	12	22	36	75	30
Burgess Hill Town	40	9	6	25	39	90	30
Whyteleafe	40	6	10	24	38	67	28

Whitehawk had 3 points deducted for fielding an ineligible player.
Burgess Hill Town had 3 points deducted for fielding an ineligible player.
Croydon Athletic had 10 points deducted for financial irregularities and then resigned from the League on 18th January 2012. The club's record was expunged when it stood at: 19 3 3 13 23 44 2
Godalming Town transferred to the Southern Football League Division One Central at the end of the season.

Division One North

Team	P	W	D	L	F	A	Pts
Grays Athletic	42	32	6	4	96	38	102
Maldon & Tiptree	42	27	8	7	101	47	89
Thamesmead Town	42	28	4	10	85	49	88
Witham Town	42	24	7	11	71	47	79
Aveley	42	24	6	12	92	58	78
Heybridge Swifts	42	21	10	11	102	55	73
Soham Town Rangers	42	22	7	13	95	75	73
Romford	42	19	7	16	72	72	64
Tilbury	42	18	9	15	69	62	63
Brentwood Town	42	17	8	17	63	62	59
Potters Bar Town	42	15	13	14	64	68	58
Cheshunt	42	16	10	16	75	73	55
Waltham Abbey	42	15	8	19	60	70	53
Chatham Town	42	13	13	16	59	65	52
Wroxham	42	12	14	16	68	64	50
Needham Market	42	12	13	17	61	62	49
A.F.C. Sudbury	42	12	9	21	57	84	45
Waltham Forest	42	10	10	22	54	72	40
Ware	42	10	6	26	59	105	36
Redbridge	42	7	6	29	42	105	26
Harlow Town	42	9	8	25	45	82	25
Ilford	42	4	8	30	32	105	20

Redbridge had one point deducted for fielding an ineligible player.
Cheshunt had 3 points deducted for fielding an ineligible player.
Harlow Town had 10 points deducted for failing to notify the league that they had failed to make repayments under their company voluntary arrangement and had extended the term of their CVA.

2012-2013

Premier Division

Team	P	W	D	L	F	A	Pts
Whitehawk	42	25	13	4	88	42	88
Lowestoft Town	42	23	11	8	71	38	80
Wealdstone	42	22	13	7	70	38	79
Concord Rangers	42	22	10	10	80	54	76
East Thurrock United	42	18	16	8	65	45	70
Metropolitan Police	42	20	10	12	65	56	70
Bury Town	42	19	9	14	66	64	66
Canvey Island	42	18	10	14	60	55	64
Margate	42	17	11	14	61	49	62
Hendon	42	16	12	14	48	50	60
Kingstonian	42	18	5	19	63	62	59
Leiston	42	13	17	12	55	57	56
Hampton & Richmond	42	13	14	15	58	56	53
Bognor Regis Town	42	15	8	19	48	58	53
Harrow Borough	42	12	9	21	53	71	45
Enfield Town	42	13	5	24	60	83	44
Cray Wanderers	42	10	13	19	60	85	43
Wingate & Finchley	42	12	6	24	56	82	42
Lewes	42	9	13	20	59	75	40
Carshalton Athletic	42	12	4	26	55	76	40
Hastings United	42	8	15	19	39	62	39
Thurrock	42	11	8	23	40	62	38

Thurrock had three points deducted after the end of the season for fielding an ineligible player. A subsequent appeal was rejected.

Division One South

Team	P	W	D	L	F	A	Pts
Dulwich Hamlet	42	28	5	9	91	42	89
Maidstone United	42	26	10	6	96	39	88
Faversham Town	42	22	11	9	74	57	77
Hythe Town	42	22	10	10	78	55	76
Folkestone Invicta	42	19	14	9	73	49	71
Leatherhead	42	22	4	16	66	44	70
Ramsgate	42	20	10	12	60	44	70
Burgess Hill Town	42	16	15	11	54	46	63
Sittingbourne	42	16	13	13	67	56	61
Worthing	42	16	9	17	77	74	57
Eastbourne Town	42	16	9	17	62	61	57
Merstham	42	16	8	18	67	76	56
Crawley Down Gatwick	42	15	10	17	72	70	55
Corinthian-Casuals	42	10	16	16	39	54	46
Horsham	42	12	9	21	54	77	45
Tooting & Mitcham United	42	12	9	21	52	75	45
Whitstable Town	42	12	8	22	53	71	44
Walton & Hersham	42	11	11	20	48	77	44
Herne Bay	42	10	13	19	44	69	43
Chipstead	42	11	9	22	54	80	42
Three Bridges	42	11	7	24	58	83	40
Walton Casuals	42	9	10	23	50	90	37

2013-2014

Premier Division

Wealdstone	46	28	12	6	99	43	96
Kingstonian	46	25	10	11	80	44	85
Bognor Regis Town	46	26	7	13	95	65	85
Lowestoft Town	46	24	12	10	76	40	84
AFC Hornchurch	46	24	11	11	83	53	83
Dulwich Hamlet	46	25	7	14	96	65	82
Maidstone United	46	23	12	11	92	57	81
Hendon	46	21	7	18	84	69	70
Leiston	46	19	10	17	73	71	67
Billericay Town	46	19	9	18	66	64	66
Margate	46	18	10	18	70	67	64
Hampton & Richmond Borough	46	18	10	18	72	70	64
Canvey Island	46	17	11	18	65	65	62
Grays Athletic	46	17	10	19	74	82	61
Bury Town	46	17	9	20	60	65	60
Lewes	46	14	17	15	67	67	59
Metropolitan Police	46	15	13	18	58	59	58
Harrow Borough	46	15	13	18	66	72	58
Enfield Town	46	13	12	21	64	90	51
East Thurrock United	46	13	10	23	66	84	49
Wingate & Finchley	46	14	7	25	57	84	49
Thamesmead Town	46	12	10	24	61	90	46
Carshalton Athletic	46	8	6	32	40	101	30
Cray Wanderers	46	7	5	34	40	138	26

Division One South

Peacehaven & Telscombe	46	33	8	5	128	55	107
Folkestone Invicta	46	27	8	11	102	59	89
Leatherhead	46	28	8	10	93	46	86
Guernsey	46	23	12	11	93	65	81
Hastings United	46	24	7	15	73	62	79
Burgess Hill Town	46	22	11	13	88	67	77
Merstham	46	23	7	16	81	63	76
Hythe Town	46	22	7	17	87	71	73
Walton Casuals	46	22	4	20	89	93	70
Faversham Town	46	18	14	14	78	69	68
Tooting & Mitcham United	46	17	12	17	79	75	63
Ramsgate	46	18	8	20	84	79	62
Chipstead	46	18	8	20	79	83	62
Sittingbourne	46	16	13	17	69	75	61
Worthing	46	17	8	21	80	98	59
Horsham	46	15	11	20	66	78	56
Corinthian-Casuals	46	15	10	21	69	73	55
Herne Bay	46	15	9	22	69	72	54
Three Bridges	46	15	8	23	71	88	53
Whitstable Town	46	14	11	21	61	78	53
Walton & Hersham	46	14	9	23	75	92	51
Redhill	46	13	6	27	72	96	45
Crawley Down Gatwick	46	9	6	31	51	139	33
Eastbourne Town	46	6	11	29	60	121	29

Leatherhead had 6 points deducted for a registration irregularity.

Division One North

VCD Athletic	46	32	3	11	116	54	99
Witham Town	46	30	8	8	109	54	98
Heybridge Swifts	46	28	9	9	108	59	93
Harlow Town	46	27	10	9	105	59	91
Needham Market	46	25	12	9	85	44	87
Thurrock	46	26	9	11	99	60	87
Dereham Town	46	22	11	13	98	65	77
Soham Town Rangers	46	24	4	18	92	75	76
Maldon & Tiptree	46	21	13	12	82	68	76
AFC Sudbury	46	21	13	12	76	63	76
Romford	46	21	5	20	76	69	68
Chatham Town	46	20	8	18	74	76	68
Aveley	46	20	5	21	81	81	65
Redbridge	46	16	11	19	78	84	59
Cheshunt	46	12	17	17	74	75	53
Tilbury	46	14	11	21	56	74	53
Burnham Ramblers	46	14	10	22	69	100	52
Waltham Abbey	46	14	8	24	71	90	50
Brentwood Town	46	11	13	22	71	92	46
Barkingside	46	12	10	24	76	120	46
Ware	46	12	9	25	73	93	45
Wroxham	46	10	6	30	77	123	36
Waltham Forest	46	6	7	33	43	118	25
Erith & Belvedere	46	6	4	36	44	137	22

NORTHERN PREMIER LEAGUE

1968-69

Team	P	W	D	L	F	A	Pts
Macclesfield Town	38	27	6	5	82	38	60
Wigan Athletic	38	18	12	8	59	41	48
Morecambe	38	16	14	8	64	37	46
Gainsborough Trinity	38	19	8	11	64	43	46
South Shields	38	19	8	11	78	56	46
Bangor City	38	18	9	11	102	64	45
Hyde United	38	16	10	12	71	65	42
Goole Town	38	15	10	13	80	78	40
Altrincham	38	14	10	14	69	52	38
Fleetwood	38	16	6	16	58	58	38
Gateshead	38	14	9	15	42	48	37
South Liverpool	38	12	13	13	56	66	37
Northwich Victoria	38	16	5	17	59	82	37
Boston United	38	14	8	16	59	65	36
Runcorn	38	12	11	15	59	63	35
Netherfield	38	12	4	22	51	69	28
Scarborough	38	9	10	19	49	68	28
Ashington	38	10	8	20	48	74	28
Chorley	38	8	9	21	46	75	25
Worksop Town	38	6	8	24	34	88	20

1969-70

Team	P	W	D	L	F	A	Pts
Macclesfield Town	38	22	8	8	72	41	52
Wigan Athletic	38	20	12	6	56	32	52
Boston United	38	21	8	9	65	33	50
Scarborough	38	20	10	8	74	39	50
South Shields	38	19	7	12	66	43	45
Gainsborough Trinity	38	16	11	11	64	49	43
Stafford Rangers	38	16	7	15	59	52	39
Bangor City	38	15	9	14	68	63	39
Northwich Victoria	38	15	8	15	60	66	38
Netherfield	38	14	9	15	56	54	37
Hyde United	38	15	7	16	59	59	37
Altrincham	38	14	8	16	62	65	36
Fleetwood	38	13	10	15	53	60	36
Runcorn	38	11	13	14	57	72	35
Morecambe	38	10	13	15	41	51	33
South Liverpool	38	11	11	16	44	55	33
Great Harwood	38	10	9	19	63	92	29
Matlock Town	38	8	12	18	52	67	28
Goole Town	38	10	6	22	50	71	26
Gateshead	38	5	12	21	37	94	22

1970-71

Team	P	W	D	L	F	A	Pts
Wigan Athletic	42	27	13	2	91	32	67
Stafford Rangers	42	27	7	8	87	51	61
Scarborough	42	23	12	7	83	40	58
Boston United	42	22	12	8	69	31	56
Macclesfield Town	42	23	10	9	84	45	56
Northwich Victoria	42	22	5	15	71	55	49
Bangor City	42	19	10	13	72	61	48
Altrincham	42	19	10	13	80	76	48
South Liverpool	42	15	15	12	67	57	45
Chorley	42	14	14	14	58	61	42
Gainsborough Trinity	42	15	11	16	65	63	41
Morecambe	42	14	11	17	67	79	39
South Shields	42	12	14	16	67	66	38
Bradford Park Avenue	42	15	8	19	54	73	38
Lancaster City	42	12	12	18	53	76	36
Netherfield	42	13	9	20	59	57	35
Matlock Town	42	10	13	19	58	80	33
Fleetwood	42	10	11	21	56	90	31
Great Harwood	42	8	13	21	66	98	29
Runcorn	42	10	5	27	58	84	25
Kirkby Town	42	6	13	23	57	93	25
Goole Town	42	10	4	28	44	98	24

1971-72

Team	P	W	D	L	F	A	Pts
Stafford Rangers	46	30	11	5	91	32	71
Boston United	46	28	13	5	87	37	69
Wigan Athletic	46	27	10	9	70	43	64
Scarborough	46	21	15	10	75	46	57
Northwich Victoria	46	20	14	12	65	59	54
Macclesfield Town	46	18	15	13	61	50	51
Gainsborough Trinity	46	21	9	16	93	79	51
South Shields	46	18	14	14	75	57	50
Bangor City	46	20	8	18	93	74	48
Altrincham	46	18	11	17	72	58	47
Skelmersdale United	46	19	9	18	61	58	47
Matlock Town	46	20	7	19	67	75	47
Chorley	46	17	12	17	66	59	46
Lancaster City	46	15	14	17	85	84	44
Great Harwood	46	15	14	17	60	74	44
Ellesmere Port Town	46	17	9	20	67	71	43
Morecambe	46	15	10	21	51	64	40
Bradford Park Avenue	46	13	13	20	54	71	39
Netherfield	46	16	5	25	51	73	37
Fleetwood	46	11	15	20	43	67	37
South Liverpool	46	12	12	22	61	73	36
Runcorn	46	8	14	24	48	80	30
Goole Town	46	9	10	27	51	97	28
Kirkby Town	46	6	12	28	38	104	24

1972-73

Team	P	W	D	L	F	A	Pts
Boston United	46	27	16	3	88	34	70
Scarborough	46	26	9	11	72	39	61
Wigan Athletic	46	23	14	9	69	38	60
Altrincham	46	22	16	8	75	55	60
Bradford Park Avenue	46	19	17	10	63	50	55
Stafford Rangers	46	20	11	15	63	46	51
Gainsborough Trinity	46	18	13	15	70	50	49
Northwich Victoria	46	17	15	14	74	62	49
Netherfield	46	20	9	17	68	65	49
Macclesfield Town	46	16	16	14	58	47	48
Ellesmere Port Town	46	18	11	17	52	56	47
Skelmersdale United	46	15	16	15	58	59	46
Bangor City	46	16	13	17	70	60	45
Mossley	46	17	11	18	70	73	45
Morecambe	46	17	11	18	62	70	45
Great Harwood	46	14	15	17	63	74	43
South Liverpool	46	12	19	15	47	57	43
Runcorn	46	15	12	19	75	78	42
Goole Town	46	13	13	20	64	73	39
South Shields	46	17	4	25	64	81	38
Matlock Town	46	11	11	24	42	80	33
Lancaster City	46	10	11	25	53	78	31
Barrow	46	12	6	28	52	101	30
Fleetwood	46	5	15	26	31	77	25

1973-74

	P	W	D	L	F	A	Pts
Boston United	46	27	11	8	69	32	65
Wigan Athletic	46	28	8	10	96	39	64
Altrincham	46	26	11	9	77	34	63
Stafford Rangers	46	27	9	10	101	45	63
Scarborough	46	22	14	10	62	43	58
South Shields	46	25	6	15	87	48	56
Runcorn	46	21	14	11	72	47	56
Macclesfield Town	46	18	15	13	48	47	51
Bangor City	46	19	11	16	65	56	49
Gainsborough Trinity	46	18	11	17	77	64	47
South Liverpool	46	16	15	15	55	47	47
Skelmersdale United	46	16	13	17	50	59	45
Goole Town	46	14	15	17	60	69	43
Fleetwood	46	14	15	17	48	68	43
Mossley	46	15	11	20	53	65	41
Northwich Victoria	46	14	13	19	68	75	41
Morecambe	46	13	13	20	62	84	39
Buxton	46	14	10	22	45	71	38
Matlock Town	46	11	14	21	50	79	36
Great Harwood	46	10	14	22	52	74	34
Bradford Park Avenue	46	9	15	22	42	84	33
Barrow	46	13	7	26	46	94	33
Lancaster City	46	10	12	24	52	67	32
Netherfield	46	11	5	30	42	88	27

1974-75

	P	W	D	L	F	A	Pts
Wigan Athletic	46	33	6	7	94	38	72
Runcorn	46	30	8	8	102	42	68
Altrincham	46	26	12	8	87	43	64
Stafford Rangers	46	25	13	8	81	39	63
Scarborough	46	24	12	10	75	45	60
Mossley	46	23	11	12	78	52	57
Gateshead United	46	22	12	12	74	48	56
Goole Town	46	19	12	15	75	71	50
Northwich Victoria	46	18	12	16	83	71	48
Great Harwood	46	17	14	15	69	66	48
Matlock Town	46	19	8	19	87	79	46
Boston United	46	16	14	16	64	63	46
Morecambe	46	14	15	17	71	87	43
Worksop Town	46	14	14	18	69	66	42
South Liverpool	46	14	14	18	59	71	42
Buxton	46	11	17	18	50	77	39
Macclesfield Town	46	11	14	21	46	62	36
Lancaster City	46	13	10	23	53	76	36
Bangor City	46	13	9	24	56	67	35
Gainsborough Trinity	46	10	15	21	46	79	35
Skelmersdale United	46	13	7	26	63	93	33
Barrow	46	9	15	22	45	72	33
Netherfield	46	12	8	26	42	91	32
Fleetwood	46	5	10	31	26	97	20

1975-76

	P	W	D	L	F	A	Pts
Runcorn	46	29	10	7	95	42	68
Stafford Rangers	46	26	15	5	81	41	67
Scarborough	46	26	10	10	84	43	62
Matlock Town	46	26	9	11	96	63	61
Boston United	46	27	6	13	95	58	60
Wigan Athletic	46	21	15	10	81	42	57
Altrincham	46	20	14	12	77	57	54
Bangor City	46	21	12	13	80	70	54
Mossley	46	21	11	14	70	58	53
Goole Town	46	20	13	13	58	49	53
Northwich Victoria	46	17	17	12	79	59	51
Lancaster City	46	18	9	19	61	70	45
Worksop Town	46	17	10	19	63	56	44
Gainsborough Trinity	46	13	17	16	58	69	43
Macclesfield Town	46	15	12	19	50	64	42
Gateshead United	46	17	7	22	64	63	41
Buxton	46	11	13	22	37	62	35
Skelmersdale United	46	12	10	24	45	74	34
Netherfield	46	11	11	24	55	76	33
Morecambe	46	11	11	24	47	67	33
Great Harwood	46	13	7	26	58	86	33
South Liverpool	46	12	9	25	45	78	33
Barrow	46	12	9	25	47	84	33
Fleetwood	46	3	9	34	36	131	15

1976-77

	P	W	D	L	F	A	Pts
Boston United	44	27	11	6	82	35	65
Northwich Victoria	44	27	11	6	85	43	65
Matlock Town	44	26	11	7	108	57	63
Bangor City	44	22	11	11	87	52	55
Scarborough	44	21	12	11	77	66	54
Goole Town	44	23	6	15	64	50	52
Lancaster City	44	21	9	14	71	58	51
Gateshead United	44	18	12	14	80	64	48
Mossley	44	17	14	13	74	59	48
Altrincham	44	19	9	16	60	53	47
Stafford Rangers	44	16	14	14	60	55	46
Runcorn	44	15	14	15	57	49	44
Worksop Town	44	16	12	16	50	58	44
Wigan Athletic	44	14	15	15	62	54	43
Morecambe	44	13	11	20	59	75	37
Gainsborough Trinity	44	13	10	21	58	74	36
Great Harwood	44	11	14	19	63	84	36
Buxton	44	11	13	20	48	63	35
Macclesfield Town	44	8	15	21	41	68	31
Frickley Athletic	44	11	8	25	53	93	30
Barrow	44	11	6	27	56	87	28
South Liverpool	44	10	8	26	51	104	28
Netherfield	44	9	8	27	47	92	26

1977-78

	P	W	D	L	F	A	Pts
Boston United	46	31	9	6	85	35	71
Wigan Athletic	46	25	15	6	83	45	65
Bangor City	46	26	10	10	92	50	62
Scarborough	46	26	10	10	80	39	62
Altrincham	46	22	15	9	84	49	59
Northwich Victoria	46	22	14	10	83	55	58
Stafford Rangers	46	22	13	11	71	41	57
Runcorn	46	19	18	9	70	44	56
Mossley	46	22	11	13	85	73	55
Matlock Town	46	21	12	13	79	60	54
Lancaster City	46	15	14	17	66	82	44
Frickley Athletic	46	15	12	19	77	81	42
Barrow	46	14	12	20	58	61	40
Goole Town	46	15	9	22	60	68	39
Great Harwood	46	13	13	20	66	83	39
Gainsborough Trinity	46	14	10	22	61	74	38
Gateshead	46	16	5	25	65	74	37
Netherfield	46	11	13	22	50	80	35
Workington	46	13	8	25	48	80	34
Worksop Town	46	12	10	24	45	84	34
Morecambe	46	11	11	24	67	92	33
Macclesfield Town	46	12	9	25	60	92	33
Buxton	46	13	6	27	60	95	32
South Liverpool	46	9	7	30	53	111	25

1978-79

	P	W	D	L	F	A	Pts
Mossley	44	32	5	7	117	48	69
Altrincham	44	25	11	8	93	39	61
Matlock Town	44	24	8	12	100	59	56
Scarborough	44	19	14	11	61	44	52
Southport	44	19	14	11	62	49	52
Boston United	44	17	18	9	40	33	52
Runcorn	44	21	9	14	79	54	51
Stafford Rangers	44	18	14	12	67	41	50
Goole Town	44	17	15	12	56	61	49
Northwich Victoria	44	18	11	15	64	52	47
Lancaster City	44	17	12	15	62	54	46
Bangor City	44	15	14	15	65	66	44
Worksop Town	44	13	14	17	55	67	40
Workington	44	16	7	21	62	74	39
Netherfield	44	13	11	20	39	69	37
Barrow	44	14	9	21	47	78	37
Gainsborough Trinity	44	12	12	20	52	67	36
Morecambe	44	11	13	20	55	65	35
Frickley Athletic	44	13	9	22	58	70	35
South Liverpool	44	12	10	22	48	85	34
Gateshead	44	11	11	22	42	63	33
Buxton	44	11	9	24	50	84	31
Macclesfield Town	44	8	10	26	40	92	26

1979-80

	P	W	D	L	F	A	Pts
Mossley	42	28	9	5	96	41	65
Witton Albion	42	28	8	6	89	30	64
Frickley Athletic	42	24	13	5	93	48	61
Burton Albion	42	25	6	11	83	42	56
Matlock Town	42	18	17	7	87	53	53
Buxton	42	21	9	12	61	48	51
Worksop Town	42	20	10	12	65	52	50
Macclesfield Town	42	18	11	13	67	53	47
Grantham	42	18	8	16	71	65	44
Marine	42	16	10	16	65	57	42
Goole Town	42	14	13	15	61	63	41
Lancaster City	42	13	13	16	74	77	39
Oswestry Town	42	12	14	16	44	60	38
Gainsborough Trinity	42	14	8	20	64	75	36
Runcorn	42	11	11	20	46	63	33
Gateshead	42	11	11	20	50	77	33
Morecambe	42	10	12	20	40	59	32
Netherfield	42	7	15	20	37	66	29
Southport	42	8	13	21	30	75	29
South Liverpool	42	7	14	21	51	84	28
Workington	42	8	12	22	50	85	28
Tamworth	42	8	9	25	26	77	25

1980-81

	P	W	D	L	F	A	Pts
Runcorn	42	32	7	3	99	22	71
Mossley	42	24	7	11	95	55	55
Marine	42	22	10	10	66	41	54
Buxton	42	21	7	14	64	50	49
Gainsborough Trinity	42	17	13	12	80	57	47
Burton Albion	42	19	8	15	63	54	46
Witton Albion	42	19	8	15	70	62	46
Goole Town	42	14	16	12	56	50	44
South Liverpool	42	19	6	17	59	64	44
Workington	42	15	13	14	57	48	43
Gateshead	42	12	18	12	65	61	42
Worksop Town	42	15	11	16	66	61	41
Macclesfield Town	42	13	13	16	52	69	39
Grantham	42	14	9	19	57	74	37
Matlock Town	42	12	12	18	57	80	36
Lancaster City	42	13	9	20	48	70	35
Netherfield	42	11	12	19	73	81	34
Oswestry Town	42	13	8	21	54	67	34
King's Lynn	42	8	18	16	46	65	34
Southport	42	11	11	20	42	68	33
Morecambe	42	11	8	23	42	74	30
Tamworth	42	9	12	21	38	76	30

1981-82

	P	W	D	L	F	A	Pts
Bangor City	42	27	8	7	108	60	62
Mossley	42	24	11	7	76	43	59
Witton Albion	42	22	10	10	75	44	54
Gateshead	42	19	14	9	65	49	52
King's Lynn	42	19	12	11	61	36	50
Grantham	42	18	13	11	65	53	49
Burton Albion	42	19	9	14	71	62	47
Southport	42	16	14	12	63	55	46
Marine	42	17	12	13	64	57	46
Macclesfield Town	42	17	9	16	67	58	43
Workington	42	18	7	17	62	60	43
Worksop Town	42	15	13	14	52	60	43
South Liverpool	42	13	13	16	55	57	39
Goole Town	42	13	13	16	56	60	39
Oswestry Town	42	14	11	17	55	59	39
Buxton	42	14	11	17	48	56	39
Lancaster City	42	13	12	17	47	50	38
Gainsborough Trinity	42	10	13	19	60	69	33
Tamworth	42	10	9	23	31	56	29
Morecambe	42	9	11	22	43	86	29
Matlock Town	42	7	12	23	38	72	26
Netherfield	42	5	9	28	31	91	19

1982-83

Gateshead	42	32	4	6	114	43	100
Mossley	42	25	9	8	77	42	84
Burton Albion	42	24	9	9	81	53	81
Chorley	42	23	11	8	77	49	80
Macclesfield Town	42	24	8	10	71	49	80
Marine	42	17	17	8	81	57	68
Workington	42	19	10	13	71	55	67
Hyde United	42	18	12	12	91	63	66
King's Lynn	42	17	13	12	62	44	64
Matlock Town	42	18	10	14	70	65	64
Witton Albion	42	17	12	13	82	52	63
Buxton	42	17	9	16	60	62	60
Morecambe	42	16	11	15	75	66	59
Grantham	42	15	13	14	49	50	58
Southport	42	11	14	17	58	65	47
Goole Town	42	13	7	22	52	66	46
Gainsborough Trinity	42	11	9	22	60	71	42
Oswestry Town	42	10	8	24	56	99	38
South Liverpool	42	7	15	20	57	91	36
Tamworth	42	7	8	27	44	97	29
Worksop Town	42	5	10	27	50	98	25
Netherfield	42	2	9	31	28	129	15

1983-84

Barrow	42	29	10	3	92	38	97
Matlock Town	42	23	8	11	72	48	77
South Liverpool	42	22	11	9	55	44	77
Grantham	42	20	8	14	64	51	68
Burton Albion	42	17	13	12	61	47	64
Macclesfield Town	42	18	10	14	65	55	64
Rhyl	42	19	6	17	64	55	63
Horwich RMI	42	18	9	15	64	59	63
Gainsborough Trinity	42	17	11	14	82	66	62
Stafford Rangers	42	15	17	10	65	52	62
Hyde United	42	17	8	17	61	63	59
Marine	42	16	10	16	63	68	58
Witton Albion	42	14	14	14	64	57	56
Chorley	42	14	11	17	68	65	53
Workington	42	14	9	19	53	57	51
Southport	42	14	8	20	57	74	50
Worksop Town	42	13	8	21	57	74	47
Goole Town	42	12	10	20	59	80	46
Morecambe	42	11	12	19	59	75	45
Oswestry Town	42	11	8	23	66	97	41
Buxton	42	11	6	25	52	91	39
Mossley	42	9	9	24	47	74	33

Mossley had 3 points deducted

1984-85

Stafford Rangers	42	26	8	8	81	40	86
Macclesfield Town	42	23	13	6	67	39	82
Witton Albion	42	22	8	12	57	39	74
Hyde United	42	21	8	13	68	52	71
Marine	42	18	15	9	59	34	69
Burton Albion	42	18	15	9	70	49	69
Worksop Town	42	19	10	13	68	56	67
Workington	42	18	9	15	59	53	63
Horwich RMI	42	16	14	12	67	50	62
Bangor City	42	17	9	16	70	61	60
Gainsborough Trinity	42	14	14	14	72	73	56
Southport	42	15	9	18	65	66	54
Matlock Town	42	14	9	19	56	66	51
Oswestry Town	42	14	9	19	59	75	51
Mossley	42	14	9	19	45	65	51
Goole Town	42	13	11	18	60	65	50
Rhyl	42	11	14	17	52	63	47
Morecambe	42	11	14	17	51	67	47
Chorley	42	12	10	20	47	63	46
South Liverpool	42	9	15	18	43	71	42
Grantham	42	8	13	21	41	69	36
Buxton	42	8	6	28	38	79	30

Grantham had 1 point deducted

1985-86

Gateshead	42	24	10	8	85	51	82
Marine	42	23	11	8	63	35	80
Morecambe	42	17	17	8	59	39	68
Gainsborough Trinity	42	18	14	10	66	52	68
Burton Albion	42	18	12	12	64	47	66
Southport	42	17	11	14	70	66	62
Worksop Town	42	17	10	15	51	48	61
Workington	42	14	18	10	54	46	59
Macclesfield Town	42	17	8	17	67	65	59
Hyde United	42	14	15	13	63	62	57
Witton Albion	42	15	13	14	56	59	57
Mossley	42	13	16	13	56	60	55
Bangor City	42	13	15	14	51	51	54
Rhyl	42	14	10	18	65	71	52
South Liverpool	42	11	17	14	43	44	50
Horwich RMI	42	15	6	21	53	63	50
Caernarfon Town	42	11	17	14	51	63	50
Oswestry Town	42	12	13	17	51	60	49
Buxton	42	11	12	19	55	76	45
Chorley	42	9	15	18	56	64	42
Matlock Town	42	9	15	18	59	75	42
Goole Town	42	7	11	24	37	78	31

Workington, Witton Albion, Horwich and Goole Town all had 1 point deducted.

1986-87

Macclesfield Town	42	26	10	6	80	47	88
Bangor City	42	25	12	5	74	35	87
Caernarfon Town	42	20	16	6	67	40	76
Marine	42	21	10	11	70	43	73
South Liverpool	42	21	10	11	58	40	73
Morecambe	42	20	12	10	66	49	72
Matlock Town	42	20	10	12	81	67	70
Southport	42	19	11	12	67	49	68
Chorley	42	16	12	14	58	59	60
Mossley	42	15	12	15	57	52	57
Hyde United	42	15	10	17	81	70	55
Burton Albion	42	16	6	20	56	68	54
Buxton	42	13	14	15	71	68	53
Witton Albion	42	15	8	19	68	79	53
Barrow	42	15	7	20	42	57	52
Goole Town	42	13	12	17	58	62	51
Oswestry Town	42	14	8	20	55	83	50
Rhyl	42	10	15	17	56	74	45
Worksop Town	42	9	13	20	56	74	40
Gainsborough Trinity	42	9	10	23	53	77	37
Workington	42	5	14	23	38	70	28
Horwich RMI	42	3	12	27	36	85	20

Workington and Horwich RMI both had 1 point deducted.

1987-88　Premier Division

Chorley	42	26	10	6	78	35	88
Hyde United	42	25	10	7	91	52	85
Caernarfon Town	42	22	10	10	56	34	76
Morecambe	42	19	15	8	61	41	72
Barrow	42	21	8	13	70	41	71
Worksop Town	42	20	11	11	74	55	71
Bangor City	42	20	10	12	72	55	70
Rhyl	42	18	13	11	70	42	67
Marine	42	19	10	13	67	45	67
Frickley Athletic	42	18	11	13	61	55	65
Witton Albion	42	16	12	14	61	47	60
Goole Town	42	17	9	16	71	61	60
Horwich RMI	42	17	9	16	46	42	60
Southport	42	15	12	15	43	48	57
South Liverpool	42	10	19	13	56	64	49
Buxton	42	11	14	17	72	76	47
Mossley	42	11	11	20	54	75	44
Gateshead	42	11	7	24	52	71	40
Matlock Town	42	10	8	24	58	89	38
Gainsborough Trinity	42	8	10	24	38	81	34
Oswestry Town	42	6	10	26	44	101	28
Workington	42	6	3	33	28	113	21

First Division

Fleetwood Town	36	22	7	7	85	45	73
Stalybridge Celtic	36	22	6	8	72	42	72
Leek Town	36	20	10	6	63	38	70
Accrington Stanley	36	21	6	9	71	39	69
Farsley Celtic	36	18	9	9	64	48	60
Droylsden	36	16	10	10	63	48	58
Eastwood Hanley	36	14	12	10	50	37	54
Winsford United	36	15	6	15	59	47	51
Congleton Town	36	12	16	8	43	39	51
Harrogate Town	36	13	9	14	51	50	48
Alfreton Town	36	13	8	15	53	54	47
Radcliffe Borough	36	11	13	12	66	62	46
Irlam Town	36	12	10	14	39	45	46
Penrith	36	11	11	14	46	51	44
Sutton Town	36	11	5	20	51	96	38
Lancaster City	36	10	6	20	45	72	36
Eastwood Town	36	8	10	18	45	65	34
Curzon Ashton	36	8	4	24	43	73	28
Netherfield	36	4	4	28	35	93	16

Congleton Town had 1 point deducted
Farsley Celtic had 3 points deducted

1988-89　Premier Division

Barrow	42	26	9	7	69	35	87
Hyde United	42	24	8	10	77	44	80
Witton Albion	42	22	13	7	67	39	79
Bangor City	42	22	10	10	77	48	76
Marine	42	23	7	12	69	48	76
Goole Town	42	22	7	13	75	60	73
Fleetwood Town	42	19	16	7	58	44	73
Rhyl	42	18	10	14	75	65	64
Frickley Athletic	42	17	10	15	64	53	61
Mossley	42	17	9	16	56	58	60
South Liverpool	42	15	13	14	65	57	58
Caernarfon Town	42	15	10	17	49	63	55
Matlock Town	42	16	5	21	65	73	53
Southport	42	13	12	17	66	52	51
Buxton	42	12	14	16	61	63	50
Morecambe	42	13	9	20	55	60	47
Gainsborough Trinity	42	12	11	19	56	73	47
Shepshed Charterhouse	42	14	8	20	49	60	44
Stalybridge Celtic	42	9	13	20	46	81	40
Horwich RMI	42	7	14	21	42	70	35
Gateshead	42	7	13	22	36	70	34
Worksop Town	42	6	5	31	42	103	23

Morecambe had 1 point deducted
Shepshed Charterhouse had 6 points deducted

First Division

Colne Dynamoes	42	30	11	1	102	21	98
Bishop Auckland	42	28	5	9	78	28	89
Leek Town	42	25	11	6	74	41	85
Droylsden	42	25	9	8	84	48	84
Whitley Bay	42	23	6	13	77	49	75
Accrington Stanley	42	21	10	11	81	60	73
Lancaster City	42	21	8	13	76	54	71
Harrogate Town	42	19	7	16	68	61	64
Newtown	42	15	12	15	65	59	57
Congleton Town	42	15	11	16	62	66	56
Workington	42	17	3	22	59	74	54
Eastwood Town	42	14	10	18	55	61	52
Curzon Ashton	42	13	11	18	74	72	50
Farsley Celtic	42	12	13	17	52	73	49
Irlam Town	42	11	14	17	53	63	47
Penrith	42	14	5	23	61	91	47
Radcliffe Borough	42	12	10	20	62	86	46
Eastwood Hanley	42	11	12	19	46	67	45
Winsford United	42	13	6	23	58	93	45
Alfreton Town	42	8	11	23	44	92	35
Netherfield	42	8	9	25	57	90	32
Sutton Town	42	7	6	29	70	109	23

Leek Town and Netherfield both had 1 point deducted
Colne Dynamo had 3 points deducted
Sutton Town had 4 points deducted

1989-90

Premier Division

Colne Dynamoes	42	32	6	4	86	40	102
Gateshead	42	22	10	10	78	58	76
Witton Albion	42	22	7	13	67	39	73
Hyde United	42	21	8	13	73	50	71
South Liverpool	42	20	9	13	89	79	69
Matlock Town	42	18	12	12	61	42	66
Southport	42	17	14	11	54	48	65
Fleetwood Town	42	17	12	13	73	66	63
Marine	42	16	14	12	59	55	62
Bangor City	42	15	15	12	64	58	60
Bishop Auckland	42	17	8	17	72	64	59
Frickley Athletic	42	16	8	18	56	61	56
Horwich RMI	42	15	13	14	66	69	55
Morecambe	42	15	9	18	58	70	54
Gainsborough Trinity	42	16	8	18	59	55	53
Buxton	42	15	8	19	59	72	53
Stalybridge Celtic	42	12	9	21	48	61	45
Mossley	42	11	10	21	61	82	43
Goole Town	42	12	5	25	54	77	41
Shepshed Charterhouse	42	11	7	24	55	82	40
Caernarfon Town	42	10	8	24	56	86	38
Rhyl	42	7	10	25	43	77	30

Rhyl had 1 point deducted
Horwich and Gainsborough Trinity both had 3 points deducted

First Division

Leek Town	42	26	8	8	70	31	86
Droylsden	42	27	6	9	81	46	80
Accrington Stanley	42	22	10	10	80	53	76
Whitley Bay	42	21	11	10	93	59	74
Emley	42	20	9	13	70	42	69
Congleton Town	42	20	12	10	65	53	69
Winsford United	42	18	10	14	65	53	64
Curzon Ashton	42	17	11	14	66	60	62
Harrogate Town	42	17	9	16	68	62	60
Lancaster City	42	15	14	13	73	54	59
Eastwood Town	42	16	11	15	61	64	59
Farsley Celtic	42	17	6	19	71	75	57
Rossendale United	42	15	9	18	73	69	54
Newtown	42	14	12	16	49	62	54
Irlam Town	42	14	11	17	61	66	53
Workington	42	14	8	20	56	64	50
Radcliffe Borough	42	14	7	21	47	63	49
Alfreton Town	42	13	8	21	59	85	47
Worksop Town	42	13	5	24	56	95	44
Netherfield	42	11	6	25	56	89	39
Eastwood Hanley	42	10	6	26	45	76	36
Penrith	42	9	9	24	44	88	36

Congleton Town 3 points deducted. Droylsden 7 points deducted.

1990-91   Premier Division

Witton Albion	40	28	9	3	81	31	93
Stalybridge Celtic	40	22	11	7	44	26	77
Morecambe	40	19	16	5	72	44	73
Fleetwood Town	40	20	9	11	69	44	69
Southport	40	18	14	8	66	48	68
Marine	40	18	11	11	56	39	65
Bishop Auckland	40	17	10	13	62	56	61
Buxton	40	17	11	12	66	61	59
Leek Town	40	15	11	14	48	44	56
Frickley Athletic	40	16	6	18	64	62	54
Hyde United	40	14	11	15	73	63	53
Goole Town	40	14	10	16	68	74	52
Droylsden	40	12	11	17	67	70	47
Chorley	40	12	10	18	55	55	46
Mossley	40	13	10	17	55	68	45
Horwich RMI	40	13	6	21	62	81	45
Matlock Town	40	12	7	21	52	70	43
Bangor City	40	9	12	19	52	70	39
South Liverpool	40	10	9	21	58	92	39
Gainsborough Trinity	40	9	11	20	57	84	38
Shepshed Charterhouse	40	6	7	27	38	83	25

Buxton had 3 points deducted. Mossley had 4 points deducted.

First Division

Whitley Bay	42	25	10	7	95	38	85
Emley	42	24	12	6	78	37	84
Worksop Town	42	25	7	10	85	56	82
Accrington Stanley	42	21	13	8	83	57	76
Rhyl	42	21	7	14	62	63	70
Eastwood Town	42	17	11	14	70	60	62
Warrington Town	42	17	10	15	68	52	61
Lancaster City	42	19	8	15	58	56	61
Bridlington Town	42	15	15	12	72	52	60
Curzon Ashton	42	14	14	14	49	57	56
Congleton Town	42	14	12	16	57	71	54
Netherfield	42	14	11	17	67	66	53
Newtown	42	13	12	17	68	75	51
Caernarfon Town	42	13	10	19	51	64	49
Rossendale United	42	12	13	17	66	67	48
Radcliffe Borough	42	12	12	18	50	69	48
Irlam Town	42	12	11	19	55	76	47
Winsford United	42	11	13	18	51	66	46
Harrogate Town	42	11	13	18	55	73	46
Workington	42	11	11	20	54	67	41
Farsley Celtic	42	11	9	22	49	78	39
Alfreton Town	42	7	12	23	41	84	33

Lancaster City had 4 points deducted. Farsley Celtic and Workington both had 3 points deducted. Rossendale United had 1 point deducted.

1991-92

Premier Division

Stalybridge Celtic	42	26	14	2	84	33	92
Marine	42	23	9	10	64	32	78
Morecambe	42	21	13	8	70	44	76
Leek Town	42	21	10	11	62	49	73
Buxton	42	21	9	12	65	47	72
Emley	42	18	11	13	69	47	65
Southport	42	16	17	9	57	48	65
Accrington Stanley	42	17	12	13	78	62	63
Hyde United	42	17	9	16	69	67	60
Fleetwood Town	42	17	8	17	67	64	59
Bishop Auckland	42	16	9	17	48	58	57
Goole Town	42	15	9	18	60	72	54
Horwich RMI	42	13	14	15	44	52	53
Frickley Athletic	42	12	16	14	61	57	52
Droylsden	42	12	14	16	62	72	50
Mossley	42	15	4	23	51	73	49
Whitley Bay	42	13	9	20	53	79	48
Gainsborough Trinity	42	11	13	18	48	63	46
Matlock Town	42	12	9	21	59	87	45
Bangor City	42	11	10	21	46	57	43
Chorley	42	11	9	22	61	82	42
Shepshed Albion	42	6	8	28	46	79	26

First Division

Colwyn Bay	42	30	4	8	99	49	94
Winsford United	42	29	6	7	96	41	93
Worksop Town	42	25	5	12	101	51	80
Guiseley	42	22	12	8	93	56	78
Caernarfon Town	42	23	9	10	78	47	78
Bridlington Town	42	22	9	11	86	46	75
Warrington Town	42	20	8	14	79	64	68
Knowsley United	42	18	10	14	69	52	64
Netherfield	42	18	7	17	54	61	61
Harrogate Town	42	14	16	12	73	69	58
Curzon Ashton	42	15	9	18	71	83	54
Farsley Celtic	42	15	9	18	79	101	53
Radcliffe Borough	42	15	9	18	67	72	51
Newtown	42	15	6	21	60	95	51
Eastwood Town	42	13	11	18	59	70	50
Lancaster City	42	10	19	13	55	62	49
Congleton Town	42	14	5	23	59	81	47
Rhyl	42	11	10	21	59	69	43
Rossendale United	42	9	11	22	61	90	38
Alfreton Town	42	12	2	28	63	98	38
Irlam Town	42	9	7	26	45	95	33
Workington	42	7	8	27	45	99	28

Farsley Celtic, Irlam Town and Workington all had 1 point deducted. Radcliffe Borough had 3 points deducted.

1992-93

Premier Division

Southport	42	29	9	4	103	31	96
Winsford United	42	27	9	6	91	43	90
Morecambe	42	25	11	6	93	51	86
Marine	42	26	8	8	83	47	86
Leek Town	42	21	11	10	86	51	74
Accrington Stanley	42	20	13	9	79	45	73
Frickley Athletic	42	21	6	15	62	52	69
Barrow	42	18	11	13	71	55	65
Hyde United	42	17	13	12	87	71	64
Bishop Auckland	42	17	11	14	63	52	62
Gainsborough Trinity	42	17	8	17	63	66	59
Colwyn Bay	42	16	6	20	80	79	54
Horwich RMI	42	14	10	18	72	79	52
Buxton	42	13	10	19	60	75	49
Matlock Town	42	13	11	18	56	79	47
Emley	42	13	6	23	62	91	45
Whitley Bay	42	11	8	23	57	96	41
Chorley	42	10	10	22	52	93	40
Fleetwood Town	42	10	7	25	50	77	37
Droylsden	42	10	7	25	47	84	37
Mossley	42	7	8	27	53	95	29
Goole Town	42	6	9	27	47	105	27

Matlock Town had 3 points deducted

First Division

Bridlington Town	40	25	11	4	84	35	86
Knowsley United	40	23	7	10	86	48	76
Ashton United	40	22	8	10	81	54	74
Guiseley	40	20	10	10	90	64	70
Warrington Town	40	19	10	11	85	57	67
Gretna	40	17	12	11	64	47	63
Curzon Ashton	40	16	15	9	69	63	63
Great Harwood Town	40	17	9	14	66	57	60
Alfreton Town	40	15	9	16	80	80	54
Harrogate Town	40	14	12	14	77	81	54
Worksop Town	40	15	9	16	66	70	54
Radcliffe Borough	40	13	14	13	66	69	53
Workington	40	13	13	14	51	61	52
Eastwood Town	40	13	11	16	49	52	50
Netherfield	40	11	14	15	68	63	47
Caernarfon Town	40	13	8	19	66	74	47
Farsley Celtic	40	12	8	20	64	77	44
Lancaster City	40	10	12	18	49	76	42
Shepshed Albion	40	9	12	19	46	66	39
Congleton Town	40	10	7	23	58	95	37
Rossendale United	40	5	5	30	50	126	20

1993-94

Premier Division

Marine	42	27	9	6	106	62	90
Leek Town	42	27	8	7	79	50	89
Boston United	42	23	9	10	90	43	78
Bishop Auckland	42	23	9	10	73	58	78
Frickley Athletic	42	21	12	9	90	51	75
Colwyn Bay	42	18	14	10	74	51	68
Morecambe	42	20	7	15	90	56	67
Barrow	42	18	10	14	59	51	64
Hyde United	42	17	10	15	80	71	61
Chorley	42	17	10	15	70	67	61
Whitley Bay	42	17	9	16	61	72	60
Gainsborough Trinity	42	15	11	16	64	66	56
Emley	42	12	16	14	63	71	52
Matlock Town	42	13	12	17	71	76	51
Buxton	42	13	10	19	67	73	49
Accrington Stanley	42	14	7	21	63	85	49
Droylsden	42	11	14	17	57	82	47
Knowsley United	42	11	11	20	52	66	44
Winsford United	42	9	11	22	50	74	38
Horwich RMI	42	8	12	22	50	75	35
Bridlington Town	42	7	10	25	41	91	28
Fleetwood Town	42	7	7	28	55	114	28

Horwich RMI 1 point deducted. Bridlington Town 3 points deducted

First Division

Guiseley	40	29	6	5	87	37	93
Spennymoor United	40	25	6	9	95	50	81
Ashton United	40	24	7	9	85	41	79
Lancaster City	40	20	10	10	74	46	70
Netherfield	40	20	6	14	68	60	66
Alfreton Town	40	18	10	12	83	70	64
Warrington Town	40	17	11	12	52	48	62
Goole Town	40	16	11	13	72	58	59
Great Harwood Town	40	15	14	11	56	60	59
Gretna	40	16	7	17	64	65	55
Workington	40	14	10	16	70	74	52
Worksop Town	40	14	9	17	79	87	51
Bamber Bridge	40	13	11	16	62	59	50
Curzon Ashton	40	13	8	19	62	71	47
Congleton Town	40	12	9	19	53	68	45
Radcliffe Borough	40	10	14	16	62	75	44
Mossley	40	10	12	18	44	68	39
Caernarfon Town	40	9	11	20	54	88	38
Farsley Celtic	40	6	16	18	42	77	34
Harrogate Town	40	8	9	23	40	86	33
Eastwood Town	40	7	11	22	47	63	32

Mossley had 3 points deducted

1994-95

Premier Division

Marine	42	29	11	2	83	27	98
Morecambe	42	28	10	4	99	34	94
Guiseley	42	28	9	5	96	50	93
Hyde United	42	22	10	10	89	59	76
Boston United	42	20	11	11	80	43	71
Spennymoor United	42	20	11	11	66	52	71
Buxton	42	18	9	15	65	62	63
Gainsborough Trinity	42	16	13	13	69	61	61
Bishop Auckland	42	16	12	14	68	55	57
Witton Albion	42	14	14	14	54	56	56
Barrow	42	17	5	20	68	71	56
Colwyn Bay	42	16	8	18	71	80	56
Emley	42	14	13	15	62	68	55
Matlock Town	42	15	5	22	62	72	50
Accrington Stanley	42	12	13	17	55	77	49
Knowsley United	42	11	14	17	64	83	47
Winsford United	42	10	11	21	56	75	41
Chorley	42	11	7	24	64	87	40
Frickley Athletic	42	10	10	22	53	79	40
Droylsden	42	10	8	24	56	93	38
Whitley Bay	42	8	8	26	46	97	32
Horwich RMI	42	9	4	29	49	94	31

Bishop Auckland had 3 points deducted

First Division

Blyth Spartans	42	26	9	7	95	55	87
Bamber Bridge	42	25	10	7	101	51	85
Warrington Town	42	25	9	8	74	40	84
Alfreton Town	42	25	7	10	94	49	82
Lancaster City	42	23	10	9	81	44	79
Worksop Town	42	19	14	9	95	68	71
Radcliffe Borough	42	18	10	14	76	70	64
Ashton United	42	18	8	16	80	70	62
Netherfield	42	17	7	18	54	56	58
Eastwood Town	42	14	13	15	67	61	55
Gretna	42	14	13	15	64	66	55
Atherton Laburnum Rovers	42	14	8	20	60	67	50
Harrogate Town	42	14	8	20	57	78	50
Caernarfon Town	42	13	10	19	59	62	49
Curzon Ashton	42	10	16	16	64	80	46
Great Harwood Town	42	11	13	18	66	87	46
Congleton Town	42	11	13	18	52	75	46
Fleetwood	42	12	11	19	51	74	44
Farsley Celtic	42	12	7	23	66	100	43
Workington	42	12	6	24	61	91	42
Goole Town	42	11	7	24	46	81	40
Mossley	42	11	5	26	52	90	37

Mossley had 1 point deducted. Fleetwood had 3 points deducted

1995-96

Premier Division

Bamber Bridge	42	20	16	6	81	49	76
Boston United	42	23	6	13	86	59	75
Hyde United	42	21	11	10	86	51	74
Barrow	42	20	13	9	69	42	73
Gainsborough Trinity	42	20	13	9	60	41	73
Blyth Spartans	42	17	13	12	75	61	64
Accrington Stanley	42	17	14	11	62	54	62
Emley	42	17	10	15	57	53	61
Spennymoor United	42	14	18	10	67	61	60
Guiseley	42	15	14	13	62	57	59
Bishop Auckland	42	16	11	15	60	55	59
Marine	42	15	14	13	59	54	59
Witton Albion	42	17	8	17	60	62	59
Chorley	42	14	9	19	67	74	48
Knowsley United	42	14	6	22	61	89	48
Winsford United	42	10	16	16	56	79	46
Leek Town	42	10	15	17	52	55	45
Colwyn Bay	42	8	21	13	43	57	45
Frickley Athletic	42	11	14	17	63	87	44
Buxton	42	9	11	22	43	72	38
Droylsden	42	10	8	24	58	100	38
Matlock Town	42	8	11	23	71	86	35

Accrington Stanley, Chorley & Frickley Town all had 3 points deducted

First Division

Lancaster City	40	24	11	5	79	38	83
Alfreton Town	40	23	9	8	79	47	78
Lincoln United	40	22	7	11	80	56	73
Curzon Ashton	40	20	7	13	73	53	67
Farsley Celtic	40	19	9	12	66	61	66
Radcliffe Borough	40	17	13	10	70	48	64
Eastwood Town	40	18	9	13	60	47	63
Whitley Bay	40	18	8	14	72	62	62
Ashton United	40	19	7	14	73	65	60
Atherton Laburnum Rovers	40	15	12	13	60	61	57
Worksop Town	40	16	8	16	84	90	56
Gretna	40	13	13	14	75	65	52
Warrington Town	40	13	10	17	75	72	49
Leigh RMI	40	14	7	19	53	59	49
Netherfield	40	13	10	17	64	73	49
Workington	40	11	12	17	50	62	45
Bradford Park Avenue	40	9	14	17	57	72	41
Congleton Town	40	11	11	18	36	59	41
Great Harwood Town	40	9	7	24	44	78	33
Fleetwood	40	7	10	23	41	81	31
Harrogate Town	40	7	10	23	54	96	31

Great Harwood Town had 1 point deducted, Congleton Town had 3 points deducted and Ashton United had 4 points deducted

1996-97

Premier Division

Leek Town	44	28	9	7	71	35	93
Bishop Auckland	44	23	14	7	88	43	83
Hyde United	44	22	16	6	93	46	82
Emley	44	23	12	9	89	54	81
Barrow	44	23	11	10	71	45	80
Boston United	44	22	13	9	74	47	79
Blyth Spartans	44	22	11	11	74	49	77
Marine	44	20	15	9	53	37	75
Guiseley	44	20	11	13	63	54	71
Gainsborough Trinity	44	18	12	14	65	46	66
Accrington Stanley	44	18	12	14	77	70	66
Runcorn	44	15	15	14	63	62	60
Chorley	44	16	9	19	69	66	57
Winsford United	44	13	14	17	50	56	53
Knowsley United	44	12	14	18	58	79	49
Colwyn Bay	44	11	13	20	60	76	46
Lancaster City	44	12	9	23	48	75	45
Frickley Athletic	44	12	8	24	62	91	44
Spennymoor United	44	10	10	24	52	68	40
Bamber Bridge	44	11	7	26	59	99	40
Alfreton Town	44	8	13	23	45	83	37
Witton Albion	44	5	14	25	41	91	29
Buxton	44	5	12	27	33	86	27

Knowsley United had 1 point deducted

First Division

Radcliffe Borough	42	26	7	9	77	33	85
Leigh RMI	42	24	11	7	65	33	83
Lincoln United	42	25	8	9	78	47	83
Farsley Celtic	42	23	8	11	75	48	77
Worksop Town	42	20	12	10	68	38	69
Stocksbridge Park Steels	42	19	11	12	66	54	68
Bradford Park Avenue	42	20	8	14	58	50	68
Ashton United	42	17	14	11	73	52	65
Great Harwood Town	42	16	12	14	56	46	60
Droylsden	42	15	14	13	69	67	59
Matlock Town	42	16	10	16	61	69	58
Whitley Bay	42	14	12	16	47	54	54
Flixton	42	15	7	20	57	72	52
Netherfield	42	12	14	16	54	56	50
Eastwood Town	42	12	14	16	42	50	50
Gretna	42	10	18	14	55	68	48
Harrogate Town	42	13	8	21	55	76	47
Congleton Town	42	12	9	21	47	64	45
Workington	42	10	12	20	45	63	42
Curzon Ashton	42	8	10	24	48	79	34
Warrington Town	42	5	18	19	42	79	33
Atherton Laburnum Rovers	42	7	9	26	45	85	30

Worksop Town had 3 points deducted

1997-98

Premier Division

Barrow	42	25	8	9	61	29	83
Boston United	42	22	12	8	55	40	78
Leigh RMI	42	21	13	8	63	41	76
Runcorn	42	22	9	11	80	50	75
Gainsborough Trinity	42	22	9	11	60	39	75
Emley	42	22	8	12	81	61	74
Winsford United	42	19	12	11	54	43	69
Altrincham	42	18	11	13	76	44	65
Guiseley	42	16	16	10	61	53	64
Bishop Auckland	42	17	12	13	78	60	63
Marine	42	15	11	16	56	59	56
Hyde United	42	13	16	13	60	55	55
Colwyn Bay	42	15	9	18	53	57	54
Spennymoor United	42	14	11	17	58	72	52
Chorley	42	14	7	21	51	70	49
Frickley Athletic	42	12	12	18	45	62	48
Lancaster City	42	13	8	21	55	74	47
Blyth Spartans	42	12	13	17	52	63	39
Bamber Bridge	42	9	12	21	51	74	39
Accrington Stanley	42	8	14	20	49	68	38
Radcliffe Borough	42	6	12	24	39	70	30
Alfreton Town	42	3	13	26	32	86	22

Spennymoor United had 1 point deducted
Blyth Spartans had 10 points deducted

First Division

Whitby Town	42	30	8	4	99	48	98
Worksop Town	42	28	7	7	93	44	91
Ashton United	42	26	9	7	93	43	87
Droylsden	42	24	8	10	70	49	80
Lincoln United	42	20	11	11	76	62	71
Farsley Celtic	42	20	10	12	72	66	70
Witton Albion	42	19	9	14	77	55	66
Eastwood Town	42	18	12	12	68	51	66
Bradford Park Avenue	42	18	11	13	62	46	65
Belper Town	42	18	7	17	68	66	61
Stocksbridge Park Steels	42	17	9	16	68	63	60
Trafford	42	16	6	20	59	61	54
Whitley Bay	42	14	12	16	60	63	54
Matlock Town	42	14	11	17	68	65	53
Gretna	42	13	9	20	58	64	48
Netherfield	42	12	11	19	55	75	47
Flixton	42	10	12	20	45	73	42
Congleton Town	42	11	8	23	65	101	41
Harrogate Town	42	8	14	20	57	80	38
Great Harwood Town	42	8	12	22	42	88	36
Workington	42	8	7	27	38	84	31
Buxton	42	7	3	32	41	87	24

1998-99

Premier Division

Altrincham	42	23	11	8	67	33	80
Worksop Town	42	22	10	10	66	48	76
Guiseley	42	21	9	12	64	47	72
Bamber Bridge	42	18	15	9	63	48	69
Gateshead	42	18	11	13	69	58	65
Gainsborough Trinity	42	19	8	15	65	59	65
Whitby Town	42	17	13	12	77	62	64
Leigh RMI	42	16	15	11	63	54	63
Hyde United	42	16	11	15	61	48	59
Stalybridge Celtic	42	16	11	15	71	63	59
Winsford United	42	14	15	13	56	52	57
Runcorn	42	12	19	11	46	49	55
Emley	42	12	17	13	47	49	53
Blyth Spartans	42	14	9	19	56	64	51
Colwyn Bay	42	12	13	17	60	71	49
Frickley Athletic	42	11	15	16	55	71	48
Marine	42	10	17	15	61	69	47
Spennymoor United	42	12	11	19	52	71	47
Lancaster City	42	11	13	18	50	62	46
Bishop Auckland	42	10	15	17	49	67	45
Chorley	42	8	15	19	45	68	39
Accrington Stanley	42	9	9	24	47	77	36

First Division

Droylsden	42	26	8	8	97	55	86
Hucknall Town	42	26	11	5	80	38	86
Ashton United	42	22	12	8	79	46	78
Lincoln United	42	20	12	10	94	65	72
Eastwood Town	42	20	8	14	65	69	68
Radcliffe Borough	42	19	8	15	78	62	65
Burscough	42	19	8	15	67	61	65
Witton Albion	42	18	9	15	70	63	63
Bradford Park Avenue	42	17	11	14	64	55	62
Stocksbridge Park Steels	42	16	13	13	64	60	61
Harrogate Town	42	17	7	18	75	77	58
Gretna	42	16	10	16	73	80	58
Belper Town	42	15	11	16	58	57	56
Trafford	42	14	11	17	50	58	53
Netherfield Kendal	42	13	10	19	51	64	49
Flixton	42	12	12	18	50	64	48
Matlock Town	42	14	6	22	53	72	48
Farsley Celtic	42	11	13	18	56	73	46
Whitley Bay	42	10	9	23	53	77	39
Congleton Town	42	8	15	19	65	91	39
Great Harwood Town	42	10	8	24	51	73	38
Alfreton Town	42	9	8	25	53	86	35

Hucknall Town had 3 points deducted

1999-2000

Premier Division

Leigh RMI	44	28	8	8	91	45	92
Hyde United	44	24	13	7	77	44	85
Gateshead	44	23	13	8	79	41	82
Marine	44	21	16	7	78	46	79
Emley	44	20	12	12	54	41	72
Lancaster City	44	20	11	13	65	55	71
Stalybridge Celtic	44	18	12	14	64	54	66
Bishop Auckland	44	18	11	15	63	61	65
Runcorn	44	18	10	16	64	55	64
Worksop Town	44	19	6	19	78	65	63
Gainsborough Trinity	44	16	15	13	59	49	63
Whitby Town	44	15	13	16	66	66	58
Barrow	44	14	15	15	65	59	57
Blyth Spartans	44	15	9	20	62	67	54
Droylsden	44	14	12	18	53	60	54
Frickley Athletic	44	15	9	20	64	85	54
Bamber Bridge	44	14	11	19	70	67	53
Hucknall Town	44	14	11	19	55	61	53
Leek Town	44	14	10	20	58	79	52
Colwyn Bay	44	12	12	20	46	85	48
Spennymoor United	44	10	13	21	41	71	42
Guiseley	44	8	17	19	52	72	41
Winsford United	44	3	7	34	40	116	16

Spennymoor United had 1 point deducted

First Division

Accrington Stanley	42	25	9	8	96	43	84
Burscough	42	22	18	2	81	35	84
Witton Albion	42	23	15	4	88	46	84
Bradford Park Avenue	42	23	9	10	77	48	78
Radcliffe Borough	42	22	12	8	71	48	78
Farsley Celtic	42	19	11	12	66	52	68
Matlock Town	42	17	16	9	72	55	67
Ossett Town	42	17	8	17	77	55	59
Stocksbridge Park Steels	42	16	8	18	55	70	56
Eastwood Town	42	15	11	16	64	65	55
Harrogate Town	42	14	12	16	65	67	54
Congleton Town	42	14	12	16	63	73	54
Chorley	42	13	15	14	53	64	54
Ashton United	42	12	16	14	65	67	52
Workington	42	13	13	16	49	55	52
Lincoln United	42	13	12	17	52	80	51
Belper Town	42	13	11	18	59	72	50
Trafford	42	11	12	19	55	63	45
Gretna	42	11	7	24	48	78	40
Netherfield Kendal	42	8	9	25	46	82	33
Flixton	42	7	9	26	47	85	30
Whitley Bay	42	7	9	26	41	87	30

Eastwood Town had 1 point deducted

2000-2001

Premier Division

Stalybridge Celtic	44	31	9	4	96	32	102
Emley	44	31	8	5	87	42	101
Bishop Auckland	44	26	7	11	88	53	85
Lancaster City	44	24	9	11	84	60	81
Worksop Town	44	20	13	11	102	60	73
Barrow	44	21	9	14	83	63	72
Altrincham	44	20	10	14	80	58	70
Gainsborough Trinity	44	17	14	13	59	56	65
Accrington Stanley	44	18	10	16	72	67	64
Hucknall Town	44	17	12	15	57	63	63
Gateshead	44	16	12	16	68	61	60
Bamber Bridge	44	17	8	19	63	65	59
Runcorn	44	15	10	19	56	70	55
Blyth Spartans	44	15	9	20	61	64	54
Burscough	44	14	10	20	59	68	52
Hyde United	44	13	12	19	72	79	51
Whitby Town	44	13	11	20	60	76	50
Marine	44	12	13	19	62	78	49
Colwyn Bay	44	12	10	22	68	102	46
Frickley Athletic	44	10	15	19	50	79	45
Droylsden	44	13	6	25	50	80	45
Leek Town	44	12	8	24	45	70	44
Spennymoor United	44	4	5	35	32	108	17

2001-2002

Premier Division

Burton Albion	44	31	11	2	106	30	104
Vauxhall Motors	44	27	8	9	86	55	89
Lancaster City	44	23	9	12	80	57	78
Worksop Town	44	23	9	12	74	51	78
Emley	44	22	9	13	69	55	75
Accrington Stanley	44	21	9	14	89	64	72
Runcorn FC Halton	44	21	8	15	76	53	71
Barrow	44	19	10	15	75	59	67
Altrincham	44	19	9	16	66	58	66
Bradford Park Avenue	44	18	5	21	77	76	59
Droylsden	44	17	8	19	65	78	59
Blyth Spartans	44	14	16	14	59	62	58
Frickley Athletic	44	16	11	17	63	69	58
Gateshead	44	14	14	16	58	71	56
Whitby Town	44	15	8	21	61	76	53
Hucknall Town	44	14	9	21	50	68	51
Marine	44	11	17	16	62	71	50
Burscough	44	15	5	24	69	86	50
Gainsborough Trinity	44	13	10	21	61	76	49
Colwyn Bay	44	12	11	21	49	82	47
Bishop Auckland	44	12	8	24	46	68	44
Hyde United	44	10	10	24	61	87	40
Bamber Bridge	44	7	10	27	38	88	30

Frickley Athletic and Bamber Bridge both had 1 point deducted.

First Division

Bradford Park Avenue	42	28	5	9	83	40	89
Vauxhall Motors	42	23	10	9	95	50	79
Ashton United	42	23	9	10	91	49	78
Stocksbridge Park Steels	42	19	13	10	80	60	70
Trafford	42	20	9	13	70	62	68
Belper Town	42	18	11	13	71	62	65
Witton Albion	42	15	16	11	51	50	61
Ossett Town	42	16	12	14	66	58	60
Radcliffe Borough	42	17	8	17	72	71	59
Chorley	42	15	14	13	71	70	59
Harrogate Town	42	15	10	17	60	70	55
Matlock Town	42	14	10	18	70	74	52
North Ferriby United	42	14	10	18	64	73	52
Workington	42	13	12	17	53	60	51
Lincoln United	42	13	12	17	60	75	51
Gretna	42	12	12	18	72	82	48
Guiseley	42	11	15	16	37	50	48
Kendal Town	42	12	12	18	60	69	47
Farsley Celtic	42	12	11	19	53	71	47
Eastwood Town	42	13	8	21	40	63	47
Winsford United	42	13	11	18	61	70	44
Congleton Town	42	8	6	28	43	94	30

Trafford and Kendal Town both had 1 point deducted
Winsford United had 6 points deducted

First Division

Harrogate Town	42	25	11	6	80	35	86
Ossett Town	42	21	13	8	73	44	76
Ashton United	42	21	12	9	90	63	75
Spennymoor United	42	22	6	14	75	73	72
Radcliffe Borough	42	20	8	14	73	51	68
Leek Town	42	20	8	14	67	51	68
Gretna	42	19	7	16	66	66	63
Eastwood Town	42	17	11	14	61	59	62
Rossendale United	42	17	10	15	69	58	61
Witton Albion	42	17	10	15	72	68	61
Guiseley	42	18	7	17	60	67	61
North Ferriby United	42	14	16	12	71	60	58
Chorley	42	16	9	17	59	57	57
Matlock Town	42	15	9	18	49	48	51
Trafford	42	14	9	19	64	80	51
Workington	42	12	12	18	51	57	48
Farsley Celtic	42	12	11	19	64	78	47
Belper Town	42	12	11	19	49	66	47
Lincoln United	42	11	14	17	62	80	47
Stocksbridge Park Steels	42	12	9	21	55	76	45
Kendal Town	42	9	9	24	52	76	36
Ossett Albion	42	8	8	26	43	92	32

Gretna had 1 point deducted.
Matlock Town had 3 points deducted.

2002-2003

Premier Division

Accrington Stanley	44	30	10	4	97	44	100
Barrow	44	24	12	8	84	52	84
Vauxhall Motors	44	22	10	12	81	46	76
Stalybridge Celtic	44	21	13	10	77	51	76
Worksop Town	44	21	9	14	82	67	72
Harrogate Town	44	21	8	15	75	63	71
Bradford Park Avenue	44	20	10	14	73	70	70
Hucknall Town	44	17	15	12	72	62	66
Droylsden	44	18	10	16	62	52	64
Whitby Town	44	17	12	15	80	69	63
Marine	44	17	10	17	63	60	61
Wakefield & Emley	44	14	18	12	46	49	60
Runcorn FC Halton	44	15	15	14	69	74	60
Altrincham	44	17	9	18	58	63	60
Gainsborough Trinity	44	16	11	17	67	66	59
Ashton United	44	15	13	16	71	79	58
Lancaster City	44	16	9	19	71	75	57
Burscough	44	14	9	21	44	51	51
Blyth Spartans	44	14	9	21	67	87	51
Frickley Athletic	44	13	8	23	45	78	47
Gateshead	44	10	11	23	60	81	41
Colwyn Bay	44	5	9	30	52	99	24
Hyde United	44	5	8	31	40	98	23

2003-2004

Premier Division

Hucknall Town	44	29	8	7	83	38	95
Droylsden	44	26	8	10	96	64	86
Barrow	44	22	14	8	82	52	80
Alfreton Town	44	23	9	12	73	43	78
Harrogate Town	44	24	5	15	79	63	77
Southport	44	20	10	14	71	52	70
Worksop Town	44	19	13	12	69	50	70
Lancaster City	44	20	9	15	62	49	69
Vauxhall Motors	44	19	10	15	78	75	67
Gainsborough Trinity	44	17	13	14	70	52	64
Stalybridge Celtic	44	18	10	16	72	66	64
Altrincham	44	16	15	13	66	51	63
Runcorn FC Halton	44	16	13	15	67	63	61
Ashton United	44	17	8	19	59	79	59
Whitby Town	44	14	11	19	55	70	53
Marine	44	13	12	19	62	74	51
Bradford Park Avenue	44	12	14	18	48	62	50
Spennymoor United	44	14	6	24	55	93	48
Burscough	44	10	15	19	47	67	45
Radcliffe Borough	44	12	6	26	74	99	42
Blyth Spartans	44	10	10	24	54	74	40
Frickley Athletic	44	11	7	26	51	83	40
Wakefield & Emley	44	8	6	30	45	99	30

Division One

Alfreton Town	42	26	9	7	106	59	87
Spennymoor United	42	27	6	9	81	42	87
Radcliffe Borough	42	25	10	7	90	46	85
North Ferriby United	42	23	9	10	78	45	78
Chorley	42	21	10	11	80	51	73
Belper Town	42	20	13	9	53	42	73
Witton Albion	42	19	15	8	67	50	72
Matlock Town	42	20	10	12	67	48	70
Leek Town	42	20	9	13	63	46	69
Workington	42	19	10	13	73	60	67
Farsley Celtic	42	17	11	14	66	67	62
Kendal Town	42	18	7	17	68	58	61
Bamber Bridge	42	15	9	18	55	59	54
Guiseley	42	14	11	17	68	63	53
Bishop Auckland	42	13	10	19	58	83	49
Lincoln United	42	12	9	21	67	77	45
Stocksbridge PS	42	11	9	22	54	81	42
Rossendale United	42	12	5	25	58	88	41
Kidsgrove Athletic	42	9	11	22	49	71	38
Ossett Town	42	8	9	25	39	80	33
Eastwood Town	42	5	8	29	33	92	23
Trafford	42	5	6	31	34	99	21

Division One

Hyde United	42	24	8	10	79	49	80
Matlock Town	42	23	7	12	78	51	76
Farsley Celtic	42	20	14	8	78	56	74
Lincoln United	42	20	11	11	73	53	71
Witton Albion	42	17	12	13	61	56	63
Gateshead	42	21	4	17	65	68	63
Workington	42	17	11	14	70	58	62
Leek Town	42	16	13	13	56	47	61
Guiseley	42	16	12	14	66	54	60
Bamber Bridge	42	16	12	14	64	53	60
Bridlington Town	42	16	10	16	70	68	58
Prescot Cables	42	16	10	16	63	65	58
Bishop Auckland	42	14	13	15	61	64	55
Ossett Town	42	15	10	17	62	73	52
Rossendale United	42	13	12	17	53	62	51
Colwyn Bay	42	14	9	19	56	82	51
North Ferriby United	42	13	11	18	64	70	50
Chorley	42	13	10	19	54	70	49
Stocksbridge Park Steels	42	12	12	18	57	69	48
Belper Town	42	9	15	18	44	58	42
Kendal Town	42	11	7	24	53	79	40
Kidsgrove Athletic	42	10	9	23	45	67	39

Gateshead had 4 points deducted. Ossett Town had 3 points deducted

2004-2005

Premier Division

Hyde United	42	25	13	4	80	43	88
Workington	42	26	7	9	73	30	85
Farsley Celtic	42	25	8	9	81	41	83
Whitby Town	42	23	11	8	65	49	80
Prescot Cables	42	21	8	13	63	54	71
Burscough	42	21	7	14	93	74	70
Leek Town	42	16	15	11	63	52	63
Witton Albion	42	15	17	10	56	44	62
Radcliffe Borough	42	16	14	12	60	60	62
Guiseley	42	16	13	13	70	64	61
Matlock Town	42	14	13	15	59	67	55
Blyth Spartans	42	13	13	16	53	55	52
Wakefield & Emley	42	14	10	18	60	67	52
Lincoln United	42	15	4	23	53	66	49
Marine	42	10	18	14	53	60	48
Ossett Town	42	11	13	18	53	62	46
Gateshead	42	11	12	19	61	84	45
Frickley Athletic	42	10	14	18	44	57	44
Bishop Auckland	42	11	7	24	51	74	40
Bridlington Town	42	7	14	21	43	66	35
Bamber Bridge	42	9	7	26	48	92	34
Spennymoor United	42	9	10	23	44	65	25

Spennymoor United had 12 points deducted.

Division One

North Ferriby United	42	25	8	9	83	49	83
Ilkeston Town	42	24	9	9	64	40	81
AFC Telford United	42	23	11	8	78	44	80
Willenhall Town	42	22	12	8	71	46	78
Kendal Town	42	21	8	13	89	69	71
Eastwood Town	42	20	9	13	73	54	69
Mossley	42	20	6	16	81	56	66
Brigg Town	42	15	19	8	59	46	64
Gresley Rovers	42	17	12	13	57	53	63
Kidsgrove Athletic	42	15	15	12	60	55	60
Woodley Sports	42	16	11	15	68	74	59
Ossett Albion	42	15	13	14	83	74	58
Colwyn Bay	42	14	13	15	54	62	55
Stocksbridge Park Steels	42	15	9	18	58	58	51
Shepshed Dynamo	42	13	11	18	53	75	50
Chorley	42	13	9	20	62	69	48
Belper Town	42	13	8	21	57	66	47
Spalding United	42	13	8	21	57	69	47
Clitheroe	42	12	10	20	47	57	46
Warrington Town	42	11	13	18	45	59	46
Rossendale United	42	10	10	22	64	87	40
Rocester	42	0	6	36	31	132	6

Stocksbridge Park Steels had 3 points deducted.

2005-2006　Premier Division

Blyth Spartans	42	26	11	5	79	32	89
Frickley Athletic	42	26	8	8	72	36	86
Marine	42	23	12	7	61	25	81
Farsley Celtic	42	23	10	9	84	34	79
North Ferriby United	42	21	10	11	77	54	73
Whitby Town	42	18	10	14	60	59	64
Burscough	42	19	6	17	64	64	63
Witton Albion	42	17	9	16	68	55	60
Matlock Town	42	16	11	15	60	55	59
AFC Telford United	42	14	17	11	54	52	59
Ossett Town	42	17	7	18	57	61	58
Leek Town	42	14	14	14	50	53	56
Prescot Cables	42	15	8	19	49	60	53
Guiseley	42	14	9	19	45	58	51
Ashton United	42	13	10	19	62	63	49
Ilkeston Town	42	12	13	17	48	51	49
Gateshead	42	12	10	20	52	77	46
Radcliffe Borough	42	12	8	22	54	62	44
Lincoln United	42	10	14	18	44	64	44
Wakefield Emley	42	11	9	22	38	69	42
Bradford Park Avenue	42	10	9	23	64	86	39
Runcorn FC Halton	42	6	11	25	36	108	29

Division One

Mossley	42	23	9	10	83	55	78
Fleetwood Town	42	22	10	10	72	48	76
Kendal Town	42	22	10	10	81	58	76
Woodley Sports	42	22	8	12	85	53	74
Gresley Rovers	42	20	10	12	79	64	70
Stocksbridge PS	42	17	16	9	66	43	67
Eastwood Town	42	16	14	12	66	58	62
Brigg Town	42	16	14	12	70	64	62
Belper Town	42	17	8	17	53	56	59
Shepshed Dynamo	42	15	13	14	57	56	58
Bridlington Town	42	16	10	16	61	68	58
Colwyn Bay	42	15	11	16	56	53	56
Bamber Bridge	42	13	15	14	65	59	54
Ossett Albion	42	15	9	18	54	64	54
Rossendale United	42	12	17	13	58	61	53
Clitheroe	42	15	8	19	54	73	53
Kidsgrove Athletic	42	14	9	19	66	69	51
Chorley	42	14	8	20	58	59	50
Warrington Town	42	11	15	16	62	74	48
Spalding United	42	10	15	17	49	70	45
Goole	42	11	11	20	55	85	43
Bishop Auckland	42	3	6	33	39	99	15

Goole had 1 point deducted.

2006-2007　Premier Division

Burscough	42	23	12	7	80	37	80
Witton Albion	42	24	8	10	90	48	80
AFC Telford United	42	21	15	6	72	40	78
Marine	42	22	8	12	70	53	74
Matlock Town	42	21	9	12	70	43	72
Guiseley	42	19	12	11	71	49	69
Hednesford Town	42	18	14	10	49	41	68
Fleetwood Town	42	19	10	13	71	60	67
Gateshead	42	17	14	11	75	57	65
Ossett Town	42	18	10	14	61	52	64
Whitby Town	42	18	6	18	63	78	60
Ilkeston Town	42	16	11	15	66	62	59
North Ferriby United	42	15	9	18	54	61	54
Prescot Cables	42	13	14	15	52	56	53
Lincoln United	42	12	15	15	40	58	51
Frickley Athletic	42	13	10	19	50	69	49
Leek Town	42	13	9	20	49	61	48
Ashton United	42	13	9	20	52	72	48
Kendal Town	42	12	11	19	59	79	47
Mossley	42	10	5	27	48	79	35
Radcliffe Borough	42	7	11	24	39	71	32
Grantham Town	42	3	8	31	39	94	17

Burscough had one point deducted.

Division One

Team							
Buxton	46	30	11	5	94	37	101
Cammell Laird	46	28	10	8	105	56	94
Eastwood Town	46	26	9	11	89	43	87
Bradford Park Avenue	46	24	10	12	77	47	82
Colwyn Bay	46	22	11	13	74	65	77
Stocksbridge Park Steels	46	22	10	14	82	49	76
Goole	46	21	9	16	80	84	72
Kidsgrove Athletic	46	21	7	18	91	80	70
Rossendale United	46	21	7	18	64	59	70
Woodley Sports	46	19	11	16	89	71	68
Ossett Albion	46	19	11	16	71	66	68
Harrogate Railway	46	21	5	20	72	78	68
Bamber Bridge	46	18	8	20	78	75	62
Alsager Town	46	18	7	21	72	75	61
Skelmersdale United	46	17	10	19	72	77	61
Clitheroe	46	18	6	22	78	75	60
Brigg Town	46	16	10	20	57	72	58
Gresley Rovers	46	16	7	23	59	75	55
Belper Town	46	17	4	25	58	86	55
Shepshed Dynamo	46	15	7	24	62	96	52
Wakefield	46	13	10	23	48	71	49
Warrington Town	46	13	8	25	64	84	47
Chorley	46	10	6	30	52	99	36
Bridlington Town	46	3	14	29	33	101	23

2007-2008

Premier Division

Team							
Fleetwood Town	40	28	7	5	81	39	91
Witton Albion	40	27	8	5	84	28	89
Gateshead	40	26	7	7	93	42	85
Eastwood Town	40	20	9	11	61	45	69
Buxton	40	20	8	12	60	50	68
Guiseley	40	19	10	11	65	43	67
Marine	40	19	4	17	70	65	61
Hednesford Town	40	15	8	17	62	65	53
Worksop Town	40	13	12	15	59	62	51
Ashton United	40	11	15	14	63	73	48
Kendal Town	40	12	11	17	61	70	47
Whitby Town	40	13	7	20	68	75	46
Prescot Cables	40	13	8	19	48	62	46
Frickley Athletic	40	11	13	16	50	68	46
North Ferriby United	40	13	7	20	53	76	46
Matlock Town	40	12	9	19	55	68	45
Ilkeston Town	40	10	14	16	64	72	44
Ossett Town	40	12	8	20	48	60	44
Leek Town	40	11	11	18	54	68	44
Stamford	40	11	10	19	59	86	43
Lincoln United	40	7	8	25	44	85	29

Prescot Cables had one point deducted.

Division One North

Team							
Bradford Park Avenue	42	25	7	10	91	43	82
FC United of Manchester	42	24	9	9	91	49	81
Skelmersdale United	42	23	9	10	94	46	78
Curzon Ashton	42	23	9	10	78	48	78
Bamber Bridge	42	22	8	12	70	54	74
Ossett Albion	42	20	10	12	77	65	70
Wakefield	42	19	7	16	58	49	64
Newcastle Blue Star	42	17	12	13	71	58	63
Rossendale United	42	16	11	15	66	74	59
Garforth Town	42	16	8	18	60	63	56
Lancaster City	42	15	9	18	54	70	54
Harrogate Railway	42	13	12	17	51	58	51
Clitheroe	42	13	11	18	63	77	50
Chorley	42	10	12	20	56	80	42
Mossley	42	12	6	24	60	100	42
Radcliffe Borough	42	9	11	22	53	75	38
Woodley Sports	42	7	13	22	38	65	33
Bridlington Town	42	8	8	26	42	99	32

Woodley Sports had one point deducted.

Division One South

Team							
Retford United	42	31	6	5	93	35	99
Cammell Laird	42	27	5	10	82	54	86
Nantwich Town	42	25	4	13	90	45	79
Sheffield	42	22	10	10	82	53	76
Stocksbridge Park Steels	42	21	9	12	72	61	72
Grantham Town	42	22	4	16	74	58	70
Colwyn Bay	42	19	8	15	86	65	65
Belper Town	42	17	13	12	73	64	64
Goole	42	18	10	14	77	69	64
Carlton Town	42	16	11	15	86	82	59
Gresley Rovers	42	18	5	19	53	69	59
Quorn	42	15	8	19	69	76	53
Warrington Town	42	13	8	21	51	78	47
Alsager Town	42	12	7	23	58	88	43
Shepshed Dynamo	42	10	8	24	44	75	38
Brigg Town	42	8	12	22	56	86	36
Kidsgrove Athletic	42	7	10	25	61	90	31
Spalding United	42	3	10	29	46	105	19

2008-2009

Premier Division

Team							
Eastwood Town	42	25	12	5	82	37	87
Ilkeston Town	42	23	13	6	59	34	82
Nantwich Town	42	22	10	10	83	41	76
Guiseley	42	22	10	10	98	60	76
Kendal Town	42	21	11	10	85	63	74
FC United of Manchester	42	21	9	12	82	58	72
Bradford Park Avenue	42	20	12	10	74	52	72
Hednesford Town	42	21	6	15	78	52	69
Ashton United	42	16	10	16	71	75	58
North Ferriby United	42	16	6	20	67	65	54
Frickley Athletic	42	13	15	14	50	58	54
Ossett Town	42	15	8	19	71	74	53
Marine	42	15	6	21	54	75	51
Buxton	42	13	10	19	56	58	49
Matlock Town	42	12	13	17	65	74	49
Boston United	42	12	13	17	38	52	49
Worksop Town	42	12	12	18	48	87	48
Cammell Laird	42	12	11	19	58	70	47
Whitby Town	42	12	10	20	58	71	46
Witton Albion	42	12	6	24	53	73	42
Leigh Genesis	42	11	7	24	42	88	40
Prescot Cables	42	5	12	25	52	107	27

Division One North

Team							
Durham City	40	25	12	3	98	41	87
Skelmersdale United	40	26	8	6	96	51	86
Newcastle Blue Star	40	21	10	9	93	54	73
Colwyn Bay	40	23	7	10	72	49	73
Curzon Ashton	40	20	8	12	66	44	68
Ossett Albion	40	19	9	12	76	61	66
Lancaster City	40	19	8	13	69	64	65
FC Halifax Town	40	17	12	11	71	52	63
Wakefield	40	16	8	16	65	62	56
Mossley	40	16	6	18	63	70	54
Bamber Bridge	40	16	5	19	69	78	53
Clitheroe	40	15	7	18	64	76	52
Woodley Sports	40	16	3	21	57	74	51
Chorley	40	13	8	19	56	66	47
Trafford	40	13	7	20	72	83	46
Garforth Town	40	13	5	22	77	99	44
Radcliffe Borough	40	12	6	22	51	66	42
Harrogate Railway	40	13	3	24	58	82	42
Warrington Town	40	11	8	21	50	73	41
Salford City	40	10	6	24	59	107	36
Rossendale United	40	8	10	22	53	83	34

Colwyn Bay had 3 points deducted.

Division One South

Retford United	38	24	9	5	88	34	81
Belper Town	38	24	9	5	79	41	81
Stocksbridge Park Steels	38	23	6	9	92	44	75
Carlton Town	38	20	10	8	83	50	70
Rushall Olympic	38	20	8	10	63	42	68
Glapwell	38	21	5	12	78	58	68
Stamford	38	15	16	7	65	51	61
Shepshed Dynamo	38	16	8	14	61	61	56
Leek Town	38	14	12	12	63	60	54
Lincoln United	38	14	9	15	58	65	51
Sheffield	38	14	8	16	67	69	50
Quorn	38	13	9	16	54	63	48
Grantham Town	38	12	11	15	49	65	47
Loughborough Dynamo	38	11	13	14	45	58	46
Kidsgrove Athletic	38	12	5	21	49	62	41
Willenhall Town	38	10	8	20	55	74	38
Spalding United	38	10	7	21	41	82	37
Goole	38	13	5	20	62	85	33
Gresley Rovers	38	6	7	25	41	78	25
Brigg Town	38	3	5	30	41	92	14

Goole had 11 points deducted.

Division One North

FC Halifax Town	42	30	10	2	108	38	100
Lancaster City	42	31	3	8	95	45	96
Curzon Ashton	42	23	12	7	93	50	75
Colwyn Bay	42	23	6	13	77	57	75
Skelmersdale United	42	22	8	12	80	56	74
Leigh Genesis	42	21	8	13	81	51	71
Mossley	42	18	11	13	73	67	65
Clitheroe	42	18	8	16	72	66	62
Warrington Town	42	18	6	18	65	69	60
Radcliffe Borough	42	17	6	19	65	78	57
Salford City	42	16	8	18	63	74	56
Trafford	42	15	8	19	79	73	53
AFC Fylde	42	15	8	19	67	79	53
Bamber Bridge	42	14	10	18	58	67	52
Prescot Cables	42	13	11	18	51	68	50
Chorley	42	13	10	19	56	76	49
Harrogate Railway Athletic	42	15	7	20	58	79	49
Wakefield	42	12	12	18	49	58	48
Woodley Sports	42	10	15	17	53	67	45
Garforth Town	42	11	7	24	64	94	40
Ossett Albion	42	7	7	28	52	91	28
Rossendale United	42	6	7	29	38	94	25

Harrogate Railway Athletic had 3 points deducted.
Curzon Ashton had 6 points deducted, 3 for fielding an ineligible player and 3 for a financial irregularity. Initially 10 points were deducted for the financial irregularity, with 5 points suspended, but on appeal this was reduced to 6 points deducted with 3 suspended.

2009-2010

Premier Division

Guiseley	38	25	4	9	73	41	79
Bradford Park Avenue	38	24	6	8	94	51	78
Boston United	38	23	8	7	90	34	77
North Ferriby United	38	22	9	7	70	38	75
Kendal Town	38	21	8	9	75	47	71
Retford United	38	18	11	9	73	46	65
Matlock Town	38	17	9	12	72	49	60
Buxton	38	16	12	10	66	43	60
Marine	38	17	6	15	60	55	57
Nantwich Town	38	16	6	16	64	69	54
Stocksbridge Park Steels	38	15	7	16	80	68	52
Ashton United	38	15	6	17	48	63	51
FC United of Manchester	38	13	8	17	62	65	47
Whitby Town	38	12	10	16	56	62	46
Frickley Athletic	38	12	9	17	50	66	45
Burscough	38	13	5	20	55	65	44
Hucknall Town	38	12	8	18	65	81	44
Worksop Town	38	7	9	22	45	68	30
Ossett Town	38	6	7	25	46	92	25
Durham City	38	2	0	36	27	168	0

Durham City had 6 points deducted.
King's Lynn folded and their record was expunged.
Newcastle Blue Star folded and resigned from the League before the start of the season.

Division One South

Mickleover Sports	42	28	5	9	93	51	89
Chasetown	42	24	10	8	78	42	82
Glapwell	42	23	12	7	73	42	81
Kidsgrove Athletic	42	22	12	8	93	50	78
Sheffield	42	21	10	11	75	51	73
Belper Town	42	21	8	13	83	55	71
Witton Albion	42	20	7	15	76	53	67
Leek Town	42	18	13	11	68	61	67
Carlton Town	42	19	9	14	74	68	66
Stamford	42	18	10	14	77	54	64
Grantham Town	42	17	11	14	62	56	62
Rushall Olympic	42	16	11	15	68	61	59
Market Drayton Town	42	16	5	21	71	81	53
Loughborough Dynamo	42	15	8	19	70	80	53
Brigg Town	42	15	7	20	60	77	52
Cammell Laird	42	13	11	18	51	66	50
Shepshed Dynamo	42	10	18	14	44	55	48
Goole	42	12	10	20	70	84	46
Lincoln United	42	13	5	24	57	67	44
Quorn	42	9	13	20	55	78	40
Spalding United	42	5	5	32	33	111	20Ü
Willenhall Town	42	5	4	33	21	109	9

Willenhall Town had 10 points deducted for entering administration.

2010-2011

Premier Division

FC Halifax Town	42	30	8	4	108	36	98
Colwyn Bay	42	24	7	11	67	56	79
Bradford Park Avenue	42	23	8	11	84	55	77
FC United of Manchester	42	24	4	14	76	53	76
North Ferriby United	42	22	7	13	78	51	73
Buxton	42	20	10	12	71	52	70
Kendal Town	42	21	5	16	80	77	68
Marine	42	20	7	15	74	64	67
Worksop Town	42	21	6	15	72	54	66
Chasetown	42	20	6	16	76	59	66
Matlock Town	42	20	6	16	74	59	66
Northwich Victoria	42	18	9	15	66	55	63
Stocksbridge Park Steels	42	17	6	19	75	75	57
Ashton United	42	16	5	21	57	62	53
Mickleover Sports	42	15	7	20	70	76	52
Whitby Town	42	14	9	19	58	77	51
Nantwich Town	42	13	7	22	68	90	46
Frickley Athletic	42	11	11	20	43	68	44
Burscough	42	12	7	23	56	73	43
Hucknall Town	42	11	10	21	57	80	43
Ossett Town	42	9	5	28	45	103	32
Retford United	42	5	2	35	31	111	17

Worksop Town had 3 points deducted.
Burscough were reprieved from relegation due to Ilkeston Town folding earlier in the season.

Division One South

Barwell	42	30	4	8	84	46	94
Newcastle Town	42	27	9	6	104	48	90
Rushall Olympic	42	26	3	13	78	45	81
Brigg Town	42	24	8	10	74	58	80
Grantham Town	42	23	10	9	69	48	79
Sutton Coldfield Town	42	23	6	13	89	60	75
Kidsgrove Athletic	42	23	6	13	88	59	75
Carlton Town	42	21	10	11	88	50	73
Glapwell	42	21	6	15	82	58	69
Romulus	42	20	7	15	71	65	67
Sheffield	42	15	10	17	73	86	55
Lincoln United	42	14	12	16	70	77	54
Goole	42	16	6	20	79	93	54
Belper Town	42	16	5	21	70	74	53
Quorn	42	11	14	17	57	61	47
Leek Town	42	14	5	23	64	74	47
Loughborough Dynamo	42	13	7	22	72	89	46
Market Drayton Town	42	13	5	24	67	91	44
Stamford	42	10	12	20	62	74	42
Rainworth Miners Welfare	42	11	7	24	53	85	40
Shepshed Dynamo	42	4	9	29	44	103	21
Spalding United	42	3	7	32	33	127	16

Glapwell resigned from the League at the end of the season.

Division One North

Chester	44	29	10	5	107	36	97
Skelmersdale United	44	30	7	7	117	48	97
Chorley	44	25	11	8	87	43	86
Curzon Ashton	44	25	10	9	85	49	85
AFC Fylde	44	24	9	11	91	59	81
Clitheroe	44	19	13	12	82	70	70
Bamber Bridge	44	20	10	14	70	60	70
Lancaster City	44	21	5	18	80	61	68
Warrington Town	44	18	16	10	70	50	67
Witton Albion	44	15	17	12	75	63	62
Woodley Sports	44	17	11	16	71	75	62
Salford City	44	17	11	16	68	73	62
Garforth Town	44	13	13	18	67	71	52
Trafford	44	15	7	22	73	92	52
Mossley	44	14	9	21	75	77	51
Wakefield	44	14	8	22	55	74	50
Durham City	44	13	10	21	75	92	48
Radcliffe Borough	44	12	12	20	60	89	48
Cammell Laird	44	13	8	23	66	94	47
Harrogate Railway Athletic	44	13	7	24	82	103	46
Prescot Cables	44	9	15	20	52	79	42
Ossett Albion	44	6	11	27	60	134	26
Leigh Genesis	44	5	8	31	39	112	23

Warrington Town and Ossett Albion both had 3 points deducted.
Durham City had 1 point deducted.

2011-2012

Premier Division

Chester	42	31	7	4	102	29	100
Northwich Victoria	42	26	8	8	73	43	83
Chorley	42	24	7	11	76	48	79
Bradford Park Avenue	42	24	6	12	77	49	78
Hednesford Town	42	21	10	11	67	49	73
FC United of Manchester	42	21	9	12	83	51	72
Marine	42	19	9	14	56	50	66
Rushall Olympic	42	17	10	15	52	51	61
North Ferriby United	42	16	10	16	56	70	58
Nantwich Town	42	15	13	14	65	61	57
Kendal Town	42	15	8	19	78	83	53
Ashton United	42	15	8	19	61	67	53
Buxton	42	15	8	19	64	77	53
Matlock Town	42	12	14	16	52	54	50
Worksop Town	42	13	10	19	56	76	49
Stafford Rangers	42	12	12	18	60	65	48
Whitby Town	42	12	11	19	57	80	47
Stocksbridge Park Steels	42	10	12	20	57	75	42
Frickley Athletic	42	10	12	20	48	69	42
Chasetown	42	10	11	21	50	75	41
Mickleover Sports	42	11	10	21	67	85	40
Burscough	42	5	11	26	54	104	26

Mickleover Sports had 3 points deducted for fielding an ineligible player.
Nantwich Town had 1 point deducted for fielding an ineligible player.
Northwich Victoria had 3 points deducted for fielding an ineligible player and were later expelled from the Northern Premier League after being found guilty of failing to comply with the League's financial rules.
On appeal this punishment was reduced to relegation from the League's Premier Division.

Division One North

AFC Fylde	42	31	6	5	90	29	99
Curzon Ashton	42	28	11	3	91	44	95
Witton Albion	42	28	6	8	101	44	90
Farsley	42	25	6	11	86	48	81
Garforth Town	42	24	7	11	95	63	79
Lancaster City	42	24	5	13	80	48	77
Skelmersdale United	42	21	12	9	94	60	75
Woodley Sports	42	22	5	15	71	51	71
Durham City	42	20	2	20	81	80	62
Bamber Bridge	42	17	9	16	69	68	60
Warrington Town	42	17	9	16	69	71	60
Trafford	42	15	11	16	70	66	56
Salford City	42	14	10	18	69	71	52
Mossley	42	10	15	17	66	75	45
Radcliffe Borough	42	13	6	23	54	75	45
Prescot Cables	42	10	12	20	53	71	42
Ossett Town	42	11	9	22	41	84	42
Ossett Albion	42	11	6	25	59	95	39
Clitheroe	42	10	8	24	51	76	38
Wakefield	42	7	12	23	38	77	33
Harrogate Railway Athletic	42	8	7	27	54	115	31
Cammell Laird	42	8	4	30	34	103	28

Woodley Sports were relegated from the League at the end of the season due to ground grading and security of tenure issues. The club subsequently changed their name to Stockport Sports and joined the North West Counties Football League.
Durham City resigned from the League at the end of the season and joined the Northern League.

Division One South

Grantham Town	42	29	7	6	92	44	93
Carlton Town	42	26	5	11	101	52	83
Ilkeston	42	26	5	11	93	44	83
Sheffield	42	22	9	11	93	62	75
Leek Town	42	22	8	12	77	60	74
Belper Town	42	23	5	14	74	57	74
Stamford	42	20	8	14	77	75	68
Loughborough Dynamo	42	18	11	13	80	61	65
New Mills	42	17	12	13	79	76	63
Goole	42	18	8	16	72	78	62
Hucknall Town	42	16	9	17	54	61	57
Sutton Coldfield Town	42	16	7	19	72	63	55
Kidsgrove Athletic	42	13	16	13	62	59	55
Coalville Town	42	15	10	17	69	72	55
Newcastle Town	42	14	10	18	59	70	52
Market Drayton Town	42	11	15	16	61	84	48
Brigg Town	42	11	12	19	52	76	45
Lincoln United	42	10	13	19	65	85	43
Rainworth Miners Welfare	42	10	11	21	38	55	41
Romulus	42	7	15	20	56	85	36
Quorn	42	6	9	27	48	85	27
Shepshed Dynamo	42	5	10	27	45	115	25

Grantham Town had 1 point deducted for fielding an ineligible player.

2012-2013

Premier Division

North Ferriby United	42	28	9	5	96	43	93
Hednesford Town	42	28	9	5	91	47	93
FC United of Manchester	42	25	8	9	86	48	83
Witton Albion	42	24	8	10	85	57	80
AFC Fylde	42	23	6	13	93	51	75
Rushall Olympic	42	20	10	12	69	55	70
Buxton	42	18	13	11	72	56	67
Chorley	42	20	7	15	63	52	67
Worksop Town	42	20	6	16	91	68	66
Ashton United	42	15	14	13	71	66	59
Marine	42	16	11	15	61	61	59
Ilkeston	42	15	13	14	67	55	58
Whitby Town	42	16	9	17	68	72	57
Nantwich Town	42	15	8	19	63	76	53
Stafford Rangers	42	12	15	15	54	60	51
Blyth Spartans	42	15	6	21	70	87	51
Matlock Town	42	12	9	21	54	80	45
Frickley Athletic	42	10	9	23	58	88	39
Grantham Town	42	9	9	24	56	75	36
Stocksbridge Park Steels	42	9	9	24	67	106	36
Kendal Town	42	9	6	27	65	112	33
Eastwood Town	42	3	6	33	36	121	15

Division One North

Skelmersdale United	42	32	6	4	110	41	102
Cammell Laird	42	26	8	8	86	58	86
New Mills	42	26	7	9	107	69	85
Trafford	42	24	8	10	93	44	80
Mossley	42	24	8	10	83	48	80
Ramsbottom United	42	24	7	11	97	49	79
Curzon Ashton	42	22	7	13	98	67	73
Clitheroe	42	21	10	11	66	63	73
Bamber Bridge	42	21	7	14	86	58	70
Warrington Town	42	19	12	11	76	54	69
Burscough	42	14	17	11	81	64	59
Ossett Town	42	14	13	15	67	65	55
Lancaster City	42	15	8	19	70	73	50
Farsley	42	13	10	19	72	80	49
Radcliffe Borough	42	11	15	16	68	69	48
Salford City	42	11	13	18	65	79	46
Prescot Cables	42	12	10	20	51	67	46
Harrogate Railway Athletic	42	11	8	23	47	89	41
Wakefield	42	6	9	27	38	119	27
Ossett Albion	42	6	7	29	49	96	25
Goole AFC	42	5	8	29	44	89	23
Garforth Town	42	4	4	34	44	157	16

Lancaster City had 3 points deducted for fielding an ineligible player.

Division One South

King's Lynn Town	42	28	8	6	86	46	92
Coalville Town	42	25	11	6	108	44	86
Belper Town	42	23	13	6	95	42	82
Stamford	42	23	7	12	97	58	76
Chasetown	42	21	11	10	83	51	74
Sutton Coldfield Town	42	22	8	12	81	61	74
Halesowen Town	42	23	5	14	79	65	74
Northwich Victoria	42	19	10	13	88	58	67
Sheffield	42	18	9	15	85	82	63
Leek Town	42	15	14	13	72	60	59
Gresley	42	16	10	16	75	77	58
Carlton Town	42	16	8	18	67	68	56
Brigg Town	42	14	11	17	62	76	53
Rainworth Miners Welfare	42	14	9	19	59	75	51
Market Drayton Town	42	13	11	18	68	78	50
Loughborough Dynamo	42	13	10	19	75	75	49
Newcastle Town	42	11	13	18	45	58	46
Kidsgrove Athletic	42	12	7	23	75	89	43
Romulus	42	11	9	22	52	78	42
Lincoln United	42	9	9	24	64	102	36
Mickleover Sports	42	7	13	22	51	92	34
Hucknall Town	42	4	4	34	39	171	16

2013-2014

Premier Division

Chorley	46	29	10	7	107	39	97
FC United of Manchester	46	29	9	8	108	52	96
AFC Fylde	46	28	9	9	97	41	93
Worksop Town	46	27	7	12	120	87	88
Ashton United	46	24	8	14	92	62	80
Skelmersdale United	46	24	5	17	92	79	77
Rushall Olympic	46	21	12	13	79	65	75
Blyth Spartans	46	20	12	14	79	78	72
Whitby Town	46	18	16	12	82	64	70
Trafford	46	20	8	18	77	73	68
King's Lynn Town	46	20	8	18	76	77	68
Matlock Town	46	18	13	15	61	53	67
Buxton	46	16	14	16	63	60	62
Barwell	46	17	11	18	62	67	62
Grantham Town	46	17	10	19	77	78	61
Witton Albion	46	17	9	20	77	80	60
Ilkeston	46	17	8	21	81	77	59
Stamford	46	17	7	22	75	85	58
Nantwich Town	46	14	14	18	77	71	56
Marine	46	13	14	19	68	76	53
Frickley Athletic	46	12	13	21	62	80	49
Stafford Rangers	46	9	8	29	56	112	35
Stocksbridge Park Steels	46	5	8	33	60	130	23
Droylsden	46	2	3	41	40	182	9

Division One South

Halesowen Town	40	29	4	7	80	38	91
Coalville Town	40	27	8	5	101	35	89
Leek Town	40	28	4	8	85	35	88
Belper Town	40	24	9	7	98	50	81
Mickleover Sports	40	22	7	11	82	62	73
Sutton Coldfield Town	40	19	7	14	74	53	64
Scarborough Athletic	40	18	7	15	73	57	61
Newcastle Town	40	18	5	17	66	65	59
Gresley	40	17	5	18	66	67	56
Carlton Town	40	15	10	15	58	55	55
Romulus	40	16	7	17	66	64	55
Chasetown	40	14	10	16	52	59	52
Goole	40	15	6	19	60	75	51
Loughborough Dynamo	40	13	8	19	62	77	47
Rainworth Miners Welfare	40	12	10	18	52	72	46
Sheffield	40	12	8	20	69	80	44
Lincoln United	40	10	6	24	55	88	36
Brigg Town	40	9	8	23	49	94	35
Market Drayton Town	40	8	11	21	56	105	35
Bedworth United	40	9	7	24	48	83	34
Kidsgrove Athletic	40	7	9	24	41	80	30

Eastwood Town resigned from the League on 9th March 2014 and their playing record (Played 27, Won 2, Drawn 5, Lost 20) was expunged. Leek Town had 3 points deducted for fielding an ineligible player in a fixture against Eastwood Town. However, as Eastwood Town's record was expunged this has no effect on their points total in the above table.

Division One North

Curzon Ashton	42	31	6	5	92	36	99
Darlington 1883	42	28	6	8	101	37	90
Warrington Town	42	27	6	9	86	47	87
Bamber Bridge	42	26	5	11	81	45	83
Ramsbottom United	42	25	8	9	112	57	80
Lancaster City	42	24	8	10	75	52	80
Farsley	42	21	12	9	76	51	75
Ossett Town	42	19	8	15	66	63	65
Northwich Victoria	42	16	15	11	73	52	63
Kendal Town	42	17	5	20	83	84	56
Cammell Laird	42	15	9	18	65	64	54
Salford City	42	15	7	20	68	80	52
Harrogate Railway Athletic	42	14	6	22	52	66	48
Burscough	42	13	9	20	58	82	48
Mossley	42	13	8	21	73	90	47
New Mills	42	12	9	21	68	95	45
Clitheroe	42	12	7	23	55	81	43
Radcliffe Borough	42	12	7	23	57	93	43
Padiham	42	12	6	24	61	92	42
Prescot Cables	42	10	10	22	63	86	40
Ossett Albion	42	7	8	27	40	80	29
Wakefield	42	7	7	28	55	127	28

Ramsbottom United had 3 points deducted for fielding an ineligible player. Cammell Laird resigned from the League at the end of the season.

LONDON LEAGUE

The London League was formed in 1896 following an initiative by Mr. George Fordham who believed that the 2-year old Southern League was causing travel difficulties for London clubs.

Note: Some of the published tables contained errors. Where it has not been possible to correct the errors, the totals for these are shown in italics below the relevant columns.

1896-97

Division One

3rd Grenadier Guards	12	9	1	2	32	13	19
Thames Ironworks	12	7	2	3	17	17	16
Barking Woodville	12	6	3	3	20	11	15
Ilford	12	7	1	4	26	14	15
Crouch End	12	4	2	6	14	19	10
Vampires	12	3	1	8	10	28	7
London Welsh	12	0	2	10	9	26	2

The 1st Scots Guards resigned from the League and their record was deleted when it stood as: 4 1 0 3 3 7 3
London Welsh were suspended towards the end of the season and their opponents were awarded wins for outstanding fixtures.

Division Two

Bromley	**16**	**11**	**3**	**2**	**42**	**16**	**25**
Brentford	**16**	**9**	**6**	**1**	**42**	**19**	**24**
Queens Park Rangers	**16**	**10**	**1**	**5**	**31**	**14**	**21**
Stanley	**16**	**7**	**6**	**3**	**22**	**10**	**20**
Hammersmith Athletic	16	5	3	8	18	25	13
Harrow Athletic	16	4	3	9	19	34	11
Fulham	16	3	4	9	17	40	10
West Croydon	16	3	4	9	12	33	10
Forest Swifts	16	3	4	9	25	37	10

Clapton Clifton were expelled from the League and their record was deleted when it stood as: 0 12 1 11 7 33 1
Orient were promoted from Division Three and Barnet joined from the North Middlesex League.

Division Three

Barking Woodville Reserves	12	8	2	2	28	9	18
Orient	12	7	2	3	27	22	16
Walthamstow Town	12	6	2	4	20	19	14
Old Tottonians	12	5	1	6	21	20	11
Guildhall	12	5	0	7	26	32	10
Ideal Wanderers	12	3	2	7	11	23	8
Crouch End Reserves	12	3	1	8	10	18	7

Division Three closed down at the end of the season.

1897-98

Division One

Thames Ironworks	16	12	3	1	47	15	27
Brentford	16	12	2	2	43	17	26
Leyton	16	8	4	4	41	33	20
3rd Grenadier Guards	16	7	3	6	34	33	17
Ilford	16	5	7	4	33	25	17
Stanley	16	5	4	7	22	22	14
Barking Woodville	16	2	6	8	16	37	10
Bromley	16	4	2	10	20	49	10
2nd Grenadier Guards	16	0	3	13	17	42	3

Queens Park Rangers withdrew from the League and their record was deleted when it stood as: 4 1 0 3 5 11 2
Thames Ironworks and Brentford both moved to the Southern League. (Thames Ironworks subsequently changed their name to West Ham United in 1900). Bromley moved to the Kent League and Ilford moved to the South Essex League.

Division Two

Barnet	18	15	2	1	63	17	32
Fulham	18	13	5	0	60	10	31
Hammersmith Athletic	18	11	1	6	40	25	23
Metropolitan Railway	18	11	1	6	41	26	23
West Hampstead	18	8	2	8	37	35	18
West Croydon	18	6	4	8	31	44	16
Orient	18	7	0	11	30	45	14
Harrow Athletic	18	4	1	13	23	58	9
Forest Swifts	18	2	3	13	18	61	7
2nd Life Guards	18	3	1	14	13	35	7

Fulham moved to the Southern League and were replaced by their reserve team. Barnet, Hammersmith Athletic, West Hampstead, Metropolitan Railway and Orient were promoted to Division One. Orient changed their name to Clapton Orient.

1898-99

Division One

Tottenham Hotspur Reserves	16	14	1	1	49	19	29
Deptford Town	16	11	2	3	45	17	24
Barnet	16	6	5	5	33	30	17
Hanwell	16	7	2	7	35	28	16
Clapton Orient	16	7	2	7	29	32	16
Willesden Town	16	5	3	8	24	32	13
Hammersmith Athletic	16	5	1	10	20	38	11
West Hampstead	16	5	1	10	22	32	9
Hounslow	16	3	1	12	20	49	7

West Hampstead had 2 points deducted. Metropolitan Railway withdrew. Hanwell, West Hampstead and Hounslow moved to the Middlesex League and Deptford Town moved to the Kent League. Bromley joined from the Kent League.

Division Two

Monsteds Athletic	**14**	**11**	**1**	**2**	**49**	**15**	**23**
Commercial Athletic	**14**	**9**	**1**	**4**	**42**	**14**	**19**
Lower Clapton Imperial	14	6	6	2	13	9	18
Eton Mission	14	5	3	6	17	19	13
Walthamstow Holborn	14	6	1	7	22	31	13
Novocastrians	14	4	3	7	24	37	11
Fulham Reserves	14	4	1	9	14	33	9
Imperial	14	2	2	10	17	40	6

South Woodford withdrew.

1899-1900

Division One

Millwall Athletic Reserves	18	16	0	2	70	15	32
Tottenham Hotspur Reserves	18	14	2	2	74	24	28
Queens Park Rangers Reserves	18	12	1	5	40	20	25
Thames Ironworks Reserves	18	10	2	6	42	23	22
Monsteds Athletic	18	10	0	8	42	42	20
Clapton Orient	18	4	5	9	40	50	13
Commercial Athletic	18	4	3	11	24	42	11
Willesden Town	18	5	1	12	27	66	11
Barnet	18	4	2	12	33	52	10
Hammersmith Athletic	18	3	0	15	13	71	6

Tottenham Hotspur Reserves had 2 points deducted.
Bromley were expelled for fielding professional players and their record was deleted when it stood as: 4 0 2 2 4 19 2

The amateurs who had been playing in the first team began playing for the reserves in Division Two which then became the first team. Thames Ironworks Reserves changed their name to West Ham United Reserves and Deptford Town returned from the Kent League.

Division Two

Fulham Reserves	14	10	2	2	31	16	22
Walthamstow Holborn	14	10	1	3	37	16	21
Lower Clapton Imperial	14	10	1	3	31	9	21
Willesden Green	14	6	1	7	17	23	13
Walthamstow Town	14	5	3	6	16	23	13
Covent Garden	14	5	2	7	14	25	12
Novocastrians	14	2	1	11	6	20	5
Bromley Reserves / Bromley	14	2	1	11	12	32	5

Please see note above about Bromley and their Reserve team.
Lower Clapton Imperial were promoted to Division One.

1900-01

Division One

Millwall Athletic Reserves	20	17	2	1	91	5	36
Woolwich Arsenal Reserves	20	15	3	2	67	12	33
Queens Park Rangers Reserves	20	13	2	5	46	19	28
West Ham United Reserves	20	11	5	4	40	23	27
Tottenham Hotspur Reserves	20	10	3	7	38	34	23
Fulham	20	8	3	9	37	35	19
Clapton Orient	20	8	2	10	36	31	18
Brentford Reserves	20	7	2	11	45	48	16
Deptford Town	20	6	3	11	19	46	15
Lower Clapton Imperial	20	1	1	18	22	77	3
Wandsworth	20	1	0	19	4	115	2

Barnet withdrew from the League and disbanded. Their record was deleted
when it stood as: 13   0   1   12   5   55   1
Brentford Reserves were relegated to Division Two.

Division Two

Excelsior	**14**	**11**	**0**	**3**	**59**	**20**	**22**
Woolwich Polytechnic	14	9	2	3	37	18	20
Fulham Reserves	14	9	0	5	36	19	18
Novocastrians	14	8	1	5	38	27	17
Bromley	14	6	3	5	19	25	15
Walthamstow Town	14	6	1	7	14	25	13
Hendon	14	3	1	10	17	49	7
West Norwood	14	0	0	14	5	42	0

Clapton Orient Reserves withdrew.
Bromley moved to the West Kent League.

1901-02

A new Premier Division was formed to provide extra games for the first XI's
of London professional clubs.

Premier Division

West Ham United	8	5	1	2	18	9	11
Tottenham Hotspur	8	3	3	2	15	13	9
Millwall Athletic	8	2	4	2	9	13	8
Queens Park Rangers	8	2	2	4	11	14	6
Woolwich Arsenal	8	2	2	4	9	13	6

Division One

Woolwich Arsenal Reserves	18	13	1	4	66	22	27
Queens Park Rangers Reserves	18	11	5	2	43	17	27
Tottenham Hotspur Reserves	18	10	2	6	53	22	22
Fulham	18	9	2	7	35	37	20
Clapton Orient	18	8	3	7	49	37	19
Millwall Athletic Reserves	18	7	4	7	32	23	18
West Ham United Reserves	18	7	4	7	29	36	18
Deptford Town	18	7	4	7	28	46	18
Wandsworth	18	3	1	14	23	52	7
Excelsior	*18*	*2*	*0*	*16*	*15*	*81*	*4*

Division One Championship play-off

Woolwich Arsenal Reserves vs Queens Park Rangers Reserves   2-0

Division Two

East Greenwich Gas Works	16	12	1	3	46	19	25
Brentford Reserves	16	12	0	4	57	21	24
Willesden Town	16	12	0	4	41	21	24
Stonebridge Park Athletic	16	10	0	6	54	27	20
Hendon	16	6	2	8	28	30	14
Fulham Reserves	16	7	0	9	32	49	14
Woolwich Polytechnic	16	5	0	11	20	35	10
Walthamstow Town	16	4	0	12	22	71	8
Neasden	16	2	1	13	23	49	5
					323	*322*	

Millwall St. Johns withdrew after being suspended by the London F.A.
Novocastrians also withdrew.

1902-03

Premier Division

Tottenham Hotspur	10	7	1	2	19	4	15
West Ham United	10	5	3	2	15	13	13
Woolwich Arsenal	10	6	0	4	14	10	12
Millwall Athletic	10	3	4	3	18	14	10
Queens Park Rangers	10	2	3	5	9	15	7
Brentford	10	1	1	8	9	28	3

Millwall Athletic changed their name to Millwall.

Division One

Tottenham Hotspur Reserves	18	13	2	3	53	12	28
Queens Park Rangers Reserves	18	10	3	5	30	31	23
Woolwich Arsenal Reserves	18	8	5	5	40	16	19
Deptford Town	18	7	4	7	22	34	18
West Ham United Reserves	18	6	5	7	26	20	17
Fulham	18	6	5	7	31	34	17
Clapton Orient	18	6	5	7	19	23	17
Millwall Athletic Reserves	18	8	2	8	24	28	16
Leyton	18	4	5	9	30	40	13
Wandsworth	18	4	0	14	22	59	8

Millwall Athletic Reserves and Woolwich Arsenal Reserves each had 2
points deducted.
Fulham were promoted to the Premier Division and were replaced by their
reserves who were promoted from Division Two.

Division Two

Brentford Reserves	**20**	**18**	**0**	**2**	**80**	**13**	**36**
Willesden Town	**20**	**15**	**2**	**3**	**82**	**25**	**32**
Finchley	20	15	1	4	52	19	31
Hanwell	20	8	4	8	36	63	20
Childs Hill Imperial	20	8	2	10	42	40	18
Stonebridge Park Athletic	20	7	3	10	38	42	17
Fulham Reserves	20	7	2	11	23	67	16
Walthamstow Town	20	6	3	11	35	45	15
Great Western Railway	20	7	1	12	48	71	15
Hendon	20	6	3	11	30	48	15
Excelsior	20	0	5	15	14	47	5

1903-04

Premier Division

Millwall	12	11	1	0	38	8	23
Tottenham Hotspur	12	7	1	4	23	14	15
Woolwich Arsenal	12	6	2	4	24	19	14
Queens Park Rangers	12	5	2	5	18	23	12
Brentford	12	2	3	7	16	19	7
Fulham	12	3	1	8	10	29	7
West Ham United	12	2	2	8	14	31	6

Division One

	P	W	D	L	F	A	Pts
Woolwich Arsenal Reserves	20	16	4	0	73	15	36
Tottenham Hotspur Reserves	20	16	3	1	62	21	35
Brentford Reserves	20	10	3	7	45	33	23
Queens Park Rangers Reserves	20	7	9	4	46	37	23
Fulham Reserves	20	9	1	10	40	38	19
Clapton Orient	20	6	6	8	26	33	18
Leyton	20	5	8	7	34	45	18
Millwall Reserves	20	7	3	10	27	31	17
West Ham United Reserves	20	6	4	10	28	38	16
Willesden Town	20	4	3	13	30	53	11
1st Grenadier Guards	20	1	2	17	19	86	4

Division Two

	P	W	D	L	F	A	Pts
Catford Southend	18	17	1	0	84	19	35
Woolwich Polytechnic	18	12	2	4	61	25	26
Childs Hill Imperial	18	9	4	5	43	29	22
Finchley	18	8	3	7	47	35	19
Enfield	18	8	3	7	35	49	19
Hanwell	18	6	5	7	35	38	17
Boleyn Castle	18	6	3	9	30	25	15
Walthamstow Town	18	6	2	10	36	56	14
Kingston-on-Thames	18	4	3	11	21	55	11
Great Western Railway	18	1	0	17	15	76	2

1904-05

The professional clubs withdrew their first teams and the League was restructured. Division One was renamed to the Premier Division, Division Two became Division One and a new Division Two was formed.

Premier Division

	P	W	D	L	F	A	Pts
Fulham Reserves	18	14	3	1	59	14	31
Tottenham Hotspur Reserves	18	12	4	2	50	16	28
Woolwich Arsenal Reserves	18	10	3	5	57	33	23
West Ham United Reserves	18	9	1	8	58	40	19
Leyton	18	7	4	7	46	46	18
Queens Park Rangers Reserves	18	8	2	8	33	39	18
Clapton Orient	18	6	3	9	37	46	15
Brentford Reserves	18	3	5	10	22	42	11
Willesden Town	18	2	6	10	21	57	10
Millwall Reserves	18	3	1	14	22	72	7

Clapton Orient were replaced by their reserves who were doubly promoted up from Division Two.

Division One

	P	W	D	L	F	A	Pts
Southall	14	11	1	2	68	22	23
Enfield	14	10	0	4	40	17	20
Finchley	14	9	2	3	43	20	20
Orpington	14	6	3	5	37	33	15
Hanwell	14	5	1	8	30	38	11
West Hampstead	14	4	1	9	23	46	9
Woolwich Polytechnic	14	3	3	8	18	54	9
City of Westminster	14	2	1	11	10	39	5

Hanwell moved to the Great Western Suburban League.

Division Two

	P	W	D	L	F	A	Pts
Clapton Orient Reserves	12	10	0	2	39	13	20
Harrow United	12	9	1	2	35	15	19
Felstead (Silvertown)	12	8	0	4	50	18	16
Barnet Alston	12	5	2	5	35	21	12
Southall Reserves	12	4	1	7	33	42	9
Willesden Town Reserves	12	3	0	9	14	42	6
Hendon	12	1	0	11	17	72	2

Felstead (Silvertown) and Barnet Alston were promoted to Division One.

1905-06

Premier Division

	P	W	D	L	F	A	Pts
Fulham Reserves	14	8	5	1	26	11	21
Tottenham Hotspur Reserves	14	7	5	2	28	15	19
Queens Park Rangers Reserves	14	7	4	3	31	11	18
Woolwich Arsenal Reserves	14	7	3	4	37	21	17
Leyton	14	4	5	5	23	22	13
West Ham United Reserves	14	4	3	7	14	24	11
Clapton Orient Reserves	14	3	1	10	14	37	7
Brentford Reserves	14	2	2	10	11	43	6

Chelsea Reserves were promoted from Division One.

Division One

	P	W	D	L	F	A	Pts
Catford Southend	14	10	2	2	39	12	22
Chelsea Reserves	14	9	1	4	46	20	19
Felstead (Silvertown)	14	8	1	5	33	26	17
Southern United	14	7	0	7	40	42	14
Barnet Alston	14	5	2	7	28	35	12
Orpington	14	5	0	9	24	44	10
Finchley	14	3	3	8	24	40	9
Enfield	14	3	3	8	20	35	9

Barnet were promoted from Division Two.

Division Two

	P	W	D	L	F	A	Pts
New Malden	10	6	3	1	22	7	15
Charlton Albion	10	6	2	2	29	12	14
Barnet	10	4	4	2	19	9	12
21st Lancers	10	3	1	6	9	19	7
Harrow United	8	2	0	6	7	19	4
Seven Kings	8	2	0	6	5	25	4

The games between Harrow United and Seven Kings were not played.

1906-07

Premier Division

	P	W	D	L	F	A	Pts
Woolwich Arsenal Reserves	18	13	3	2	61	15	29
Tottenham Hotspur Reserves	18	10	5	3	42	22	25
Queens Park Rangers Reserves	18	12	1	5	33	24	25
Fulham Reserves	18	9	5	4	30	22	23
West Ham United Reserves	18	8	4	6	42	28	20
Chelsea Reserves	18	4	5	9	35	44	13
Crystal Palace Reserves	18	5	3	10	27	33	13
Leyton Reserves	18	5	3	10	25	41	13
Clapton Orient Reserves	18	4	2	12	25	52	10
Brentford Reserves	18	3	3	12	20	59	9

Division One

	P	W	D	L	F	A	Pts
Barnet Alston	14	11	3	0	45	7	25
Finchley	13	8	0	5	39	25	16
Enfield	12	6	3	3	34	21	15
Catford Southend	13	5	2	6	24	33	12
Custom House	13	5	1	7	23	29	11
Orpington	14	3	3	8	19	38	9
Barnet	13	3	2	8	17	38	8
Eltham	10	3	0	7	22	32	6

Southern United withdrew during the season.
Finchley and Enfield were declared joint runners-up to allow for their unplayed games. The following games were left unplayed:
Barnet vs Custom House, Eltham vs Catford Southend, Eltham vs Enfield, Eltham vs Finchley and Enfield vs Eltham.
Tufnell Park joined as a newly formed club.

Division Two

	P	W	D	L	F	A	Pts
Deptford Invicta	10	7	2	1	27	8	16
North Woolwich	10	7	1	2	35	13	15
Walthamstow Grange	10	6	2	2	17	6	14
Waltham	10	3	1	6	15	26	7
Charlton Albion	9	2	2	5	14	22	6
Ponders End United	9	0	0	9	5	38	0

Harrow United withdrew during the season.
Charlton Albion vs Ponders End United was not played.

1907-08

Premier Division

	P	W	D	L	F	A	Pts
Fulham Reserves	16	12	2	2	46	12	26
West Ham United Reserves	16	12	2	2	41	20	26
Woolwich Arsenal Reserves	16	12	1	3	61	19	25
Barnet Alston	16	5	4	7	23	24	14
Clapton Orient Reserves	16	4	6	6	24	35	14
Millwall Reserves	16	4	4	8	17	27	12
Crystal Palace Reserves	16	4	4	8	20	33	12
Brentford Reserves	16	4	0	12	16	38	8
Leyton Reserves	16	3	1	12	18	58	7

Brentford Reserves were relegated to Division One.

Division One

	P	W	D	L	F	A	Pts
Deptford Invicta	16	11	3	2	42	14	25
Catford Southend	16	11	3	2	51	24	25
Tufnell Park	16	9	3	4	42	19	21
Custom House	16	6	3	7	28	27	15
North Woolwich	16	6	2	8	32	32	14
Orpington	16	6	1	9	33	45	13
Finchley	16	5	2	9	29	45	12
Enfield	16	5	0	11	32	46	10
West Hampstead	16	3	3	10	22	59	9

Deptford Invicta and Tufnell Park were promoted to the Premier Division.

Division Two

	P	W	D	L	F	A	Pts
Walthamstow Grange	**12**	**9**	**2**	**1**	**27**	**7**	**20**
Summerstown	**12**	**8**	**2**	**2**	**34**	**11**	**18**
Waltham	12	6	2	4	30	25	14
Croydon Common Reserves	12	6	1	5	27	17	13
Eton Mission	12	4	3	5	20	24	11
Brimsdown	12	3	2	7	16	29	8
Acton United & Aldine	12	0	0	12	3	44	0

1908-09

Premier Division

	P	W	D	L	F	A	Pts
West Ham United Reserves	16	11	4	1	46	18	26
Woolwich Arsenal Reserves	16	10	3	3	40	17	23
Millwall Reserves	16	7	4	5	30	26	18
Clapton Orient Reserves	16	7	3	6	34	22	17
Deptford Invicta	16	5	5	6	21	36	15
Fulham Reserves	16	4	6	6	21	24	14
Barnet Alston	16	4	3	9	21	38	11
Leyton Reserves	16	3	4	9	24	39	10
Tufnell Park	16	4	2	10	19	36	10

Division One

	P	W	D	L	F	A	Pts
Brentford Reserves	**16**	**11**	**1**	**4**	**48**	**20**	**23**
North Woolwich	15	8	1	6	38	38	17
Finchley	16	8	1	7	24	31	17
Summerstown	15	8	0	7	29	42	16
Custom House	14	7	0	7	29	26	14
Walthamstow Grange	16	7	0	9	36	43	14
Catford Southend	15	5	2	8	41	39	12
West Hampstead	15	5	1	9	33	34	11
Enfield	12	4	2	6	22	27	10

5 games were not played.

Division Two

	P	W	D	L	F	A	Pts
Clapham Reserves	12	9	0	3	27	22	18
Croydon Common Reserves	10	6	0	4	25	11	12
Norwood Association	12	6	0	6	23	22	12
Waltham	10	4	3	3	27	15	11
Brimsdown	11	5	1	5	18	19	11
Eton Mission	12	3	2	7	22	30	8
Shepherds Bush Reserves	11	3	0	8	13	36	6

3 games were not played.
Brimsdown and Waltham were promoted to Division One.

1909-10

Premier Division

	P	W	D	L	F	A	Pts
Chelsea Reserves	18	13	3	2	58	18	29
West Ham United Reserves	18	13	3	2	41	16	29
Fulham Reserves	18	10	4	4	47	22	24
Clapton Orient Reserves	18	7	7	4	22	18	21
Brentford Reserves	18	7	5	6	40	35	19
Barnet Alston	18	6	4	8	29	50	16
Deptford Invicta	18	5	3	10	27	51	13
Millwall Reserves	18	3	6	9	22	38	12
Queens Park Rangers Reserves	18	3	3	12	15	40	9
Leyton Reserves	18	3	2	13	41	54	8

Division One was split into two sections – A and B.

Division One – Section A

	P	W	D	L	F	A	Pts
Barking	12	11	1	0	35	8	23
Custom House	12	9	1	2	27	10	19
Summerstown	12	5	1	6	22	26	11
Orpington	12	4	2	6	27	20	10
Catford Southend	11	5	0	6	28	23	10
North Woolwich	12	2	1	9	12	41	5
Brimsdown	11	1	2	8	8	31	4

Barking and Catford Southend were promoted to the Premier Division.

Division One – Section B

	P	W	D	L	F	A	Pts
Wood Green Town	**12**	**8**	**2**	**2**	**35**	**15**	**18**
Tufnell Park	**12**	**7**	**2**	**3**	**33**	**11**	**16**
Finchley	12	6	3	3	22	17	15
Walthamstow Grange	12	5	2	5	22	25	12
Enfield	12	5	1	6	29	23	11
West Hampstead	12	2	2	8	24	49	6
Waltham	12	3	0	9	18	43	6

Division Two

	P	W	D	L	F	A	Pts
Ravenscourt Amateurs	**14**	**10**	**1**	**3**	**45**	**19**	**21**
Bronze Athletic	**14**	**8**	**1**	**5**	**29**	**20**	**17**
Shepherds Bush Reserves	14	7	2	5	37	31	16
Peel Institute	14	7	2	5	26	34	16
Eton Mission	14	5	3	6	32	40	13
Charlton Albion	14	5	2	7	22	22	12
Croydon Common Reserves	14	4	2	8	22	25	10
Woodford	14	2	3	9	19	41	7

Croydon Common Reserves were promoted to the Premier Division.

1910-11

Premier Division was split into two sections – A and B.

Premier Division – Section A

	P	W	D	L	F	A	Pts
Millwall Reserves	14	11	0	3	39	14	22
Leyton Reserves	14	10	0	4	29	19	20
West Ham United Reserves	14	9	1	4	33	11	19
Clapton Orient Reserves	14	8	0	6	27	18	16
Croydon Common Reserves	14	5	1	8	25	20	11
Barking	14	5	1	8	13	27	11
Catford Southend	14	4	2	8	12	29	10
Deptford Invicta	*14*	*1*	*1*	*12*	*8*	*48*	*3*

Premier Division – Section B

	P	W	D	L	F	A	Pts
Queens Park Rangers Reserves	14	11	1	2	40	13	23
Fulham Reserves	14	11	1	2	37	15	23
Chelsea Reserves	14	9	2	3	33	14	20
Crystal Palace Reserves	14	5	5	4	22	22	15
Tufnell Park	14	5	2	7	23	21	12
Brentford Reserves	14	4	3	7	22	21	11
Barnet Alston	14	3	0	11	22	37	6
Wood Green Town	*14*	*0*	*2*	*12*	*10*	*66*	*2*

Championship play-off:

Millwall Reserves vs Queens Park Rangers Reserves   2-1

Division One Section A and Section B merged into a single division.

Division One

Walthamstow Grange	14	12	1	1	51	10	25
Custom House	14	10	1	3	35	16	21
Enfield	14	6	2	6	19	30	14
Kilburn	14	5	3	6	24	32	13
Bronze Athletic	14	4	3	7	18	19	11
North Woolwich	14	4	3	7	18	22	11
Finchley	14	4	1	9	19	35	9
Ravenscourt Amateurs	14	3	2	9	21	41	8

Ravenscourt Amateurs moved to the Great Western Suburban League.

Division Two

Metrogas	12	9	1	2	52	15	19
Pinner	10	6	2	2	27	15	14
West London Old Boys	12	7	0	5	27	18	14
Peel Institute	11	5	1	5	21	20	11
Eton Mission	11	3	2	6	16	32	8
West Norwood	12	4	0	8	13	42	8
Shepherds Bush Reserves	12	2	2	8	14	28	6

Pinner vs Eton Mission and Pinner vs Peel Institute were not played.

1911-12

Premier Division – Section A

West Ham United Reserves	12	9	3	0	48	15	21
Millwall Reserves	12	7	3	2	32	13	17
Clapton Orient Reserves	12	6	3	3	31	12	15
Leyton Reserves	12	6	1	5	22	18	13
Walthamstow Grange	12	2	3	7	18	28	7
Catford Southend	12	2	2	8	14	55	6
Barking	*12*	*1*	*3*	*8*	*9*	*33*	*5*

Premier Division – Section B

Crystal Palace Reserves	12	11	0	1	37	12	22
Queens Park Rangers Reserves	12	9	0	3	32	12	18
Fulham Reserves	12	4	4	4	22	23	12
Brentford Reserves	12	4	3	5	18	19	11
Tufnell Park	12	4	2	6	13	20	10
Barnet Alston	12	3	0	9	13	38	6
Custom House	12	2	1	9	13	24	5

Barnet Alston and Tufnell Park left to become founder members of the Athenian League.

Championship play-off:

West Ham United Reserves vs Crystal Palace Reserves   3-2

Division One

Enfield	14	11	2	1	41	14	24
Bronze Athletic	14	8	2	4	44	21	18
Finchley	14	8	1	5	31	17	17
Kilburn	14	5	4	5	26	22	14
Deptford Invicta	14	4	3	7	25	31	11
Metrogas	13	4	2	7	23	40	10
Pinner	14	2	6	6	23	44	10
Wood Green Town	13	3	0	10	24	48	6

Metrogas vs Wood Green Town was not played.
Finchley left to become founder members of the Athenian League.

Division Two

Ilford Reserves	12	9	0	3	33	12	18
Wealdstone	12	7	2	3	39	15	16
West Norwood	12	7	2	3	23	21	16
Hampstead Town	11	6	0	5	23	21	12
Brabys Ironworks	12	5	0	7	21	30	10
Nunhead Reserves	12	2	2	8	15	35	6
West London Old Boys	11	2	0	9	14	34	4

Hampstead Town vs West London Old Boys was not played.
Ilford Reserves and Hampstead Town were promoted to Division One.

1912-13

Premier Division – Section A

West Ham United Reserves	8	7	0	1	25	7	14
Millwall Reserves	8	6	0	2	14	4	12
Clapton Orient Reserves	8	3	1	4	18	12	7
Custom House	8	2	0	6	8	25	4
Walthamstow Grange	8	1	1	6	4	21	3

Premier Division – Section B

Croydon Common Reserves	10	6	2	2	23	12	14
Crystal Palace Reserves	10	6	2	2	26	15	14
Catford Southend	10	6	1	3	20	14	13
Queens Park Rangers Reserves	10	4	0	6	17	17	8
Brentford Reserves	10	3	0	7	18	29	6
Enfield	10	2	1	7	12	29	5

Championship play-off:

West Ham United Reserves vs Croydon Common Reserves   2-1

Division One

Bronze Athletic	14	12	0	2	43	15	24
Hampstead Town	14	9	1	4	34	14	19
Wood Green Town	14	7	0	7	27	26	14
Kilburn	14	5	3	6	31	33	13
Ilford Reserves	14	5	2	7	26	34	12
Deptford Invicta	14	4	2	8	26	40	10
Pinner	14	4	2	8	23	36	10
Barking	14	3	4	7	17	29	10

Bronze Athletic, Hampstead Town and Barking were all promoted to the Premier Division.
Charlton Athletic joined Division One.

Division Two

Wealdstone	12	9	1	2	37	11	19
Brabys Ironworks	12	9	0	3	16	10	18
West Norwood	12	6	4	2	22	13	16
Custom House Reserves	12	6	0	6	24	23	12
West London Old Boys	12	3	3	6	17	19	9
Fulham St. Andrews	12	3	1	8	14	26	7
Tufnell Park Reserves	12	0	3	9	10	38	3

Wealdstone, Custom House Reserves, West London Old Boys and Tufnell Park Reserves were all promoted to Division One.
Division Two then closed down.

1913-14

The Premier Division was re-organised into separate professional and amateur sections.

Premier Division – Professional Section

Fulham Reserves	16	10	3	3	37	17	23
West Ham United Reserves	16	9	1	6	36	17	19
Croydon Common Reserves	16	8	2	6	18	20	18
Crystal Palace Reserves	16	8	1	7	43	28	17
Clapton Orient Reserves	16	7	3	6	29	37	17
Millwall Reserves	16	8	0	8	32	32	16
Arsenal Reserves	16	5	3	8	20	23	13
Queens Park Rangers Reserves	16	5	1	10	26	43	11
Brentford Reserves	16	4	2	10	13	37	10

Premier Division – Amateur Section

Hampstead Town	12	8	3	1	25	12	19
Walthamstow Grange	12	8	2	2	31	13	18
Bronze Athletic	12	5	3	4	24	14	13
Custom House	12	5	2	5	28	17	12
Barking	12	3	5	4	18	22	11
Woolwich	12	3	2	7	15	34	8
2nd Battalion Grenadier Guards	12	0	3	9	11	40	3

Grays Athletic, Catford Southend and Finchley all joined from the Athenian League.

Championship play-off:

Fulham Reserves vs Hampstead Town	4-1

Division One

West London Old Boys	14	11	3	0	38	8	25
Charlton Athletic	14	12	1	1	42	10	25
Wealdstone	14	6	2	6	30	30	14
Barking Reserves	14	6	2	6	30	31	14
Hampstead Town Reserves	14	4	2	8	24	26	10
Tufnell Park Reserves	14	5	0	9	27	44	10
Custom House Reserves	14	4	1	9	30	46	9
Ilford Reserves	14	1	3	10	14	40	5

Charlton Athletic were promoted to the Premier Division – Amateur Section. West London Old Boys moved to the Spartan League.

1914-15

Premier Division – Professional Section

West Ham United Reserves	16	10	3	3	41	19	23
Queens Park Rangers Reserves	16	9	3	4	31	24	21
Tottenham Hotspur Reserves	16	9	2	5	25	16	20
Fulham Reserves	16	9	1	6	46	29	19
Arsenal Reserves	16	8	2	6	29	25	18
Millwall Reserves	16	7	2	7	23	24	16
Crystal Palace Reserves	16	5	1	10	17	43	11
Clapton Orient Reserves	16	4	1	11	16	31	9
Croydon Common Reserves	16	3	1	12	24	41	7

Premier Division – Amateur Section

Grays Athletic	12	11	1	0	53	13	23
Walthamstow Grange	12	8	2	2	37	9	18
Catford Southend	14	6	3	5	25	29	15
Page Green Old Boys	14	6	2	6	29	32	14
Custom House	14	5	3	6	27	25	13
Barking	14	3	3	8	28	44	9
Finchley	14	4	0	10	26	43	8
Romford Town	14	3	2	9	18	48	8

Charlton Athletic resigned from the League in March 1915 and their record was deleted when it stood as: 9 6 0 3 22 18 12
The games between Grays Athletic and Walthamstow Grange were not played.

Championship play-off:

West Ham United Reserves vs Grays Athletic	3-1

Division One

Grays Athletic Reserves	4	3	1	0	8	4	7
Catford Southend Reserves	4	2	1	1	6	5	5
Hampstead Town Reserves	3	2	0	1	7	5	4
Charlton Athletic Reserves	5	0	2	3	7	11	2
Tufnell Park Reserves	4	0	2	2	3	6	2

The remaining games were not played as the division was abandoned because of the war.

1915-19

The London League was suspended from 1915 to 1919 due to the war. When the League restarted in 1919, it was without the Professional Section of the Premier Division. Meanwhile Barking had changed their name to Barking Town and Sterling Athletic joined Division One as a newly formed club.

1919-20

Premier Division

Custom House	14	12	2	0	40	9	26
Charlton Athletic	14	9	2	3	37	17	20
Grays Athletic	14	8	1	5	37	25	17
Walthamstow Grange	14	6	1	7	20	17	13
Ordnance	14	5	2	7	27	32	12
Barking Town	14	5	1	8	27	22	11
Catford Southend	14	4	3	7	21	31	11
Islington Town	14	1	0	13	10	66	2

Ordnance were relegated to Division One and Charlton Athletic moved to the Southern League.

Division One

London Generals	**16**	**13**	**1**	**2**	**57**	**17**	**27**
Harrow Weald	16	11	1	4	57	17	23
Sterling Athletic	16	11	0	5	54	14	22
Wealdstone	16	9	2	5	41	18	20
Grays Athletic Reserves	16	10	0	6	42	24	20
Charlton Athletic Reserves	16	6	3	7	28	34	15
Catford Southend Reserves	16	5	1	10	26	44	11
Pearl Assurance	16	2	0	14	15	92	4
Great Northern Railway	16	1	0	15	14	74	2

Division Two was revived for the 1920-21 season and Grays Athletic Reserves were relegated to it.

1920-21

Premier Division

Barking Town	18	12	4	2	58	22	28
Grays Athletic	18	13	1	4	47	21	27
Enfield	18	9	4	5	54	32	22
Custom House	18	9	4	5	40	31	22
Walthamstow Grange	18	6	8	4	25	24	20
Catford Southend	18	8	4	6	43	42	20
London Generals	18	5	3	10	31	67	13
Belvedere & District	18	5	2	11	26	42	12
Chiswick Town	18	4	2	12	33	48	10
Gnome Athletic	18	1	4	13	26	54	6

Enfield moved to the Athenian League.

Division One

Sterling Athletic	30	24	4	2	136	30	52
Temple Mills	30	17	7	6	81	37	41
Harrow Weald	30	17	5	8	90	49	39
Cray Wanderers	30	14	9	7	88	54	37
Catford Southend Reserves	30	16	5	9	77	50	37
Harlesden Town	30	14	5	11	74	54	33
Ordnance	30	14	3	13	64	64	31
Summerstown Reserves	30	12	6	12	47	64	30
Blackwell & Thames Ironworks	30	9	11	10	64	60	29
Hampstead Town Reserves	30	12	3	15	59	69	27
Metropolitan Railway	30	9	7	14	70	82	25
Bexleyheath Labour	30	11	2	17	59	87	24
Waterlows	30	9	5	16	47	69	23
Old Aloysians	30	8	5	17	66	104	21
Wealdstone	30	8	4	18	32	76	20
Willesden Town	30	4	3	23	33	138	11

Division Two

Wall End United	22	17	3	2	76	21	37
Grays Athletic Reserves	22	18	1	3	81	28	37
North Woolwich Invicta	22	16	1	5	54	26	33
Transport Workers	22	14	4	4	67	23	32
Chiswick Town Reserves	22	14	3	5	65	26	31
R.A.F. Kidbrooke	22	9	3	10	58	57	21
Brymay Athletic	22	5	7	10	37	41	17
R.A.F. Record Office	22	6	5	11	41	48	17
Deptford Town	22	4	4	14	26	66	12
Harrow Weald Reserves	22	3	6	13	27	95	12
Derrick Wanderers	22	3	2	17	36	92	8
Roehampton	22	3	1	18	26	71	7

Grays Athletic Reserves and Transport Workers were both promoted to Division One.

Division One

Barking Town Reserves	30	25	1	4	96	29	51
Grays Athletic Reserves	30	22	4	4	95	31	48
Cray Wanderers	30	21	3	6	87	40	45
Summerstown Reserves	30	18	3	9	82	53	39
S.T.D. Athletic	30	16	5	9	59	38	37
Cheshunt Reserves	30	15	3	12	73	53	33
Harlesden Town	30	13	6	11	62	56	32
Custom House Reserves	30	12	6	12	59	58	30
Catford Southend Reserves	30	11	5	14	57	57	27
Blackwell & Thames Ironworks	30	11	2	17	62	83	24
Wealdstone	30	8	7	15	45	69	23
Metropolitan Railway	30	8	5	17	51	83	21
Hampstead Town Reserves	30	7	6	17	52	68	20
Old Aloysians	30	7	6	17	65	102	20
H.M.S.O. Press	30	6	5	19	49	99	17
Transport Workers	30	4	5	21	26	101	13

Wealdstone moved to the Spartan League.

Division Two

Wall End United	20	12	6	2	56	18	30
Brymay Athletic	20	13	4	3	45	22	30
Chiswick Town Reserves	20	12	3	5	38	21	27
Deptford Town	20	11	2	7	52	38	24
Depot R.H.A.	20	9	5	6	29	21	23
Algernon Athletic	20	9	2	9	39	38	20
North Woolwich Invicta	20	8	3	9	33	36	19
Bromley Old Boys	20	6	5	9	39	40	17
Artillery College	20	7	2	11	30	44	16
R.A.F. Kidbrooke	20	4	2	14	23	56	10
University	20	1	2	17	4	54	4

Brymay Athletic were promoted to Division One.

1921-22

Premier Division

Grays Athletic	30	24	4	2	78	24	52
Catford Southend	30	18	5	7	69	42	41
Bostall Heath	30	16	8	6	74	40	40
Redhill	30	18	4	8	78	44	40
Barking Town	30	18	4	8	84	51	40
Edmonton	30	13	6	11	47	40	32
Leyton	30	14	3	13	60	59	31
Custom House	30	13	4	13	53	48	30
Earlsfield Town	30	14	2	14	53	49	30
Belvedere & District	30	11	8	11	55	62	30
Gnome Athletic	30	11	5	14	55	63	27
Walthamstow Grange	30	10	4	16	60	69	24
Chiswick Town	30	8	2	20	40	79	18
Tooting Town	30	6	5	19	39	68	17
Temple Mills	30	5	5	20	35	100	15
Sterling Athletic	30	5	3	22	26	68	13

Belvedere & District changed their name to Erith & Belvedere and moved to the Kent League.
Cray Wanderers were promoted from Division One.

1922-23

Premier Division

Custom House	30	19	6	5	72	33	44
Redhill	30	20	3	7	97	46	43
Leyton	30	20	3	7	92	44	43
Grays Athletic	30	18	3	9	91	43	39
Barking Town	30	15	9	6	71	34	39
Bostall Heath	30	17	5	8	66	34	39
Edmonton	30	14	7	9	72	42	35
Gnome Athletic	30	10	12	8	56	48	32
Gwynnes Athletic	30	11	4	15	54	65	26
Tooting Town	30	10	6	14	48	78	26
Sterling Athletic	30	9	5	16	38	56	23
Catford Southend	30	8	7	15	45	69	23
Cray Wanderers	30	10	1	19	58	87	21
Walthamstow Grange	30	8	4	18	43	90	20
Burberry	30	8	1	21	59	116	17
Temple Mills	30	4	2	24	31	108	10

Redhill and Barking Town both moved to the Athenian League.
Finchley joined from the Spartan League and West Norwood joined from the Isthmian League.

Division One

Millwall United	28	20	3	5	72	26	43
Van Den Bergh	28	20	3	5	80	40	43
Barking Town Reserves	28	17	3	8	76	45	37
Mitcham Wanderers	28	16	5	7	68	47	37
Custom House Reserves	28	12	6	10	52	46	30
Catford Southend Reserves	28	13	4	11	54	49	30
Grays Athletic Reserves	28	11	7	10	52	49	29
Livesey United	28	11	6	11	60	57	28
S.T.D. Athletic	28	11	5	12	60	65	27
Summerstown Reserves	28	11	4	13	63	73	26
Bush Hill Park	28	11	3	14	46	38	25
Metropolitan Railway	28	7	4	17	41	77	18
Enfield Reserves	28	7	4	17	31	62	18
Brymay Athletic	28	7	2	19	35	80	16
Cheshunt Reserves	28	4	5	19	48	84	13

Millwall United and Mitcham Wanderers were promoted to the Premier Division. Port of London Authority Police and North Woolwich Invicta were both promoted from Division Two.
Carshalton Athletic joined from the Surrey Senior League.

Division Two

Hendon Town	22	16	4	2	94	26	36
Port of London Authority Police	22	15	4	3	59	19	34
Algernon Athletic	22	14	2	6	61	30	30
Telcon Athletic	22	11	5	6	63	38	27
Wren Athletic	22	11	5	6	46	29	27
North Woolwich Invicta	22	12	1	9	52	49	25
New Barnet	22	10	2	10	34	45	22
Wall End United	22	7	7	8	32	49	21
Deptford Town	22	7	3	12	45	36	17
Chingford United	22	5	1	16	38	91	11
Commercial Gas	22	4	1	17	20	72	9
R.N.V.R.	22	2	1	19	20	80	5

1923-24

Premier Division

Leyton	30	19	7	4	75	22	45
Millwall United	30	20	3	7	70	29	43
Bostall Heath	30	18	6	6	85	37	42
Mitcham Wanderers	30	19	4	7	66	41	42
Grays Athletic	30	15	6	9	82	43	36
Finchley	30	13	9	8	48	32	35
Tooting Town	30	14	7	9	46	40	35
Custom House	30	11	7	12	60	60	29
West Norwood	30	10	8	12	31	48	28
Walthamstow Town	30	9	8	13	51	60	26
Metrogas	30	9	7	14	49	66	25
Cray Wanderers	30	8	6	16	36	54	22
Old Charlton	30	7	6	17	39	80	20
Walthamstow Grange	30	6	7	17	38	70	19
Edmonton	30	8	3	19	41	80	19
Sterling Athletic	30	3	8	19	32	87	14

Grays Athletic moved to the Kent League, West Norwood moved to the Athenian League and Sterling Athletic withdrew from senior football.
Chelmsford joined having previously been playing in both the Middlesex League and the Essex & Suffolk Border League.

Division One

S.T.D. Athletic	30	24	3	3	113	27	51
Custom House Reserves	30	20	5	5	86	41	45
Grays Athletic Reserves	30	19	4	7	73	39	42
Van Den Bergh	30	18	3	9	84	51	39
Barking Town Reserves	30	16	3	11	84	49	35
Port of London Authority Police	30	14	5	11	69	48	33
Perrycobow	30	14	5	11	63	50	33
Metropolitan Railway	30	15	3	12	75	62	33
Carshalton Athletic	30	15	2	13	69	63	32
Erith & Belvedere Reserves	30	13	3	14	72	69	29
Enfield Reserves	30	12	3	15	55	72	27
Barnet Reserves	30	11	3	16	54	76	25
Beckenham	30	10	2	18	53	73	22
Bush Hill Park	30	9	2	19	44	81	20
Metrogas Reserves	30	3	3	24	22	145	9
North Woolwich Invicta	30	2	1	27	20	90	5

Bush Hill Park moved to the Spartan League.
Hendon Town and Siemens Sports were promoted from Division Two.

Division Two

Savoy Hotel	18	16	0	2	66	12	32
Siemens Sports	18	15	1	2	77	17	31
Hendon Town	18	10	3	5	70	29	23
Perrycobow Reserves	18	10	1	7	39	41	21
Wren Athletic	18	8	2	8	55	33	18
Walthamstow Town Reserves	17	8	1	8	42	38	17
Algernon Athletic	18	6	2	10	37	43	14
Beckenham Reserves	17	5	1	11	28	53	11
Old Ignatians	18	3	3	12	41	65	9
British Legion	18	1	0	17	10	134	2

One game was not played.
Division Two closed down at the end of the season.

1924-25

Premier Division

Leyton	26	18	3	5	58	21	39
Millwall United	26	16	5	5	77	36	37
Bostall Heath	26	15	7	4	60	33	37
Mitcham Wanderers	26	16	4	6	57	29	36
Tooting Town	26	9	10	7	42	34	28
Walthamstow Grange	26	11	4	11	49	42	26
Custom House	26	11	3	12	44	57	25
Hanwell Town	26	10	4	12	47	53	24
Edmonton	26	10	3	13	37	58	23
Chelmsford	26	9	3	14	45	53	21
Metrogas	26	8	5	13	42	62	21
Cray Wanderers	26	8	4	14	46	60	20
Finchley	26	5	5	16	25	52	15
Walthamstow Town	26	6	0	20	23	62	12

Division One

Bromley Reserves	30	25	1	4	127	43	51
Barking Town Reserves	30	21	3	6	114	50	45
Erith & Belvedere Reserves	30	21	3	6	101	46	45
Bexleyheath Town Reserves	30	17	3	10	72	57	37
Carshalton Athletic	30	16	3	11	86	48	35
Hendon Town	30	13	5	12	56	62	31
Siemens Sports	30	12	6	12	59	59	30
Port of London Authority Police	30	11	8	11	64	76	30
Custom House Reserves	30	13	3	14	75	75	29
S.T.D. Athletic	30	12	4	14	67	53	28
Beckenham	30	13	2	15	65	61	28
Woolwich Polytechnic	30	12	2	16	55	74	26
Barnet Reserves	30	10	3	17	52	85	23
Cheshunt Reserves	30	7	2	21	56	112	16
Metropolitan Railway	30	6	2	22	50	121	14
Merton Town	30	5	2	23	40	117	12

Metropolitan Railway moved to the Spartan League.

1925-26

Premier Division

Leyton	26	21	1	4	94	28	43
Tooting Town	26	15	5	6	73	38	35
Millwall United	26	16	2	8	76	42	34
Custom House	26	14	6	6	64	41	34
Cray Wanderers	26	13	4	9	54	50	30
Finchley	26	10	3	13	61	62	23
Walthamstow Grange	26	8	7	11	54	67	23
Mitcham Wanderers	26	10	3	13	51	66	23
Hanwell Town	26	8	7	11	58	76	23
Bostall Heath	26	10	3	13	54	71	23
Chelmsford	26	11	0	15	68	58	22
Walthamstow Town	26	7	5	14	46	81	19
Edmonton	26	8	2	16	35	66	18
Metrogas	26	6	2	18	58	100	14

Walthamstow Town changed their name to Walthamstow Borough.
Edmonton were relegated to Division One.
Grays Athletic joined from the Kent League.

Division One

Bromley Reserves	30	21	4	5	128	64	46
Erith & Belvedere Reserves	30	15	8	7	100	56	38
Barking Town Reserves	30	15	6	9	78	71	36
Carshalton Athletic	30	16	3	11	84	67	35
Siemens Sports	30	12	10	8	87	64	34
Chelmsford Reserves	30	15	4	11	92	71	34
Callender Athletic	30	15	4	11	65	57	34
Hendon Town	30	12	6	12	66	69	30
Beckenham	30	11	6	13	71	82	28
Port of London Authority Police	30	8	11	11	50	58	27
Barnet Reserves	30	10	7	13	67	85	27
Bostall Athletic	30	10	6	14	50	76	26
S.T.D. Athletic	30	8	9	13	53	78	25
Bexleyheath Town Reserves	30	9	4	17	72	91	22
Woolwich Polytechnic	30	7	6	17	65	101	20
Hampstead Town Reserves	30	8	2	20	62	100	18

Carshalton Athletic were promoted to the Premier Division.

1926-27

Premier Division

Grays Athletic	26	22	3	1	106	28	47
Leyton	26	18	7	1	103	33	43
Millwall United	26	16	5	5	73	38	37
Finchley	26	13	6	7	73	44	32
Tooting Town	26	14	2	10	63	51	30
Mitcham Wanderers	26	11	6	9	66	43	28
Chelmsford	26	12	3	11	77	60	27
Custom House	26	13	1	12	61	63	27
Cray Wanderers	26	12	2	12	80	76	26
Carshalton Athletic	26	8	4	14	58	95	20
Bostall Heath	26	7	3	16	60	91	17
Walthamstow Grange	26	6	3	17	40	75	15
Hanwell Town	26	2	5	19	19	75	9
Walthamstow Borough	26	3	0	23	18	125	6

Leyton moved to the Athenian League and Epsom Town joined from the
Surrey Senior League.

Division One

Callender Athletic	24	15	6	3	70	28	36
Hendon Town	24	14	7	3	69	33	35
Bostal Athletic	24	14	2	8	79	54	30
Fulham "A"	24	13	4	7	68	59	30
Beckenham	24	11	5	8	82	62	27
Erith & Belvedere Reserves	24	12	2	10	58	60	26
Chelmsford Reserves	24	11	3	10	58	58	25
Brentwood Mental Hospital	24	10	2	12	64	74	22
Edmonton	24	8	4	12	49	67	20
Hays Wharf	24	9	2	13	46	64	20
Leyton Reserves	24	7	5	12	54	65	19
Siemens Sports	24	5	7	12	52	72	17
Woolwich Polytechnic	24	1	3	20	31	84	5

Bostall Athletic moved to the Kent League.

1927-28

Premier Division

Epsom Town	24	17	4	3	73	33	38
Grays Athletic	24	17	2	5	83	32	36
Cray Wanderers	24	12	6	6	78	60	30
Carshalton Athletic	24	14	2	8	63	51	30
Chelmsford	24	11	3	10	75	54	25
Mitcham Wanderers	24	10	5	9	56	42	25
Finchley	24	10	3	11	64	55	23
Millwall United	24	10	2	12	61	77	22
Custom House	24	9	4	11	33	49	22
Bostall Heath	24	9	2	13	60	80	20
Tooting Town	24	7	4	13	47	61	18
Callender Athletic	24	6	5	13	48	72	17
Walthamstow Grange	24	3	0	21	31	106	6

Division One

Beckenham	24	17	5	2	97	47	39
Hounslow	24	17	3	4	92	36	37
Hendon Town	24	17	2	5	89	40	36
Fulham "A"	24	17	2	5	88	50	36
Brentwood Mental Hospital	24	11	5	8	53	58	27
Chelmsford Reserves	24	10	4	10	83	63	24
Tate Institute	24	9	3	12	51	63	21
Epsom Town Reserves	24	6	6	12	65	68	18
Hays Wharf	24	7	2	15	56	70	16
Erith & Belvedere Reserves	24	6	4	14	55	81	16
Woolwich Polytechnic	24	5	6	13	46	80	16
Siemens Sports	24	6	1	17	61	120	13
Woolwich	24	6	1	17	39	99	13

Leavesden Mental Hospital joined from the Hertfordshire County League.

1928-29

Premier Division

Mitcham Wanderers	24	18	3	3	70	20	39
Grays Athletic	24	18	3	3	87	32	39
Finchley	24	18	1	5	87	31	37
Cray Wanderers	24	13	4	7	84	56	30
Epsom Town	24	13	2	9	64	49	28
Chelmsford	24	11	5	8	53	42	27
Bostall Heath	24	11	1	12	71	79	23
Tooting Town	24	8	2	14	44	69	18
Custom House	24	8	2	14	36	70	18
Walthamstow Grange	24	6	4	14	35	78	16
Callender Athletic	24	5	4	15	33	64	14
Beckenham	24	4	5	15	46	70	13
Carshalton Athletic	24	3	4	17	47	97	10

Finchley moved to the Athenian League and Erith & Belvedere joined from
the Kent League. Romford joined as a newly formed club and a mid-week
club called Lombardians formed a Saturday side who joined the League as
Dagenham Town.

Division One

Holland Athletic	24	19	2	3	87	35	40
Hotel Cecil	24	17	2	5	99	37	36
Hounslow	24	14	3	7	84	63	31
Leavesden Mental Hospital	24	15	0	9	90	56	30
Woolwich Polytechnic	24	11	2	11	51	59	24
Standard Telephones	24	11	0	13	65	68	22
Hendon Town	24	11	0	13	48	65	22
Chelmsford Reserves	24	7	6	11	60	69	20
Fulham "A"	24	8	4	12	48	58	20
Brentwood Mental Hospital	24	8	4	12	51	68	20
Erith & Belvedere Reserves	24	7	4	13	44	67	18
Tate Institute	24	7	2	15	35	82	16
Epsom Town Reserves	24	6	1	17	41	76	13

Hounslow moved to the Spartan League.

1929-30

Premier Division

Grays Athletic	26	16	7	3	73	36	39
Mitcham Wanderers	26	16	6	4	56	28	38
Tooting Town	26	16	4	6	70	53	36
Chelmsford	26	11	6	9	70	44	28
Dagenham Town	26	11	6	9	46	49	28
Walthamstow Grange	26	10	7	9	46	49	27
Epsom Town	26	11	4	11	66	57	26
Erith & Belvedere	26	9	7	10	51	55	25
Carshalton Athletic	26	11	2	13	52	72	24
Romford	26	10	2	14	60	55	22
Bostall Heath	26	8	4	14	42	61	20
Cray Wanderers	26	8	3	15	55	68	19
Whyteleafe Albion	26	6	5	15	60	91	17
Beckenham	*26*	*7*	*1*	*18*	*55*	*84*	*15*

Finchley joined from the Athenian League.

Division One

Park Royal	24	21	1	2	111	24	43
Leavesden Mental Hospital	24	17	4	3	97	23	38
U.G.B.M. Sports (Charlton)	24	16	4	4	80	29	36
Woolwich Polytechnic	24	15	1	8	71	47	31
Standard Telephones	24	12	4	8	77	57	28
Epsom Town Reserves	24	12	2	10	70	56	26
Brentwood Mental Hospital	24	9	3	12	66	73	21
Tate Institute	24	8	3	13	45	73	19
Romford Reserves	24	8	1	15	57	86	17
Erith & Belvedere Reserves	24	5	4	15	46	88	14
Watney's Sports	24	6	2	16	44	89	14
Chelmsford Reserves	24	5	3	16	32	75	13
Beckenham Reserves	24	4	4	16	40	116	12

1930-31

Premier Division

Chelmsford	26	20	2	4	106	51	42
Grays Athletic	26	16	5	5	82	41	37
Romford	26	15	3	8	77	39	33
Epsom Town	26	14	4	8	66	63	32
Mitcham Wanderers	26	15	1	10	73	40	31
Finchley	26	12	7	7	79	57	31
Dagenham Town	26	12	3	11	63	55	27
Erith & Belvedere	26	10	3	13	54	61	23
Cray Wanderers	26	9	4	13	45	55	22
Bostall Heath	26	9	4	13	48	65	22
Whyteleafe Albion	26	8	2	16	59	88	18
Tooting Town	26	6	6	14	48	78	18
Carshalton Athletic	26	4	7	15	44	97	15
Walthamstow Grange	26	6	1	19	52	106	13

Erith & Belvedere moved to the Kent League and Romford moved to the Athenian League.
Tilbury joined from the Kent League and Park Royal, Beckenham and Hendon town were all promoted from Division One.

Division One

Park Royal	26	25	0	1	158	28	50
Beckenham	26	17	6	3	84	35	40
Leavesden Mental Hospital	26	16	4	6	102	45	36
U.G.B.M. Sports (Charlton)	26	14	6	6	79	47	34
Hendon Town	26	13	5	8	63	59	31
Chelmsford Reserves	26	12	5	9	67	74	29
Finchley Reserves	26	12	2	12	55	59	26
Epsom Town Reserves	26	9	5	12	50	66	23
Brentwood Mental Hospital	26	9	3	14	60	63	21
Woolwich Polytechnic	26	8	4	14	67	97	20
Standard Telephones	26	8	3	15	41	77	19
Mitcham Wanderers Reserves	26	5	5	16	38	86	15
Romford Reserves	26	5	2	19	34	91	12
Erith & Belvedere Reserves	26	2	4	20	32	103	8

U.G.B.M. Sports changed their name to U.G.B. Sports.

1931-32

Premier Division

Park Royal	26	19	7	0	106	27	45
Epsom Town	26	16	5	5	69	33	37
Bostall Heath	26	17	3	6	67	34	37
Chelmsford	26	14	5	7	57	32	33
Dagenham Town	26	11	9	6	61	45	31
Finchley	26	11	5	10	61	46	27
Grays Athletic	26	10	4	12	63	63	24
Mitcham Wanderers	26	7	9	10	60	58	23
Tooting Town	26	8	6	12	50	67	22
Carshalton Athletic	26	8	3	15	52	72	19
Hendon Town	26	8	2	16	44	87	18
Tilbury	26	6	5	15	39	76	17
Cray Wanderers	26	6	4	16	56	104	16
Beckenham	26	4	7	15	33	74	15

Tooting Town and Mitcham Wanderers merged to form Tooting & Mitcham United.

Division One

Chelmsford Reserves	20	16	2	2	70	21	34
Jurgens (Purfleet)	20	13	4	3	66	33	30
Leavesden Mental Hospital	20	14	1	5	93	34	29
U.G.B. Sports (Charlton)	20	10	3	7	35	34	23
Grays Town	20	10	2	8	39	49	22
Finchley Reserves	20	8	5	7	44	40	21
Epsom Town Reserves	20	9	2	9	51	49	20
Woolwich Polytechnic	20	6	5	9	43	51	17
Mitcham Wanderers Reserves	20	3	4	13	35	57	10
Tate Institute	20	2	4	14	23	71	8
Hendon Town Reserves	20	2	2	16	21	81	6

1932-33

Premier Division

Park Royal	26	20	3	3	72	31	43
Epsom Town	26	16	7	3	92	45	39
Finchley	26	16	2	8	67	37	34
Chelmsford	26	14	5	7	88	59	33
Tooting & Mitcham United	26	13	3	10	61	48	29
Bostall Heath	26	12	5	9	52	59	29
Dagenham Town	26	11	5	10	62	59	27
Carshalton Athletic	26	10	4	12	52	64	24
Cray Wanderers	26	9	5	12	54	58	23
Hendon Town	26	10	1	15	50	61	21
Tilbury	26	7	7	12	44	59	21
Grays Athletic	26	6	5	15	45	60	17
Shepherds Bush	*26*	*5*	*2*	*19*	*50*	*99*	*12*
Beckenham	*26*	*4*	*4*	*18*	*34*	*84*	*12*

Streatham Town joined from the Surrey Senior League. Leavesden Mental Hospital and Post Office Engineers were promoted from Division One. Shepherds Bush also joined the Spartan League in 1933. It seems likely but is not certain that, from 1933 to 1935, the first team played in the Spartan League and the team that played in the London League – Division One was the reserves.

Division One

Leavesden Mental Hospital	26	21	2	3	120	25	44
Jurgens (Purfleet)	26	18	4	4	69	32	40
Post Office Engineers	26	13	8	5	69	36	34
Finchley Reserves	26	16	1	9	63	48	33
U.G.B. Sports (Charlton)	26	13	5	8	71	43	31
Dagenham Town Reserves	26	15	1	10	62	56	31
Epsom Town Reserves	26	14	2	10	78	63	30
Tooting & Mitcham United Reserves	26	10	6	10	51	50	26
Grays Athletic Reserves	26	10	4	12	47	68	24
South West Ham	26	9	5	12	49	50	23
Chelmsford Reserves	26	8	2	16	44	88	18
Tillings Athletic	26	4	2	20	43	85	10
Hendon Town Reserves	26	4	2	20	31	86	10
Woolwich Polytechnic	26	4	2	20	33	100	10

Jurgens (Purfleet) moved to the Spartan League.

1933-34

Premier Division

Park Royal	26	22	3	1	107	30	47
Leavesden Mental Hospital	26	17	3	6	76	41	37
Epsom Town	26	14	4	8	75	51	32
Finchley	26	13	5	8	58	40	31
Chelmsford	26	14	2	10	81	51	30
Bostall Heath	26	13	1	12	57	55	27
Tooting & Mitcham United	26	11	4	11	54	66	26
Tilbury	26	9	5	12	49	61	23
Streatham Town	26	9	4	13	54	63	22
Grays Athletic	26	9	4	13	52	81	22
Dagenham Town	26	9	3	14	54	60	21
Post Office Engineers	26	8	2	16	42	68	18
Carshalton Athletic	26	6	4	16	35	71	16
Cray Wanderers	26	4	4	18	41	97	12

Cray Wanderers moved to the Kent League.
Epsom Town changed their name to Epsom.

Division One

Eton Manor	30	20	5	5	72	38	45
U.G.B. Sports (Charlton)	30	21	2	7	90	36	44
Beckenham	30	17	7	6	78	45	41
Jurgens (Purfleet) Reserves	30	16	9	5	75	55	41
Northmet	30	18	4	8	87	46	40
Finchley Reserves	30	17	4	9	74	51	38
Epsom Town Reserves	30	15	8	7	67	48	38
Dagenham Town Reserves	30	14	3	13	72	63	31
Park Royal Reserves	30	13	2	15	94	72	28
Chelmsford Reserves	30	10	6	14	66	80	26
Woolwich Polytechnic	30	11	2	17	72	105	24
Acton	30	6	8	16	47	79	20
Streatham Town Reserves	30	8	3	19	35	63	19
Tooting & Mitcham United Reserves	30	7	3	20	51	89	17
Post Office Engineers Reserves	30	6	3	21	42	112	15
Grays Athletic Reserves	30	5	3	22	42	82	13

Acton were known as Shepherds Bush before they changed their name in December 1933.

1934-35

Premier Division

Park Royal	26	20	1	5	99	36	41
Epsom	26	16	2	8	70	51	34
Leavesden Mental Hospital	26	15	4	7	79	60	34
Post Office Engineers	26	15	2	9	71	47	32
Finchley	26	15	2	9	63	44	32
Dagenham Town	26	11	5	10	47	42	27
Streatham Town	26	11	4	11	61	52	26
Chelmsford	26	10	3	13	51	54	23
Grays Athletic	26	9	5	12	56	63	23
Bostall Heath	26	10	3	13	47	53	23
Tilbury	26	10	3	13	44	69	23
Eton Manor	26	9	2	15	43	63	20
Tooting & Mitcham United	26	4	9	13	31	58	17
Carshalton Athletic	26	4	1	21	26	96	9

Chelmsford moved to the Eastern Counties League.

Division One

Northmet	28	20	4	4	89	39	44
Dagenham Town Reserves	28	15	7	6	70	45	37
Chelmsford Reserves	28	16	4	8	88	50	36
Grays Athletic Reserves	28	15	5	8	66	48	35
Post Office Engineers Reserves	28	15	5	8	74	64	35
U.G.B. Sports (Charlton)	28	13	5	10	81	52	31
Epsom Reserves	28	11	9	8	75	51	31
Eton Manor Reserves	28	10	7	11	45	49	27
Finchley Reserves	28	10	6	12	64	72	26
London Labour	28	12	2	14	72	101	26
Streatham Town Reserves	28	11	3	14	67	63	25
Acton	28	7	7	14	45	72	21
Woolwich Polytechnic	28	6	5	17	54	96	17
Tooting & Mitcham United Reserves	28	3	10	15	36	66	16
Beckenham	28	5	3	20	32	90	13

Ford Sports and Briggs Motor Bodies both joined from the South Essex League. Acton disbanded.

1935-36

Premier Division

Leavesden Mental Hospital	24	16	3	5	67	34	35
Finchley	24	16	3	5	76	39	35
Post Office Engineers	24	15	5	4	68	35	35
Tilbury	24	12	3	9	64	46	27
Carshalton Athletic	24	11	3	10	64	59	25
Tooting & Mitcham United	24	11	3	10	42	45	25
Eton Manor	24	10	4	10	44	43	24
Dagenham Town	24	10	4	10	46	51	24
Grays Athletic	24	10	3	11	54	49	23
Epsom	24	7	3	14	58	64	17
Bostall Heath	24	7	3	14	35	76	17
Streatham Town	24	5	3	16	40	65	13
Park Royal	24	5	2	17	44	96	12

Park Royal left after merging with Southall of the Athenian League. Royal Naval Depot (Chatham) joined from the Kent League and West Norwood joined from the Surrey Senior League.

Division One

Ford Sports	32	25	1	6	107	44	51
U.G.B. Sports (Charlton)	32	22	5	5	78	36	49
Eton Manor Reserves	32	19	8	5	82	35	46
Briggs Motor Bodies	32	21	4	7	98	45	46
Hayesco	32	18	5	9	93	60	41
Post Office Engineers Reserves	32	16	4	12	88	66	36
Tilbury Reserves	32	15	5	12	69	56	35
Northmet	32	17	0	15	95	84	34
Venner Sports	32	11	7	14	57	65	29
Chelmsford Reserves	32	11	7	14	67	79	29
Woolwich Polytechnic	32	11	4	17	83	94	26
Grays Athletic Reserves	32	10	4	18	46	83	24
Finchley Reserves	32	9	4	19	60	89	22
Jurgens (Purfleet) Reserves	32	8	4	20	41	108	20
Epsom Reserves	32	6	7	19	51	82	19
Tooting & Mitcham United Reserves	32	8	3	21	48	93	19
Dagenham Town Reserves	32	7	4	21	53	97	18

1936-37

Premier Division

Finchley	26	15	5	6	94	43	35
Epsom	26	14	7	5	77	49	35
Grays Athletic	26	17	1	8	72	53	35
Eton Manor	26	14	5	7	71	38	33
Streatham Town	26	15	2	9	65	45	32
Leavesden Mental Hospital	26	13	5	8	59	60	31
Post Office Engineers	26	12	3	11	71	59	27
Tooting & Mitcham United	26	11	4	11	46	54	26
Royal Naval Depot	26	11	2	13	63	80	24
Dagenham Town	26	9	4	13	53	68	22
Carshalton Athletic	26	8	2	16	50	73	18
Tilbury	26	7	4	15	41	64	18
West Norwood	26	4	6	16	42	80	14
Bostall Heath	26	5	4	17	35	73	14

Dagenham Town moved to become founder members of the Essex County League, Tooting & Mitcham United moved to the Athenian League and West Norwood moved to the Surrey Senior League. Walton-on-Thames joined from the Surrey Senior League.

Division One

Briggs Motor Bodies	24	19	4	1	81	32	42
Ford Sports	24	18	2	4	77	27	38
Northmet	24	14	3	7	74	45	31
Venner Sports	24	11	7	6	47	32	29
Eton Manor Reserves	24	11	5	8	48	46	27
CWS (Silvertown)	24	11	4	9	64	59	26
U.G.B. Sports (Charlton)	24	12	1	11	65	65	25
Post Office Engineers Reserves	24	8	5	11	65	66	21
Woolwich Polytechnic	24	8	3	13	49	54	19
Tilbury Reserves	24	6	4	14	33	67	16
Grays Athletic Reserves	24	5	5	14	52	63	15
Jurgens (Purfleet) Reserves	24	6	2	16	32	84	14
Wandgas Athletic	24	2	5	17	45	92	9

1937-38

Premier Division

Eton Manor	24	19	2	3	61	20	40
Epsom	24	16	3	5	80	37	35
Walton-on-Thames	24	16	1	7	71	45	33
Tilbury	24	15	3	6	69	46	33
Finchley	24	15	2	7	70	32	32
Post Office Engineers	24	11	5	8	49	40	27
Leavesden Mental Hospital	24	12	2	10	67	50	26
Wandsworth United	24	11	1	12	55	71	23
Grays Athletic	24	9	3	12	54	52	21
Guildford City Reserves	24	6	1	17	33	88	13
Carshalton Athletic	24	4	3	17	33	79	11
Bostall Heath	24	4	2	18	21	58	10
Royal Naval Depot	24	3	2	19	31	76	8

Dagenham Town returned from the Essex County League which closed down after one season. Uxbridge joined from the Spartan League.

Division One

Northmet	26	20	1	5	91	38	41
Ford Sports	26	18	4	4	96	31	40
Eton Manor Reserves	26	14	6	6	78	44	34
Briggs Motor Bodies	26	14	3	9	56	33	31
CWS (Silvertown)	26	14	2	10	52	38	30
U.G.B. Sports (Charlton)	26	12	4	10	65	46	28
Finchley Reserves	26	13	2	11	62	56	28
Post Office Engineers Reserves	26	11	4	11	65	60	26
Woolwich Polytechnic	26	9	7	10	66	61	25
Venner Sports	26	7	9	10	39	44	23
Grays Athletic Reserves	26	8	3	15	40	75	19
Wandgas Athletic	26	6	3	17	40	109	15
Royal Ordnance Factories	26	3	8	15	33	76	14
Tilbury Reserves	26	3	4	19	38	110	10

Venner Sports moved to the Surrey Senior League.

1938-39

Premier Division

Dagenham Town	28	20	2	6	86	38	42
Leavesden Mental Hospital	28	20	1	7	106	53	41
Epsom	28	20	1	7	78	43	41
Finchley	28	18	4	6	68	26	40
Guildford City Reserves	28	14	4	10	77	77	32
Eton Manor	28	13	5	10	60	40	31
Carshalton Athletic	28	14	3	11	69	59	31
Tilbury	28	13	3	12	61	60	29
Post Office Engineers	28	11	6	11	66	58	28
Walton-on-Thames	28	9	9	10	73	74	27
Grays Athletic	28	11	3	14	59	64	25
Uxbridge	28	9	6	13	61	62	24
Royal Naval Depot	28	4	4	20	38	98	12
Bostall Heath	28	4	3	21	48	112	11
Wandsworth United	28	2	2	24	41	127	6

Finchley moved to the Athenian League. Hersham joined from the Surrey Senior League and Wembley joined as a newly formed club.

Division One

Briggs Motor Bodies	28	21	4	3	114	35	46
Finchley Reserves	28	20	3	5	83	20	43
Woolwich Polytechnic	28	18	1	9	110	59	37
Ford Sports	28	15	6	7	91	49	36
CWS (Silvertown)	28	17	2	9	65	46	36
U.G.B. Sports (Charlton)	28	15	5	8	56	30	35
Eton Manor Reserves	28	16	2	10	82	58	34
Northmet	28	13	3	12	76	74	29
Royal Ordnance Factories	28	8	7	13	47	70	23
Uxbridge Reserves	28	7	8	13	42	76	22
Port of London Authority	28	8	3	17	54	91	19
Grays Athletic Reserves	28	7	5	16	42	86	19
Post Office Engineers Reserves	28	6	5	17	62	95	17
Wandgas Athletic	28	4	4	20	61	115	12
Walton-on-Thames Reserves	28	4	4	20	52	133	12

1939-45

War broke out soon after the start of the 1939-40 season and the League then closed down. It did not restart until 1945 when it was re-formed with two regional divisions, East and West.

However, several pre-war members were not ready to resume and not all of those that were ready chose to rejoin the league. Grays Athletic joined the newly formed Corinthian League, Briggs Motor Bodies changed their name to Briggs Sports and joined the Spartan League and Ford Sports also joined the Spartan League. Neither Dagenham Town nor Wembley were able to resume at all and so effectively disbanded. Walton-on-Thames merged with Hersham to form Walton & Hersham who, like Grays Athletic, became founder members of the Corinthian League.

Amongst the new members were Crittall Athletic and Chelmsford City Reserves who had been members of the Eastern Counties League before the war, De Havilland who had been members of the Hertfordshire County League, Vickers Armstrong (ex-Surrey Senior League) and Edgware Town (ex-Middlesex Senior League). Epsom changed their name back to Epsom Town.

1945-46

East Division

Woolwich Polytechnic	20	16	2	2	77	23	34
Crittall Athletic	20	15	2	3	77	26	32
Ekco	20	14	0	6	72	39	28
Royal Naval Depot (Chatham)	20	13	2	5	66	38	28
Eton Manor	20	11	4	5	50	29	26
Chelmsford City Reserves	20	10	1	9	59	54	21
Woodford Town	20	8	1	11	72	67	17
Snaresbrook United	20	3	4	13	44	60	10
Ford Sports Reserves	20	5	0	15	27	84	10
London Transport Central Buses	20	4	14	36	90	8	
Briggs Sports Reserves	20	2	2	16	30	100	6

Those above the line qualified for the Premier Division in 1946-47, the remainder (except Snaresbrook United) played in Division One.

West Division

Edgware Town	14	10	2	2	49	20	22
Uxbridge	14	9	0	5	47	43	18
Guildford City Reserves	14	7	0	7	45	33	14
De Havilland	14	4	5	5	29	33	13
Epsom Town	14	6	1	7	40	51	13
Walton & Hersham Reserves	14	4	3	7	37	36	11
Vickers Armstrong	14	4	3	7	32	49	11
Carshalton Athletic	14	4	2	8	32	46	10

Championship decider:

Woolwich Polytechnic vs Edgware Town   2-1

Edgware Town, Uxbridge and Carshalton Athletic moved to the Corinthian League and Vickers Armstrong moved to the Surrey Senior League. Guildford City Reserves and Epsom Town were placed in the Premier Division for 1946-47 while De Havilland were placed in Division One.

Pre-war members Leavesden Mental Hospital and Tilbury returned to the Premier Division as did Post Office Engineers who had changed their name to London Telecoms.

Pre-war members Royal Ordnance Factories and Eton Manor Reserves returned to Division One for 1946-47 as did Port of London Authority who had added 'Police' to their name. Ruislip Manor joined from the Middlesex Senior League and there were also two newly formed clubs in Division One, Cheshunt and Dagenham British Legion.

1946-47

Premier Division

Chelmsford City Reserves	26	19	5	2	93	36	43
Tilbury	26	17	4	5	62	32	38
Eton Manor	26	16	4	6	76	37	36
Crittall Athletic	26	14	5	7	70	50	33
Guildford City Reserves	26	12	7	7	59	47	31
Ekco	26	10	8	8	74	57	28
Leavesden Mental Hospital	26	12	4	10	80	63	28
Woodford Town	26	8	7	11	45	55	23
Woolwich Polytechnic	26	6	7	13	51	77	19
Epsom Town	26	8	3	15	50	77	19
Bedford Town Reserves	26	6	6	14	47	62	18
Dartford Reserves	26	6	5	15	43	66	17
Royal Naval Depot (Chatham)	26	5	7	14	45	77	17
London Telecoms	26	6	2	18	41	100	14

London Telecoms changed their name to Post Office Telecoms.

Division One

Dagenham British Legion	26	20	4	2	77	36	44
Cheshunt	26	19	2	5	122	42	40
De Havilland	26	18	1	7	88	60	37
Ruislip Manor	26	17	2	7	75	48	36
Ford Sports Reserves	26	13	5	8	65	57	31
Eton Manor Reserves	26	11	4	11	93	67	26
Briggs Sports Reserves	26	9	7	10	62	70	25
London Transport Central Buses	26	10	4	12	73	66	24
Britannia	26	10	4	12	67	63	24
Stanmore	26	10	3	13	68	71	23
Woodford Town Reserves	26	6	5	15	50	85	17
Royal Ordnance Factories	26	6	4	16	50	93	16
Ilford Electrical	26	5	4	17	41	74	14
Port of London Authority Police	26	3	1	22	42	141	7

Britannia closed down but Chadwell Heath took over both their ground and their place in the league.

A new Division Two was formed for 1947-48 that included West Thurrock Athletic from the South Essex League and Vickers Armstrong from the Surrey Senior League.

1947-48

Premier Division

Chelmsford City Reserves	28	21	2	5	126	37	44
Tilbury	28	17	6	5	78	35	40
Crittall Athletic	28	18	4	6	78	42	40
Guildford City Reserves	28	16	1	11	81	51	33
Leavesden Mental Hospital	28	13	6	9	74	63	32
Eton Manor	28	12	8	8	58	52	32
Ekco	28	12	3	13	58	70	27
Woolwich Polytechnic	28	10	7	11	55	67	27
Dartford Reserves	28	11	4	13	43	57	26
Edmonton Borough	28	10	4	14	62	65	24
Woodford Town	28	11	2	15	59	82	24
Bedford Town Reserves	28	10	4	14	50	76	24
Epsom Town	28	7	5	16	45	80	19
Royal Naval Depot (Chatham)	28	6	5	17	50	98	17
Post Office Telecoms	28	4	3	21	31	73	11

Chelmsford City Reserves left, continuing in the Eastern Counties League. A newly formed club called Chingford Town placed their reserves in the league.

Division One

Cheshunt	22	16	4	2	95	25	36
Ruislip Manor	22	16	1	5	103	39	33
De Havilland	22	12	3	7	63	49	27
Dagenham British Legion	22	9	8	5	54	45	26
Woodford Town Reserves	22	11	4	7	52	44	26
London Transport Central Buses	22	9	5	8	52	59	23
Eton Manor Reserves	22	9	5	8	45	53	23
Ford Sports Reserves	22	9	3	10	40	64	21
Chadwell Heath	22	8	1	13	42	64	17
Briggs Sports Reserves	22	6	3	13	49	71	15
Port of London Authority Police	*22*	*5*	*0*	*17*	*40*	*60*	*10*
Royal Ordnance Factories	*22*	*3*	*1*	*18*	*21*	*83*	*7*

Ford Sports joined from the Spartan League and their reserves were relegated to Division Two.

Division Two

West Thurrock Athletic	**26**	**20**	**4**	**2**	**87**	**21**	**44**
De Havilland Vampires	**26**	**17**	**5**	**4**	**77**	**37**	**39**
Rainham Town	**26**	**17**	**4**	**5**	**82**	**38**	**38**
Edmonton Borough Reserves	**26**	**16**	**3**	**7**	**70**	**42**	**35**
Vickers Armstrong	26	14	4	8	82	40	32
U.G.B.M. Sports	26	11	6	9	74	62	28
Epsom Town Reserves	26	12	3	11	50	53	27
Brentwood & Warley Reserves	26	9	7	10	60	60	25
Eton Manor "A"	26	11	1	14	62	61	23
Ekco Reserves	26	10	1	15	59	71	21
London Trans. Central Buses Res.	26	7	5	14	42	74	19
Dagenham British Legion Reserves	26	8	2	16	36	88	18
Standard Telephones	26	3	6	17	23	62	12
Enfield Cables	26	0	3	23	19	114	3

1948-49

Premier Division

Guildford City Reserves	26	19	2	5	61	24	40
Eton Manor	26	16	2	8	66	31	34
Epsom Town	26	16	1	9	72	52	33
Tilbury	26	15	2	9	60	32	32
Bedford Town Reserves	26	13	3	10	60	48	29
Woolwich Polytechnic	26	14	1	11	61	56	29
Dartford Reserves	26	12	3	11	54	48	27
Woodford Town	26	12	3	11	68	65	27
Chingford Town Reserves	26	10	6	10	40	44	26
Edmonton Borough	26	12	2	12	51	60	26
Crittall Athletic	26	9	7	10	49	47	25
Leavesden Mental Hospital	26	10	3	13	62	66	23
Royal Naval Depot (Chatham)	26	3	3	20	31	96	9
Ekco	26	1	2	23	20	85	4
					755	754	

Epsom Town moved to the Corinthian League and Chingford Town Reserves moved to the Metropolitan League. Tonbridge Reserves and Gravesend & Northfleet Reserves both joined from the Kent League. Cheshunt and Rainham Town were promoted from Division One.

Division One

Cheshunt	26	21	2	3	73	24	44
West Thurrock Athletic	26	18	3	5	82	42	39
Ruislip Manor	26	17	2	7	73	48	36
London Transport Central Buses	26	15	3	8	73	61	33
Rainham Town	26	13	5	8	52	33	31
Ford Sports	26	10	10	6	51	43	30
Dagenham British Legion	26	13	3	10	62	45	29
Briggs Sports Reserves	26	12	2	12	60	50	26
De Havilland Vampires	26	11	4	11	44	43	26
De Havilland	26	10	2	14	42	65	22
Eton Manor Reserves	26	6	3	17	39	64	15
Chadwell Heath	26	4	7	15	32	71	15
Edmonton Borough Reserves	*26*	*4*	*3*	*19*	*41*	*74*	*11*
Woodford Town Reserves	*26*	*2*	*3*	*21*	*34*	*95*	*7*

Vickers Armstrong, Crittall Athletic Reserves, Rainham Town Reserves, Lea Bridge Gas and Brentwood & Warley Reserves were all promoted from Division Two.

Division Two

Vickers Armstrong	26	20	4	2	97	25	44
Crittall Athletic Reserves	26	15	4	7	68	44	34
Rainham Town Reserves	26	14	5	7	61	44	33
Tilbury Reserves	26	13	6	7	59	39	32
Lea Bridge Gas	26	12	7	7	43	42	31
Brentwood & Warley Reserves	26	11	6	9	58	50	28
Cheshunt Reserves	26	11	5	10	45	54	27
Eton Manor "A"	26	9	7	10	38	44	25
Royal Ordnance Factories	26	7	8	11	44	54	22
U.G.B.M. Sports	26	7	6	13	50	69	20
Epsom Town Reserves	26	7	5	14	62	79	19
Port of London Authority Police	26	6	6	14	39	61	18
Ford Sports Reserves	26	5	6	15	29	52	16
Dagenham British Legion Reserves	26	5	5	16	35	70	15
					728	727	

Harris Lebus joined from the Middlesex Senior League and Aveley joined from the Thurrock Combination.

1949-50

Premier Division

Cheshunt	30	23	3	4	115	39	49
Tilbury	30	21	5	4	62	29	47
Dartford Reserves	30	21	3	6	69	36	45
Crittall Athletic	30	15	5	10	69	57	35
Tonbridge Reserves	30	12	7	11	42	41	31
Rainham Town	30	12	6	12	50	46	30
Bedford Town Reserves	30	11	7	12	56	60	29
Woodford Town	30	14	1	15	63	70	29
Guildford City Reserves	30	11	5	14	57	56	27
Gravesend & Northfleet Reserves	30	10	5	15	58	61	25
Hastings United Reserves	30	9	7	14	47	71	25
Eton Manor	30	9	5	16	47	62	23
Edmonton Borough	30	9	4	17	49	68	22
Woolwich Polytechnic	30	8	6	16	44	63	22
Leavesden Mental Hospital	30	9	3	18	48	86	21
Royal Naval Depot (Chatham)	30	7	6	17	41	72	20

Tilbury moved to the Corinthian League and Hastings United Reserves moved to the Metropolitan League. Edmonton Borough merged with Tufnell Park of the Isthmian League to form Tufnell Park Edmonton. West Thurrock Athletic and Ruislip Manor were promoted from Division One.

Division One

Vickers Armstrong	26	21	2	3	97	25	44
Briggs Sports Reserves	26	18	3	5	81	26	39
Chadwell Heath	26	18	2	6	86	48	38
West Thurrock Athletic	26	15	4	7	66	42	34
Dagenham British Legion	26	14	3	9	65	53	31
Ruislip Manor	26	13	4	9	69	54	30
London Transport Central Buses	26	10	5	11	56	61	25
Rainham Town Reserves	26	10	4	12	59	51	24
Eton Manor Reserves	26	10	4	12	44	65	24
Crittall Athletic Reserves	26	9	3	14	48	72	21
Ford Sports	26	8	2	16	48	74	18
Brentwood & Warley Reserves	26	7	1	18	51	76	15
De Havilland	*26*	*3*	*5*	*18*	*24*	*80*	*11*
Lea Bridge Gas	*26*	*3*	*4*	*19*	*26*	*93*	*10*

Vickers Armstrong moved to the Metropolitan League and Ford Sports moved to the Spartan League.

Division Two

Bata Sports	28	22	3	3	108	23	47
Harris Lebus	28	20	6	2	84	24	46
Port of London Authority Police	28	18	5	5	85	42	41
Aveley	28	16	7	5	78	40	39
Cheshunt Reserves	28	14	5	9	57	44	33
Tilbury Reserves	28	12	7	9	56	39	31
Ruislip Manor Reserves	28	10	8	10	55	58	28
Royal Ordnance Factories	28	10	5	13	57	71	25
Woodford Town Reserves	28	7	8	13	52	69	22
Ford Sports Reserves	28	9	4	15	40	61	22
Eton Manor "A"	28	6	9	13	41	70	21
Dagenham British Legion Reserves	28	7	5	16	38	92	19
Vickers Armstrong Reserves	28	7	4	17	46	83	18
U.G.B.M. Sports	28	7	4	17	42	77	18
Edmonton Borough Reserves	28	2	6	20	41	86	10
					880	879	

The top five clubs and Ford Sports Reserves were all promoted to Division One. Barkingside joined from the Walthamstow League and Dagenham Cables joined from the South Essex League.

1950-51

Premier Division

Dartford Reserves	28	21	4	3	75	26	46
Woodford Town	28	22	1	5	106	41	45
Cheshunt	28	14	10	4	83	40	38
Gravesend & Northfleet Reserves	28	16	2	10	56	35	34
Ruislip Manor	28	11	8	9	56	61	30
Eton Manor	28	12	5	11	56	46	29
Bedford Town Reserves	28	11	7	10	51	59	29
Guildford City Reserves	28	11	6	11	56	45	28
West Thurrock Athletic	28	12	3	13	48	51	27
Tonbridge Reserves	28	11	4	13	46	47	26
Rainham Town	28	9	3	16	38	48	21
Leavesden Mental Hospital	28	7	6	15	48	66	20
Crittall Athletic	28	6	7	15	49	87	19
Woolwich Polytechnic	28	9	1	18	38	89	19
Royal Naval Depot (Chatham)	28	3	3	22	38	103	9

Bedford Town Reserves moved to the United Counties League, Tonbridge Reserves moved to the Metropolitan League and Woodford Town, Cheshunt and Rainham Town all moved to the Delphian League. Beckenham and Cray Wanderers joined from the Kent Amateur League, Welwyn Garden City joined from the Spartan League and Aylesford Paper Mills joined from the Kent League.

Division One

Aveley	24	18	1	5	73	43	37
Briggs Sports Reserves	24	14	5	5	83	56	33
Bata Sports	24	13	4	7	61	36	30
Harris Lebus	24	13	4	7	62	46	30
Port of London Authority Police	24	12	4	8	61	51	28
London Transport Central Buses	24	12	2	10	77	50	26
Cheshunt Reserves	24	9	6	9	47	45	24
Rainham Town Reserves	24	9	6	9	40	49	24
Dagenham British Legion	24	10	2	12	53	61	22
Eton Manor Reserves	24	8	6	10	44	51	22
Chadwell Heath	24	6	4	14	41	74	16
Brentwood & Warley Reserves	24	4	3	17	36	76	11
Ford Sports Reserves	24	4	1	19	22	63	9
					700	701	

Eton Manor Reserves and Ford Sports Reserves were both relegated to Division Two. Storey Athletic joined from the South Essex League.

Division Two

Woodford Town Reserves	24	17	4	3	78	37	38
Barkingside	24	14	6	4	73	32	34
Wapping Sports	24	14	5	5	62	40	33
Stones Athletic	24	14	4	6	61	35	32
Ruislip Manor Reserves	24	11	5	8	52	45	27
Eton Manor "A"	24	9	5	10	44	48	23
Lea Bridge Gas	24	10	3	11	47	63	23
Lathol Athletic	24	8	6	10	49	56	22
Royal Ordnance Factories	24	7	7	10	36	38	21
Dagenham Cables	24	8	3	13	39	58	19
Bata Sports Reserves	24	5	8	11	45	54	18
U.G.B.M. Sports	24	4	4	16	32	64	12
De Havilland	24	5	0	19	29	77	10

Barkingside, Dagenham Cables, Lathol Athletic, Stones Athletic, Royal Ordnance Factories and U.G.B.M. Sports were all promoted to Division One.

1951-52

Premier Division

West Thurrock Athletic	28	22	3	3	69	34	47
Ruislip Manor	28	20	2	6	88	46	42
Guildford City Reserves	28	15	10	3	70	28	40
Crittall Athletic	28	14	7	7	83	51	35
Gravesend & Northfleet Reserves	28	13	6	9	75	46	32
Eton Manor	28	13	4	11	71	47	30
Beckenham	28	8	10	10	49	59	26
Welwyn Garden City	28	10	5	13	43	57	25
Dartford Reserves	28	10	4	14	47	48	24
Cray Wanderers	28	10	4	14	52	72	24
Leavesden Mental Hospital	28	9	4	15	48	83	22
Woolwich Polytechnic	28	9	2	17	54	74	20
Aylesford Paper Mills	28	7	6	15	57	79	20
Royal Naval Depot (Chatham)	28	7	3	18	49	100	17
Post Office Engineers (L.T.R.)	28	6	4	18	47	78	16

Crittall Athletic moved to the Eastern Counties League. Wingate joined from the Parthenon League.

Division One

London Transport Central Buses	24	16	4	4	83	35	36
Storey Athletic	24	16	4	4	71	31	36
Bata Sports	24	15	4	5	52	29	34
Barkingside	24	13	3	8	52	34	29
Harris Lebus	24	12	3	9	57	44	27
Port of London Authority Police	24	13	0	11	56	45	26
Dagenham Cables	24	11	4	9	46	44	26
Lathol Athletic	24	10	5	9	53	63	25
Aveley	24	11	2	11	62	39	24
Stones Athletic	24	10	3	11	48	58	23
Dagenham British Legion	24	6	3	15	45	65	15
Royal Ordnance Factories	24	2	4	18	28	72	8
U.G.B.M. Sports	24	1	1	22	20	114	3

Aveley were promoted to the Premier Division. Stones Athletic were relegated to Division Two.

Division Two

Pitsea United	24	19	3	2	87	24	41
Wapping Sports	24	19	2	3	107	35	40
Storey Athletic Reserves	24	15	3	6	54	38	33
Lea Bridge Gas	24	12	5	7	52	42	29
Ruislip Manor Reserves	24	10	5	9	55	49	25
Aylesford Paper Mill Reserves	24	7	10	7	41	42	24
Bata Sports Reserves	24	8	5	11	52	65	21
Welwyn Garden City Reserves	24	8	3	13	46	67	19
Eton Manor Reserves	24	6	6	12	43	46	18
Beckenham Reserves	24	7	3	14	47	74	17
Ford Sports Reserves	24	5	6	13	39	68	16
Aveley Reserves	24	4	7	13	36	62	15
Post Office Engineers (L.T.R.) Res.	24	6	2	16	39	87	14
					698	699	

1952-53

Premier Division

Eton Manor	30	17	9	4	83	34	43
Dartford Reserves	30	16	10	4	68	37	42
Ruislip Manor	30	13	13	4	78	41	39
Gravesend & Northfleet Reserves	30	16	4	10	69	47	36
Guildford City Reserves	30	12	11	7	61	49	35
Leavesden Mental Hospital	30	14	7	9	53	45	35
Aveley	30	14	7	9	60	54	35
Wingate	30	14	3	13	58	62	31
West Thurrock Athletic	30	10	9	11	55	55	29
Beckenham	30	9	9	12	55	53	27
Woolwich Polytechnic	30	11	4	15	54	71	26
Cray Wanderers	30	9	6	15	56	60	24
Aylesford Paper Mills	30	9	6	15	65	87	24
Post Office Engineers (L.T.R.)	30	8	5	17	44	82	21
Royal Naval Depot (Chatham)	30	6	6	18	47	88	18
Welwyn Garden City	30	5	5	20	46	87	15

Dartford Reserves, Gravesend & Northfleet Reserves and Guildford City Reserves all moved to the Metropolitan League.

Division One

Storey Athletic	**24**	**21**	**2**	**1**	**89**	**26**	**44**
London Transport Central Buses	24	17	2	5	84	32	36
Pitsea United	24	14	4	6	58	47	32
Bata Sports	24	12	5	7	55	36	29
Harris Lebus	24	9	6	9	52	50	24
Barkingside	24	9	5	10	48	46	23
Parkhill (Chingford)	24	10	3	11	50	53	23
Lathol Athletic	24	9	4	11	45	56	22
Port of London Authority Police	24	7	7	10	47	53	21
Dagenham Cables	24	9	3	12	37	49	21
Downshall	24	5	5	14	31	60	15
Dagenham British Legion	24	3	7	14	22	57	13
Royal Ordnance Factories	24	2	5	17	19	72	9

Wapping Sports and Stones Athletic promoted from Division Two.

Division Two

Wapping Sports	28	22	5	1	148	34	49
Eton Manor Reserves	28	17	7	4	79	38	41
Harris Lebus Reserves	28	17	5	6	77	48	39
Bata Sports Reserves	28	15	6	7	85	48	36
Beckenham Reserves	28	13	9	6	77	48	35
Stones Athletic	28	15	4	9	68	47	34
Wingate Reserves	28	14	5	9	70	60	33
Ruislip Manor Reserves	28	14	2	12	81	63	30
Storey Athletic Reserves	28	10	7	11	54	60	27
West Thurrock Athletic Reserves	28	8	5	15	48	88	21
Ford Sports Reserves	28	8	4	16	49	81	20
Lea Bridge Gas	28	7	6	15	56	100	20
London Trans. Central Buses Res.	28	9	1	18	56	73	19
Aylesford Paper Mill Reserves	28	3	2	23	34	110	8
Post Office Engineers (L.T.R.) Res.	28	2	4	22	32	116	8

Division Two closed down and a separate division was set up exclusively for reserve sides.

1953-54

Premier Division

Eton Manor	26	19	4	3	61	25	42
Cray Wanderers	26	15	6	5	66	46	36
Aveley	26	14	5	7	55	37	33
Beckenham	26	13	4	9	56	43	30
Ruislip Manor	26	13	3	10	61	44	29
Woolwich Polytechnic	26	12	5	9	51	47	29
Wingate	26	10	5	11	37	42	25
Storey Athletic	26	8	8	10	37	35	24
Leavesden Mental Hospital	26	9	4	13	57	58	22
West Thurrock Athletic	26	8	6	12	35	45	22
Welwyn Garden City	26	8	6	12	42	57	22
Aylesford Paper Mills	26	8	4	14	38	51	20
Post Office Engineers (L.T.R.)	26	5	7	14	35	55	17
Royal Naval Depot (Chatham)	26	5	3	18	22	68	13

Aylesford Paper Mills and Royal Naval Depot (Chatham) both moved to the Kent Amateur League. Harlow Town joined from the Spartan League.

Division One

London Transport Central Buses	26	21	1	4	108	42	43
Wapping Sports	26	19	1	6	74	45	39
Barkingside	26	14	6	6	50	34	34
Lathol Athletic	26	13	4	9	67	49	30
Bata Sports	26	12	5	9	66	54	29
Pitsea United	26	11	5	10	51	46	27
Harris Lebus	26	9	8	9	53	53	26
Parkhill (Chingford)	26	12	2	12	50	56	26
Stones Athletic	26	10	3	13	47	60	23
Dagenham British Legion	26	8	6	12	58	70	22
Port of London Authority Police	26	7	7	12	41	53	21
Dagenham Cables	26	6	8	12	43	46	20
Stansted	26	6	6	14	44	61	18
Royal Ordnance Factories	26	1	4	21	23	82	6

Dagenham British Legion changed their name to Dagenham Park.

1954-55

Premier Division

Aveley	22	17	2	3	62	24	36
Cray Wanderers	22	16	3	3	53	29	35
Ruislip Manor	22	15	2	5	70	37	32
Eton Manor	22	13	2	7	68	37	28
Beckenham	22	12	2	8	43	34	26
Storey Athletic	22	11	1	10	47	34	23
Welwyn Garden City	22	7	4	11	34	52	18
West Thurrock Athletic	22	7	3	12	39	52	17
Woolwich Polytechnic	22	7	3	12	33	44	17
Wingate	22	7	2	13	34	52	16
Harlow Town	22	4	4	14	28	58	12
Leavesden Mental Hospital	22	1	2	19	24	82	4

Storey Athletic changed their name to East Ham United. Leavesden Mental Hospital moved to the Hertfordshire County League and Welwyn Garden City moved to the Spartan League. Basildon Town and Epping Town both joined from the Parthenon League and Cheshunt joined from the Delphian League.

Division One

Wapping Sports	26	21	2	3	90	24	44
Parkhill (Chingford)	26	18	5	3	86	44	41
Barkingside	26	13	8	5	51	30	34
London Transport Central Buses	26	12	6	8	75	62	30
Bata Sports	26	13	2	11	57	47	28
Dagenham Cables	26	9	5	12	63	68	23
Lathol Athletic	26	9	4	13	51	64	22
Harris Lebus	26	9	3	14	47	49	21
Stansted	26	8	5	13	47	61	21
Stones Athletic	26	8	5	13	52	76	21
Royal Ordnance Factories	26	7	7	12	43	70	21
Port of London Authority Police	26	8	4	14	55	76	20
Pitsea United	26	8	3	15	45	66	19
Dagenham Park	26	6	7	13	43	68	19

Parkhill (Chingford) changed their name to Chingford.

1955-56

Premier Division

Eton Manor	24	16	5	3	70	21	37
Aveley	24	13	7	4	61	35	33
Cray Wanderers	24	14	4	6	50	37	32
Ruislip Manor	24	15	1	8	64	43	31
East Ham United	24	13	5	6	56	44	31
Basildon Town	24	14	3	7	68	37	29
Cheshunt	24	9	7	8	55	59	25
Beckenham	24	11	2	11	51	51	24
Wingate	24	6	4	14	47	59	16
West Thurrock Athletic	24	5	5	14	27	51	15
Epping Town	24	5	4	15	33	67	14
Harlow Town	24	4	5	15	38	63	13
Woolwich Polytechnic	24	3	4	17	31	84	10

Basildon Town had 2 points deducted.
Woolwich Polytechnic moved to the Kent Amateur League.
Barkingside, Chingford and Pitsea United were promoted from Division
One.

Division One

Bata Sports	26	18	3	5	76	32	39
Lathol Athletic	26	15	6	5	51	36	36
London Transport Central Buses	26	13	8	5	81	50	34
Barkingside	26	13	5	8	62	23	31
Chingford	26	13	5	8	61	47	31
Wapping Sports	26	14	2	10	82	46	30
Dagenham Cables	26	13	4	9	79	55	30
Port of London Authority Police	26	13	4	9	57	52	30
Harris Lebus	26	9	8	9	54	59	26
Pitsea United	26	7	4	15	54	83	18
Royal Ordnance Factories	26	6	5	15	35	62	17
Dagenham Park	26	6	3	17	46	101	15
Stones Athletic	26	4	6	16	40	76	14
Stansted	26	5	3	18	34	90	13

Harris Lebus changed their name to Finsbury and moved to the Parthenon
League. Royal Ordnance Factories moved to the Kent Amateur League.
Division One closed down, leaving just one senior division.

1956-57

Cray Wanderers	28	23	2	3	118	54	48
Cheshunt	28	19	3	6	88	56	41
Aveley	28	18	4	6	75	46	40
Basildon Town	28	17	5	6	90	45	39
Eton Manor	28	16	5	7	78	49	37
East Ham United	28	16	2	10	79	47	34
Ruislip Manor	28	12	8	8	67	53	32
Wingate	28	13	5	10	74	50	31
Harlow Town	28	12	3	13	49	88	27
Chingford	28	9	4	15	57	82	22
Beckenham	28	8	1	19	51	89	17
West Thurrock Athletic	28	8	1	19	42	81	17
Barkingside	28	6	4	18	38	66	16
Epping Town	28	4	4	20	46	89	12
Pitsea United	28	3	1	24	29	86	7

Aveley moved to the Delphian League. Tilbury joined from the Corinthian
League and Willesden joined from the Parthenon League.

1957-58

Cray Wanderers	30	23	5	2	102	35	51
Eton Manor	30	21	3	6	92	49	45
Tilbury	30	17	5	8	67	61	39
East Ham United	30	17	4	9	98	54	38
Wingate	30	16	4	10	81	60	36
West Thurrock Athletic	30	12	11	7	53	39	35
Ruislip Manor	30	14	6	10	73	68	34
Harlow Town	30	13	6	11	82	69	32
Willesden	30	11	9	10	58	48	31
Basildon Town	30	13	4	13	65	83	30
Barkingside	30	11	6	13	54	52	28
Cheshunt	30	10	4	16	59	76	24
Chingford	30	6	5	19	44	91	17
Epping Town	30	4	8	18	47	76	16
Beckenham	30	4	5	21	55	104	13
Pitsea United	30	2	7	21	36	101	11

Ruislip Manor moved to the Spartan League.
Arlesey Town joined from the Parthenon League.

1958-59

Tilbury	28	22	3	3	78	27	47
East Ham United	28	22	1	5	96	36	45
Cray Wanderers	28	15	4	9	79	51	34
Eton Manor	28	15	3	10	68	57	33
West Thurrock Athletic	28	15	3	10	52	45	33
Willesden	28	11	7	10	51	43	29
Barkingside	28	11	5	12	55	53	27
Epping Town	28	10	6	12	44	56	26
Wingate	28	10	5	13	52	50	25
Cheshunt	28	10	5	13	75	80	25
Arlesey Town	28	11	2	15	66	67	24
Basildon Town	28	8	5	15	58	84	21
Beckenham	28	7	6	15	42	81	20
Harlow Town	28	8	1	19	40	72	17
Chingford	28	5	4	19	43	97	14

Cray Wanderers, Eton Manor, Willesden and Cheshunt all moved to become
founder members of the Aetolian League and Basildon Town and
Chingford moved to the Parthenon League. Hatfield Town and Baldock
Town joined from the Parthenon League and Bletchley United joined from
the South Midlands League.

1959-60

Tilbury	22	17	4	1	85	22	38
East Ham United	22	11	6	5	61	34	28
Wingate	22	11	6	5	57	43	28
West Thurrock Athletic	22	10	6	6	43	30	26
Arlesey Town	22	10	4	8	47	52	24
Barkingside	22	9	5	8	46	36	23
Bletchley United	22	7	9	6	50	42	23
Harlow Town	22	7	9	6	36	33	23
Epping Town	22	7	7	8	42	38	21
Beckenham	22	5	3	14	33	56	13
Hatfield Town	22	3	5	14	24	74	11
Baldock Town	22	2	2	18	19	83	6

Arlesey Town lost the lease of their ground and ceased activity for a season. They subsequently joined the South Midlands League in 1961. Chingford and Chalfont St. Peter joined from the Parthenon League.

1960-61

Tilbury	24	21	2	1	90	21	44
East Ham United	24	14	1	9	60	38	29
Harlow Town	24	12	5	7	38	30	29
Bletchley United	24	10	7	7	55	44	27
Hatfield Town	24	11	4	9	44	51	26
Epping Town	24	11	2	11	59	43	24
Beckenham	24	9	6	9	47	53	24
Wingate	24	11	2	11	46	53	24
Baldock Town	24	9	6	9	38	46	24
Chingford	24	7	3	14	37	53	17
Barkingside	24	6	4	14	33	61	16
Chalfont St. Peter	24	6	3	15	42	72	15
West Thurrock Athletic	24	5	3	16	26	50	13

Harlow Town moved to the Delphian League, Bletchley United moved to the United Counties League and Beckenham moved to the Aetolian League. Amersham Town joined from the Hellenic League, Chalfont National joined from the Parthenon League and Slade Green Athletic joined from the Kent Amateur League.

1961-62

Tilbury	24	19	5	0	105	26	43
Chingford	24	17	2	5	66	27	36
West Thurrock Athletic	24	14	2	8	51	36	30
East Ham United	24	11	5	8	55	43	27
Chalfont St. Peter	24	11	4	9	47	53	26
Wingate	24	9	5	10	48	35	23
Slade Green Athletic	24	8	7	9	49	60	23
Barkingside	24	9	3	12	55	47	21
Baldock Town	24	8	2	14	44	64	18
Epping Town	24	6	5	13	27	51	17
Amersham Town	24	7	3	14	49	87	17
Hatfield Town	24	5	6	13	32	51	16
Chalfont National	24	5	5	14	42	90	15

Tilbury and Wingate both moved to the Delphian League, East Ham United moved to the Aetolian League, Chalfont St. Peter moved to the Spartan League and Amersham Town moved to the Hellenic League. Northern Polytechnic joined from the Nemean Amateur League and London Transport joined from the Parthenon League.

1962-63

Chingford	20	16	0	4	56	25	32
West Thurrock Athletic	20	15	1	4	66	36	31
Barkingside	20	14	1	5	50	23	29
Epping Town	20	11	2	7	58	39	24
Slade Green Athletic	20	10	4	6	53	41	24
Northern Polytechnic	20	10	2	8	36	33	22
Hermes	20	8	2	10	61	49	18
Ulysses	20	6	4	10	31	33	16
Baldock Town	20	6	3	11	38	55	15
London Transport	20	1	4	15	14	62	6
Hatfield Town	20	1	1	18	23	89	3
					486	485	

Chingford moved to the Metropolitan League and Baldock Town moved to the South Midlands League. Woolwich Polytechnic and R.O.F. Sports both joined from the Kent Amateur League and Tunbridge Wells Rangers Reserves joined from the Seanglian League. The existing division reverted to being the Premier Division as Division One was re-formed. Amongst the clubs in the new Division One were C.A.V. Athletic, Canvey Island and Harold Hill from the Parthenon Legaue.

1963-64

Premier Division

Epping Town	22	15	3	4	65	29	33
Hermes	22	14	2	6	52	32	30
R.O.F. Sports	22	11	3	8	46	38	25
West Thurrock Athletic	22	11	2	9	56	30	24
Barkingside	22	9	6	7	53	37	24
Woolwich Polytechnic	22	10	3	9	51	39	23
Hatfield Town	22	10	2	10	45	41	22
Ulysses	22	9	4	9	30	31	22
Northern Polytechnic	22	7	6	9	42	51	20
Slade Green Athletic	22	7	5	10	45	63	19
Tunbridge Wells Rangers Reserves	22	8	2	12	45	63	18
London Transport	22	1	2	19	30	106	4

Division One

C.A.V. Athletic	26	22	1	3	107	22	45
Highfield	26	20	3	3	102	18	43
Harold Hill	26	16	6	4	89	39	38
Metropolitan Police Reserves	26	16	2	8	80	47	34
Epping Town Reserves	26	15	4	7	75	53	34
Canvey Island	26	14	3	9	65	35	31
Rolenmill	26	14	2	10	76	51	30
Chingford Reserves	26	8	4	14	52	67	20
Ulysses Reserves	26	8	2	16	39	72	18
Barkingside Reserves	26	7	3	16	51	98	17
Hatfield Town Reserves	26	7	2	17	44	81	16
Hermes Reserves	26	6	2	18	34	75	14
Slade Green Athletic Reserves	26	6	1	19	39	113	13
Northern Polytechnic Reserves	26	4	3	19	25	106	11
					878	877	

In 1964, the London League merged with the Aetolian League to form the Greater London League. All first teams playing in either division joined the Greater London League with the exception of Northern Polytechnic.

AETOLIAN LEAGUE

The Aetolian League was formed in 1959 by a group of former Kent League clubs left behind when many of their fellow members were elected to a new division of the Southern League. This forced those remaining clubs to recruit members for a new league from further afield.

The 14 founder members were: Chatham Town, Deal Town, Faversham Town, Herne Bay, Sheppey United, Snowdown Colliery Welfare and Whitstable Town, all from the Kent League; Cheshunt, Cray Wanderers, Eton Manor and Willesden, all from the London League; Ford United recently formed by a merger of Ford Sports from the London Business Houses League and Briggs Sports of the Spartan League; Crockenhill from the Kent Amateur League and Charlton Athletic "A".

There was also a Second Division of 12 clubs which consisted mainly of the reserve sides of the First Division clubs and included just one first team, Medway Corinthians. There was no promotion or relegation between the two divisions.

1959-60

Division One

Ford United	26	15	7	4	65	32	37
Deal Town	26	14	7	5	68	35	35
Faversham Town	26	11	8	7	64	39	30
Chatham Town	26	12	6	8	48	40	30
Eton Manor	26	10	7	9	55	49	27
Crockenhill	26	9	9	8	47	55	27
Snowdown Colliery Welfare	26	8	10	8	47	47	26
Willesden	26	11	2	13	53	50	24
Cray Wanderers	26	11	2	13	52	56	24
Cheshunt	26	10	4	12	47	68	24
Charlton Athletic "A"	26	8	7	11	52	53	23
Herne Bay	26	8	7	11	51	61	23
Sheppey United	26	8	4	14	48	68	20
Whitstable Town	26	5	4	17	29	73	14

Whitstable Town moved to the Kent Amateur League.

Division Two

Ford United Reserves	22	15	4	3	63	25	34
Willesden Reserves	22	14	5	3	57	27	33
Faversham Town Reserves	22	14	2	6	66	38	30
Cray Wanderers Reserves	22	13	2	7	70	45	28
Snowdown Colliery Welfare Res.	22	9	4	9	49	41	22
Sheppey United Reserves	22	8	2	12	44	54	18
Medway Corinthians	22	5	8	9	43	53	18
Herne Bay Reserves	22	8	2	12	42	62	18
Deal Town Reserves	22	7	4	11	48	72	18
Canterbury City Reserves	22	8	1	13	38	53	17
Eton Manor Reserves	22	6	3	13	26	50	15
Cheshunt Reserves	22	5	3	14	39	65	13

Orpington Athletic joined from the Kent Amateur League.

1960-61

Division One

Snowdown Colliery Welfare	24	18	2	4	81	40	38
Ford United	24	14	3	7	68	39	31
Cray Wanderers	24	14	3	7	79	52	31
Herne Bay	24	11	9	4	50	40	31
Sheppey United	24	9	6	9	62	60	24
Cheshunt	24	10	3	11	44	53	23
Crockenhill	24	9	4	11	55	61	22
Chatham Town	24	10	2	12	37	50	22
Eton Manor	24	9	3	12	43	53	21
Deal Town	24	8	5	11	52	66	21
Faversham Town	24	5	8	11	45	60	18
Charlton Athletic "A"	24	5	6	13	39	58	16
Willesden	24	5	4	15	33	56	14

Beckenham joined from the London League.

Division Two

Faversham Town Reserves	20	12	3	5	45	29	27
Sheppey United Reserves	20	12	3	5	54	39	27
Willesden Reserves	20	12	1	7	59	38	25
Eton Manor Reserves	20	10	3	7	35	27	23
Ford United Reserves	20	9	4	7	50	34	22
Cheshunt Reserves	20	9	3	8	37	35	21
Herne Bay Reserves	20	9	2	9	49	38	20
Orpington Athletic	20	8	3	9	51	43	19
Snowdown Colliery Welfare Res.	20	7	1	12	38	53	15
Medway Corinthians	20	6	3	11	37	63	15
Deal Town Reserves	20	3	0	17	24	80	6

Medway Corinthians left the League.

1961-62

Division One

Ford United	26	16	6	4	61	22	38
Snowdown Colliery Welfare	26	14	6	6	71	51	34
Cheshunt	26	13	6	7	67	49	32
Sheppey United	26	14	4	8	64	57	32
Deal Town	26	13	5	8	56	50	31
Herne Bay	26	14	2	10	53	55	30
Cray Wanderers	26	12	4	10	60	52	28
Willesden	26	10	4	12	60	61	24
Chatham Town	26	10	4	12	55	57	24
Charlton Athletic "A"	26	11	0	15	65	58	22
Eton Manor	26	6	9	11	41	41	21
Faversham Town	26	8	4	14	47	69	20
Beckenham	26	8	4	14	36	64	20
Crockenhill	26	3	2	21	48	98	8

Cheshunt moved to the Spartan League.
East Ham United joined from the London League.

Division Two

Ford United Reserves	20	13	4	3	72	12	30
Cray Wanderers Reserves	20	13	4	3	63	31	30
Herne Bay Reserves	20	13	3	4	58	29	29
Faversham Town Reserves	20	11	5	4	69	34	27
Willesden Reserves	20	7	5	8	28	34	19
Orpington Athletic	20	6	5	9	42	44	17
Beckenham Reserves	20	8	1	11	36	67	17
Snowdown Colliery Welfare Res.	20	5	5	10	34	45	15
Eton Manor Reserves	20	6	3	11	41	55	15
Sheppey United Reserves	20	6	2	12	41	64	14
Deal Town Reserves	20	2	3	15	12	81	7

1962-63

Division One

Cray Wanderers	24	16	5	3	58	30	37
Chatham Town	24	16	3	5	69	24	35
Herne Bay	24	14	6	4	59	27	34
Ford United	24	16	2	6	54	29	34
Deal Town	24	11	5	8	47	41	27
Faversham Town	24	10	5	9	43	36	25
Eton Manor	24	10	4	10	46	35	24
Snowdown Colliery Welfare	24	9	6	9	38	34	24
Sheppey United	24	6	7	11	48	61	19
East Ham United	24	9	1	14	34	59	19
Willesden	24	6	4	14	33	50	16
Beckenham	24	4	2	18	29	76	10
Crockenhill	24	3	2	19	28	84	8

Deal Town moved to the Southern League and Willesden moved to the Spartan League. Whitstable Town joined from the Seanglian League.

Division Two

Herne Bay Reserves	21	14	4	3	57	31	32
Rainham Town Reserves	22	13	5	4	55	33	31
Ford United Reserves	22	13	4	5	63	23	30
Faversham Town Reserves	22	11	2	9	56	40	24
Sheppey United Reserves	22	9	5	8	60	49	23
Eton Manor Reserves	22	10	3	9	47	41	23
East Ham United Reserves	22	9	4	9	41	61	22
Orpington Athletic	21	9	2	10	43	46	20
Snowdown Colliery Welfare Res.	22	6	6	10	36	44	18
Beckenham Reserves	22	7	4	11	30	52	18
Willesden Reserves	22	3	5	14	28	54	11
Deal Town Reserves	22	3	4	15	31	73	10

Orpington Athletic vs Herne Bay Reserves was not played.

1963-64

Division One

Chatham Town	22	16	4	2	73	24	36
Herne Bay	22	16	3	3	70	23	35
Cray Wanderers	22	15	5	2	76	27	35
Sheppey United	22	12	4	6	64	49	28
Ford United	22	12	2	8	55	38	26
Snowdown Colliery Welfare	21	9	1	11	43	37	19
Faversham Town	22	8	2	12	38	51	18
Beckenham	21	5	4	12	36	69	14
Eton Manor	22	6	2	14	25	62	14
Crockenhill	22	6	1	15	39	65	13
Whitstable Town	22	5	2	15	38	76	12
East Ham United	22	5	2	15	36	72	12

Beckenham vs Snowdown Colliery Welfare was abandoned but was not subsequently replayed.
Chatham Town moved to the Metropolitan League and Herne Bay moved to the Athenian League.

Division Two

Herne Bay Reserves	24	18	2	4	80	26	38
Ford United Reserves	24	16	4	4	64	39	36
Sheppey United Reserves	23	14	4	5	63	34	32
Rainham Town Reserves	24	12	6	6	66	45	30
Eton Manor Reserves	24	13	2	9	55	42	28
Chatham Town Reserves	24	11	5	8	56	51	27
Eastbourne United Reserves	23	11	4	8	45	48	26
Cray Wanderers Reserves	24	10	2	12	48	47	22
Orpington Athletic	24	9	3	12	54	61	21
Snowdown Colliery Welfare Res.	24	7	1	16	35	59	15
Beckenham Reserves	24	6	2	16	49	69	14
East Ham United Reserves	24	3	5	16	38	87	11
Faversham Town Reserves	24	3	4	17	33	78	10

Sheppey United Reserves and Eastbourne United reserves met only once.
Orpington Athletic moved to the Parthenon League.

In 1964, the Aetolian League merged with the London League to form the Greater London League and the remaining Aetolian League clubs joined the new league.

SPARTAN LEAGUE

The Spartan League was formed in1907 after Mr J.R. Schumacher successfully canvassed support for his belief that a new league would be welcomed by those southern amateur clubs of suitable status who had been unable to gain entry to the 2-year-old Isthmian League. Of the 6 founder members, Bromley, Dulwich Hamlet, Nunhead and West Norwood had been playing in the South Suburban League, Shepherd's Bush had been playing in the Great Western Suburban League and Leytonstone had been playing in the South Essex League.

1907-08

Bromley	10	8	0	2	24	12	16
Shepherd's Bush	10	6	1	3	23	13	13
Nunhead	10	5	2	3	18	13	12
Dulwich Hamlet	10	4	1	5	19	20	9
West Norwood	10	4	1	5	15	19	9
Leytonstone	10	0	1	9	12	34	1

All 6 members left after being elected to the Isthmian League for the 1908-09 season and the Spartan League was re-formed with two 6-club divisions, Eastern and Western. Chelmsford and South Weald of the South Essex League joined the Eastern Division as did Hitchin Town of the South-Eastern League while for St. Albans City, this was their first league competition. Walthamstow Grange of the London League also joined the Eastern Division while Summerstown were also playing in the London League but joined the Western Division.

1908-09

Eastern Division

Luton Clarence	8	4	1	3	41	20	9
Walthamstow Grange	8	4	1	3	19	15	9
Chelmsford	8	4	0	4	24	30	8
South Weald	8	4	0	4	19	22	8
St. Albans City	8	2	2	4	12	28	4

St. Albans City had 2 points deducted for fielding an ineligible player. Hitchin Town resigned and disbanded on 28th October. Their only game was a 6-0 defeat away to Walthamstow Grange. Chelmsford and South Weald left but continued in the South Essex League and Walthamstow Grange left but continued in the London League.

Western Division

Aylesbury United	10	7	2	1	31	14	16
Summerstown	10	6	1	3	25	16	13
2nd Coldstream Guards	10	4	3	3	21	17	11
Newportonians	10	2	4	4	19	22	8
Marlow	10	2	3	5	12	28	7
Clapham	10	2	1	7	16	27	5

Summerstown left the League but continued to play in the London League and Clapham also left the League

Championship play-off:

Aylesbury United vs Luton Clarence   4-1
(played at Aylesbury)

1909-10

The Spartan League again re-formed, with two divisions, "A" and "B". The four remaining ex-Western Division clubs joined Division "A" except for Newportonians, who joined Division "B" along with the two remaining ex-Eastern Division clubs. Division "A" was made up to 7 clubs by the election of Chesham Generals and Redhill from the South-Eastern League, Wimbledon from the West Surrey League, and Sutton Court. Division "B" was made up to 6 clubs by the election of 3rd Grenadier Guards, East Ham and the re-formed Hitchin Town.

Division "A"

2nd Coldstream Guards	12	9	1	2	47	13	19
Aylesbury United	12	6	3	3	25	21	15
Redhill	12	5	3	4	34	17	13
Sutton Court	12	4	3	5	19	25	11
Marlow	12	3	4	5	15	34	10
Wimbledon	12	3	2	7	17	31	8
Chesham Generals	12	3	2	7	16	32	8

Wimbledon disbanded and Redhill moved to the South Suburban League.

Division "B"

St. Albans City	10	9	0	1	59	7	18
Luton Clarence	10	7	0	3	37	14	14
3rd Grenadier Guards	10	6	0	4	21	26	12
East Ham	10	4	0	6	15	32	8
Hitchin Town	10	3	0	7	12	29	6
Newportonians	10	1	0	9	8	44	2

Luton Clarence left the League.

Championship play-off:

St. Albans City vs 2nd Coldstream Guards   0-1
(played at St. Albans)

1910-11

The League re-formed with a single division. The existing members were joined by Tufnell Park who also continued in the London League.

2nd Coldstream Guards	18	14	3	1	49	11	31
Tufnell Park	18	13	3	2	57	19	29
St. Albans City	18	14	1	3	60	24	29
Aylesbury United	18	8	5	5	37	27	21
Chesham Generals	18	8	3	7	37	35	19
East Ham	18	7	4	7	36	36	18
3rd Grenadier Guards	18	6	2	10	33	46	14
Sutton Court	18	4	4	10	31	36	12
Newportonians	18	1	1	16	14	52	3
Hitchin Town	18	1	2	15	17	74	2
					371	360	

Hitchin Town had 2 points deducted and subsequently disbanded at the end of the season.
Marlow resigned from the League and their record was deleted when it stood as: 7   1   0   6   4   27   2
Marlow joined the Great Western Suburban League for the 1911-12 season. Cambridge United joined from the East Anglian League, Polytechnic joined from the South Suburban League and Tufnell Spartans joined as a new club after being formed by members of Tufnell Park's reserve team.

1911-12

St. Albans City	24	21	1	2	71	15	43
2nd Coldstream Guards	24	19	3	2	71	19	41
Sutton Court	24	13	1	10	56	41	27
Chesham Generals	24	11	4	9	53	41	26
Aylesbury United	24	10	5	9	49	44	25
3rd Grenadier Guards	24	10	5	9	37	41	25
Cambridge United	24	11	2	11	50	46	24
East Ham	24	10	4	10	25	29	24
1st Grenadier Guards	24	9	4	11	48	53	22
Polytechnic	24	8	3	13	28	70	19
Tufnell Spartans	24	6	4	14	35	53	16
Tufnell Park	24	2	8	14	28	51	12
Newportonians	24	3	2	19	25	73	8

Tufnell Park moved to the Athenian League. Woodford Albion joined from the Olympian League and Watford Orient joined as a newly formed club.

1912-13

2nd Coldstream Guards	24	20	1	3	73	20	41
St. Albans City	24	16	4	4	77	24	36
Chesham Generals	24	16	4	4	60	29	36
Newportonians	24	13	3	8	48	37	29
Watford Orient	24	11	6	7	72	44	28
Aylesbury United	24	11	2	11	40	61	24
Cambridge United	24	9	5	10	39	52	23
Tufnell Spartans	24	9	3	12	39	47	21
Polytechnic	24	6	9	9	26	40	21
3rd Grenadier Guards	24	8	3	13	34	53	19
Sutton Court	24	6	5	13	47	59	17
East Ham	24	5	1	18	19	57	11
Woodford Albion	24	2	2	20	19	70	6

East Ham moved to the Middlesex League and Cambridge United moved to the Haverhill & District League. Tunbridge Wells joined from the Isthmian League.

1913-14

Chesham Generals	22	17	2	3	48	21	36
Aylesbury United	22	16	2	4	69	27	34
St. Albans City	22	16	3	3	54	16	33
2nd Coldstream Guards	22	11	3	8	41	33	25
Newportonians	22	7	6	9	26	38	20
Polytechnic	22	7	5	10	35	41	19
Great Western Railway	22	8	3	11	36	50	19
Sutton Court	22	7	4	11	41	51	18
Tufnell Spartans	22	6	5	11	34	41	17
Woodford Albion	22	7	3	12	25	39	17
Tunbridge Wells	22	5	6	11	22	41	16
Watford Orient	22	3	2	17	25	58	6

St. Albans City and Watford Orient each had 2 points deducted.
Tunbridge Wells disbanded. Wycombe Wanderers joined from the Great Western Suburban League and West London Old Boys joined from the London League.

1914-19

Wycombe Wanderers and 2nd Coldstream Guards resigned during August 1914. On 5th September 1914, Chesham Generals beat West London Old Boys 4-0 but that was the only game played before 11th September when the league held a special meeting and suspended all activities until the end of the war.

In 1917, Chesham Generals merged with Chesham Town of the Athenian League to form Chesham United who replaced Chesham Generals in the Spartan League. After the war, Watford Orient moved to the Watford & District League and Woodford Albion did not re-form. West London Old Boys did not re-form until 1920 when they joined the Athenian League. Hoffman Athletic joined from the Essex & Suffolk Border League and G.E.R. (Romford) joined as a newly formed club.

1919-20

Wycombe Wanderers	20	18	1	1	114	24	37
G.E.R. (Romford)	20	17	1	2	88	19	35
St. Albans City	20	13	1	6	64	35	27
Aylesbury United	20	12	2	6	49	31	26
Chesham United	20	11	2	7	58	46	24
Sutton Court	20	11	2	7	54	45	24
Polytechnic	19	6	0	13	42	65	12
Tufnell Spartans	20	5	1	14	41	70	11
Newportonians	20	4	3	13	25	67	11
Great Western Railway	20	3	0	17	20	79	6
2nd Coldstream Guards	19	2	1	16	19	93	5

2nd Coldstream Guards vs Polytechnic was not played.
Hoffman Athletic resigned from the League and their record was deleted when it stood as:

	2	0	1	1	3	10	1

Tufnell Spartans changed their name to Wood Green. St. Albans City moved to the Athenian League and Hoffman Athletic moved to the South Essex League. 2nd Coldstream Guards were transferred to Salisbury and were replaced in the Spartan League by 1st Welsh Guards. Slough joined from the Great Western Suburban League and Leavesden Mental Hospital joined from the Hertfordshire County League.

1920-21

A Second Division was formed, mostly for reserve sides but it also included Cubitts Recreation Club from the Aylesbury & District League, R.A.F. (Uxbridge), a newly formed club, and Lighthouse Old Boys (Streatham).

Division One

Wycombe Wanderers	22	19	2	1	108	29	40
Slough	22	16	4	2	73	20	36
Chesham United	22	16	3	3	88	34	35
G.E.R. (Romford)	22	15	1	6	67	36	31
Leavesden Mental Hospital	22	13	4	5	42	29	30
Wood Green	22	9	5	8	55	54	23
Aylesbury United	22	10	1	11	44	52	21
Sutton Court	22	6	4	12	47	71	16
Polytechnic	22	5	5	12	37	53	15
Great Western Railway	22	2	2	18	34	100	6
1st Welsh Guards	22	1	4	17	24	79	6
Newportonians	22	0	5	17	16	78	5

Wycombe Wanderers moved to the Isthmian League and Newportonians also left the League. Walthamstow Avenue joined from the South Essex League, Hertford Town joined from the Middlesex League, Railway Clearing House joined from the Northern Suburban League, Leyland Motors joined as a newly formed club and Finchley also joined. Great Western Railway were relegated to Division Two.

Division Two

Wycombe Wanderers Reserves	14	10	3	1	61	18	23
Cubitts Recreation Club	14	9	2	3	37	29	20
Chesham United Reserves	14	6	2	6	44	39	14
Aylesbury United Reserves	14	6	2	6	32	35	14
Polytechnic Reserves	14	7	0	7	25	34	14
R.A.F. (Uxbridge)	14	4	1	9	31	41	9
Slough Reserves	14	4	1	9	26	43	9
G.E.R. (Romford) Reserves	14	3	3	8	21	39	9
						277	278

Lighthouse Old Boys (Streatham) resigned from the League before playing a game.
R.A.F. (Uxbridge) moved to the Great Western Suburban League.

1921-22

Division One

Chesham United	26	19	2	5	113	29	40
Slough	26	18	4	4	101	40	40
Finchley	26	15	4	7	67	36	34
Leavesden Mental Hospital	26	11	11	4	44	31	33
Aylesbury United	26	14	3	9	69	55	31
G.E.R. (Romford)	26	14	2	10	70	47	30
Wood Green	26	12	5	9	56	46	29
Walthamstow Avenue	26	13	2	11	56	47	28
Polytechnic	26	10	6	10	53	49	26
Hertford Town	26	10	5	11	58	65	25
Sutton Court	26	9	3	14	59	70	21
Leyland Motors	26	5	3	18	24	76	13
Railway Clearing House	26	4	4	18	25	105	12
1st Welsh Guards	26	1	0	25	22	121	2

Sutton Court changed their name to Old Latymerians. Leyland Motors moved to the Surrey Senior League and 1st Welsh Guards also left. Maidenhead United joined from the Great Western Suburban League, Wealdstone joined from the London League and Old Lyonians joined from the Middlesex League. Railway Clearing House were relegated to Division Two.

Division Two

Chesham United Reserves	18	14	1	3	71	23	29
Aylesbury United Reserves	18	12	3	3	47	25	27
Finchley Reserves	18	10	5	3	56	28	25
Cubitts Recreation Club	18	11	2	5	75	26	24
G.E.R. (Romford) Reserves	18	8	3	7	43	42	19
Slough Reserves	18	8	1	9	40	49	17
Walthamstow Avenue Reserves	18	7	2	9	40	40	16
Polytechnic Reserves	18	4	2	12	24	56	10
Great Western Railway	18	4	1	13	20	57	9
Leyland Motors Reserves	18	1	2	15	25	95	4

Cubitts Recreation club disbanded. Wendover joined from the Aylesbury & District League and Apsley joined from the Hertfordshire County League. Berkhamsted Town also joined from the Hertfordshire County League after changing their name from Berkhamsted Comrades. Leighton United joined as a new club formed by a merger of The Comrades and Morgan's Ivy Leaf.

1922-23

Division One

Chesham United	26	20	3	3	106	29	43
Wealdstone	26	16	3	7	72	44	35
Slough	26	15	2	9	68	51	32
Maidenhead United	26	12	8	6	47	51	32
Leavesden Mental Hospital	26	13	3	10	50	40	29
G.E.R. (Romford)	26	13	3	10	52	50	29
Walthamstow Avenue	26	11	6	9	58	51	28
Wood Green	26	11	2	13	48	68	24
Hertford Town	26	9	5	12	55	50	23
Aylesbury United	26	10	2	14	47	60	22
Old Latymerians	26	10	0	16	65	80	20
Polytechnic	26	8	4	14	35	59	20
Finchley	26	6	3	17	36	61	15
Old Lyonians	26	3	6	17	38	83	12

Finchley moved to the London League. R.A.F. (Uxbridge) re-joined.

Division Two

Wendover	24	16	5	3	70	27	37
Leighton United	24	16	3	5	75	38	35
Chesham United Reserves	24	15	3	6	75	47	33
Slough Reserves	24	13	5	6	49	37	31
Aylesbury United Reserves	24	12	3	9	60	40	27
Railway Clearing House	24	11	5	8	67	51	27
Wealdstone Reserves	24	10	3	11	39	46	23
Finchley Reserves	24	7	8	9	38	47	22
Berkhamsted Town	22	9	2	11	45	50	20
Walthamstow Avenue Reserves	22	8	2	12	42	55	18
Apsley	24	8	1	15	45	58	17
Polytechnic Reserves	24	4	3	17	32	71	11
Great Western Railway	24	3	1	20	20	90	7

Berkhamsted Town and Walthamstow Avenue Reserves did not meet. Amersham Town and L.M.S. Railway joined the League.

1923-24

Division One

Leavesden Mental Hospital	25	21	1	3	66	14	43
G.E.R. (Romford)	26	18	3	5	77	29	39
Slough	26	18	2	6	90	33	38
Aylesbury United	26	15	4	7	70	46	34
Wealdstone	26	14	5	7	71	47	33
Chesham United	26	14	1	11	68	59	29
Wood Green	26	10	3	13	67	62	23
Hertford Town	26	11	1	14	61	77	23
Polytechnic	26	11	1	14	42	57	23
Walthamstow Avenue	25	7	8	10	52	65	22
Old Lyonians	26	7	4	15	39	68	18
Maidenhead United	26	7	3	16	44	67	17
R.A.F. (Uxbridge)	26	5	3	18	39	95	13
Old Latymerians	26	3	1	22	33	100	7

Leavesden Mental Hospital vs Walthamstow Avenue was not played. Old Lyonians moved to the Southern Amateur League and Leavesden Mental Hospital moved to the Great Western Suburban League. Botwell Mission and Staines Lagonda both joined from the Great Western Suburban League.

Division Two

Leighton United	26	21	3	2	92	34	45
Apsley	26	16	5	5	78	40	37
Wealdstone Reserves	26	15	4	7	72	42	34
Amersham Town	26	16	1	9	73	46	33
Berkhamsted Town	26	15	3	8	59	46	33
Slough Reserves	26	12	5	9	55	51	29
Walthamstow Avenue Reserves	26	12	3	11	63	51	27
Aylesbury United Reserves	25	10	2	13	56	67	22
Chesham United Reserves	26	9	4	13	69	76	20
L.M.S. Railway	26	9	2	15	51	89	20
Wendover	26	7	4	15	37	60	18
Railway Clearing House	26	5	5	16	53	63	15
Polytechnic Reserves	26	7	1	18	33	70	15
Great Western Railway	25	3	6	16	32	70	12

Chesham United Reserves had 2 points deducted. Aylesbury United Reserves vs Great Western Railway was not played. Great Western Railway left the League. Bush Hill Park joined from the London League and Lyons Club joined from the West London Sports League.

1924-25

Division One

Chesham United	26	21	4	1	107	32	46
G.E.R. (Romford)	26	17	4	5	74	37	38
Slough	26	17	1	8	90	54	35
Botwell Mission	26	13	3	10	69	42	29
Staines Lagonda	26	12	5	9	57	51	29
Walthamstow Avenue	26	11	5	10	59	64	27
R.A.F. (Uxbridge)	26	11	5	10	56	73	27
Hertford Town	26	11	4	11	56	52	26
Maidenhead United	26	9	2	15	55	66	20
Wealdstone	26	7	6	13	48	62	20
Wood Green	26	8	4	14	53	73	20
Aylesbury United	26	8	3	15	51	79	19
Old Latymerians	26	6	3	17	37	81	15
Polytechnic	26	5	3	18	38	84	13

Staines Lagonda changed their name to Staines Town.
Colchester Town joined from the Essex & Suffolk Border League.

Division Two

Wealdstone Reserves	26	20	1	5	87	35	41
Lyons Club	26	17	4	5	74	32	38
Apsley	26	15	5	6	81	38	36
Berkhamsted Town	26	16	3	7	76	46	35
Bush Hill Park	26	15	3	8	62	35	33
Walthamstow Avenue Reserves	26	13	3	10	58	46	29
Wendover	26	12	4	10	43	43	28
Chesham United Reserves	26	11	5	10	69	55	27
Amersham Town	26	11	3	12	55	52	25
Leighton United	26	11	1	14	67	69	23
Railway Clearing House	26	6	3	17	34	76	15
Polytechnic Reserves	26	6	3	17	25	59	15
L.M.S. Railway	26	5	2	19	43	103	12
Aylesbury United Reserves	26	3	1	22	30	115	7

L.M.S. Railway left the League.

1925-26

Division One

G.E.R. (Romford)	28	21	3	4	97	47	45
Botwell Mission	28	20	3	5	109	51	43
Maidenhead United	28	19	3	6	122	64	41
Walthamstow Avenue	28	17	5	6	103	61	39
Chesham United	28	15	6	7	100	59	36
Slough	28	17	2	9	81	50	36
Wealdstone	28	13	4	11	79	80	30
Aylesbury United	28	13	2	13	78	86	28
Wood Green	28	9	7	12	62	83	25
Colchester Town	28	10	4	14	63	94	24
Staines Town	28	6	6	16	75	90	18
Polytechnic	28	6	5	17	60	98	17
Hertford Town	28	7	3	18	73	120	17
Old Latymerians	28	5	2	21	59	111	12
R.A.F. (Uxbridge)	28	4	1	23	74	141	9

R.A.F. (Uxbridge) were relegated to Division Two (A).

Division Two was expanded and split into two sections, "A" and "B".
Great Western Railway rejoined the League while amongst the new clubs
were Hoddesdon Town and Ware from the Hertfordshire County League,
Hazells (Aylesbury) from the Aylesbury & District League and Metropolitan
Railway from the London League.

Division Two (A)

Lyons Club	23	18	3	2	99	28	39
Chesham United Reserves	24	16	3	5	80	48	35
Leighton United	24	13	4	7	98	49	30
Hazells (Aylesbury)	24	11	6	7	72	65	28
Apsley	24	13	2	9	72	42	28
Slough Reserves	24	10	5	9	73	67	25
Wealdstone Reserves	24	10	4	10	81	69	24
Wendover	24	10	3	11	54	69	23
Berkhamsted Town	24	8	5	11	74	69	21
Amersham Town	24	8	4	12	56	82	20
R.A.F. (Halton)	24	8	1	15	58	78	17
Aylesbury United Reserves	23	7	1	15	47	75	15
Metropolitan Railway	24	2	1	21	41	164	5

Lyons Club vs Aylesbury United Reserves was not played.
Metropolitan Railway left the League. Watford Old Boys and Yiewsley both
joine
d from the Great Western Suburban League.

Division Two (B)

Artillery College	24	19	1	4	117	45	39
Ware	24	17	1	6	81	43	35
Bush Hill Park	24	13	6	5	64	44	32
Great Western Railway	24	13	5	6	69	53	31
Finchley Reserves	24	13	4	7	58	44	30
Hoddesdon Town	24	13	3	8	80	58	29
Walthamstow Avenue Reserves	24	12	2	10	69	46	26
Northampton Polytechnic	24	11	2	11	68	55	24
Hertford Town Reserves	24	9	3	12	55	92	21
G.E.R. (Romford) Reserves	24	6	4	14	54	90	16
Polytechnic Reserves	24	5	3	16	45	83	13
Wood Green Reserves	24	6	0	18	60	98	12
Railway Clearing House	24	2	0	22	32	101	4

Railway Clearing House and Bush Hill Park both left the League.
1st Scots Guards and R.A.S.C. Feltham joined the League and Great Western
Railway transferred to Division Two (A).

Division Two Championship play-off:

Lyons Club vs Artillery College   6-1
(played at Aylesbury United)

1926-27

Division One

Maidenhead United	28	19	5	4	116	51	43
Chesham United	28	18	4	6	83	41	40
Slough	28	18	4	6	96	53	40
Wealdstone	28	18	3	7	100	67	39
G.E.R. (Romford)	28	16	4	8	85	68	36
Walthamstow Avenue	28	15	5	8	97	61	35
Botwell Mission	28	14	2	12	71	57	30
Aylesbury United	28	12	5	11	79	86	29
Lyons Club	28	10	8	10	64	55	28
Staines Town	28	10	6	12	84	93	26
Colchester Town	28	10	4	14	64	74	24
Wood Green	28	6	3	19	57	92	15
Hertford Town	28	6	3	19	61	119	15
Polytechnic	28	4	6	18	54	102	14
Old Latymerians	28	1	4	23	38	130	6

Old Latymerians were relegated to Division Two (B).

Division Two (A)

Berkhamsted Town	24	21	0	3	97	33	42
Apsley	24	18	2	4	96	40	38
Wealdstone Reserves	24	14	3	7	85	53	31
Leighton United	24	13	2	9	78	61	28
R.A.F. (Halton)	24	11	5	8	50	56	27
R.A.F. (Uxbridge)	24	10	3	11	80	81	23
Chesham United Reserves	24	9	4	11	69	55	22
Aylesbury United Reserves	24	9	4	11	57	63	22
Hazells (Aylesbury)	24	8	2	14	61	75	18
Watford Old Boys	24	8	1	15	57	112	17
Great Western Railway	24	7	2	15	46	80	16
Amersham Town	24	7	1	16	62	89	15
Wendover	24	6	1	17	56	96	13

Yiewsley resigned from the League and their record was deleted when it stood as:

	7	1	0	6	13	30	2

Lyons Club vs Aylesbury United Reserves was not played.
Pinner joined from the Harrow & District League.

Division Two (B)

Ware	23	19	2	2	114	39	40
Slough Reserves	24	16	2	6	81	38	34
1st Scots Guards	23	13	4	6	55	43	30
Walthamstow Avenue Reserves	24	12	5	7	77	51	29
Hoddesdon Town	24	13	3	8	72	62	29
Finchley Reserves	24	12	4	8	56	49	28
Artillery College	24	12	2	10	57	56	26
R.A.S.C. Feltham	24	10	2	12	56	64	22
Northampton Polytechnic	24	8	4	12	53	61	20
Polytechnic Reserves	24	7	5	12	39	56	19
G.E.R. (Romford) Reserves	24	5	4	15	45	75	14
Hertford Town Reserves	24	3	5	16	48	96	11
Wood Green Reserves	24	3	2	19	30	93	8

1st Scots Guards vs Ware was not played.
Artillery College, 1st Scots Guards and R.A.S.C. Feltham all left the League.
Haywards Sports (Enfield) joined from the Northern Intermediate League,
Lea Bridge Gas joined from the Walthamstow & District League and
Welwyn Garden City joined from the Bedford & District League.

Division Two Championship play-off:

Berkhamsted Town vs Ware	4-0
(played at Apsley)	

1927-28

Division One

Botwell Mission	28	22	2	4	106	46	46
Walthamstow Avenue	28	21	2	5	106	48	44
Chesham United	28	18	5	5	101	44	41
Wealdstone	28	17	3	8	90	62	37
Maidenhead United	28	15	4	9	103	57	34
G.E.R. (Romford)	28	11	8	9	74	67	30
Staines Town	28	12	6	10	65	76	30
Aylesbury United	28	13	2	13	89	69	28
Slough	28	12	4	12	82	73	28
Lyons Club	28	11	6	11	47	58	28
Colchester Town	28	10	5	13	69	74	25
Berkhamsted Town	28	10	1	17	52	82	21
Hertford Town	28	7	4	17	52	114	18
Polytechnic	28	2	2	24	33	101	6
Wood Green	28	2	0	26	46	144	4

Wealdstone moved to the Athenian League.

Division Two (A)

Leighton United	24	19	4	1	92	29	42
R.A.F. (Uxbridge)	24	15	6	3	90	29	36
R.A.F. (Halton)	24	14	3	7	63	55	31
Watford Old Boys	24	13	3	8	86	57	29
Hazells (Aylesbury)	24	12	4	8	59	55	28
Wealdstone Reserves	24	11	3	10	64	69	25
Chesham United Reserves	24	10	2	12	63	58	22
Great Western Railway	24	8	5	11	52	71	21
Apsley	24	8	4	12	74	72	20
Amersham Town	24	8	3	13	58	89	19
Aylesbury United Reserves	24	5	5	14	35	68	15
Pinner	24	5	3	16	42	78	13
Wendover	24	4	3	17	47	95	11

Leighton United, R.A.F. (Uxbridge) and Watford Old Boys were all promoted
to Division One. Farnham United joined from the Slough, Windsor &
District League and Marlow joined from the Reading & District League.
Division Two (A) changed its name to Division Two (West).

Division Two (B)

Hoddesdon Town	24	18	5	1	82	30	41
Walthamstow Avenue Reserves	24	18	4	2	85	32	40
Haywards Sports (Enfield)	24	17	2	5	73	37	36
Finchley Reserves	24	13	6	5	71	46	32
Welwyn Garden City	24	15	2	7	64	43	32
Lea Bridge Gas	24	14	2	8	59	39	30
Ware	24	8	3	13	50	68	19
Wood Green Reserves	24	8	1	15	71	89	17
Polytechnic Reserves	24	8	0	16	48	73	16
Slough Reserves	24	7	2	15	51	82	16
G.E.R. (Romford) Reserves	24	4	4	16	42	77	12
Old Latymerians	24	5	1	18	56	93	11
Northampton Polytechnic	24	4	2	18	46	89	10

Haywards Sports (Enfield) were promoted to Division One. Old Latymerians
moved to the Southern Olympian League. Poplar Rovers joined from the
Walthamstow & District League, Waltham Comrades joined from the
Northern Suburban League, Hitchin Town joined as a newly formed club
and Ministry of Health also joined.
Division Two (B) changed its name to Division Two (East).
Slough Reserves transferred to Division Two (West).

Division Two Championship play-off:

Leighton Town vs Hoddesdon Town	4-0
(played at Berkhamsted Town)	

1928-29

Division One was enlarged and split into two sections, West and East.

Division One West: Three new members joined – Cowley (Oxford) from
the Oxfordshire Senior League, Egham from the Surrey Senior League and
Leagrave & District from the Northamptonshire League.

Division One East: Five new members joined – Chadwell Heath from the
South Essex League having changed their name from Eagle Park,
Brentwood & Warley also from the South Essex League, Crittall Athletic
from the Essex & Suffolk Border League, Eastbourne Old Comrades from
the Sussex County League and Metropolitan Police.

Division One (West)

Aylesbury United	24	18	2	4	113	47	38
Maidenhead United	24	17	3	4	91	45	37
Botwell Mission	24	14	4	6	87	64	32
Chesham United	24	14	1	9	78	50	29
Staines Town	24	11	5	8	73	62	27
Egham	24	10	7	7	45	49	27
Leighton United	24	11	2	11	59	66	24
Slough	24	10	2	12	54	65	22
Cowley (Oxford)	24	6	7	11	47	59	19
Leagrave & District	24	7	4	13	45	65	18
Berkhamsted Town	24	5	7	12	42	64	17
Watford Old Boys	24	5	3	16	48	91	13
R.A.F. (Uxbridge)	24	3	3	18	32	87	7

R.A.F. (Uxbridge) had 2 points deducted.
Botwell Mission changed their name to Hayes.

Division One (East)

Metropolitan Police	24	18	2	4	97	29	38
Walthamstow Avenue	24	18	2	4	94	34	38
Brentwood & Warley	24	17	2	5	64	42	36
Colchester Town	24	13	3	8	75	63	29
G.E.R. (Romford)	24	12	5	7	54	47	29
Crittall Athletic	24	14	1	9	59	54	29
Lyons Club	24	10	6	8	57	46	26
Haywards Sports (Enfield)	24	9	3	12	54	54	21
Eastbourne Old Comrades	24	6	4	14	55	69	16
Wood Green	24	7	1	16	47	89	15
Hertford Town	24	3	7	14	48	83	13
Chadwell Heath	24	5	3	16	44	83	13
Polytechnic	24	4	1	19	36	91	9

Championship play-off:

Metropolitan Police vs Aylesbury United	8-0

(played at Maidenhead United)

The two Division One geographical sections were re-organised into a new Premier Division and Division One.

Premier Division: Formed by the top 6 teams plus Slough from Division One (West) together with Wood Green and the top 7 (excluding Walthamstow Avenue) from Division One (East).

Division One: Formed by those clubs in the two Division One geographical sections who were excluded from the Premier Division, apart from Walthamstow Avenue who moved to the Athenian League, and Chadwell Heath who also left. These two were replaced by Hounslow from the London League and Windsor & Eton from the Athenian League.

Division Two (West)

R.A.F. (Halton)	24	17	3	4	77	48	37
Chesham United Reserves	24	17	3	4	91	34	35
Apsley	24	13	5	6	78	54	31
Maidenhead United Reserves	24	12	7	5	69	50	31
Farnham United	24	13	2	9	61	33	28
Great Western Railway	24	12	1	11	61	64	25
Hazells (Aylesbury)	24	12	1	11	51	64	25
Marlow	24	11	2	11	66	68	24
Amersham Town	24	9	1	14	69	77	19
Slough Reserves	24	7	4	13	53	78	18
Aylesbury United Reserves	24	7	2	15	67	67	16
Pinner	24	5	4	15	48	84	14
Wendover	24	2	3	19	40	110	7

Chesham United Reserves had 2 points deducted.
Apsley were promoted to Division One. Wendover moved to the Aylesbury & District League and Amersham Town moved to the Chesham League. Willesden Polytechnic joined from the Neasden & District League.

Division Two (East)

Metropolitan Police Reserves	24	19	4	1	113	37	42
Hitchin Town	24	19	3	2	111	45	41
Ware	24	13	8	3	76	33	34
Lea Bridge Gas	24	15	2	7	68	38	30
Walthamstow Avenue Reserves	24	13	4	7	78	60	30
Welwyn Garden City	24	12	3	9	60	41	27
Poplar Rovers	24	11	2	11	52	63	24
Finchley Reserves	24	9	3	12	52	70	21
Hoddesdon Town	24	7	5	12	63	75	19
Waltham Comrades	24	5	3	16	37	80	13
Ministry of Health	24	5	3	16	33	93	13
Polytechnic Reserves	24	4	1	19	33	76	9
Northampton Polytechnic	24	3	1	20	34	99	7

Lea Bridge Gas had 2 points deducted.
Hitchin Town were promoted to Division One. Northampton Polytechnic moved to the Nemean Amateur League. Letchworth Town joined from the Bedfordshire County League and Bishop's Stortford joined from the Stansted & District League. Poplar Rovers changed their name to the Rovers (Poplar).

Division Two Championship play-off:

Metropolitan Police Reserves vs R.A.F. (Halton)	8-0

(played at Hitchin Town)

1929-30

Premier Division

Metropolitan Police	26	19	4	3	98	26	42
Chesham United	26	19	2	5	85	51	40
Hayes	26	15	6	5	92	53	36
Egham	26	16	2	8	58	28	34
Maidenhead United	26	14	3	9	86	56	31
Brentwood & Warley	26	12	5	9	61	50	29
Crittall Athletic	26	12	4	10	62	44	28
Slough	26	10	4	12	57	63	24
Colchester Town	26	9	6	11	53	71	24
Aylesbury United	26	8	3	15	64	96	19
Lyons Club	26	7	5	14	35	70	19
G.E.R. (Romford)	26	6	2	18	43	83	14
Wood Green	26	4	5	17	39	90	13
Staines Town	26	3	5	18	35	87	9

Staines Town had 2 points deducted.
Hayes moved to the Athenian League. G.E.R. (Romford) changed their name to G.E.R. (Loughton) and Wood Green changed their name to Wood Green Town.

Division One

Haywards Sports (Enfield)	26	22	2	2	105	33	46
Hounslow	26	20	3	3	105	37	43
Hertford Town	26	15	3	8	76	44	33
Hitchin Town	26	15	1	10	103	44	31
Cowley (Oxford)	26	9	9	8	54	58	27
Windsor & Eton	26	13	2	11	79	75	26
Eastbourne Old Comrades	26	11	3	12	55	65	25
Leighton United	26	10	3	13	63	75	23
Berkhamsted Town	26	10	3	13	63	76	23
Apsley	26	10	2	14	62	65	22
Leagrave & District	26	10	2	14	38	67	22
Watford Old Boys	26	8	1	17	56	78	17
R.A.F. (Uxbridge)	26	6	5	15	40	95	17
Polytechnic	26	1	5	20	31	118	7

Windsor & Eton had 2 points deducted.
R.A.F. (Uxbridge) were relegated to Division Two (West) and Polytechnic were relegated to Division Two (East). Waterlows (Dunstable) joined from the Bedfordshire County League. Watford Old Boys changed their name to Watford Spartans.

Division Two (West)

Marlow	24	17	3	4	75	38	37
Chesham United Reserves	24	16	2	6	89	48	34
Hayes Reserves	24	15	3	6	92	49	33
Willesden Polytechnic	24	12	3	9	79	64	27
Pinner	24	11	1	12	64	72	23
Maidenhead United Reserves	24	9	4	11	63	73	22
Farnham United	24	8	5	11	39	63	21
Aylesbury United Reserves	24	9	3	12	58	73	21
Great Western Railway	24	6	7	11	55	59	19
Hazells (Aylesbury)	24	8	3	13	50	75	19
R.A.F. (Halton)	24	10	1	13	76	85	19
Berkhamsted Town Reserves	24	7	3	14	56	70	17
Slough Reserves	24	8	2	14	50	77	16

R.A.F. (Halton) and Slough Reserves each had 2 points deducted.

Division Two (East)

Letchworth Town	22	17	3	2	94	38	37
Lea Bridge Gas	22	13	6	3	64	35	32
Hoddesdon Town	22	12	5	5	57	46	29
Ware	22	12	4	6	72	41	28
Hitchin Town Reserves	22	10	4	8	58	40	24
Waltham Comrades	22	9	6	7	61	42	24
Bishop's Stortford	22	9	4	9	57	45	22
Lyons Club Reserves	22	9	2	11	43	69	20
The Rovers (Poplar)	22	5	6	11	31	49	16
Welwyn Garden City	22	6	4	12	39	63	16
Polytechnic Reserves	22	5	3	14	39	77	13
Ministry of Health	22	1	1	20	21	91	3

Ministry of Health left and Callender Athletic joined.

Division Two Championship play-off:

Marlow vs Letchworth Town	1-0
(played at Aylesbury United)	

1930-31

Premier Division

Haywards Sports (Enfield)	26	21	2	3	130	48	44
Maidenhead United	26	18	5	3	94	39	41
Metropolitan Police	26	18	2	6	78	39	38
Chesham United	26	16	2	8	81	53	34
Slough	26	14	2	10	73	53	30
Hounslow	26	11	4	11	59	59	26
Brentwood & Warley	26	11	3	12	56	57	25
Crittall Athletic	26	10	6	10	54	67	24
Colchester Town	26	10	0	16	72	81	20
Aylesbury United	26	10	1	15	71	98	19
Egham	26	8	2	16	42	67	18
Lyons Club	26	8	1	17	55	88	17
Wood Green Town	26	8	1	17	47	87	17
G.E.R. (Loughton)	26	3	1	22	41	117	7

Crittall Athletic and Aylesbury United each had 2 points deducted for fielding an ineligible player.
Haywards Sports (Enfield) lost their ground in Lincoln Road, Ponders End for building and subsequently disbanded. Hounslow changed their name to Hounslow Town.

Division One

Windsor & Eton	26	21	1	4	108	49	43
Hitchin Town	26	19	3	4	103	36	41
Waterlows (Dunstable)	26	17	3	6	101	48	37
Marlow	26	16	2	8	80	53	34
Apsley	26	12	5	9	77	64	29
Berkhamsted Town	26	12	5	9	49	55	29
Eastbourne Old Comrades	26	10	5	11	78	87	25
Letchworth Town	26	9	6	11	80	75	24
Staines Town	26	9	4	13	76	81	22
Leighton Town	26	10	0	16	79	76	20
Cowley (Oxford)	26	9	4	13	65	82	20
Hertford Town	26	9	2	15	58	94	20
Leagrave & District	26	4	4	18	37	109	12
Watford Spartans	26	2	2	22	33	115	6

Cowley (Oxford) had 2 points deducted for fielding an ineligible player.
Leagrave & District left and Watford Spartans were relegated to Division One (West). Luton Amateur joined from the South Midlands League.

Division Two (West)

Maidenhead United Reserves	26	17	3	6	92	57	37
Chesham United Reserves	26	16	4	6	111	68	36
Hazells (Aylesbury)	26	12	7	7	91	50	31
Farnham United	26	12	7	7	78	47	31
Pinner	26	14	3	9	86	86	31
Berkhamsted Town Reserves	26	12	6	8	70	70	30
Aylesbury United Reserves	26	11	5	10	70	71	27
R.A.F. (Halton)	26	10	5	11	86	79	25
Egham Reserves	26	9	6	11	64	75	24
R.A.F. (Uxbridge)	26	11	2	13	99	79	22
Hounslow Reserves	26	9	2	15	78	91	20
Slough Reserves	26	7	5	14	73	106	19
Willesden Polytechnic	26	4	7	15	53	110	15
Great Western Railway	26	5	4	17	39	101	10

R.A.F. (Uxbridge) had 2 points deducted for fielding an ineligible player.
Great Western Railway had 4 points deducted for fielding ineligible players.
Great Western Railway left and Henley Town joined from the Reading & District League.

Division Two (East)

Callender Athletic	26	23	3	0	117	23	49
Lea Bridge Gas	26	18	4	4	105	53	40
Bishop's Stortford	26	19	0	7	81	40	38
Hitchin Town Reserves	26	16	2	8	103	67	32
Hoddesdon Town	26	12	4	10	87	65	26
Polytechnic	26	10	5	11	65	73	25
Welwyn Garden City	26	11	4	11	68	83	24
The Rovers (Poplar)	26	8	4	14	31	42	20
Ware	26	7	5	14	48	72	19
Hertford Town Reserves	26	7	5	14	57	91	19
Apsley Reserves	26	6	6	14	52	87	18
Letchworth Town Reserves	26	8	1	17	52	75	17
Waltham Comrades	26	8	1	17	57	97	17
Lyons Club Reserves	26	6	2	18	44	99	14

Hitchin Town Reserves, Hoddesdon Town and Welwyn Garden City each had 2 points deducted for fielding an ineligible player. R.A.F. Henlow joined from the South Midlands League and Bushey United also joined. Apsley Reserves transferred to Division Two (West).

Division Two Championship play-off:

Callender Athletic vs Maidenhead United Reserves	4-1
(played at Egham)	

1931-32

Premier Division

Maidenhead United	24	18	3	3	76	37	39
Slough	24	13	7	4	68	46	33
Chesham United	24	14	4	6	64	41	32
Hitchin Town	24	13	3	8	56	46	29
Colchester Town	24	12	3	9	71	63	27
Metropolitan Police	24	11	4	9	57	40	26
Aylesbury United	24	11	4	9	64	50	26
Hounslow Town	24	11	1	12	48	54	23
Windsor & Eton	24	8	2	14	57	66	18
Brentwood & Warley	24	7	4	13	49	66	18
Crittall Athletic	24	7	3	14	44	72	17
Lyons Club	*24*	*6*	*4*	*14*	*36*	*65*	*16*
Egham	*24*	*3*	*2*	*19*	*39*	*83*	*8*

Division One

Callender Athletic	**24**	**17**	**4**	**3**	**91**	**48**	**38**
Apsley	**24**	**18**	**1**	**5**	**80**	**40**	**37**
Waterlows (Dunstable)	24	16	3	5	82	53	35
Wood Green Town	24	16	2	6	81	48	34
Marlow	24	15	3	6	89	46	33
Berkhamsted Town	24	10	2	12	55	55	22
Leighton United	24	9	3	12	59	72	21
Letchworth Town	24	8	4	12	61	68	20
Staines Town	24	7	4	13	59	81	18
Hertford Town	24	7	3	14	57	74	17
Cowley (Oxford)	24	3	7	14	46	78	13
Eastbourne Old Comrades	24	5	3	16	44	101	13
Luton Amateur	24	3	5	16	23	63	11

G.E.R. (Loughton) resigned and disbanded and their record was deleted when it stood as follows: 3 1 0 2 8 26 2
Wood Green Town were promoted to the Premier Division along with Callender Athletic and Apsley. Eastbourne Old Comrades moved to the Brighton, Hove & District League as Eastbourne Comrades.

Division Two (West)

R.A.F. (Uxbridge)	**26**	**20**	**5**	**1**	**110**	**38**	**45**
Chesham United Reserves	26	21	0	5	98	42	42
Hazells (Aylesbury)	26	13	5	8	74	50	31
Maidenhead United Reserves	26	13	3	10	86	68	29
Aylesbury United Reserves	26	14	0	12	78	68	28
Watford Spartans	26	13	2	11	64	65	28
R.A.F. (Halton)	26	11	3	12	77	76	25
Apsley Reserves	26	11	3	12	62	72	25
Henley Town	26	9	5	12	55	78	23
Farnham United	26	9	4	13	59	69	22
Egham Reserves	26	9	4	13	45	59	22
Pinner	26	7	4	15	55	89	18
Berkhamsted Town Reserves	26	7	4	15	51	88	18
Willesden Polytechnic	26	2	4	20	45	97	8

Watford Spartans changed their name to Watford British Legion.

Division Two (East)

Bishop's Stortford	**26**	**21**	**1**	**4**	**80**	**26**	**43**
Hoddesdon Town	**26**	**19**	**5**	**2**	**110**	**43**	**43**
Lea Bridge Gas	26	17	1	8	98	72	35
Polytechnic	26	16	3	7	63	55	35
Hitchin Town Reserves	26	14	2	10	80	67	30
R.A.F. (Henlow)	26	14	1	11	79	67	29
Bushey United	26	13	1	12	96	72	27
Waltham Comrades	26	12	3	11	75	67	27
Letchworth Town Reserves	26	12	1	13	63	61	25
Lyons Club Reserves	26	8	2	16	46	79	18
Ware	26	6	4	16	41	68	16
Hertford Town Reserves	26	6	1	19	51	110	13
Welwyn Garden City	26	5	2	19	52	105	12
The Rovers (Poplar)	26	3	5	18	36	78	11

The Rovers (Poplar) moved to the Leytonstone & District League.
Harlow Town joined from the East Hertfordshire League, Hoxton Manor joined from the Northern Suburban League and Stevenage Town joined from the South Midlands League.

Division Two Championship play-off:

R.A.F. (Uxbridge) vs Bishop's Stortford 2-0
(played at Hitchin Town)

1932-33

Premier Division

Chesham United	26	18	1	7	78	39	37
Slough	26	17	0	9	81	58	34
Callender Athletic	26	14	5	7	62	46	33
Crittall Athletic	26	14	3	9	55	48	31
Colchester Town	26	14	3	9	78	75	31
Metropolitan Police	26	15	0	11	56	42	30
Brentwood & Warley	26	13	2	11	61	61	28
Hitchin Town	26	11	5	10	74	57	27
Maidenhead United	26	11	4	11	68	64	26
Wood Green Town	26	9	3	14	47	67	21
Hounslow Town	26	9	3	14	46	70	21
Windsor & Eton	26	8	1	17	46	75	17
Apsley	*26*	*5*	*4*	*17*	*59*	*77*	*14*
Aylesbury United	*26*	*6*	*2*	*18*	*41*	*73*	*14*

Division One

Waterlows (Dunstable)	**26**	**18**	**5**	**3**	**98**	**43**	**41**
Letchworth Town	**26**	**17**	**3**	**6**	**79**	**41**	**37**
Hertford Town	26	14	8	4	78	43	36
Bishop's Stortford	26	14	3	9	66	52	31
Hoddesdon Town	26	12	6	8	85	52	30
Berkhamsted Town	26	9	8	9	61	51	26
Staines Town	26	9	6	11	42	72	24
Cowley (Oxford)	26	10	3	13	39	47	23
Egham	26	9	5	12	51	63	23
Marlow	26	8	5	13	71	71	21
Lyons Club	26	8	3	15	53	78	19
R.A.F. (Uxbridge)	26	8	3	15	61	84	19
Leighton United	26	7	5	14	54	96	19
Luton Amateur	*26*	*6*	*3*	*17*	*28*	*73*	*15*

Egham Town moved to the Surrey Senior League.
Luton Amateur were relegated to Division Two (East).
Shepherds Bush joined from the London League.

Division Two (West)

Maidenhead United Reserves	26	18	2	6	110	68	38
Chesham United Reserves	26	17	4	5	107	67	38
Pinner	26	15	7	4	106	57	37
Hazells (Aylesbury)	26	14	8	4	95	61	36
Farnham United	26	15	5	6	72	61	35
R.A.F. (Halton)	26	12	5	9	89	68	29
Watford British Legion	26	12	3	11	81	72	27
Slough Reserves	26	11	4	11	86	74	26
Henley Town	26	11	4	11	58	59	26
Aylesbury United Reserves	26	6	5	15	64	79	17
Berkhamsted Town Reserves	26	6	4	16	56	76	16
Apsley Reserves	26	6	2	18	59	111	14
Egham Reserves	26	5	3	18	50	108	13
Willesden Polytechnic	26	6	0	20	45	117	12

West Kensington Sports Club joined the League.

Division Two (East)

Hoxton Manor	26	24	1	1	102	29	49
R.A.F. (Henlow)	26	16	3	7	87	48	35
Bushey United	26	16	3	7	98	68	35
Hitchin Town Reserves	26	15	3	8	100	64	33
Stevenage Town	26	13	2	11	85	71	28
Lea Bridge Gas	26	13	2	11	82	73	28
Harlow Town	26	12	2	12	71	88	26
Polytechnic	26	10	4	12	68	73	24
Ware	26	10	3	13	62	66	23
Letchworth Town Reserves	26	10	2	14	60	79	22
Hertford Town Reserves	26	8	4	14	57	79	20
Welwyn Garden City	26	4	6	16	39	82	14
Lyons Club Reserves	26	5	4	17	35	82	14
Waltham Comrades	26	5	3	18	43	87	13

Waltham Comrades left the League and Lyons Club Reserves transferred to Division Two (West). Jurgens (Purfleet) joined from the London League and Saffron Walden Town joined from the North Essex League.

Division Two Championship play-off:

Hoxton Manor vs Maidenhead United Reserves	4-1
(played at Letchworth Town)	

1933-34

Premier Division

Maidenhead United	26	19	6	1	84	40	44
Chesham United	26	17	3	6	68	38	37
Metropolitan Police	26	15	2	9	79	59	32
Waterlows (Dunstable)	26	13	3	10	72	54	29
Hitchin Town	26	12	4	10	52	46	28
Letchworth Town	26	11	5	10	49	49	27
Windsor & Eton	26	11	5	10	49	66	27
Colchester Town	26	11	4	11	71	66	26
Crittall Athletic	26	10	5	11	56	59	25
Callender Athletic	26	11	1	14	50	54	23
Slough	26	9	3	14	57	64	21
Hounslow Town	26	8	3	15	48	69	19
Brentwood & Warley	26	5	4	17	34	68	14
Wood Green Town	*26*	*5*	*2*	*19*	*34*	*71*	*12*

Brentwood & Warley moved to the South Essex League.

Division One

Apsley	26	19	5	2	93	37	43
Hoxton Manor	26	17	4	5	85	37	38
Hertford Town	26	17	3	6	85	43	37
Aylesbury United	26	15	2	9	96	52	32
Berkhamsted Town	26	12	5	9	80	59	29
Leighton United	26	14	1	11	84	75	29
Hoddesdon Town	26	12	3	11	57	59	27
Lyons Club	26	10	6	10	65	68	26
Marlow	26	11	2	13	66	73	24
Bishop's Stortford	26	7	5	14	50	58	19
Acton	26	5	6	15	34	62	16
Cowley (Oxford)	26	6	3	17	50	73	15
R.A.F. (Uxbridge)	26	6	3	17	35	137	15
Staines Town	26	6	2	18	43	90	14

Shepherds Bush changed their name to Acton during December 1933. Cowley (Oxford) moved to the Oxfordshire Senior League and R.A.F. (Uxbridge) also left the League.

Division Two (West)

Henley Town	24	21	2	1	85	29	44
Hazells (Aylesbury)	24	18	3	3	94	35	39
Chesham United Reserves	24	15	3	6	83	52	33
Willesden Polytechnic	24	13	4	7	59	36	30
Pinner	24	11	4	9	51	44	26
Maidenhead United Reserves	24	12	2	10	82	78	26
Aylesbury United Reserves	24	11	3	10	66	55	25
Watford British Legion	24	7	5	12	68	79	19
Farnham United	24	8	2	14	58	96	18
R.A.F. (Halton)	24	6	5	13	50	64	17
Apsley Reserves	24	6	3	15	53	95	15
West Kensington Sports Club	24	4	5	15	35	61	13
Lyons Club Reserves	24	3	1	20	35	95	7

Slough Reserves resigned from the League and their record was deleted when it stood as follows: 12 3 2 7 17 36 8
Lyons Club Reserves transferred to Division Two (East).
Willesden Polytechnic changed their name to Kilburn Polytechnic.
Roxonian joined from the Harrow & District League.

Division Two (East)

Jurgens (Purfleet)	26	21	3	2	102	21	45
Stevenage Town	26	21	3	2	100	44	45
R.A.F. (Henlow)	26	21	2	3	110	26	44
Polytechnic	26	13	6	7	81	47	32
Lea Bridge Gas	26	14	1	11	82	70	29
Bushey United	26	11	6	9	80	74	28
Ware	26	11	6	9	39	47	28
Bishop's Stortford Reserves	26	8	3	15	48	77	19
Saffron Walden Town	26	7	5	14	42	71	19
Harlow Town	26	9	1	16	51	87	19
Letchworth Town Reserves	26	7	3	16	72	82	17
Hertford Town Reserves	26	6	3	17	39	89	15
Luton Amateur	26	5	4	17	38	70	14
Welwyn Garden City	26	3	4	19	22	111	10

R.A.F. (Henlow) were promoted to Division One along with Jurgens (Purfleet). The 2nd Coldstream Guards joined the League.

Division Two Championship play-off:

Henley Town vs Jurgens (Purfleet)	4-1
(played at Maidenhead United)	

1934-35

Premier Division

Hitchin Town	26	18	2	6	65	33	38
Metropolitan Police	26	17	4	5	53	28	38
Hoxton Manor	26	13	3	10	61	39	29
Slough	26	13	3	10	67	52	29
Waterlows (Dunstable)	26	13	2	11	85	67	28
Maidenhead United	26	10	7	9	63	61	27
Colchester Town	26	12	2	12	60	76	26
Callender Athletic	26	8	8	10	42	42	24
Chesham United	26	9	6	11	55	64	24
Windsor & Eton	26	10	2	14	47	52	22
Crittall Athletic	26	8	6	12	48	59	22
Letchworth Town	26	10	2	14	45	69	22
Apsley	26	10	1	15	57	65	21
Hounslow Town	*26*	*6*	*2*	*18*	*39*	*80*	*14*

Colchester Town and Crittall Athletic both left to join the new Eastern Counties League. Cambridge Town joined from the Southern Amateur League.

Division One

Jurgens (Purfleet)	26	19	3	4	70	34	41
Aylesbury United	26	19	2	5	80	34	40
Hoddesdon Town	26	11	10	5	74	43	32
Hertford Town	26	15	2	9	79	65	32
Marlow	26	13	6	7	70	60	32
Wood Green Town	26	14	1	11	75	72	29
Berkhamsted Town	26	13	2	11	84	43	28
Lyons Club	26	12	1	13	65	60	25
R.A.F. (Henlow)	26	10	4	12	66	68	24
Henley Town	26	10	3	13	51	61	23
Bishop's Stortford	26	8	3	15	44	77	19
Acton	26	5	6	15	49	78	16
Leighton United	26	4	7	15	28	79	15
Staines Town	26	2	4	20	34	95	8

Staines Town left the League and Acton disbanded.

Division Two (West)

Pinner	26	17	6	3	89	37	40
Marlow Reserves	26	17	3	6	101	53	37
R.A.F. (Halton)	26	16	4	6	64	40	36
Hazells (Aylesbury)	26	16	2	8	80	56	34
Chesham United Reserves	26	12	4	10	74	63	28
Apsley Reserves	26	11	4	11	56	79	26
Aylesbury United Reserves	26	11	3	12	63	75	25
Maidenhead United Reserves	26	9	6	11	64	70	24
Roxonian	26	9	5	12	50	67	23
Watford British Legion	26	9	4	13	64	59	22
Farnham United	26	8	5	13	50	64	21
Kilburn Polytechnic	26	9	3	14	51	68	21
West Kensington Sports Club	26	4	6	16	38	67	14
Windsor & Eton Reserves	26	6	1	19	55	101	13

R.A.F. (Halton) were promoted to Division One along with Pinner.
Amersham Town joined from the Chesham League.
West Kensington Sports Club disbanded.

Division Two (East)

Lea Bridge Gas	26	18	3	5	101	40	39
Stevenage Town	26	18	4	4	79	36	38
Welwyn Garden City	26	18	0	8	77	50	36
Ware	26	12	7	7	47	38	31
Bushey United	26	12	3	11	94	75	27
Harlow Town	26	12	2	12	61	47	26
2nd Coldstream Guards	26	10	6	10	56	51	26
Saffron Walden Town	26	10	5	11	75	58	25
Polytechnic	26	10	5	11	57	64	25
Letchworth Town Reserves	26	10	3	13	46	66	23
Hertford Town Reserves	26	9	2	15	50	69	20
Luton Amateur	26	8	2	16	50	84	18
Bishop's Stortford Reserves	26	8	1	17	55	87	17
Lyons Club Reserves	26	4	3	19	30	113	11

Stevenage Town had 2 points deducted for fielding an ineligible player.
Welwyn Garden City ceased playing for 2 years because they could not take
a gate at their ground. Dagenham Cables joined from the Dagenham &
District League.

Division Two Championship play-off:

Lea Bridge Gas vs Pinner	4-1

(played at Wood Green Town)

1935-36

Premier Division

Waterlows (Dunstable)	26	19	2	5	107	55	40
Callender Athletic	26	18	2	6	90	61	38
Cambridge Town	26	13	4	9	67	53	30
Chesham United	26	13	4	9	59	57	30
Metropolitan Police	26	13	2	11	57	52	28
Hitchin Town	26	10	5	11	60	59	25
Maidenhead United	26	10	5	11	67	72	25
Windsor & Eton	26	11	2	13	63	55	24
Slough	26	11	2	13	53	67	24
Hoxton Manor	26	10	3	13	49	50	23
Jurgens (Purfleet)	26	11	1	14	54	66	23
Aylesbury United	26	8	5	13	51	77	21
Apsley	*26*	*8*	*2*	*16*	*68*	*83*	*18*
Letchworth Town	*26*	*7*	*1*	*18*	*59*	*97*	*15*

Division One

Hoddesdon Town	26	20	1	5	105	48	41
Lyons Club	26	16	5	5	66	41	37
Wood Green Town	26	16	3	7	89	56	35
Henley Town	26	14	3	9	93	77	31
Hertford Town	26	13	4	9	68	48	30
Berkhamsted Town	26	14	2	10	72	59	30
Hounslow Town	26	13	1	12	71	60	27
Marlow	26	11	3	12	67	72	25
R.A.F. (Henlow)	26	9	4	13	52	71	22
Lea Bridge Gas	26	8	6	12	57	84	22
Bishop's Stortford	26	9	2	15	72	72	20
Leighton United	26	8	3	15	48	90	19
Pinner	*26*	*6*	*2*	*18*	*44*	*80*	*14*
R.A.F. (Halton)	*26*	*5*	*1*	*20*	*59*	*105*	*11*

Pinner and R.A.F. (Halton) were both relegated to Division One (West).

Division Two (West)

Hazells (Aylesbury)	24	19	4	1	101	27	42
Windsor & Eton Reserves	24	10	8	6	80	55	28
Marlow Reserves	24	12	4	8	87	67	28
Maidenhead United Reserves	24	13	2	9	56	46	28
Aylesbury United Reserves	24	10	5	9	56	55	25
Amersham Town	24	10	4	10	60	61	24
Apsley Reserves	24	9	6	9	60	63	24
Farnham United	24	10	4	10	64	70	24
Kilburn Polytechnic	24	9	4	11	67	79	22
Chesham United Reserves	24	8	5	11	66	68	21
Watford British Legion	24	8	3	13	75	92	19
Berkhamsted Town Reserves	24	7	3	14	38	80	17
Roxonian	24	3	4	17	28	74	10

Watford British Legion moved to the Hertfordshire County League,
Farnham United moved to the Slough & Windsor Junior League and
Kilburn Polytechnic also left the League. Wendover joined from the
Aylesbury & District League.

Division Two (East)

Letchworth Town Reserves	24	18	4	2	83	30	40
Dagenham Cables	24	16	4	4	65	32	36
Polytechnic	24	15	4	5	67	41	34
Saffron Walden Town	24	13	6	5	71	47	32
2nd Coldstream Guards	24	13	5	6	62	45	31
Stevenage Town	24	12	4	8	65	44	28
Harlow Town	24	8	9	7	62	63	25
Bushey United	24	7	6	11	75	84	20
Bishop's Stortford Reserves	24	6	6	12	48	64	18
Ware	24	6	4	14	34	64	16
Hertford Town Reserves	24	4	7	13	42	66	15
Luton Amateur	24	5	2	17	38	71	12
Lyons Club Reserves	24	2	1	21	33	94	5

Polytechnic were promoted to Division One. Bushey United and the 2nd Coldstream Guards transferred to Division Two (West). Epping Town joined from the South Essex League, Sawbridgeworth Town joined from the East Hertfordshire League, White City joined from the Mid-Hertfordshire League and the 1st Coldstream Guards also joined the League.

Division Two Championship play-off:

Letchworth Town Reserves vs Hazells (Aylesbury)	4-1
(played at Apsley)	

1936-37

Premier Division

Metropolitan Police	26	16	4	6	90	47	36
Windsor & Eton	26	16	3	7	81	60	35
Waterlows (Dunstable)	26	16	2	8	99	65	34
Hitchin Town	26	14	4	8	66	44	32
Callender Athletic	26	15	2	9	76	58	32
Cambridge Town	26	11	8	7	59	49	30
Hoxton Manor	26	11	3	12	56	54	25
Chesham United	26	10	4	12	55	68	24
Maidenhead United	26	10	2	14	67	67	22
Aylesbury United	26	9	4	13	57	81	22
Lyons Club	26	9	3	14	57	77	21
Slough	26	8	3	15	62	73	19
Hoddesdon Town	*26*	*6*	*5*	*15*	*51*	*82*	*17*
Jurgens (Purfleet)	*26*	*7*	*1*	*18*	*44*	*95*	*15*

Jurgens (Purfleet) left the League.

Division One

Henley Town	**26**	**17**	**3**	**6**	**93**	**48**	**37**
Letchworth Town	**26**	**16**	**4**	**6**	**68**	**51**	**36**
Hounslow Town	26	14	6	6	61	41	34
Bishop's Stortford	26	14	4	8	63	48	32
Apsley	26	13	5	8	79	60	31
Wood Green Town	26	13	4	9	64	45	30
Polytechnic	26	13	3	10	54	49	29
Marlow	26	11	4	11	76	71	26
Berkhamsted Town	26	10	3	13	51	61	23
Lea Bridge Gas	26	10	3	13	70	85	23
Hertford Town	26	8	3	15	63	63	19
Leighton United	26	6	6	14	46	82	18
R.A.F. (Henlow)	*26*	*5*	*4*	*17*	*39*	*74*	*14*
Hazells (Aylesbury)	*26*	*5*	*2*	*19*	*33*	*82*	*12*

R.A.F. (Henlow) were relegated to Division Two (East) and Hazells (Aylesbury) were relegated to Division Two (West).
Uxbridge joined from the Athenian League.

Division Two (West)

Wendover	**26**	**18**	**2**	**6**	**79**	**50**	**38**
Windsor & Eton Reserves	26	17	3	6	92	47	37
2nd Coldstream Guards	26	16	1	9	65	49	33
Pinner	26	14	4	8	72	44	32
Roxonian	26	11	4	11	56	61	26
Apsley Reserves	26	10	5	11	70	61	25
Berkhamsted Town Reserves	26	10	5	11	70	74	25
Bushey United	26	12	1	13	70	77	25
R.A.F. (Halton)	26	10	4	12	73	74	24
Maidenhead United Reserves	26	8	6	12	57	68	22
Aylesbury United Reserves	26	8	6	12	56	72	22
Amersham Town	26	8	6	12	43	63	22
Chesham United Reserves	26	7	6	13	52	77	20
Marlow Reserves	26	4	5	17	56	94	13

The 2nd Coldstream Guards left the League.

Division Two (East)

Saffron Walden Town	**26**	**20**	**1**	**5**	**93**	**50**	**41**
Letchworth Town Reserves	26	18	3	5	98	49	39
Epping Town	26	16	5	5	99	51	37
White City	26	15	0	11	87	61	30
Ware	26	12	5	9	63	52	29
Harlow Town	26	12	4	10	79	75	28
Bishop's Stortford Reserves	26	12	4	10	68	74	28
1st Coldstream Guards	26	11	4	11	83	71	26
Dagenham Cables	26	11	3	12	74	62	25
Stevenage Town	26	9	7	10	55	59	25
R.A.F. (Henlow) Reserves	26	9	6	11	66	74	24
Lyons Club Reserves	26	6	2	18	54	109	14
Sawbridgeworth Town	26	4	2	20	28	105	10
Luton Amateur	26	3	2	21	52	107	8

The 1st Coldstream Guards left the League. Welwyn Garden City rejoined after a 2-year absence having obtained the use of Shredded Wheat's ground.

Division Two Championship play-off:

Saffron Walden Town vs Wendover	2-1
(played at Ware)	

1937-38

Premier Division

Waterlows (Dunstable)	26	18	4	4	95	53	40
Windsor & Eton	26	17	3	6	67	42	37
Callender Athletic	26	15	5	6	62	41	35
Chesham United	26	14	6	6	74	30	34
Hitchin Town	26	14	4	8	71	36	32
Slough	26	14	3	9	77	61	31
Metropolitan Police	26	15	1	10	67	47	31
Cambridge Town	26	11	4	11	67	65	26
Maidenhead United	26	8	7	11	52	55	23
Hoxton Manor	26	8	4	14	46	63	20
Lyons Club	26	6	7	13	36	62	19
Letchworth Town	26	8	2	16	46	83	18
Aylesbury United	*26*	*4*	*4*	*18*	*44*	*81*	*12*
Henley Town	*26*	*1*	*4*	*21*	*39*	*124*	*6*

Division One

Marlow	26	14	6	6	82	54	34
Wood Green Town	26	14	5	7	72	46	33
Uxbridge	26	18	2	6	75	44	32
Hoddesdon Town	26	14	4	8	80	51	32
Hertford Town	26	13	6	7	73	55	32
Bishop's Stortford	26	12	4	10	43	50	28
Apsley	26	11	4	11	61	52	26
Saffron Walden Town	26	11	2	13	54	56	24
Berkhamsted Town	26	10	3	13	59	69	23
Wendover	26	8	5	13	56	72	21
Hounslow Town	26	9	2	15	48	73	20
Leighton United	26	8	3	15	43	69	19
Polytechnic	26	7	4	15	54	62	18
Lea Bridge Gas	*26*	*7*	*2*	*17*	*45*	*92*	*16*

Uxbridge had 6 points deducted and moved to the London League.
Lea Bridge Gas were relegated to Division Two (East).

Division Two (West)

Pinner	26	21	2	3	95	32	44
Roxonian	26	18	1	7	59	29	37
R.A.F. (Halton)	26	14	8	4	96	59	36
Windsor & Eton Reserves	26	16	3	7	58	34	35
Berkhamsted Town Reserves	26	14	4	8	80	61	32
Bushey United	26	10	7	9	68	65	27
Aylesbury United Reserves	26	11	4	11	66	63	26
Maidenhead United Reserves	26	10	6	10	64	61	26
Hazells (Aylesbury)	26	9	4	13	67	86	22
Chesham United Reserves	26	9	3	14	63	76	21
Marlow Reserves	26	8	3	15	63	90	19
Amersham Town	26	4	8	14	52	84	16
Lyons Club Reserves	26	6	2	18	44	81	14
Apsley Reserves	26	3	3	20	47	101	9

Roxonian changed their name to Harrow Town.

Division Two (East)

R.A.F. (Henlow)	26	18	2	6	92	47	38
Stevenage Town	26	17	4	5	84	56	38
Epping Town	26	16	5	5	86	43	37
White City	26	12	8	6	63	47	32
Bishop's Stortford Reserves	26	11	5	10	54	52	27
Uxbridge Reserves	26	10	6	10	56	59	26
Dagenham Cables	26	11	3	12	55	51	25
Ware	26	10	5	11	54	59	25
Luton Amateur	26	9	5	12	64	64	23
Sawbridgeworth Town	26	9	4	13	43	67	22
Letchworth Town Reserves	26	7	6	13	46	68	20
Harlow Town	26	9	1	16	53	60	19
Polytechnic Reserves	26	6	6	14	42	66	18
Welwyn Garden City	26	5	4	17	36	89	14

Dagenham Cables moved to the London Business Houses League and Polytechnic Reserves transferred to Division Two (West). Vauxhall Motors joined from the South Midlands League, Upminster joined from the Romford & District League and Ford Sports also joined.

Division Two Championship play-off:

R.A.F. (Henlow) vs Pinner   6-3
(played at Chesham United)

1938-39

Premier Division

Metropolitan Police	26	17	6	3	92	33	40
Slough	26	15	6	5	72	43	36
Hitchin Town	26	15	5	6	93	39	35
Waterlows (Dunstable)	26	13	7	6	71	47	33
Cambridge Town	26	12	8	6	49	39	32
Chesham United	26	12	5	9	60	59	29
Windsor & Eton	26	12	3	11	84	56	27
Wood Green Town	26	11	5	10	57	69	27
Maidenhead United	26	7	8	11	50	71	22
Callender Athletic	26	7	6	13	46	63	20
Lyons Club	26	7	5	14	39	85	19
Marlow	26	7	3	16	52	83	17
Hoxton Manor	26	4	6	16	32	63	14
Letchworth Town	26	6	1	19	34	81	13

Hitchin Town moved to the Athenian League and Callender Athletic also left the League.

Division One

Aylesbury United	26	19	2	5	92	47	40
Hertford Town	26	19	1	6	101	47	39
Apsley	26	18	1	7	96	42	37
Hoddesdon Town	26	15	3	8	81	48	33
Bishop's Stortford	26	14	3	9	66	56	31
Berkhamsted Town	26	12	2	12	59	66	26
Polytechnic	26	11	4	11	53	64	26
Saffron Walden Town	26	11	3	12	59	76	25
Hounslow Town	26	10	3	13	55	64	23
Leighton United	26	11	0	15	55	65	22
Pinner	26	9	1	16	55	76	19
Henley Town	26	6	4	16	69	101	16
Wendover	26	6	2	18	42	84	14
R.A.F. (Henlow)	*26*	*6*	*1*	*19*	*56*	*103*	*13*

R.A.F. (Henlow) were relegated to Division Two (East).

Division Two (West)

Harrow Town	26	20	1	5	89	25	41
Polytechnic Reserves	26	18	1	7	69	43	37
Hazells (Aylesbury)	26	15	3	8	68	57	33
R.A.F. (Halton)	26	13	3	10	75	55	29
Amersham Town	26	13	3	10	62	55	29
Chesham United Reserves	26	12	4	10	55	50	28
Marlow Reserves	26	11	5	10	65	66	27
Apsley Reserves	26	11	5	10	49	54	27
Maidenhead United Reserves	26	12	2	12	68	70	26
Windsor & Eton Reserves	26	10	3	13	66	65	23
Bushey United	26	10	2	14	49	59	22
Berkhamsted Town Reserves	26	8	1	17	50	82	17
Aylesbury United Reserves	26	7	3	16	51	95	17
Lyons Club Reserves	26	3	2	21	50	90	8

Briggs Sports joined from the London League, Redford Sports joined from the Reading Senior League and Yiewsley joined from the South-West Middlesex League.

Division Two (East)

	P	W	D	L	F	A	Pts
Ford Sports	26	20	0	6	99	25	40
Ware	26	19	0	7	60	44	38
Vauxhall Motors	26	14	5	7	74	45	33
Lea Bridge Gas	26	16	1	9	72	58	33
Luton Amateur	26	13	4	9	63	53	30
Stevenage Town	26	14	2	10	71	65	30
White City	26	13	3	10	79	56	29
Upminster	26	12	3	11	68	53	27
Epping Town	26	11	4	11	59	59	26
Welwyn Garden City	26	11	2	13	50	56	24
Bishop's Stortford Reserves	26	5	6	15	32	76	16
Sawbridgeworth Town	26	6	3	17	50	88	15
Harlow Town	26	5	4	17	46	83	14
Saffron Walden Town Reserves	26	3	3	20	29	91	9

Hatfield United joined from the Hertfordshire County League and Stansted joined from the East Hertfordshire League.

Division Two Championship play-off:

Ford Sports vs Harrow Town   3-2
(played at Ford Sports)

1939-40

Three games were played before war was declared and the league then closed down until 1945. The results of these 3 games were as follows:

Premier Division

Cambridge Town vs Hoxton Manor   1-2
Lyons Club vs Waterlows (Dunstable)   1-3

Division One

Saffron Walden Town vs Apsley   1-3

1945

The league restarted in 1945 with three geographical divisions, Central, East and West but no reserve sides. A number of pre-war members did not rejoin:
Amersham Town, Epping Town, Harlow Town, Hazells (Aylesbury), Redford Sports, Sawbridgeworth Town, Stansted and Upminster did not resume in 1945 but all eight clubs rejoined the Spartan League in 1946.
Bushey United did not re-form after the war.
White City did not re-join.
Hoxton Manor merged with Crown F.C. to form Crown and Manor who joined the North London Alliance in 1945.
Slough had merged with Slough Centre in 1943 to form Slough United who became a founder member of the Corinthian League in 1945.
Maidenhead United and Windsor & Eton both also became founder members of the Corinthian League in 1945.
R.A.F. (Henlow) and Waterlows (Dunstable) did not resume until 1946 when they both joined the South Midlands League.
Lea Bridge Gas did not resume until 1946 when they joined the Northern Suburban League.
Wendover and R.A.F. (Halton) did not resume until 1948 when they both joined the Great Western Combination.

1945-46

Central Division

Metropolitan Police	18	17	1	0	89	23	35
Pinner	18	14	2	2	79	29	30
Wood Green Town	18	12	2	4	80	37	26
Ford Sports	18	10	2	6	64	38	22
Harrow Town	18	10	1	7	51	40	21
Hoddesdon Town	18	6	3	9	54	62	15
Briggs Sports	18	7	0	11	42	74	14
Ware	18	4	1	13	44	72	9
Lyons Club	18	2	2	14	21	67	6
Hertford Town	18	1	0	17	28	110	2

Eastern Division

Cambridge Town	16	13	1	2	65	18	27
Vauxhall Motors	16	12	1	3	60	24	25
Letchworth Town	16	10	3	3	64	27	23
Welwyn Garden City	16	7	2	7	51	44	16
Saffron Walden Town	16	7	1	8	43	46	15
Luton Amateur	16	4	5	7	35	44	13
Hatfield United	16	4	2	10	39	68	10
Stevenage Town	16	3	3	10	20	68	9
Bishop's Stortford	16	1	4	11	21	59	6

Western Division

Hounslow Town	18	12	1	5	61	23	25
Aylesbury United	18	11	1	6	70	47	23
Chesham United	18	9	4	5	55	39	22
Marlow	18	9	2	7	60	64	20
Leighton United	18	10	0	8	47	62	20
Polytechnic	18	7	5	6	44	37	19
Yiewsley	18	7	4	7	51	46	18
Berkhamsted Town	18	6	2	10	42	54	14
Henley Town	18	5	2	11	55	71	12
Apsley	18	2	3	13	32	74	7

1946

The League re-organised with a Premier Division, Division One (East) and Division One (West).
7 Central Division clubs became members of the Premier Division whilst Briggs Sports, Ford Sports and Ware all joined Division One (East).
5 Eastern Division clubs moved to Division One (East) while Bishop's Stortford, Cambridge Town, Letchworth Town and Vauxhall Motors all moved to the Premier Division.
7 Western Division clubs moved to Division One (West) while Aylesbury United and Chesham United moved to the Premier Division and Hounslow Town moved to the Corinthian League.
The Premier Division was made up to 14 clubs by Crown & Manor who joined from the North London Alliance.
Division One (East) was made up to 14 clubs by 5 pre-war members who rejoined — Epping Town, Harlow Town, Sawbridgeworth Town, Stansted, and Upminster, together with Biggleswade Town who had played in the United Counties League before the war and did not play in 1945-46.
Division One (West) was made up to 12 clubs by 3 pre-war members who rejoined — Amersham Town, Hazells (Aylesbury) and Redford Sports, together with Huntley & Palmers who joined from the Reading & District League and Wolverton Town who had played in the South Midlands League before the war and did not play in 1945-46.

1946-47

Premier Division

Metropolitan Police	26	21	2	3	100	29	44
Vauxhall Motors	26	20	2	4	112	50	42
Letchworth Town	26	16	5	5	74	54	37
Hoddesdon Town	26	15	4	7	96	73	34
Cambridge Town	26	13	3	10	95	40	29
Wood Green Town	26	12	5	9	79	65	29
Harrow Town	26	13	2	11	62	55	28
Chesham United	26	12	2	12	74	74	26
Bishop's Stortford	26	7	5	14	58	70	19
Aylesbury United	26	8	3	15	51	78	19
Pinner	26	6	5	15	43	72	17
Lyons Club	26	8	1	17	51	106	17
Crown & Manor	26	7	2	17	41	94	16
Hertford Town	26	3	1	22	34	110	7

Cambridge Town vs Chesham United and Cambridge Town vs Harrow Town were not played. Chesham United and Harrow Town were each awarded 2 points.
Chesham United moved to the Corinthian League, Crown & Manor moved to the Middlesex Senior League and Hertford Town stopped playing for a season as their ground was unavailable.

Division One (East)

Briggs Sports	**26**	**19**	**3**	**4**	**102**	**28**	**41**
Luton Amateur	26	16	4	6	73	35	36
Ford Sports	26	15	3	8	69	41	33
Upminster	26	15	3	8	72	45	33
Sawbridgeworth Town	26	13	4	9	73	54	30
Saffron Walden Town	26	12	5	9	49	53	29
Biggleswade Town	26	13	2	11	69	67	28
Harlow Town	26	12	3	11	48	63	27
Welwyn Garden City	26	11	3	12	54	49	25
Stevenage Town	26	10	1	15	55	82	21
Ware	26	7	6	13	55	85	20
Hatfield United	26	9	1	16	52	77	19
Epping Town	26	4	3	19	53	89	11
Stansted	26	5	1	20	29	85	11

Brentwood & Warley joined from the South Essex League.

Division One (West)

Huntley & Palmers	**22**	**18**	**1**	**3**	**111**	**39**	**37**
Wolverton Town	**22**	**18**	**1**	**3**	**99**	**40**	**37**
Yiewsley	22	17	2	3	123	44	36
Berkhamsted Town	22	15	2	5	97	51	32
Marlow	22	14	2	6	72	49	30
Apsley	22	11	1	10	74	56	23
Polytechnic	22	8	2	12	63	78	18
Redford Sports	22	5	2	15	47	80	12
Henley Town	22	5	2	15	49	101	12
Leighton United	22	4	2	16	35	84	10
Amersham Town	22	3	3	16	36	116	9
Hazells (Aylesbury)	22	3	2	17	46	114	8

Apsley merged with Hemel Hempstead Rovers to form Hemel Hempstead Town who continued in Division One (West). Willesden joined from the Middlesex Senior League and Headington United joined from the Oxfordshire Senior League. Slough Centre joined after de-merging from Slough United who continued in the Corinthian League as Slough Town. Chelsea Mariners joined as a new club.

Division One Championship play-off:

Briggs Sports vs Huntley & Palmers	7-3
(played at Aylesbury United)	

1947-48

Premier Division

Cambridge Town	26	21	2	3	97	34	44
Metropolitan Police	26	18	3	5	69	38	39
Vauxhall Motors	26	15	2	9	56	43	32
Hoddesdon Town	26	14	3	9	55	53	31
Wolverton Town	26	13	4	9	81	55	30
Aylesbury United	26	13	3	10	68	41	29
Briggs Sports	26	13	3	10	54	51	29
Huntley & Palmers	26	12	4	10	69	64	28
Bishop's Stortford	26	8	5	13	56	50	21
Harrow Town	26	8	5	13	50	68	21
Letchworth Town	26	5	6	15	33	58	16
Pinner	26	6	4	16	32	65	16
Wood Green Town	*26*	*6*	*2*	*18*	*44*	*82*	*14*
Lyons Club	*26*	*6*	*2*	*18*	*40*	*102*	*14*

Wood Green Town were relegated to Division One (East).
Lyons Club were relegated to Division One (West).

Division One (East)

Brentwood & Warley	**26**	**21**	**2**	**3**	**100**	**24**	**44**
Stevenage Town	26	19	3	4	82	35	41
Upminster	26	15	5	6	67	37	35
Welwyn Garden City	26	14	6	6	59	40	34
Biggleswade Town	26	13	6	7	76	48	32
Harlow Town	26	13	3	10	62	66	29
Luton Amateur	26	8	10	8	61	60	26
Ware	26	11	1	14	75	56	23
Sawbridgeworth Town	26	9	4	13	66	71	22
Ford Sports	26	9	3	14	47	62	21
Saffron Walden Town	26	7	6	13	40	71	20
Stansted	26	7	3	16	49	86	17
Hatfield United	26	4	6	16	52	89	14
Epping Town	26	1	4	21	26	117	6

Hatfield United changed their name to Hatfield Town. Luton Amateur transferred to Division One (West) and Ford Sports moved to the London League. Hertford Town rejoined after a year's inactivity and Histon Institute joined from the Cambridgeshire League.

Division One (West)

Willesden	**24**	**17**	**3**	**4**	**74**	**43**	**37**
Hemel Hempstead Town	24	17	2	5	91	33	36
Slough Centre	24	15	5	4	78	55	35
Yiewsley	24	16	3	5	87	41	35
Headington United	24	14	5	5	78	36	33
Berkhamsted Town	24	12	7	5	68	33	31
Marlow	24	10	7	7	33	39	27
Polytechnic	24	9	4	11	51	50	22
Chelsea Mariners	24	6	1	17	43	76	13
Amersham Town	24	4	4	16	43	102	12
Henley Town	24	4	3	17	36	97	11
Redford Sports	24	4	2	18	30	74	10
Leighton United	24	3	4	17	35	88	10

Hazells (Aylesbury) resigned early in the season and their record was deleted when it stood as:

	2	0	0	2	0	20	0

They joined the Great Western Combination in 1948.
Redford Sports also left the League and Rickmansworth Town joined from the Hertfordshire County League.

Division One Championship play-off:

Brentwood & Warley vs Willesden	7-2
(played at Berkhamsted Town)	

1948-49

Premier Division

Cambridge Town	26	20	4	2	85	34	44
Brentwood & Warley	26	18	4	4	75	39	40
Vauxhall Motors	26	17	4	5	83	46	38
Briggs Sports	26	17	2	7	61	31	36
Metropolitan Police	26	14	4	8	57	45	32
Harrow Town	26	11	4	11	58	57	26
Huntley & Palmers	26	11	4	11	75	81	26
Willesden	26	10	5	11	48	52	25
Letchworth Town	26	10	4	12	46	60	24
Aylesbury United	26	9	2	15	45	72	20
Wolverton Town	26	6	3	17	63	76	15
Hoddesdon Town	26	6	3	17	46	75	15
Pinner	*26*	*4*	*5*	*17*	*42*	*86*	*13*
Bishop's Stortford	*26*	*4*	*2*	*20*	*37*	*67*	*10*

Pinner were relegated to Division One (West).
Bishop's Stortford were relegated to Division One (East).
Wolverton Town changed their name to Wolverton Town & B.R..

Division One (East)

Stevenage Town	**26**	**21**	**2**	**3**	**91**	**36**	**44**
Hatfield Town	26	14	6	6	58	47	34
Histon Institute	26	15	3	8	74	51	33
Upminster	26	13	7	6	58	44	33
Biggleswade Town	26	14	3	9	62	45	31
Hertford Town	26	15	1	10	70	56	31
Wood Green Town	26	11	6	9	62	46	28
Ware	26	8	6	12	63	70	22
Stansted	26	9	3	14	60	74	21
Epping Town	26	10	1	15	46	62	21
Harlow Town	26	9	2	15	61	69	20
Welwyn Garden City	26	7	5	14	43	61	19
Saffron Walden Town	26	7	3	16	50	93	17
Sawbridgeworth Town	26	3	4	19	27	71	10

Division One (West)

Slough Centre	**26**	**20**	**5**	**1**	**81**	**19**	**45**
Yiewsley	26	21	2	3	106	34	44
Hemel Hempstead Town	26	21	0	5	84	37	42
Headington United	26	16	1	9	87	48	33
Rickmansworth Town	26	15	3	8	77	52	33
Luton Amateur	26	14	5	7	84	59	33
Berkhamsted Town	26	13	3	10	66	45	29
Marlow	26	12	3	11	59	55	27
Polytechnic	26	6	5	15	28	58	17
Chelsea Mariners	26	6	4	16	55	87	16
Leighton United	26	6	3	17	43	76	15
Henley Town	26	5	3	18	47	110	13
Amersham Town	26	3	3	20	39	111	9
Lyons Club	26	4	0	22	37	102	8

Headington United turned professional and joined the Southern League.
Wembley joined from the Middlesex Senior League.

Division One Championship play-off:

Stevenage Town vs Slough Centre	2-0
(played at Cambridge Town)	

1949-50

Premier Division

Briggs Sports	26	22	3	1	91	20	47
Cambridge Town	26	15	4	7	73	39	34
Aylesbury United	26	14	6	6	69	48	34
Wolverton Town & B.R.	26	13	6	7	78	43	32
Brentwood & Warley	26	13	4	9	59	44	30
Letchworth Town	26	13	2	11	53	50	28
Slough Centre	26	10	6	10	50	62	26
Vauxhall Motors	26	10	4	12	50	55	24
Metropolitan Police	26	8	7	11	53	65	23
Huntley & Palmers	26	9	4	13	60	72	22
Harrow Town	26	8	3	15	53	89	19
Willesden	26	8	2	16	39	57	18
Stevenage Town	*26*	*6*	*5*	*15*	*51*	*79*	*17*
Hoddesdon Town	*26*	*4*	*2*	*20*	*41*	*97*	*10*

Stevenage Town and Hoddesdon Town were both relegated to Division One (East). Cambridge Town moved to the Athenian League.

Division One (East)

Hertford Town	**26**	**22**	**1**	**3**	**91**	**29**	**45**
Histon Institute	26	17	5	4	99	51	39
Bishop's Stortford	26	14	4	8	65	45	32
Welwyn Garden City	26	13	6	7	47	36	32
Upminster	26	12	7	7	75	45	31
Biggleswade Town	26	12	7	7	71	47	31
Ware	26	10	6	10	55	59	26
Wood Green Town	26	9	4	13	47	53	22
Hatfield Town	26	7	7	12	38	46	21
Harlow Town	26	8	3	15	43	58	19
Saffron Walden Town	26	7	5	14	53	84	19
Epping Town	26	6	4	16	40	84	16
Sawbridgeworth Town	26	7	2	17	30	80	16
Stansted	26	6	3	17	37	74	15

Biggleswade Town and Wood Green Town both transferred to Division One (West). Ford Sports joined from the London League.

Division One (West)

Yiewsley	**26**	**22**	**1**	**3**	**106**	**32**	**45**
Berkhamsted Town	**26**	**21**	**2**	**3**	**107**	**34**	**44**
Wembley	26	17	1	8	79	46	35
Hemel Hempstead Town	26	15	3	8	77	45	33
Rickmansworth Town	26	15	2	9	70	37	32
Marlow	26	13	2	11	80	74	28
Amersham Town	26	11	3	12	62	86	25
Luton Amateur	26	8	5	13	48	55	21
Pinner	26	9	3	14	49	67	21
Polytechnic	26	8	4	14	46	59	20
Chelsea Mariners	26	7	6	13	39	75	20
Lyons Club	26	6	2	18	36	100	14
Leighton United	26	5	3	18	43	76	13
Henley Town	26	5	3	18	37	93	13

Lyons Club moved to the West End Amateur League. Abingdon Town joined from the Reading & District League.

Division One Championship play-off:

Yiewsley vs Hertford Town	6-1
(played at Yiewsley)	

1950-51

Premier Division

Yiewsley	26	18	4	4	87	37	40
Briggs Sports	26	16	3	7	68	25	35
Aylesbury United	26	15	5	6	70	37	35
Metropolitan Police	26	13	5	8	78	53	31
Wolverton Town & B.R.	26	12	6	8	70	67	30
Huntley & Palmers	26	14	0	12	70	62	28
Berkhamsted Town	26	11	4	11	49	50	26
Letchworth Town	26	11	2	13	59	66	24
Slough Centre	26	11	2	13	41	66	24
Brentwood & Warley	26	8	4	14	48	54	20
Willesden	26	8	4	14	46	57	20
Harrow Town	26	6	5	15	38	66	17
Hertford Town	26	6	5	15	45	85	17
Vauxhall Motors	26	8	1	17	43	87	17

Yiewsley, Aylesbury United, Berkhamsted Town, Slough Centre, Brentwood & Warley and Willesden all left to become founder members of the Delphian League.

Division One (East)

Histon Institute	26	21	1	4	106	35	43
Stevenage Town	26	20	2	4	101	42	42
Hoddesdon Town	26	17	1	8	73	49	35
Bishop's Stortford	26	15	4	7	72	48	34
Upminster	26	15	3	8	82	59	33
Hatfield Town	26	14	2	10	61	48	30
Ware	26	11	7	8	79	49	29
Ford Sports	26	14	1	11	65	47	29
Harlow Town	26	10	2	14	51	72	22
Welwyn Garden City	26	5	8	13	51	77	18
Saffron Walden Town	26	7	3	16	47	80	17
Epping Town	26	7	3	16	35	69	17
Stansted	26	3	2	21	37	112	8
Sawbridgeworth Town	26	3	1	22	31	104	7

Histon Institute, Hoddesdon Town and Upminster were all promoted to the Premier Division. Stevenage Town and Bishop's Stortford both left to become founder members of the Delphian League and Welwyn Garden City moved to the London League.

Division One (West)

Wembley	26	21	2	3	94	35	44
Hemel Hempstead Town	26	22	0	4	100	39	44
Biggleswade Town	26	13	7	6	57	44	33
Wood Green Town	26	14	3	9	66	55	31
Chelsea Mariners	26	13	4	9	67	50	30
Rickmansworth Town	26	11	3	12	61	48	25
Polytechnic	26	9	7	10	44	59	25
Abingdon Town	26	8	7	11	63	62	23
Luton Amateur	26	9	5	12	65	64	23
Marlow	26	10	1	15	62	69	21
Leighton United	26	9	3	14	67	85	21
Amersham Town	26	9	1	16	69	97	19
Pinner	26	3	7	16	38	82	13
Henley Town	26	5	2	19	54	118	12

Hemel Hempstead Town, Wood Green Town and Marlow were all promoted to the Premier Division. Wembley left to become founder members of the Delphian League. Biggleswade Town moved to the United Counties League and Pinner moved to the Southern Amateur League.

Division One Championship play-off:

Wembley vs Histon Institute	3-2
(played at Letchworth Town)	

1951-52

The two sections of Division One merged into a single division.

Premier Division

Briggs Sports	26	21	4	1	86	17	46
Wolverton Town & B.R.	26	18	4	4	96	48	40
Histon Institute	26	15	5	6	67	47	35
Hertford Town	26	12	4	10	59	56	28
Hemel Hempstead Town	26	12	3	11	68	58	27
Huntley & Palmers	26	9	8	9	49	56	26
Harrow Town	26	10	6	10	45	60	26
Wood Green Town	26	9	6	11	56	65	24
Upminster	26	9	5	12	53	53	23
Metropolitan Police	26	10	2	14	62	64	22
Letchworth Town	26	8	4	14	48	77	20
Vauxhall Motors	26	8	2	16	51	71	18
Hoddesdon Town	26	5	5	16	47	76	15
Marlow	26	5	4	17	53	92	14

Hemel Hempstead Town moved to the Delphian League.
Upminster changed their name to Hornchurch & Upminster and also moved to the Delphian League. Histon Institute changed their name to Histon. Tufnell Park Edmonton joined from the Isthmian League.

Division One

Ware	**30**	**23**	**4**	**3**	**131**	**44**	**50**
Polytechnic	**30**	**20**	**9**	**1**	**95**	**34**	**49**
Ford Sports	**30**	**21**	**5**	**4**	**90**	**49**	**47**
Saffron Walden Town	30	16	5	9	84	59	37
Amersham Town	30	16	3	11	93	82	35
Epping Town	30	13	7	10	60	66	33
Luton Amateur	30	13	4	13	103	72	30
Chelsea Mariners	30	11	7	12	73	82	29
Abingdon Town	30	10	8	12	62	74	28
Hatfield Town	30	12	3	15	77	86	27
Leighton United	30	11	4	15	81	81	26
Rickmansworth Town	30	10	5	15	84	86	25
Harlow Town	30	8	9	13	72	80	25
Stansted	30	4	6	20	50	114	14
Sawbridgeworth Town	30	5	3	22	46	131	13
Henley Town	30	5	2	23	56	117	12

Henley Town moved to the Great Western Combination and Bletchley Town joined from the South Midlands League.

1952-53

Premier Division

Ware	30	24	4	2	88	36	52
Briggs Sports	30	22	5	3	105	26	49
Metropolitan Police	30	20	4	6	93	40	44
Histon	30	18	3	9	78	47	39
Hertford Town	30	13	8	9	82	60	34
Hoddesdon Town	30	13	5	12	80	69	31
Harrow Town	30	13	2	15	52	57	28
Wolverton Town & B.R.	30	10	7	13	68	75	27
Tufnell Park Edmonton	30	11	3	16	54	61	25
Vauxhall Motors	30	9	7	14	63	80	25
Huntley & Palmers	30	10	3	17	73	89	23
Ford Sports	30	10	3	17	48	72	23
Marlow	30	9	4	17	51	106	22
Wood Green Town	30	10	1	19	47	88	21
Letchworth Town	*30*	*7*	*5*	*18*	*43*	*82*	*19*
Polytechnic	*30*	*8*	*2*	*20*	*46*	*83*	*18*

Division One

Bletchley Town	24	17	1	6	93	30	35
Hatfield Town	24	16	2	6	79	43	34
Luton Amateur	24	14	3	7	70	47	31
Saffron Walden Town	24	12	6	6	69	45	30
Amersham Town	24	13	3	8	78	61	29
Harlow Town	24	13	2	9	60	46	28
Rickmansworth Town	24	11	4	9	57	46	26
Leighton United	24	10	4	10	70	68	24
Epping Town	24	11	1	12	57	53	23
Abingdon Town	24	9	4	11	56	56	22
Chelsea Mariners	24	11	0	13	61	62	22
Stansted	24	4	0	20	27	105	8
Sawbridgeworth Town	24	0	0	24	16	131	0

Amersham Town, Leighton United and Abingdon Town left to become founder members of the Hellenic League. Stansted moved to the London League and Sawbridgeworth Town moved to the Hertfordshire County League. Tring Town joined from the Great Western Combination.

1953-54

Premier Division

Metropolitan Police	30	25	2	3	103	41	52
Briggs Sports	30	23	3	4	86	23	49
Vauxhall Motors	30	16	5	9	76	60	37
Huntley & Palmers	30	15	5	10	60	51	35
Ware	30	15	3	12	87	61	33
Tufnell Park Edmonton	30	14	4	12	69	64	32
Wolverton Town & B.R.	30	13	5	12	77	69	31
Histon	30	10	8	12	60	66	28
Marlow	30	13	2	15	64	71	28
Harrow Town	30	10	8	12	57	68	28
Ford Sports	30	10	5	15	55	64	25
Hertford Town	30	8	6	16	57	82	22
Bletchley Town	30	7	8	15	50	74	22
Wood Green Town	30	7	8	15	42	66	22
Hoddesdon Town	30	8	3	19	40	86	19
Hatfield Town	30	6	5	19	49	86	17

Hatfield Town moved to the Parthenon League and Tufnell Park Edmonton moved to the Delphian League. Bletchley Town changed their name to Bletchley & Wipac Sports.

Division One

Letchworth Town	16	14	1	1	68	16	29
Tring Town	16	11	1	4	56	23	23
Epping Town	16	9	1	6	38	31	19
Rickmansworth Town	16	6	4	6	37	36	16
Harlow Town	16	7	2	7	46	45	16
Polytechnic	16	7	2	7	35	41	16
Luton Amateur	16	3	4	9	20	49	10
Saffron Walden Town	16	4	0	12	19	42	8
Chelsea Mariners	16	2	3	11	21	57	7

Epping Town and Saffron Walden Town both moved to the Parthenon League, Rickmansworth Town moved to the Hellenic League, Harlow Town moved to the London League and Polytechnic moved to the Southern Amateur League. Luton Amateur and Chelsea Mariners also left. The League was then reduced to a single division.

1954-55

Metropolitan Police	30	24	4	2	85	37	52
Briggs Sports	30	22	3	5	108	34	47
Huntley & Palmers	30	19	4	7	86	55	42
Vauxhall Motors	30	18	4	8	80	61	40
Wolverton Town & B.R.	30	16	6	8	90	57	38
Ford Sports	30	15	7	8	79	59	37
Histon	30	14	4	12	81	61	32
Letchworth Town	30	13	6	11	76	60	32
Harrow Town	30	12	4	14	55	54	28
Hertford Town	30	9	9	12	60	70	27
Tring Town	30	9	2	19	41	115	20
Ware	30	8	3	19	66	74	19
Marlow	30	8	3	19	55	95	19
Hoddesdon Town	30	6	6	18	42	76	18
Wood Green Town	30	7	3	20	47	88	17
Bletchley & Wipac Sports	30	2	8	20	34	89	12

Bletchley & Wipac Sports moved to the South Midlands League and Ware moved to the Delphian League. Welwyn Garden City joined from the London League.

1955-56

Briggs Sports	28	23	2	3	117	26	48
Hertford Town	28	22	4	2	93	26	48
Huntley & Palmers	28	18	4	6	81	49	40
Histon	28	15	4	9	83	65	34
Wolverton Town & B.R.	28	16	1	11	58	60	33
Letchworth Town	28	13	6	9	73	58	32
Metropolitan Police	28	12	7	9	66	59	31
Marlow	28	12	7	9	53	50	31
Harrow Town	28	12	4	12	75	71	28
Vauxhall Motors	28	8	7	13	58	67	23
Welwyn Garden City	28	7	5	16	50	79	19
Ford Sports	28	7	4	17	29	61	18
Wood Green Town	28	5	4	19	50	87	14
Hoddesdon Town	28	6	2	20	38	88	14
Tring Town	28	2	3	23	28	106	7

Letchworth Town moved to the Delphian League.

1956-57

Briggs Sports	26	20	3	3	51	17	43
Hertford Town	26	16	5	5	59	24	37
Huntley & Palmers	26	17	2	7	78	43	36
Harrow Town	26	16	3	7	73	37	35
Vauxhall Motors	26	14	2	10	66	57	30
Marlow	26	13	1	12	71	47	27
Wolverton Town & B.R.	26	10	4	12	63	66	24
Metropolitan Police	26	10	2	14	51	64	22
Wood Green Town	26	10	2	14	47	63	22
Histon	26	8	5	13	57	80	21
Welwyn Garden City	26	8	4	14	61	79	20
Hoddesdon Town	26	6	8	12	47	63	20
Ford Sports	26	7	1	18	37	76	15
Tring Town	26	4	4	18	38	77	12

Boreham Wood and Rayners Lane joined from the Parthenon League.

1957-58

Briggs Sports	30	25	3	2	111	26	53
Harrow Town	30	22	4	4	94	30	48
Vauxhall Motors	30	19	6	5	87	44	44
Metropolitan Police	30	16	6	8	79	58	38
Marlow	30	15	5	10	63	60	35
Wood Green Town	30	13	6	11	76	68	32
Wolverton Town & B.R.	30	12	7	11	75	54	31
Histon	30	14	2	14	65	70	30
Hertford Town	30	11	8	11	54	69	30
Boreham Wood	30	13	0	17	70	77	26
Welwyn Garden City	30	10	5	15	53	62	25
Tring Town	30	10	3	17	52	96	23
Hoddesdon Town	30	7	6	17	48	83	20
Huntley & Palmers	30	6	7	17	64	92	19
Rayners Lane	30	7	3	20	55	84	17
Ford Sports	30	0	9	21	29	102	9

Harrow Town moved to the Delphian League and Ford Sports moved to the London Business Houses League. Ruislip Manor joined from the London League and Staines Town joined from the Hellenic League.

1958-59

Briggs Sports	30	24	2	4	92	37	50
Vauxhall Motors	30	20	2	8	93	42	42
Histon	30	19	3	8	95	56	41
Hertford Town	30	17	5	8	72	49	39
Huntley & Palmers	30	17	2	11	83	69	36
Wolverton Town & B.R.	30	16	1	13	72	74	33
Wood Green Town	30	14	5	11	53	62	33
Staines Town	30	14	4	12	69	61	32
Marlow	30	13	5	12	59	64	31
Rayners Lane	30	12	2	16	61	71	26
Boreham Wood	30	10	5	15	71	75	25
Tring Town	30	10	5	15	48	56	25
Ruislip Manor	30	10	3	17	53	60	23
Metropolitan Police	30	6	5	19	52	86	17
Welwyn Garden City	30	6	4	20	45	97	16
Hoddesdon Town	30	5	1	24	35	94	11

Briggs Sports merged with Ford Sports of the London Business Houses League and left to become founder members of the Aetolian League. Hertford Town moved to the Delphian League and Welwyn Garden City moved to the Hertfordshire County League. Bletchley Town joined from the Hellenic League and Molesey joined from the Surrey Senior League.

1959-60

Staines Town	28	18	4	6	60	36	40
Molesey	28	17	4	7	80	41	38
Vauxhall Motors	28	17	2	9	70	36	36
Histon	28	16	4	8	68	43	36
Wolverton Town & B.R.	28	17	1	10	81	49	35
Boreham Wood	28	15	4	9	70	61	34
Wood Green Town	28	12	8	8	68	47	32
Metropolitan Police	28	13	6	9	66	57	32
Ruislip Manor	28	8	5	15	49	62	21
Rayners Lane	28	8	5	15	45	63	21
Tring Town	28	9	3	16	41	68	21
Huntley & Palmers	28	7	7	14	40	67	21
Marlow	28	7	6	15	51	65	20
Bletchley Town	28	6	5	17	38	90	17
Hoddesdon Town	28	6	4	18	37	79	16

Bletchley Town moved to the United Counties League, Metropolitan Police moved to the Metropolitan League and Histon moved to the Delphian League. Crown & Manor and Kingsbury Town both joined from the Parthenon League and Petters Sports joined from the Surrey Senior League.

1960-61

Vauxhall Motors	28	16	5	7	79	41	37
Petters Sports	28	15	7	6	69	45	37
Wolverton Town & B.R.	28	15	5	8	87	62	35
Marlow	28	14	7	7	60	48	35
Staines Town	28	14	6	8	67	41	34
Molesey	28	15	4	9	59	42	34
Crown & Manor	28	13	6	9	61	50	32
Tring Town	28	15	2	11	66	61	32
Wood Green Town	28	12	7	9	57	50	31
Ruislip Manor	28	10	6	12	62	67	26
Huntley & Palmers	28	8	3	17	46	70	19
Hoddesdon Town	28	8	3	17	52	81	19
Rayners Lane	28	7	4	17	48	77	18
Boreham Wood	28	5	6	17	40	71	16
Kingsbury Town	28	6	3	19	39	86	15

Wolverton Town & B.R. moved to the United Counties League.

1961-62

Petters Sports	26	17	5	4	65	42	39
Vauxhall Motors	26	17	4	5	71	36	38
Ruislip Manor	26	15	7	4	72	38	37
Marlow	26	14	5	7	64	36	33
Crown & Manor	26	10	7	9	47	43	27
Staines Town	26	11	3	12	51	49	25
Hoddesdon Town	26	9	6	11	46	61	24
Wood Green Town	26	7	9	10	43	57	23
Boreham Wood	26	8	6	12	48	62	22
Tring Town	26	9	3	14	51	48	21
Huntley & Palmers	26	6	8	12	33	44	20
Molesey	26	7	6	13	41	60	20
Kingsbury Town	26	7	6	13	44	70	20
Rayners Lane	26	3	9	14	42	72	15

Chalfont St. Peter joined from the London League and Cheshunt joined from the Aetolian League.

1962-63

Cheshunt	30	27	1	2	122	42	55
Vauxhall Motors	30	18	3	9	94	41	39
Ruislip Manor	30	16	6	8	72	39	38
Tring Town	30	15	7	8	60	48	37
Boreham Wood	30	15	4	11	69	53	34
Chalfont St. Peter	30	14	6	10	69	59	34
Molesey	30	11	8	11	57	66	30
Marlow	30	11	7	12	65	71	29
Petters Sports	30	13	3	14	67	75	29
Staines Town	30	11	6	13	56	60	28
Rayners Lane	30	12	4	14	46	65	28
Wood Green Town	30	8	9	13	52	69	25
Crown & Manor	30	10	5	15	44	59	25
Huntley & Palmers	30	8	5	17	44	75	21
Kingsbury Town	30	5	6	19	42	80	16
Hoddesdon Town	30	4	4	22	38	95	12

Croydon Amateurs joined from the Surrey Senior League and Willesden joined from the Aetolian League.

1963-64

Croydon Amateurs	34	29	2	3	123	28	60
Boreham Wood	34	21	7	6	88	45	49
Petters Sports	34	22	4	8	75	47	48
Hoddesdon Town	34	19	9	6	86	45	47
Cheshunt	34	22	2	10	105	38	46
Chalfont St. Peter	34	17	7	10	77	62	41
Vauxhall Motors	34	15	9	10	68	39	39
Molesey	34	12	8	14	60	72	32
Wood Green Town	34	13	5	16	77	73	31
Willesden	34	11	9	14	53	65	31
Staines Town	34	13	4	17	71	83	30
Ruislip Manor	34	11	8	15	68	80	30
Marlow	34	11	6	17	66	76	28
Huntley & Palmers	34	8	9	17	38	84	25
Crown & Manor	34	8	6	20	46	91	22
Tring Town	34	5	9	20	38	101	19
Kingsbury Town	34	7	4	23	46	88	18
Rayners Lane	34	6	4	24	43	111	16

Croydon Amateurs and Cheshunt both moved to the Athenian League. Hampton and Addlestone both joined from the Surrey Senior League.

1964-65

Hampton	34	25	6	3	87	23	56
Hoddesdon Town	34	19	11	4	85	40	49
Vauxhall Motors	34	20	7	7	94	45	47
Wood Green Town	34	22	2	10	86	52	46
Staines Town	34	20	6	8	84	55	46
Willesden	34	17	5	12	61	45	39
Chalfont St. Peter	34	16	7	11	72	54	39
Boreham Wood	34	15	9	10	61	55	39
Addlestone	34	13	8	13	59	63	34
Tring Town	34	11	11	12	43	58	33
Crown & Manor	34	13	6	15	47	42	32
Marlow	34	13	3	18	79	77	29
Kingsbury Town	34	10	7	17	56	87	27
Molesey	34	9	7	18	42	82	25
Rayners Lane	34	8	7	19	57	89	23
Ruislip Manor	34	6	6	22	47	61	18
Huntley & Palmers	34	6	5	23	38	98	17
Petters Sports	34	4	5	25	34	106	13

Marlow and Ruislip Manor both moved to the Athenian League. Banstead Athletic joined from the Surrey Senior League and Leavesden Hospital joined from the Hertfordshire County League.

1965-66

Hampton	34	29	2	3	123	31	60
Boreham Wood	34	25	5	4	101	34	55
Vauxhall Motors	34	22	5	7	78	30	49
Willesden	34	19	7	8	71	39	45
Molesey	34	19	5	10	76	53	43
Banstead Athletic	34	17	8	9	67	55	42
Staines Town	34	16	9	9	77	81	41
Leavesden Hospital	34	15	7	12	71	68	37
Chalfont St. Peter	34	15	6	13	61	50	36
Hoddesdon Town	34	13	5	16	65	65	31
Tring Town	34	12	5	17	53	62	29
Kingsbury Town	34	9	9	16	60	69	27
Rayners Lane	34	9	7	18	49	77	25
Crown & Manor	34	7	7	20	46	86	21
Huntley & Palmers	34	8	4	22	51	83	20
Addlestone	34	8	4	22	55	98	20
Petters Sports	34	7	5	22	51	105	19
Wood Green Town	34	3	6	25	40	109	12

Boreham Wood moved to the Athenian League and Willesden moved to the Greater London League. Berkhamsted Town joined from the Athenian League.

1966-67

Hampton	32	25	4	3	100	23	54
Addlestone	32	23	4	5	92	34	50
Vauxhall Motors	32	21	5	6	72	41	47
Hoddesdon Town	32	18	7	7	67	34	43
Tring Town	32	16	7	9	76	49	39
Banstead Athletic	32	15	7	10	65	47	37
Chalfont St. Peter	32	14	5	13	58	60	33
Kingsbury Town	32	12	7	13	57	70	31
Huntley & Palmers	32	10	10	12	44	52	30
Rayners Lane	32	12	5	15	60	57	29
Crown & Manor	32	12	5	15	47	64	29
Staines Town	32	12	4	16	60	70	28
Leavesden Hospital	32	11	4	17	47	62	26
Molesey	32	9	7	16	50	63	25
Petters Sports	32	6	6	20	40	88	18
Berkhamsted Town	32	5	5	22	35	84	15
Wood Green Town	32	3	4	25	36	108	10

Leavesden Hospital moved to the Hertfordshire County League and Wood Green Town moved to the Northern Suburban League. Chertsey Town joined from the Greater London League, Egham Town joined from the Surrey Senior League and Leighton Town joined from the South Midlands League.

1967-68

Tring Town	34	25	7	2	105	40	57
Hampton	34	26	4	4	108	21	56
Leighton Town	34	22	4	8	86	37	48
Addlestone	34	20	7	7	82	32	47
Vauxhall Motors	34	18	11	5	81	40	47
Staines Town	34	19	7	8	84	45	45
Hoddesdon Town	34	18	9	7	70	39	45
Molesey	34	16	6	12	63	58	38
Egham Town	34	11	8	15	65	68	30
Huntley & Palmers	34	11	6	17	44	67	28
Rayners Lane	34	10	8	16	37	62	28
Banstead Athletic	34	7	13	14	48	63	27
Berkhamsted Town	34	8	10	16	37	86	26
Crown & Manor	34	10	5	19	49	79	25
Kingsbury Town	34	9	6	19	47	78	24
Chalfont St. Peter	34	5	8	21	39	83	18
Chertsey Town	34	4	10	20	45	96	18
Petters Sports	34	0	5	29	33	129	5

Petters Sports disbanded. Feltham joined from the Surrey Senior League.

1968-69

Vauxhall Motors	34	24	8	2	80	27	56
Tring Town	34	24	6	4	89	24	54
Feltham	34	24	6	4	72	40	54
Hampton	34	19	9	6	74	32	47
Leighton Town	34	21	4	9	68	43	46
Staines Town	34	18	7	9	75	54	43
Addlestone	34	18	5	11	68	40	41
Hoddesdon Town	34	14	6	14	47	42	34
Molesey	34	13	7	14	51	52	33
Chertsey Town	34	11	10	13	58	60	32
Kingsbury Town	34	13	5	16	54	65	31
Egham Town	34	9	10	15	63	74	28
Chalfont St. Peter	34	10	7	17	45	70	27
Rayners Lane	34	10	6	18	49	80	26
Berkhamsted Town	34	6	9	19	51	71	21
Huntley & Palmers	34	8	4	22	49	105	20
Banstead Athletic	34	5	3	26	29	72	13
Crown & Manor	34	1	4	29	31	102	6

1969-70

Hampton	34	25	6	3	82	21	56
Addlestone	34	24	6	4	71	24	54
Leighton Town	34	19	5	10	54	30	43
Staines Town	34	18	7	9	67	45	43
Vauxhall Motors	34	19	4	11	61	43	42
Hoddesdon Town	34	15	10	9	57	36	40
Banstead Athletic	34	17	6	11	57	44	40
Berkhamsted Town	34	14	8	12	41	41	36
Kingsbury Town	34	15	5	14	42	36	35
Tring Town	34	14	7	13	51	56	35
Chertsey Town	34	14	5	15	59	59	33
Crown & Manor	34	10	9	15	36	51	29
Molesey	34	8	12	14	38	52	28
Feltham	34	8	8	18	41	55	24
Chalfont St. Peter	34	7	9	18	35	80	23
Egham Town	34	6	8	20	31	55	20
Rayners Lane	34	5	9	20	30	73	19
Huntley & Palmers	34	3	6	25	36	88	12

Rayners Lane moved to the Middlesex League.
Bracknell Town joined from the Surrey Senior League.

1970-71

Hoddesdon Town	34	26	3	5	101	26	55
Staines Town	34	22	8	4	85	27	52
Hampton	34	22	7	5	88	32	51
Addlestone	34	20	10	4	88	37	50
Vauxhall Motors	34	18	8	8	71	43	44
Leighton Town	34	16	10	8	67	35	42
Egham Town	34	17	5	12	61	46	39
Bracknell Town	34	16	5	13	51	65	37
Banstead Athletic	34	13	5	16	61	69	31
Kingsbury Town	34	11	8	15	47	44	30
Molesey	34	12	5	17	48	68	29
Tring Town	34	12	5	17	38	79	29
Berkhamsted Town	34	11	6	17	44	65	28
Crown & Manor	34	7	10	17	27	56	24
Chertsey Town	34	9	5	20	38	58	23
Chalfont St. Peter	34	7	6	21	31	64	20
Feltham	34	6	8	20	32	70	20
Huntley & Palmers	34	1	6	27	20	114	8

Staines Town, Hampton and Addlestone all moved to the Athenian League and Huntley & Palmers moved to the Reading & District League.
Farnham Town joined from the Surrey Senior League and Harefield United joined from Middlesex County League.

1971-72

Egham Town	30	22	4	4	58	19	48
Hoddesdon Town	30	18	9	3	63	15	45
Molesey	30	15	11	4	40	23	41
Vauxhall Motors	30	17	5	8	61	29	39
Bracknell Town	30	14	10	6	58	33	38
Kingsbury Town	30	12	10	8	48	34	34
Farnham Town	30	12	8	10	51	58	32
Feltham	30	11	7	12	46	46	29
Harefield United	30	11	7	12	36	39	29
Berkhamsted Town	30	10	5	15	41	58	25
Chalfont St. Peter	30	8	9	13	29	40	25
Chertsey Town	30	8	8	14	44	53	24
Leighton Town	30	9	5	16	39	61	23
Banstead Athletic	30	8	3	19	33	72	19
Tring Town	30	6	5	19	32	65	17
Crown & Manor	30	2	8	20	22	56	12

Amersham Town joined from the Hellenic League and Farnborough Town joined from the Surrey Senior League.

1972-73

Farnborough Town	34	23	8	3	87	25	54
Hoddesdon Town	34	25	3	6	93	34	53
Feltham	34	19	10	5	67	39	48
Egham Town	34	19	8	7	78	40	46
Leighton Town	34	18	8	8	69	35	44
Kingsbury Town	34	16	12	6	60	34	44
Bracknell Town	34	18	5	11	72	52	41
Molesey	34	15	10	9	49	34	40
Vauxhall Motors	34	15	8	11	58	44	38
Harefield United	34	13	6	15	43	49	32
Banstead Athletic	34	11	9	14	48	42	31
Tring Town	34	10	9	15	52	59	29
Farnham Town	34	10	9	15	44	64	29
Crown & Manor	34	6	12	16	39	56	24
Chalfont St. Peter	34	7	8	19	40	71	22
Berkhamsted Town	34	5	6	23	36	83	16
Chertsey Town	34	4	7	23	33	97	15
Amersham Town	34	1	4	29	18	128	6

Feltham and Molesey both moved to the Athenian League.
Camberley Town joined from the Surrey Senior League and Rayners Lane joined from the Middlesex County League.

1973-74

Farnborough Town	34	28	5	1	88	16	61
Hoddesdon Town	34	24	6	4	92	36	54
Egham Town	34	24	5	5	80	28	53
Vauxhall Motors	34	19	8	7	71	29	46
Banstead Athletic	34	20	5	9	62	41	45
Bracknell Town	34	15	9	10	64	50	39
Berkhamsted Town	34	15	9	10	48	39	39
Leighton Town	34	16	4	14	48	43	36
Harefield United	34	15	5	14	49	39	35
Camberley Town	34	12	9	13	46	59	33
Rayners Lane	34	10	6	18	50	70	26
Kingsbury Town	34	9	8	17	41	58	26
Farnham Town	34	9	7	18	38	73	25
Crown & Manor	34	7	10	17	38	54	24
Chertsey Town	34	8	7	19	45	64	23
Tring Town	34	8	7	19	39	62	23
Chalfont St. Peter	34	5	10	19	33	67	20
Amersham Town	34	1	2	31	14	118	4

Vauxhall Motors and Leighton Town both moved to the United Counties League and Egham Town moved to the Athenian League.
Frimley Green joined from the Surrey Senior League.

1974-75

Farnborough Town	30	26	3	1	97	17	55
Chertsey Town	30	21	5	4	77	32	47
Harefield United	30	20	4	6	66	24	44
Hoddesdon Town	30	19	4	7	75	30	42
Banstead Athletic	30	17	3	10	63	38	37
Berkhamsted Town	30	16	5	9	55	40	37
Bracknell Town	30	14	8	8	68	34	36
Camberley Town	30	13	6	11	61	51	32
Kingsbury Town	30	11	8	11	49	39	30
Tring Town	30	9	6	15	34	48	24
Farnham Town	30	8	7	15	43	54	23
Rayners Lane	30	9	3	18	35	62	21
Crown & Manor	30	7	6	17	57	78	20
Chalfont St. Peter	30	6	4	20	43	93	16
Frimley Green	30	5	6	19	33	85	16
Amersham Town	30	0	0	30	17	148	0

Harefield United, Camberley Town and Tring Town all moved to the Athenian League and Rayners Lane moved to the Middlesex County League.

The Spartan League merged with the Metropolitan-London League at the end of the season to form the London Spartan League.